7 Day Loan

D0183677

AQA AS
PHILOSOPHY

Jeremy Hayward
Gerald Jones
Daniel Cardinal

HODDER
EDUCATION
AN HACHETTE UK COMPANY

Acknowledgements

The Publishers would like to thank the following for permission to reproduce copyright material:

Text credits: p.xi, xiv, xv, 127, 128, 129, 222, 280 Jonathan Bennett, for René Descartes, *Meditations*, copyright 2010-2015. All rights reserved; *www.earlymoderntexts.com*. **p.44** United Agents, for Ronald Knox, 'There was a young man who said, 'God...', from Langford Reed, *The Complete Limerick Book* (Jarrolds Publishers, 1924); **p.267** Alfred Music Publishing UK, for Barenaked Ladies, 'Big Bang Theme', lyrics by Ed Robertson, from the sitcom *Big Bang Theory*.

Photo credits: p.255 © Peter Willi/SuperStock/Getty Images

Every effort has been made to trace all copyright holders, but if any have been inadvertently overlooked the Publishers will be pleased to make the necessary arrangements at the first opportunity.

Although every effort has been made to ensure that website addresses are correct at time of going to press, Hodder Education cannot be held responsible for the content of any website mentioned in this book. It is sometimes possible to find a relocated web page by typing in the address of the home page for a website in the URL window of your browser.

Hachette's policy is to use papers that are natural, renewable and recyclable products and made from wood grown in sustainable forests. The logging and manufacturing processes are expected to conform to the environmental regulations of the country of origin.

Orders: please contact Bookpoint Ltd, 130 Milton Park, Abingdon, Oxon OX14 4SB. Telephone: +44 (0)1235 827720. Fax: +44 (0)1235 400454. Lines are open 9.00a.m.–5.00p.m., Monday to Saturday, with a 24-hour message answering service. Visit our website at www.hoddereducation.co.uk.

First published in 2014 by Hodder Education,

an Hachette UK company

338 Euston Road

London NW1 3BH

Impression number   5   4   3

Year   2018   2017   2016   2015

Cover photo © Vectorfactory/iStockphoto

Illustrations by Barking Dog Art and Tony Randell

Typeset in Integra Software Services Pvt. Ltd, Pondicherry, India

Printed and bound by CPI Group (UK) Ltd, Croydon, CR0 4YY

A catalogue record for this title is available from the British Library.

ISBN 978 1471 83535 3

Contents

Key to features

Activity

A practical task to help you to understand the arguments or concepts under investigation.

Experimenting with ideas

Plays around with some of the concepts discussed; looks at them from different angles.

Criticism

Highlights and evaluates the issues raised by an argument or a concept.

Quotation

A direct quotation from a key thinker.

Learn More

Learn more

Introduces related ideas or arguments that aren't required by the AS Level specification, but which provides useful additional material.

anthology
0.00

Anthology extracts

When you see the Anthology icon in the margin of the book then you should refer to the relevant extract in the Anthology extracts section at the end of the book.

Glossary

Words or phrases that appear in CAPITAL LETTERS are key terms and ideas that are explained in the Glossary at the end of the book.

Introduction

This AS Level may represent the first time you have formally studied philosophy, although you may well have debated many philosophical issues with friends, family or even with yourself. Unlike other A Levels such as mathematics, history, business studies or biology, the nature of the subject is not immediately clear from the name alone. This is because the term 'philosophy' is used to cover a great many things and is used differently by different people. To see this, you only have to wander into the philosophy section of your local bookshop or library, where the chances are you will find books covering such diverse topics as UFOs, tarot cards and personal therapy.

Even amongst philosophers themselves there is no clear consensus as to what the subject involves. Indeed, John Campbell in his book *Philosophers* photographed over 50 philosophers and asked them each to describe the subject. Perhaps not surprisingly, over 50 different answers were given. For example:

> *Philosophy is thinking in slow motion. It breaks down, describes and assesses moves we ordinarily make at great speed – to do with our natural motivations and beliefs. It then becomes evident that alternatives are possible.*[1]

Steve Pyke, *Philosophers*, page 22

Philosophy can be divided up into separate disciplines, each of which, even if not having its own methodology, does have its own area of interest and in many respects its own language. The three key areas are: METAPHYSICS – the study of the ultimate nature of reality; EPISTEMOLOGY – the study of what we can know; and ETHICS – the study of how we should live and act. Underpinning all of these areas is a fourth discipline, which includes the skills of critical thinking, of analysis and of logic.

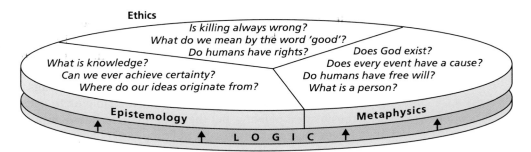

Figure 0.1 The different areas of philosophy.

Within these key areas there are further subdivisions: in metaphysics we will find questions grouped around the philosophy of mind (Do I have a SOUL? How does my mind work? What is consciousness?) and within this the question of PERSONS (Who am I? Am I the same person I was ten years ago?). However, some of this categorisation is artificial, for example the CONCEPT of personhood will also raise epistemological and ethical issues. Some other subdivisions of philosophy include: philosophy of language, philosophy of religion, aesthetics, logic and political philosophy.

Philosophy also deals with the cutting-edge and abstract questions at the forefront of most other fields of KNOWLEDGE. So there is a philosophy of history, critical theory (in English literature and the arts), philosophy of science, philosophy of maths, and so on. Indeed, if you ask enough difficult questions about any aspect of the world, you will end up with a philosophical question.

Why did the car start?

Because I turned the key.

But why?

Because it links the battery to the spark plugs which ignited the fuel.

Why does this happen?

Because fuel ignites at a certain temperature.

Yeah, but why?

Well that's the laws of physics.

But why is that a law of physics?

Because that's the way the universe was made.

And why was it made this way?

Eventually this discussion leaves science proper and drifts into the metaphysical and epistemological questions that make up the philosophy of science. Seen this way, philosophy is all around us; it's just a matter of asking the right questions. Most of the time though, we are happy to get on with our lives and so don't ask these difficult questions. As soon as we do, we start to realise that our explanations about life and the world come up a little short and we find ourselves philosophising. But why should we bother with these questions?

In one sense we can't avoid them. The unreflective life takes for granted common-sense assumptions which enable us to get on with the business of living. But these common-sense assumptions themselves represent answers to philosophical questions, and so relying on these is still to rely on a particular philosophy. However, the common-sense approach is just one possible view of things and one which is often beset with inconsistencies that we ignore. If you scratch beneath the surface, problems can arise.

Consider someone who just wants to live their life and get on with things. Perhaps they want to get a job, earn some money, get a set of wheels and buy a house, and so on. But why does this person want to do these things? Is it because they think it will make them happy? Do they think happiness is a goal worth pursuing? Is it achievable? Is the term even meaningful? If the person hasn't asked themselves these questions then it would seem they are just going about their life with no clear idea of what it is they are ultimately pursuing. We might want to ask: although such a life is possible, is it a GOOD life? The Greek philosopher Socrates would say it was not:

The unexamined life is not worth living.

Socrates, *Apology*, 38a

By avoiding these philosophical questions – all these questions still left hanging – our friends and neighbours are choosing to live the unexamined life. So congratulations for not hiding away from these issues and choosing to confront them head on. Congratulations for choosing to live the examined life.

Structure of the book

This book covers the AS Level philosophy specification published by the AQA, and which is the first year of the full A Level in philosophy. It has two main sections: Epistemology and the Philosophy of Religion, and within these two sections there are chapters that correspond to the AQA specification. Before these two sections we have included an introduction to Descartes' *Meditations*, which is a book that can be seen as a thread through much of the AS and A Level specification.

As a combination, epistemology and the philosophy of religion offer an accessible and engaging introduction to most of the areas of philosophy, as shown in **Figure 0.1** on page v. The chapters on epistemology obviously cover:

- the **theory of knowledge** (What is knowledge? What can we know?),
- but they also introduce **logic** and conceptual and critical analysis,
- as well as **metaphysics** (What is the world 'out there', beyond our PERCEPTION, really like?).

As part of your study of epistemology you will be reading and analysing extracts from the works of some great minds of western thought, including Plato, Descartes, Leibniz, Locke, Hume and Russell.

The chapters on the philosophy of religion also encompass several other areas of philosophy that go far beyond the study of theological or religious BELIEFS:

- **metaphysics** (Is there a God? What is causation? Do humans have FREE WILL?),
- and **logic** (There are many different ARGUMENTS that prove the existence of God, but how successful are they?),
- as well as **ethics** (Can all the pain and suffering in the world be justified by some higher good?)
- and finally the **philosophy of language**, which has become one of the most important branches of philosophy in the last hundred years.

It may well be the case that at university the philosophy of religion is not prioritised as a topic to study, in the way epistemology and other areas are, but you will be in good company by studying it now. Some of the most influential thinkers that the world has known have contributed to the philosophy of religion, and analysing their arguments will provide an excellent introduction to their broader philosophical ideas. The thinkers you will encounter include: Plato, Aristotle, Aquinas, Descartes, Hume and Wittgenstein. Even if you are not religious, you can hone your critical skills and your understanding of how arguments are built and knocked down by studying the philosophy of religion.

Towards the end of the book, Section 3 gives you guidance and tips on passing the AS exam, and includes an important sub-section on 'how to read philosophy'. Here we have provided some ideas, or 'lenses', which will help you to read and understand these texts and so improve your philosophical analysis. You might want to read this when you first come across an 'anthology icon'. The anthology icon appears when we are summarising a philosopher's ideas. It prompts you to flick to Section 4 where we have provided *extracts* of all texts found in the AQA online Anthology, so you can read the philosopher's original words.

Throughout this book you will find activities and advice on developing philosophical skills, such as analysing arguments and communicating concepts in a logical way. Crucially, they will help you learn to think critically and develop your own point of view. Studying philosophy will also help you develop the ability to sift through lots of information and ideas.

Now, let us turn to one of the most important books in western philosophy, the *Meditations* by René Descartes, as this will prove to be a useful introduction to many of the ideas that you will be encountering on your journey through philosophy.

Introduction to Descartes' *Meditations*

Descartes' *Meditations on First Philosophy* is one of the most significant texts in the history of western philosophy. Its project is ambitious, for in it Descartes attempts to establish the foundations for the whole of human knowledge. Along the way he calls into question the very existence of the physical universe; attempts to prove the existence of God; discovers the essential nature of matter and provides an account of the relation of body and soul. In so doing, Descartes set the agenda for debate in much of modern philosophy.

Because of its importance, it is widely studied on philosophy courses at university and has now been set as the key text to accompany the AQA A Level topics of Epistemology, Philosophy of religion and Philosophy of mind. In this introduction, we provide a brief introduction to Descartes and his six *Meditations*. At the end we also include a summary flowchart of all the key ideas contained within the text.

Brief biography

In 1596, René Descartes was born into a relatively wealthy family living in La Haye, a small town in the north west of France. At around the age of nine, the young Descartes was sent to study at a nearby Jesuit college in La Flèche. Because of ill health, Descartes was allowed the unusual privilege of lying in bed until 11am each morning – a habit that stayed with him for the rest of his life.

After completing his studies at university, Descartes travelled to Holland to enlist as a volunteer in the army of Prince Maurice of Nassau, effectively becoming a cadet in a military academy. Over the next few years Descartes served in several armies – as a volunteer he received no pay, and part of his motive was the opportunity a military career provided both to think and to travel. Actual fighting was not likely for someone of Descartes' background!

It was during this period, when shut away in a small stove-heated room in Germany, that Descartes claimed to have experienced a series of visions, which he interpreted as bestowing on him a divine mission to seek the truth through the use of REASON.

After leaving the army, he travelled around Europe, living for a while in Paris before finally settling in Holland. In his later life he was persuaded to move to Sweden to teach Queen Christina. The Queen required her philosophy lessons to begin at five in the morning. Descartes, being accustomed to much later starts, died after about six months of this new regime.

After a slow start, Descartes' fame had grown steadily throughout his lifetime, particular in his later years. After his death he became increasingly renowned. A measure of his fame is that during the

> *So I shall suppose that some malicious, powerful, cunning demon has done all he can to deceive me ... I shall think that the sky, the air, the earth, colours, shapes, sounds and all external things are merely dreams that the demon has contrived as traps for my judgement. I shall consider myself as having no hands or eyes, or flesh, or blood or senses, but as having falsely believed that I had all these things.[2]*
>
> **Descartes, *Meditations on First Philosophy, Meditation 1*, page 3**

A powerful demon such as this could make anything appear to be the case. Your whole life could have been a fiction created by the demon. Descartes came up with the idea of a deceiving demon nearly 400 years ago, and it can seem rather far-fetched to the modern imagination. Yet the central insight can be readily made with more up-to-date scenarios, for example as in *The Matrix* or the idea of a brain in a vat (page 147).

▶ **ACTIVITY**

1   Can you be 100 per cent sure that you are not being deceived in this way at this very moment?
2   If it is possible that there is such a demon deceiving you, can you know anything for certain?

The cogito

If you concede that this is a possibility, however absurd or remote, then surely you can never be 100 per cent certain of anything again. Nothing is certain – perhaps you don't even exist at all. At this point Descartes produces a response that is probably the best-known philosophical ARGUMENT of all.

My own existence cannot be doubted because, when I attempt to doubt it, I recognise that there must be something doing the doubting, and that something is me. So at the time of thinking, Descartes cannot in fact be nothing. His own existence can be known for certain in the face of his most radical doubts. Here Descartes discovers the first principle, the first certainty that he has been searching for, what is often termed the *COGITO*, after the Latin formulation from Descartes' *Principles of Philosophy* (1644), namely: *cogito ergo sum*, meaning 'I am thinking, therefore I exist', or 'I think, therefore I am.'

> *Even then, if he is deceiving me I undoubtedly exist: let him deceive me all he can, he will never bring it about that I am nothing while I think I am something. So after thoroughly thinking the matter through I conclude that this proposition, I am, I exist, must be true whenever I assert it or think it.*[3]

Descartes, *Meditations on First Philosophy*, Meditation 2, page 4

Descartes was looking for a way of defeating the sceptic, something that could not be doubted, and it looks as if he has found it. It is impossible to doubt your own existence, for the very fact that you are doubting implies that you exist. What is so significant about the *cogito* is that we can know it to be true just by thinking it. It is knowable *A PRIORI* and tells us about something that actually exists – myself. Here my conviction in my own existence appears unshakable. It doesn't depend for its truth upon anything else, and so appears to justify itself.

But has Descartes really defeated the sceptic? And, if so, what exactly has he established? What exactly is this *I*? Descartes realises that he has not yet established the existence of himself as a human being, for the evil demon could still be deceiving him as to his earthly form. He may not even have a body. But he claims, however, that the *I* must be something, and that the very least it must be is a thing that can think – a thinking thing, or, in other words, a conscious being. Of this he feels sure, so that any demon could not deceive him.

But is this so? Some commentators feel that Descartes has only established the existence of some thoughts or conscious experiences; can Descartes assert that these experiences belong to any self or *I*? Perhaps thoughts can exist by themselves, not owned by any thinker?

Clear and distinct ideas

Descartes, with his *cogito*, has finally reached a point of certainty. His belief that he exists is so 'clear and distinct' in his mind that he can immediately 'intuit' its truth by reason. Descartes argues that any other ideas that are as clear and distinct as this must also be true and suggests that the basic claims of logic, geometry and mathematics can also be known this way.

This, in essence, is Descartes' approach for starting to build up his new 'house' of knowledge. Through CLEAR AND DISTINCT IDEAS he has found the secure foundations and can start to reason outwards from this base. This approach makes Descartes the classic rationalist, which is the belief that the best way to achieve knowledge is to use reason alone.

The rest of the *Meditations*

However, Descartes still has a problem. It is hard to move beyond these few clear and distinct ideas to knowing about the world while there is still a possibility that he is being deceived by a powerful demon. To erase the possibility, Descartes feels he needs to prove that God exists: if he can do this, then he can be certain that God, who is good, would not be deceiving him. We present this argument on page 125.

The key arguments in the whole of the *Meditations* are presented in the following flowchart.

Comment   **Central argument**   **Comment**

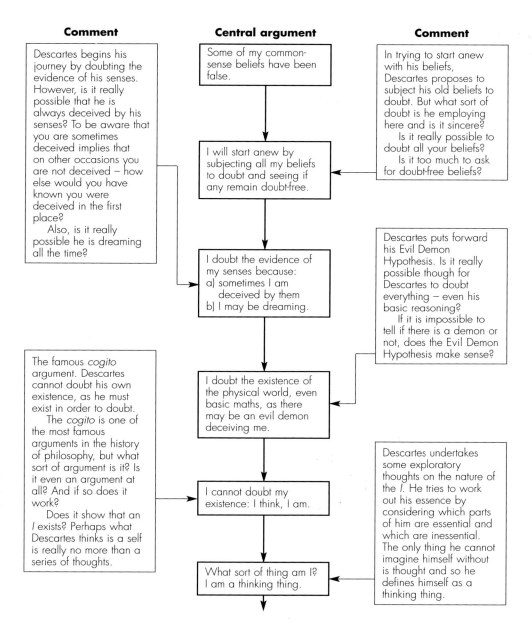

Comment

Descartes claims the *cogito* works because it is so 'clear' and 'distinct'.

However, how meaningful are these terms? Can Descartes really tell that he knows something for certain just by looking at how clear and distinct his thoughts are? And can he universalise this claim?

The Cartesian Circle. Descartes has been accused of making a serious error at this point – an error of form not just substance.

Descartes wants to prove that clear and distinct ideas are reliable. In order to do so he proves that God exists, so showing there could be no evil demon deceiving him. But the claim is that his proof relies on clear and distinct ideas. In attempting to show that clear and distinct ideas are always reliable he relies on clear and distinct ideas. The problem is that this approach is circular.

The Ontological Argument. Descartes is claiming that, by analysing the very concept of God, he can prove that God exists.

Is this a trick argument? Does the idea of perfection really entail existence?

For an analysis of the ontological argument see page 212 onwards.

Central argument

It is surprising that I know the nature of myself before that of material objects. But, after considering what I know about wax, I shouldn't really be surprised at all.

I know I exist. This cannot be doubted because it is so clear and distinct.

Anything that is perceived clearly and distinctly must be true.

… unless a Demon is deceiving me.

I know that God exists because my idea of an infinite and perfect being must have been caused by one.

I can be certain that anything clearly and distinctly perceived must be true, as God is no deceiver.

Any properties I clearly and distinctly perceive in the idea of God will be properties God has.

God is perfect and existence is part of being perfect, so God must exist.

Comment

Descartes is a bit surprised that his own nature is one of the first certainties he reaches. Before his doubts he felt convinced that he could be more certain about the objects around him than he could be about his own elusive nature. He overcomes this puzzle by considering a piece of wax – suggesting it is the mind, not the senses, that truly understands its nature. The wax cannot be known through the senses as there is no sense datum that remains the same through the various changes undergone by the wax as it melts. So the essence of matter is recognised by the understanding. Also, when he perceives anything he must also be aware of himself. To even perceive the wax requires a human mind. Descartes is now more confident about the way he arrived at an understanding of his own nature.

Descartes puts forward the 'Trademark' Argument for the existence of God.

How convincing is this? Does anyone really have an idea of a perfect and infinite being? And, if so, must this be caused by one?

For analysis of this argument see page 125 onwards.

Comment

Descartes attempts to establish his dualist thesis. As he can clearly and distinctly conceive of his non-extended mind distinct from his body, he claims it must be a separate substance.

Many critics claim that Descartes is guilty of committing the *masked-man fallacy*. The suggestion is that it is dangerous to argue that because you can think about objects differently they must be different.

Descartes has established that God is no deceiver and that all clear and distinct beliefs must be true. This presents him with the tricky task of accounting for error. Sometimes we appear to be very clear and distinct about something, but yet are still in error – how is this possible if God is no deceiver? Descartes gives the example of amputees who clearly feel that they have an arm when they don't or people who are ill and want to drink even when it is bad for them. In these cases he claims that error occurs because our body is a machine and all machines break down from time to time. He claims that such thoughts are not really clear and distinct so we are not really being deceived by God.

Central argument

My imagination and sense perceptions involve the ideas of extended bodies (matter). What causes these ideas?

I can conceive of myself clearly and distinctly as a non-extended thing existing distinctly from my body therefore I am distinct from my body.

I cannot be making up the ideas of extended bodies because:
a) I receive sense perceptions passively or against my will and
b) they involve the concept of extension and I am unextended.
As God is no deceiver, my perceptions must be caused by extended objects.

The external world exists but is not exactly how it appears.

Material objects are essentially extended. Extension is a mathematical concept understood by the mind. The world is best understood through the mind not the senses.

God is no deceiver. Everything I conceive clearly and distinctly must be true. The external world exists. The only time I am mistaken is when I make hasty judgements.

Comment

Descartes sets out to prove that the external world exists. In doing so he is overcoming the doubts of *Meditation 1* and discovering the nature of the mind–body relationship.

Immediately after proving that the external world exists, Descartes goes on to say that it is not exactly how it appears. He outlines a primary/secondary quality distinction, suggesting that objects only really have the properties of size, shape, quantity, motion, which we can perceive clearly and distinctly. The properties of colour, sound, taste, smell, etc. are caused by the primary qualities. and are not really properties of the objects themselves.

Section 1: Epistemology

1.1 Perception: What are the immediate objects of perception?

Introduction

How do we acquire KNOWLEDGE of the world? An obvious answer is that we learn about it through our senses. We know that the cat is on the mat because we can see it there. We know that it is a hot day because we can feel the warmth of the sun on our backs. However, it is undoubtedly TRUE that our senses can deceive us from time to time. Optical illusions are a case in point; take these two examples:

a)

b)

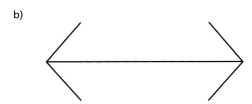

Figure 1.1 The Müller-Lyer illusion
The two horizontal lines appear to be of different lengths, but are in reality the same length.

In the Müller-Lyer illusion the horizontal line in a) appears to be longer than in b). However, if you measure the two they turn out to be the same length. Our eyes appear to have deceived us. Another case of our eyes deceiving us is when an oar appears to bend when half-immersed in water (see **Figure 1.2**). It looks bent, but we know it's really straight. Such observations raise doubts about the reliability of our sense organs in telling us about the world. So just how accurate are they as indicators of the way the world really is?

It is interesting to observe in this connection that other animals have senses that are far more sensitive than our own. Dogs, for example, can hear sounds that are too high for us to hear, and they can smell all kinds of things that we can't. Does this mean they are perceiving the world more accurately than us? Other

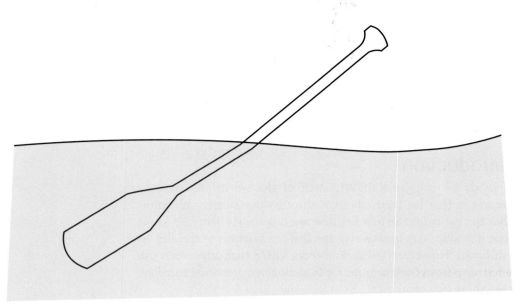

Figure 1.2 An oar half immersed in water appears crooked, but we know that in reality it remains straight.[1]

creatures have senses completely different from ours. The ability of sharks to sense the electric field created by living things, or of bats to use sound to navigate, raises the question of what the world must seem like to these animals. How do their senses represent the world in their minds? In colours and shapes? In textures and sounds? Or in some way we simply cannot imagine? Perhaps these animals have a truer PERCEPTION of the world than we do. Or perhaps no animal sees the world as it truly is.

Experimenting with ideas

1 a) Do you think your favourite food tastes the same to a dog as it does to you?

   b) Do you think dog food tastes the same to you as to a dog?

   c) Who has a truer perception of the world: dogs or humans?

2 Some creatures lack the senses we have. They may be blind or deaf. Others have senses that we don't have. They may detect electricity or magnetic fields. How many senses must a creature have for it to get a true picture of the world? Make a list of the necessary senses.

3 Dogs can hear high-frequency sound waves that we do not register. Likewise, elephants hear frequencies lower than we can register. Does it follow that all humans are partially deaf? Are some sounds so low and others so high that no creature can hear them?

4 As with sound waves, we only perceive light waves within a particular bandwidth. Imagine meeting an alien who does not perceive the frequencies of light that we do, but perceives a whole set of higher ones, such as ultra-violet and beyond. The alien represents these waves in a range of colours much as we do. Who sees the true colours of the world: humans or aliens? If neither of us does, does that mean that no colours are the real colours?

5 Can you be sure that, when you and your friend share a piece of chicken, the flavour you are experiencing is actually the same for both of you? Similarly, is there any way of telling that you are seeing exactly the same colours as someone else?

6 Sound is caused by compression waves of air hitting your ear drum. If a tree fell down in a forest and there were no ears around (human or otherwise), would it:
   a) make a sound?
   b) just produce airwaves?

7 Where are rainbows? Are they in the sky, in rain droplets, in people's minds or nowhere?

The questions above raise deep puzzles about how what we perceive connects up with the world around us. Are we perceiving reality directly or is there some indirect relationship between what we perceive and what is really there? In other words, is there something which *mediates* or gets between us and the world and which might mean that our perception may not always reveal things as they truly are?

What should be evident from your reflections on the activity questions is that we need to be clear about what is going on in perception before we can be completely confident about our answers. In other words, we need to develop some kind of theory of perception. In this chapter we will consider some of the main philosophical theories of perception, each of which offers different accounts of how we acquire knowledge of the world around us.

Realism

He thought he saw an Elephant,
That practised on a fife:
He looked again, and found it was
A letter from his wife.
'At length I realise,' he said,
'The bitterness of Life!'
'The Mad Gardener's Song', Lewis Carroll

Much of the philosophical debate over perception hinges on the question of how much of what we perceive is really a feature of the world and how much is a feature of our minds. In other words, how much of what we are perceiving is really out there? This question of what is real or not is also central to many other areas of philosophy. If you are a REALIST about something, then you believe it exists independently of our minds. If you are an ANTI-REALIST about something, you think it is mind-dependent. The following activity should draw out whether you are a realist or an anti-realist about a range of entities.

► **ACTIVITY**

For each of the following, consider whether the object or topic in question is real or not. For this exercise, take 'real' to mean 'has an existence independent of minds – human or otherwise'. Copy and complete the table.

	Real	Not real	Don't know
1 Numbers, e.g. number 7			
2 Your reflection in the mirror			
3 Colours, e.g. red			
4 Smells, e.g. coffee			
5 Morality, e.g. the wrongness of murder			
6 Electrons			
7 Scientific laws, e.g. e = mc²			
8 Ghosts			
9 Matter, i.e. physical stuff			
10 Beauty			

Real or not?

1 **Numbers**, e.g. the number 7. Whether numbers are real or not has vexed many a philosopher and is still a current debate. Plato famously thought that numbers exist independently of humans, not in the world that we see and touch, but in a world we can only perceive with our minds; a world of ideas or 'forms'. One reason for thinking this is that it would seem that mathematical truths remain true whether or not there is anyone around to recognise them: 7 + 5 has always equalled 12, even before human beings first appeared on earth. The times-tables you learnt at school will reflect truths about numbers which will remain true long after you leave school, and (if you have any) your children and grandchildren leave school. Plato was greatly influenced by another ancient Greek philosopher, Pythagoras, who thought that to understand the world truly, one must look for the mathematical structures that lie behind appearances. Pythagoras sought to uncover these structures and, among other things, revealed how music and harmony have a mathematical basis.

2 **Your reflection in the mirror.** Is your reflection behind the mirror, in the mirror, in your mind or nowhere? The mirror seems to be a window into another world but one that doesn't exist in real physical space. So is your reflection a part of the physical world? Or is the mirror world just an illusion in the mind? What mirrors seem to show is that the way we locate objects in the world around us is a result of the direction that rays of light enter our eyes. So sometimes these rays can enter our eyes at angles that suggest to our minds the presence of an object that is really somewhere else.

3 **Colours**, e.g. red. Some will argue that the word 'red' refers to the way humans see a particular wavelength of light when it hits their retinas. Others see it as the name for the particular wavelength itself. It could also be the name for a physical object's propensity to bounce back visible light at a particular frequency. So red could be in the head, in the air or on the tomato. The same, of course, is true of colours generally, such as the colour green and trees (see **Figure 1.3**).

4 **Smell.** This is discussed on page 18.

5 Morality. Are good and evil objectively real? This is a key question in ETHICS, which is studied at A Level. Those who think that morality exists independently of human minds and that there is a fact of the matter about whether or not murder is wrong, are ethical realists. Those who think that morality is in some sense a product of human minds are ethical anti-realists.

6 Electrons. Some take the view that electrons and other theoretical entities that cannot be directly observed are just a useful story we invent to make sense of experimental data. They are part of a model which helps to explain what we can observe. Others believe that such objects do actually exist and exist as we conceive them.

7 Scientific laws. These are formulated in the minds of humans, but to be successful they must be able to explain and predict aspects of the world. This raises the question of how real they are and whether there is something out there to which the law could correspond. Some anti-realists take the view that the laws do not correspond to anything and cannot really be said to be true or false – they are merely instrumental in helping humans manipulate the world. A realist may take the view that scientific laws, as they slowly evolve, edge ever closer to the truth – that is, to matching the laws of the universe.

8 Ghosts. We leave this for you to decide.

9 Matter. Some philosophers argue that the only things of which we are ever aware are ideas or sensations in our minds and that matter is just a convenient way of talking about these sensations. Most people, however, believe that there really is a material universe that we perceive all around us and that it exists independently of our minds. This is a realist view about physical objects and is the subject we explore below (page 6).

10 Beauty. Some may argue that the concept of beauty – whether in the setting of the sun or the song of the nightingale – is so universal that there must be an external standard of beauty to which these things refer. Others think that beauty is subjective – or at most culturally ingrained – and is thus solely in the eye of the beholder. This second view is probably more common these days. However, consider that it does seem odd to suppose that *anything* could be beautiful. We might think a person didn't really understand the meaning of the word, if they claimed that their chewed pen lid was a thing of beauty.

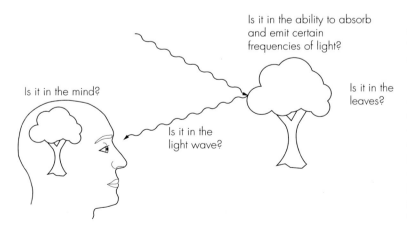

Figure 1.3 Where is the green of the tree? The word 'green' appears to have various meanings. It can refer to something in the leaves themselves: the objective property that the naïve realist says they have. It can refer to the power the leaves have to absorb and emit various wavelengths of light. It can refer to the specific wavelength itself that leaves typically emit. Or it can refer to the experience of the colour as it appears to us in our minds.

Realist theories of perception

If you examine your ordinary assumptions about the way perception works, then you'll probably find you hold a realist view. Common sense, in other words, is committed to REALISM about the world around us; it believes that physical objects exist independently of our minds. Common sense also tends to support DIRECT REALISM: the idea that we perceive things immediately, that is, without anything getting between us and the objects we perceive. So let us sketch out an initial version of this common-sense view, a view often called *NAÏVE* DIRECT REALISM since it is what people tend to adhere to before really engaging in philosophical reflection on the matter.

Direct realism

Direct realism claims that objects are composed of matter; they occupy space, and have properties such as size, shape, texture, smell, taste and colour. These properties are perceived directly. In other words, when we look at, listen to and touch things, we see, hear and feel those things themselves with no intermediary. The naïve view tends to suppose this means that we must perceive objects as they truly are. So, when you look at your red door the reason you see it as red is that it really is red. And when others come to visit, they also see the same objects with the same properties. Importantly, objects also retain their properties whether or not there is anyone present to observe them; when you turn out the light to go to bed, the objects you can no longer see remain where they are and with the same shapes and colours as before. You may not be able to see it, but your door is still red.

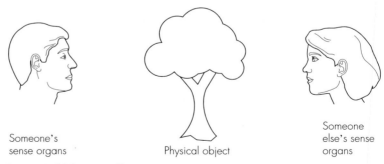

Someone's sense organs   Physical object   Someone else's sense organs

Figure 1.4 Direct realism
Direct realism identifies two elements in perception: the perceiver and the thing perceived. We perceive mind-independent objects and our senses put us in immediate contact with them. Our sense organs detect properties of objects which exist out there in the world, and all of us perceive the same objects with the same properties.

► **ACTIVITY**

If a tree falls in a forest and no animal or person is there to hear it, then does it make a noise?

a) What do you personally think?

b) What would a direct realist say?

The direct realist would say that the tree does make a noise. The world is how is appears to be and whenever someone is present as a tree falls, they are immediately aware of the noise it creates. If we can observe falling trees making noises, we can be confident that this is what they do, regardless of whether anyone happens to be present. In sum, the direct realist is saying that we perceive objects with certain properties because they are there and have those properties, and we know they are there and have the properties they do because we can perceive them.

Issues with direct realism

Most philosophers have felt that direct realism, at least in its naïve version as we have so far characterised it, cannot be maintained. The philosopher David Hume, for example, claimed that once one had engaged in 'the slightest philosophy'[2] one would be forced to give it up.

Criticism 1: Perceptual variation

Many of the difficulties that direct realism faces were highlighted by the great British empiricist philosopher, George Berkeley (1685– 1753) in his *Three Dialogues between Hylas and Philonous* (1713). The character of Philonous, Berkeley's spokesman, asks Hylas to consider what the colour of some distant clouds is (see **Figure 1.5**).

Since the clouds may appear red from a distance, and any number of colours from different perspectives, according to Berkeley it makes no sense to suppose that they have any real colour. This goes just as well for any objects. If we look closely at a flower through a microscope its colour will be different from how it looks to the naked eye. The conclusion that may be drawn is that the colour is merely an effect made upon us by physical things, and not something in the objects themselves. In other words, colour is an appearance to us, not something objectively real.

Someone far off

Someone close

Figure 1.5 Berkeley's example of observing clouds

The clouds appear different colours to different observers. But who is right? No one has any privileged perspective, and so no one can observe the true colour. Therefore colour is an appearance to observers, and not something real.

7

Bertrand Russell makes this same point in *The Problems of Philosophy* when discussing the appearance of his table, which, because of the way light reflects off its surface, appears to be different colours from different points of view. He concludes that the colour cannot be something which is really in the table itself. Rather it is an appearance which depends upon how the light falls upon it and the position of the spectator. Russell then considers a possible objection. You might be tempted to claim that the real colour is the colour as seen by a person standing near the object under normal lighting conditions. This certainly seems to be what we ordinarily mean when we talk about *the* colour of the table (see **Figure 1.6**).

anthology
1.1

Figure 1.6 Russell contemplates his table

'When, in ordinary life, we speak of *the* colour of the table, we only mean the sort of colour which it will seem to have to a normal spectator from an ordinary point of view under usual conditions of light. But the other colours which appear under other conditions have just as good a right to be considered real; and therefore, to avoid favouritism, we are compelled to deny that, in itself, the table has any one particular colour.'[3]

anthology
1.2

However, the difficulty for this defence is to determine which distance and lighting conditions should be given the privileged status of revealing reality. The apparent colour of an object will change throughout the day, from the bright light of noon to the soft light of the evening, so that it would be impossible to determine which time of day reveals the 'true' colours. The French impressionist painter Claude Monet painted a series of haystacks at different times of day in order to explore the different effects different light had on their appearance. But it makes no sense to ask which painting reveals the true colour since we have no way of choosing. And even if certain colours appear more commonly than others, this is still no basis for favouring them over the less common.

Locke discusses our perception of heat in the same vein. He asks us to imagine putting a hot hand and a cold hand into the same bucket of lukewarm water. The water then feels cold to one hand and hot to the other. But clearly the same small area of water cannot really be both hot and cold at the same time. This would be a contradiction. So the conclusion follows that it must merely appear to be hot and cold. Heat and cold, therefore, are not real properties of objects but appearances; they are effects such objects have on observers like us. (Leibniz provides a telling objection to this ARGUMENT when commenting on it in *The New Essays*. You can read his comment in the Anthology.)

anthology 1.3

Hume and Russell extend this line of reasoning to the size and shape of objects.[4] Russell points out that his table appears to take on different apparent geometric forms when observed from different angles. If we attend carefully to the appearance in the way we might if trying to draw the table, we will note that the sides, which in reality we suppose are parallel, converge slightly the further away from the spectator they go. And the angles at the corners of the table hardly ever appear as right angles. The apparent shape also changes as we move around the table (see **Figure 1.7**).

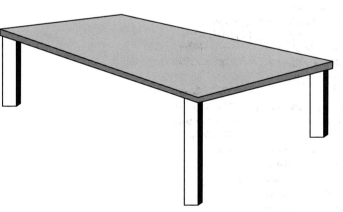

Figure 1.7 How a rectangular table appears in perspective
The way the table actually appears to us may be accurately represented by an artist and the appearance has a different shape from what we take the real shape to be. The angles are either obtuse or acute, and the sides are not parallel. And yet the real table is rectangular.

Since the table cannot really be changing its colour and shape continually, and neither can different observers be accurately perceiving it to be different colours and shapes at the same time, it seems that the direct realist must concede that objects cannot be exactly as we perceive them to be. What Russell, following Locke and Hume, concludes is that what we are directly aware of is not the table itself, but the appearance of the table to our minds. The appearance is a trapezium, the reality is a rectangle. The appearance will change with point of view, while the reality remains relatively constant.

Sense data

Russell calls these appearances SENSE DATA. Sense data are the immediate objects of perception. They are what we are directly aware of, as distinct from the physical objects which cause them. It is on the basis of our awareness of sense data that we infer the existence of the table, so that the table itself is only perceived indirectly. Sense data are thought to be certain. That is, I cannot be mistaken about how objects appear to me.

> *Let us give the name of 'sense-data' to the things that are immediately known in sensation: such things as colours, sounds, smells, hardnesses, roughnesses, and so on ... if we are to know anything about the table, it must be by means of the sense-data – brown colour, oblong shape, smoothness, etc. – which we associate with the table.*
>
> **Bertrand Russell, *Problems of Philosophy*, Chapter 1**

Defending direct realism

However, this may not mean we are forced to reject direct realism. After all, we are rarely fooled by the perspective we take into mistaking the real colours or shapes of objects. Moreover, we can explain how it is that objects will appear differently from different angles because of the lighting conditions, the point of view taken, and so on. Monet's haystacks appear to be different colours because of the colour of the light at different times of day – but we still know that hay is yellowy-brown. The science of optics explains why the shape of a table will appear different when viewed from different points of view – but we still know it is rectangular.

While direct realists must concede that we don't perceive the world precisely as it is, they can deny that this implies that we don't perceive it directly. The conditions may alter the way we perceive objects and yet it is still the objects themselves that we are directly perceiving. Defenders of direct realism accuse Russell of making an unwarranted inference from the FACT that a table appears different from how it is, to supposing that we must be immediately aware of an apparent table and only indirectly aware of the real table. But a direct realist interprets the situation differently. To say that the table appears different from how it is doesn't commit us to saying we are not directly aware of it or that there is something distinct from the real table, its appearance, which we are directly aware of. Rather the table remains the immediate object of perception, but it can nonetheless appear differently from how it is.

Criticism 2: Illusion

The second problem is one we have already begun to consider: the fact that our senses are subject to illusions. It happens on occasion that I perceive an object which appears to be one thing, when in reality it is another. A straw half immersed in my glass of water may appear to be bent when in fact it is straight, or a tower which appears round from a distance looks square when observed from close to.[5] The conclusion is drawn that what we immediately perceive cannot be what is in the world, since what we are perceiving is not the same as what is really there. The appearance of which I am directly aware, my sense data, are certain since I cannot go wrong when making judgements about how things appear to me. I know the straw appears bent, even though I may be uncertain of what it is really like. So errors only occur when I make judgements on the basis of sense data concerning what causes them (see **Figure 1.8a**).

▶ ACTIVITY

Can you think of occasions when you have been deceived by your senses in this way? Take a note of your own examples of perceptual illusions.

Defending direct realism

It may be that the direct realist can respond by claiming that in such situations the senses accurately reveal the world to us, but it's just that we can misinterpret what we perceive. Normally we are not fooled by the way water refracts light differently from air, but if ever we are fooled, it is because we have misinterpreted the information given us by our eyes.[6]

The argument from illusion also assumes that if we misperceive something that we must be immediately perceiving something which is distinct from the reality. But we can explain misperception in another way – by simply saying we misperceive the reality. We can perceive a straight straw as bent without this implying that we directly perceive a bent straw and only indirectly a straight one.

Criticism 3: Hallucinations

If illusions happen when I perceive a real thing as if it were something else, when hallucinating I am appearing to perceive something when in reality there is nothing there at all. During an hallucination it may not be possible for me to distinguish my experience from genuine perception. The visible appearance of the dagger is exactly the same to Macbeth as if he were seeing a real dagger before him. But since what the hallucinator is perceiving does not exist in the world, it must exist only as a 'dagger of the mind'. But to say that an experience is subjectively indistinguishable from a genuine experience is to say that it is the same to me whether or not there is a dagger. The argument concludes that what I am immediately aware of even when truly perceiving a dagger cannot be the real dagger (see **Figure 1.8b**).

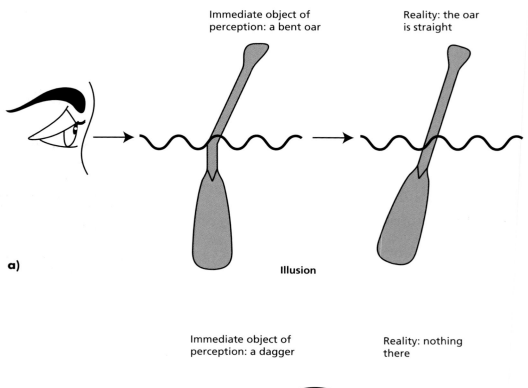

Immediate object of perception: a bent oar

Reality: the oar is straight

a)

Illusion

Immediate object of perception: a dagger

Reality: nothing there

b)

Hallucination

Figure 1.8 Illusions and hallucinations according to critics of direct realism

According to critics of direct realism, when I perceive an oar as bent when it is straight in reality, this is because I don't directly perceive the oar itself, but an appearance of the oar. And when I hallucinate, what I am directly perceiving is an appearance indistinguishable from the perceptions I might have when not hallucinating. The only difference is that there is no real object corresponding to the perception.

Defending direct realism

One response to the hallucination argument is to point out that we can, as a matter of fact, identify when we are hallucinating. Macbeth knows the dagger is not real precisely because he cannot grasp it with his hands. In other words, another sense helps him detect the deception. Indeed, if we couldn't detect hallucinations, then we would remain unaware that we were ever subject to them. It seems to follow that if hallucinations were really subjectively indistinguishable from veridical (that is, truthful or accurate) perception, then we wouldn't know we had had them and so the hallucination argument could not get started.

Another response is to deny that hallucinations are really perceptions at all. Even supposing that a hallucination and a veridical perception are indistinguishable to the person having them, it doesn't mean they are not in reality distinct kinds of phenomenon. While I may be unable to tell that I'm hallucinating at the time, this doesn't mean that hallucinations are not very different in terms of how they are produced from genuine perception. Macbeth's vision proceeds from his 'heat-oppressed brain', not from light entering his eyes reflecting off the surface of any real dagger. Thus there is no reason to suppose that genuine perception must involve the same kind of immediate object of perception as we are aware of when hallucinating.

In his *Meditations* Descartes explores a similar train of thought when suggesting that dreams are often indistinguishable from real life. When immersed in a vivid dream I may be unable to determine whether it is a dream or reality. And if such dreams are qualitatively indistinguishable from real life, I may conclude that I cannot be certain that I am not dreaming now. It appears to follow that what we are immediately aware of is not the same as what is real.

anthology
1.4

In the same way we could complain about Descartes' dreaming argument that the fact that the person enjoying their dream cannot distinguish between the dream and reality doesn't mean that there is no difference. And if dreams are different in nature from veridical perception, again we have no reason to conclude that perception generally must involve an immediate awareness of an appearance as distinct from reality.

Criticism 4: Time lag argument

The light which reaches us from the stars has travelled across trillions of miles and taken many years to arrive. For example, there was a supernova explosion that became visible on earth in AD1054 and was recorded by Chinese astronomers. We can still see the remnants of this explosion in the Crab Nebula in the constellation of Taurus. But the Nebula is over six thousand light years away, which means that the explosion those astronomers saw actually took place six thousand years before they recorded it. What we observe today is similarly out of date, so that we cannot even be sure of whether the Crab Nebula still exists. But if it might no longer exist then we can't really be perceiving it now. If we aren't perceiving the real Crab Nebula now then what we are perceiving must be an appearance: a mental image, not the real thing.

Now, while the time lag between us and the Crab Nebula is very great, there is also a time lag, albeit a very small one, between us and the physical objects around us. The light from the table in front of me takes some time to arrive and so, it appears to follow, we are not directly perceiving the objects around us.

Russell makes the same observation in the *Problems of Philosophy* when drawing the distinction between sense data and objects:

anthology
1.5

> *It takes about eight minutes for the sun's light to reach us; thus, when we see the sun we are seeing the sun eight minutes ago … if the physical sun had ceased to exist within the last eight minutes, that would make no difference to the sense data which we call 'seeing the sun'.*

(***The Problems of Philosophy,*** chapter 3)

Defending direct realism

In response, the direct realist can accept that there is a time lag in perception, but can deny that this implies that we don't directly perceive physical objects or that we must introduce something distinct from the object which we are directly aware of: a sense datum. All that follows from the fact of a time lag is that we perceive objects as they were. And this is exactly what astronomers say: 'We can see today the Crab Nebula as it was over six thousand years ago', 'Chinese astronomers recorded the supernova explosion six thousand years after it happened.' But they still saw it. So while this argument shows that we must give up the naïve view that we perceive objects instantaneously and therefore that we cannot be aware of objects as they are now, but as they were, this doesn't refute direct realism. We are not aware of the Crab Nebula as it is now, but we are nonetheless directly aware of it as it was.

Learn More

Criticism 5: The causal argument

Locke was heavily influenced by the physics of Robert Boyle (1627–1691), according to which all physical things are made up of collections of tiny indestructible particles or atoms. This world view gives Locke a particular picture of the processes which must underlie perception. In sight, for example, there is a distance between us and the objects we perceive and therefore there must be a causal process which connects our perception to the object. Locke supposes, therefore, that 'some singly imperceptible bodies must come from them to the eyes'.[7] These days scientists would concur: particles of light – photons – emitted from objects travel through the intervening space and enter our eyes, causing us to see. Hearing is no different. Boyle himself showed that sound cannot travel in a vacuum and so the air must function as a medium through which the information from sound-emitting objects travels to our ears. Subsequently, there is a further internal process whereby our visual or auditory systems process the information received until, finally, these processes result in perception. As Locke has it, the particles of light coming from external objects 'convey to the brain some motion, which produces these ideas which we have of them'.[8] So the particles which convey information from the world around us are not perceptible themselves, but they produce in us a perception or 'idea' which represents the EXTERNAL WORLD. Thus what we are immediately aware of, once again, is not the external world itself, but an appearance of the world within our minds. We perceive the world indirectly.

Defending direct realism

Defenders of direct realism can accept that I am aware of objects around me via a causal process, but deny that this implies that I am aware of the appearance of the object first and the real object only indirectly. Locke's mistake is to think that if the process leading to perception ends in the brain, that there must be something – an appearance, idea or sense datum – in the brain.

In fact, reflection on our experience appears to bear out direct realism. Indeed, if Locke's picture were correct we would surely be aware of sense data as distinct from the objects which cause them. But when I look around my room, I seem to see objects themselves and it is impossible to disentangle the two. I am not aware of the appearance or of an inference to objects, but only of the objects themselves.

▶ **ACTIVITY**

There is a 'blind spot' in your vision. This is caused by an area on the retina without light receptors where the optic nerve takes the information to the brain. To find your blind spot, follow these instructions.

In the margin we have printed a circle and a square. In a moment:

- tip the book on its side so that the square is on the right and the circle on the left
- close your right eye
- hold the book at arm's length and focus on the square
- move the book slowly toward you
- at some point the circle will 'disappear' as the light bouncing off it falls on your blind spot.

not include the colour of the coin, only the wavelength of light the coin bounces back. Yet the alien's description would not be lacking in any important way, so it seems we must conclude that the coin does not have the property of being coloured in the same way that it has other properties such as shape and density.

Now consider smell. One theory is that different smells are caused by the different shapes of airborne molecules. On the inside of our noses are thousands of receptors. When we inhale, millions of molecules whizz up through our noses and, if they are the right shape and size, some of these molecules will lodge briefly in these receptors. If enough molecules of the same type do this then we perceive a particular odour. So molecules are not coated with a smelly property that we somehow perceive. They merely have a shape which, in humans, causes the subjective experience of a smell and there is no resemblance between our sensation of smell and the shape of the molecule.

Descartes argues that the sensation of heat also cannot accurately resemble any real property of fire. Rather we should suppose that there is something in the fire which causes us to feel heat, but which is of a completely different nature from the sensation. He points out that we do not suppose that the pain fire may cause us when we get too close is really in the fire, so by the same logic, we ought to reckon that the heat it causes in us is also not in the fire.

anthology
1.6

Although I feel heat when I approach a fire and feel pain when I go too near, there is no good reason to think that something in the fire resembles the heat, or resembles the pain. There is merely reason to suppose that something or other in the fire causes feelings of heat or pain in us.

Locke agrees. He supposes that the qualities of objects that cause certain sensations in us have something to do with the minute particles from which they are composed and their movements. The relationship between these qualities of the object which cause us to, for example, see blue or smell a sweet scent, is an *arbitrary* one, meaning that there is no resemblance between the sensation of blue and whatever it is in the flower which cause it. Locke points out that we can conceive that God might have arranged things differently. The fact that we can imagine whatever it is that causes us to see blue actually causing a different sensation shows that the relationship between the sensation and the objective property is not one of resemblance.[9]

He tells us that the relationship between the immediate objects of perception and the qualities in objects causing them is like that between a word and the idea it invokes in our minds. Just as the word 'flower' doesn't resemble a real flower but is arbitrarily associated with it, so too the blue colour doesn't resemble the quality of the flower which produces it. The immediate objects of perception are not 'exactly the images and *resemblances* of something inherent in the subject: most of those sensations being in the mind no more the likeness of something existing without us, than the names that stand for them are the likeness of our *ideas*, which yet upon hearing they are apt to excite in us.'[10] For this reason, we cannot directly know what it is that causes us to see blue.[11]

Thus it would seem that objects physically possess some properties, whereas other properties are related to the minds experiencing them. Primary qualities are those that exist independently of our perceiving them, while secondary are those that require a perceiving mind. This is how Locke defines the two: Secondary qualities are:

> ... *such qualities which in truth are nothing in the objects themselves, but powers to produce various sensations in us by their primary qualities, i.e. by the bulk, figure, texture, and motion of their insensible parts, as colours, sounds, tastes, etc. these I call secondary qualities*

anthology 1.7

Essay, II, viii.10

Perceived object   Real object

Figure 1.9 Indirect realism and primary and secondary qualities
Indirect realism distinguishes what we are immediately aware of in sensation from the world itself. The immediate objects of perception are mind-dependent sense data which represent for us the mind-independent reality. But only some aspects of the representation are accurate. Our perception of primary qualities gives us an accurate picture of the size, shape and position of objects. But our perception of colours, smells and sounds do not. These are imperfect representations of the secondary qualities which cause them. Locke likens the relationship between sensations of secondary qualities to the relationship between words and ideas because it is arbitrary.

Leibniz wrote an extended commentary of Locke's *Essay Concerning Human Understanding*, published as the *New Essays Concerning Human Understanding*. He has an interesting response to Locke's primary/secondary quality distinction. In Leibniz's view nothing happens without a reason (this is his Principle of

anthology 1.8   Learn More

Sufficient Reason, see pages 277–278); or, as he puts it, to make an arbitrary decision on how to link the sensation with the secondary quality is not God's way. So, he argues, there must be a resemblance between our sensations and what causes them, even though we may not be able to recognise it. Leibniz's disagreement hangs on the fact that he denies the Cartesian assumption that Locke adopts that sense data are simple and that we have a complete idea of their true nature. Leibniz believes instead that sensations are compounds of smaller and unperceived sensations, or 'minute perceptions'. So the sound of the sea is not a simple sense datum, but is compounded out of smaller perceptions which lie below the threshold of consciousness. Since our sensations of secondary qualities are complex not simple, there is no reason to suppose that there is not some relationship of resemblance between them and the secondary qualities, it is just that we cannot bring this resemblance to consciousness in the way we can with primary qualities.[12]

► ACTIVITY

Here are some possible properties of things. Which of these properties do you think are primary – properties that actually belong to objects? Which are secondary – reliant on humans or minds?

Primary and secondary qualities are not always defined or divided up in precisely the same way by philosophers. But a traditional division is set out in the table below. Did you agree? How would you place these various qualities?

Primary qualities, i.e. real, physical qualities	Secondary qualities, i.e. the 'powers' of the object to produce experiences in humans (and other animals)	Other associated properties, often a social concept but in part a result of the primary or secondary qualities
• Position (i.e. where the object is) • Number (i.e. how many there are) • Shape • Size (i.e. how big it is) • Motion (i.e. how fast it is moving) • Colour • Heat and cold • Smell • Sound • Taste • Beauty • Value • Addictive • Important • Disposable		

People often find it difficult to recall which are the primary and which the secondary qualities. One way to think about the difference and so remember the terminology is to regard the primary qualities as those that are in objects from the beginning or primarily; that is, before anyone comes along to perceive them. By contrast, the secondary qualities are those which appear only secondarily, when minds arrive on the scene to perceive things. In a world without perceivers there would be lots of objects with primary qualities reacting to each other; they would collide, melt, dissolve, and so forth. The objects in this world can also be said to have secondary qualities as they would still have the potential to produce subjective experiences in perceivers should any appear. But without the perceivers there would be no experiences of the secondary qualities and no sensations of colour, sound or smell (see **Figure 1.9**).

Another way of conceiving the difference between primary and secondary qualities is to consider how physical objects behave. Physical objects act and interact with one another on the basis of their primary qualities. The outcome of a collision between two moving objects, say billiard balls, depends on their mass, direction of movement, speed and how they are held together by the atoms that compose them. In other words, the outcome depends entirely on the primary qualities of the objects involved. Secondary qualities have nothing to do with how objects behave. Secondary qualities are just the powers of an object to produce experiences in perceivers and so do not have an effect on how physical objects interact with each other.

Also, note that for Locke secondary qualities ultimately boil down to primary qualities. Consider the example of smell given above. A smell is a secondary quality – the power of a molecule to produce a subjective experience in a perceiver. However, a molecule has this power in virtue of the organisation of its parts and this organisation is a matter of the primary qualities (shape, size, and so on) alone. So although objects can be said to have secondary qualities, in terms of physics alone they have only primary qualities. These primary qualities have the potential to cause specific experiences in humans, and it is this potential we term a secondary quality. Thus it can be said that a secondary quality is simply the potential of a primary quality to produce an experience in a perceiver.

Locke lists the properties he considers to be primary: 'These I call original or primary qualities of body, which I think we may observe to produce simple ideas in us, viz. solidity, extension, figure, motion or rest, and number'.[13] However, the list changes slightly later in the *Essay* when he adds texture, size and situation and leaves out number, extension and solidity.

There are other considerations which have led philosophers to draw the primary/secondary quality distinction.

1   All the primary qualities lend themselves readily to mathematical or geometric description. They are measurable. The positions of any objects relative to any others can be precisely described, as can their number, shape, speed, and so on. So I can say that one object is moving three times as fast as another, that it is twice as big, and so on. And I can meaningfully say that a hexagon has twice the number of sides as a triangle. However, subjectively experienced smells, colours, and so on just don't behave like this. We cannot add, subtract, divide or multiply tastes, flavours, colours, touches or smells in the same way that we can sizes, shapes, speeds, masses and quantities.

    In *Meditation 6* Descartes draws the primary/secondary quality distinction in this way. Only those qualities that can be represented geometrically are real and this leads him to exclude weight and hardness, which have no shape, position or size.

2   Developments in natural science may also lead us to suppose that the world cannot be precisely as it appears to be. We have seen that Locke adhered to the corpuscular physics of his day, according to which the universe is made up of imperceptible atoms or corpuscles which possess the properties of size, solidity and shape.[14] Secondary qualities are the microstructures of these particles which cause sensations in us. And contemporary science is not so far removed from this sort of view. For example, physics tells us that light is a form of electromagnetic radiation and that what we perceive as different colours are in reality simply light waves of different lengths reflecting off the surfaces of objects. Light in itself, in other words, is not coloured. In reality it possesses only the primary qualities of having a certain magnitude of wavelength, of travelling at a particular speed, and so on. Similarly, heat in objects cannot properly be said to be hot or cold. Rather, our experience of hot and cold is produced by our coming into contact with physical objects with differing mean kinetic energy levels among their component atoms and molecules. The sounds we experience are not things with independent existences. Rather they are produced in us by compression waves of air impacting on our eardrums.

3   Another way of marking the distinction between primary and secondary qualities is to reflect on which

properties appear to be essential to objects and which do not. Essential properties are those an object cannot be without and remain an object and so these must be primary. Secondary qualities, by contrast, since they only appear in conjunction with perceivers, are inessential. There are different ways of distinguishing the essential from the inessential properties of an object. One very attractive method can be performed in your imagination now. You simply need to reflect on which properties you can or cannot conceive of an object lacking. Inessential properties will be those that you can imagine an object without. And the essential properties will be those you cannot.

To illustrate this approach, consider the following thought experiment about a bachelor. Can you imagine a bachelor who is hungry? Would he still be a bachelor if he were bald? Clearly yes. So being well fed and having a full head of hair are not essential properties of a bachelor. However, would a man still be a bachelor if he got married? Clearly not. You can't be a married bachelor. Such a thing is inconceivable. Would he still be a bachelor if he had a sex change? No. You can't be a bachelor unless you are male. So we have shown that being unmarried and being male are essential properties of being a bachelor.

Now let us apply this same method to physical objects and their properties. Think of an object, say an apple. If you imagine it is making no sound (which is not difficult to do) then you are still thinking of an object (a silent apple). So making a noise cannot be an essential property of an object like an apple. Similarly, if you suppose it to have no odour, then you are still thinking of an object. Next subtract its flavour. Still you are thinking of an object, albeit not a very appetising one. You may say that it is no longer an apple, but certainly it is still an object of some sort. But now let us go further and imagine it without any colour. Again, it is plausible to argue that you are still thinking of an object, only now it is invisible. Perhaps it has been 'cloaked' by some alien technology that bends the light waves around its surface so that our eyes cannot detect it; or had a wizard's invisibility cloak thrown over it. So here we have subtracted sound, odour, flavour and colour but we are still thinking of an object. This suggests that these qualities are inessential and so that it is possible for an object to exist without them.

But let us return to our apple and imagine it devoid of any shape, size, position or motion, neither still or moving. Here, it seems our imagination fails us. An object cannot lack these properties and remain an object. An object cannot be neither moving nor still. It cannot be completely without shape. It must have a particular size and occupy a specific position in space. It would seem, then, that these properties are not properties an object could lack in reality. If they are essential to the object they cannot be properties that we merely perceive in it, but which aren't really there. It follows that they must be primary qualities. At the same time, those qualities that we can imagine an object doing without must be inessential, and so plausibly they exist only through their relations with perceiving beings like ourselves. (Does this example convince you? We will return to it later.)

Locke makes a similar point when he asks us to imagine dividing up a grain of wheat. He says that the primary qualities will remain no matter how small we cut it up – even when we can no longer see the parts – and therefore that they are essential to any portion of matter.[15]

Qualities thus considered in bodies are, first, such as are utterly inseparable from the body, in what state soever it be; such as in all the alterations and changes it suffers, all the force can be used upon it, it constantly keeps; and such as sense constantly finds in every particle of matter which has bulk enough to be perceived; and the mind finds inseparable from every particle of matter [...] : e.g. take a grain of wheat, divide it into two parts; each part has still solidity, extension, figure, and mobility: divide it again, and it retains still the same qualities; and so divide it on, till the parts become insensible; they must retain still each of them all those qualities.

(**Essay**, II.viii.9)

4   Locke also draws our attention to the apparent fact that primary qualities are accessible to more than one sense. So I can both see and hear the movement of a bus. And I can feel and see the shape and position of a die. However, secondary qualities can only be picked out by one sense. I cannot hear the redness of an apple, smell the song of a blackbird or see the warmth of a cup of tea. Since a primary quality detected by one sense admits of an independent check, it must have real existence independent of the way a particular sense organ happens to be constituted.

▶ **ACTIVITY: How convincing do you find the distinction?**

Does the fact that they are accessible to more than one sense necessarily show that they are objective? Would shape be a secondary quality if we were all blind?

Does the fact that they are amenable to mathematical description show they are objective? Just because judgements in maths provide us with NECESSARY TRUTHS, doesn't itself show that objects in the world necessarily obey these rules.

Does the fact that we can't imagine them without primary qualities show that objects must have those qualities? Perhaps our imaginations are limited.

Is it really possible to imagine an object with no secondary qualities? When you imagined the colourless, odourless apple earlier, didn't the image in your mind's eye have to have *some* colour for it to be an image at all?

Indirect realism readily accommodates the primary and secondary quality distinction. Some of those properties that we perceive to be in objects really are there, and some are not. So the former are accurate reflections of the way the world is in reality and so should form the basis for our scientific knowledge of it, while the latter are a kind of illusion. This is not to say, however, that they aren't useful or that they tell us nothing of interest about the world around us. Our sensations of colour, sound, smell, and so on are not completely misleading, since they do map onto real differences in the objects but at a scale too small for us to detect. Matter might not be coloured in the sense that redness as we experience it is out there on the surfaces of things. But an apple does have certain properties to do with its ability to absorb, emit and reflect light that we succeed in picking out by seeing it as red, and it is often useful to be able to recognise these properties. For example, the ability to see red helps up pick out ripe fruits from a leafy background. Similarly food stuffs might not be objectively bitter, but foods that taste bitter are often poisonous to us. And the sweet taste of an apple signals to us that it is rich in energy-giving sugars.

A final way to understand what the indirect realist is saying is to imagine yourself reduced to the size of a molecule of air inside some miniature flying ship in which to get around the world. Imagine observing what happens when a person smells a smell, hears a sound or sees a colour. Nothing in what you observe would be smelly, noisy or colourful. The molecules producing the smell wouldn't themselves smell, nor would the compression waves of air you observe have any sound. The wavelengths of light entering someone's eyes would have a particular length, but no colour, and the surfaces of the things that reflect these wavelengths would also have no colour. (How precisely one would observe the real world if so reduced in size is a difficulty we will ignore.) So, from the point of view of this microscopic ship, the real world is odourless, colourless and silent: a world describable only in the language of particles and forces. However, you would be able to see how perceptual system distorts reality, then it will distort it in the same way for all humans. The fact that we both see bananas as bent tells us about the way we see bananas, rather than the way bananas are. Using another human doesn't get round the question of how accurate human perception is.

In this connection it may be useful to consider the film *The Matrix*. This is premised on the idea that everyone is connected to a vast super-computer that feeds data directly to the human brain in such a way that the humans consider what is portrayed to be reality. In many ways this idea is similar to that presented by Descartes' demon (see page xvi), although the whole of humanity is being deceived this time, not just one person. For those in the 'matrix' there is a big difference between reality and what appears to them to be real. This difference arises because their perceptions are not caused by what they think is reality but by a machine. What we perceive as colours and smells, and three-dimensional space, is all produced by the zeros and ones of computer code. For the people in the matrix, appealing to fellow matrix 'dwellers' to confirm that what they see is real is futile, for they too are being deceived. Likewise, without needing to resort to the idea of a deceptive matrix, if somehow human experience in general doesn't accurately mirror reality then the testimony of others will not help us one jot.

Criticism 2: Scepticism about the existence of the external world

But there is a worse problem for indirect realism. Recall Descartes' evil demon scenario, according to which our sense data could be caused by something entirely different from what we ordinarily suppose they are. If this were the case there is nothing in our sense experience that would reveal it, and so we cannot be certain that there really is a physical world out there.

Russell raises this 'uncomfortable possibility' in Chapter 2 of *The Problems of Philosophy*, accepting that we cannot strictly prove FALSE the idea that ' the whole outer world is nothing but a dream'. Nonetheless he does think we have very good reasons for rejecting it and an initial solution he considers is, once again, to appeal to the testimony of other people. Surely, when we sit around the dinner table we are all perceiving the same table. Since we all perceive something which is more or less similar, it seems reasonable to suppose there is a real object there which causes our perceptions.

However, this solution will not do, argues Russell. For this presupposes that there really do exist other people. But if I am questioning whether there really exist physical objects independently of my sense data, I must also be questioning whether other people exist independently of my sense data. The sceptical worry we have been led into encompasses not just all the things around me, but all the people as well.

> *Thus, when we are trying to show that there must be objects independent of our own sense-data, we cannot appeal to the testimony of other people, since this testimony itself consists of sense-data, and does not reveal other people's experiences unless our own sense-data are signs of things existing independently of us.*

Russell, *The Problems of Philosophy*, Chapter 2, page 7

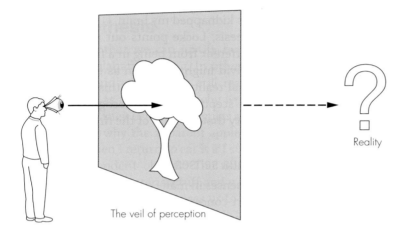

The veil of perception

Reality

Figure 1.11 The veil of perception and the trap of solipsism
All we have direct access to are our own sensations. We cannot peer beyond the veil of perception to perceive the world as it really is. But if we can't penetrate the veil of perception, then not only can we not know what the world is really like, but we can never know that the real world exists at all. Perhaps something else entirely is causing our sensations.

Locke's defences

Locke draws our attention to certain features of our sense experience which strongly suggest that they are caused by an external world.[19] His argument is not a complete proof, which, for reasons we have discussed, he recognises must be beyond him, but rather an argument to the best explanation. That is to say, the features he draws attention to are, he believes, best explained by supposing there is an external world. We will focus on two of these features.

1 The lack of choice over our experiences

One such feature is that sense experiences cannot be controlled in the way that remembered experiences can. For example, I can conjure in my imagination the smell of a rose or the taste of sugar at will. However, sensations 'force themselves upon me' so that I have no choice about whether or not to perceive something. '[I]f I turn my eyes at noon towards the sun, I cannot avoid the ideas which the light or sun then produces in me.'[20] The fact that I cannot control what sensations I have suggests that there is something external to me which produces them within me. Descartes makes the same point in his *Meditations*.

anthology
1.9

anthology
1.10

Russell develops the point that it is far simpler to suppose objects exist independently of us than that my experience is an extended dream using the example of his cat. 'If the cat exists whether I see it or not, we can understand from our own experience how it gets hungry between one meal and the next.' But if we suppose it ceases to exist, just why the cat should become hungry in the interim becomes mysterious. Thus the hypothesis that the cat continues to exist makes best sense of the available evidence.

Learn More

We cannot even talk about the real world

Some philosophers have gone further still in analysing the consequences of this gap between sensation and reality. Immanuel Kant argued that we cannot know anything about the 'real' world (which he called the noumenal world). Our mind receives data from this world, which it then processes. What we perceive (which he termed the phenomenal world) has been processed by the mind. This post-processed world is all we have access to. All the words and concepts we learn during our lives are learned by dealing with the world as we perceive it: the world of colours, smells, tastes and textures. As such, our concepts are designed to match and apply to this world of sensation. If this is the case, then there is no reason at all why our concepts should apply to the noumenal world – the world as it really is. For example, earlier we said that the real world is the cause of our sensations. However, can we really say this? After all, causation is a concept that (as far as we can know) applies only to the world of sense experience. It is only within our experience that we observe one event causing another, but we cannot observe the real world causing the perceived world, nor can we suppose the real world exhibits causal relations at all. The same applies to space and time. All of our sensations appear to us in space and time, but we cannot know whether the real world behind the veil is spatio-temporal. We, of course, cannot imagine what a world would be like that did not involve space, time or causality. But that is to be expected, since we can only understand and imagine the world of our experience. The real world lies totally beyond our comprehension. We shouldn't even call it a world at all. We should say nothing about it whatsoever.

Kant suggests that we should call the perceived world the real world, as this is the world we inhabit and is the only world of which we can meaningfully speak.

Is there a physical world?

We have seen the indirect realist introduce a gap between the nature of our experiences and the nature of the physical world in order to account for the possibility of sense deception and the apparent fact that not everything we perceive is real. But in the process it appears we have to accept that our claims to know things about a physical world that is supposed to exist independently of our experience cannot be fully justified. Sceptical doubts have forced us to retreat behind the veil of perception. If direct knowledge of the physical world is impossible and we can find no conclusive reason to suppose that the world exists at all, then belief in the external world begins to look like an irrational superstition, something which for practical purposes we cannot doubt, but which serious philosophers must reject. This is the position of the SOLIPSIST. The solipsist has a rich interior life of her own sense experiences, but denies that anything exists other than such experiences. The universe of the solipsist is a purely mental universe of one.

Few, if any, philosophers have defended SOLIPSISM. This may be because any sincere solipsists would have no reason to write down their arguments since they would not believe there was anyone else around to read them. If I were ever to encounter someone defending solipsism I could be sure that they were mistaken since if I could understand their arguments then someone other than the solipsist (namely myself) must exist. But just because no one else could be correct in their solipsism does not refute it as a philosophical position. The possibility that no external world and no other minds exist remains a possibility for me; that is, for the subject of experience. If solipsism is true, then what you are reading was not written by someone else – it is nothing more than an aspect of your consciousness.

While it may be problematic to prove that the external world exists, for everyday purposes this appears not to matter to us a great deal. We cannot but believe that we are surrounded by independently existing objects and other people and Hume and Russell have both pointed out that this belief appears to be instinctive.[25] So where philosophical arguments fail, perhaps we must make do with instinct.

▶ **ACTIVITY**

Imagine you actually believe that you are the only being in existence and everything else is some kind of illusion.

1 What would you do?
2 Would you change your life?
3 Can you think of a specific action that you might do differently?
4 Would you still have a sense of morality?
5 Is there a difference between genuine doubt and philosophical doubt?

anthology
1.11

But I desire anyone to reflect and try whether he can, by any abstraction of thought, conceive the extension and motion of a body without all other sensible qualities. For my own part, I see evidently that it is not in my power to frame an idea of a body extended and moved, but I must in addition give it some quality which is acknowledged to exist only in the mind. In short, extension, figure, and motion, abstracted from all other qualities, are inconceivable.[28]

If he is right, then when we pretended to imagine an apple divested of its secondary qualities, we could not really do so. Berkeley's thought is that the image we try to conjure in our minds of an odourless, colourless, silent apple is no image at all. To picture it in our mind's eye we must imagine it with some colour, just as a painter could not paint a colourless apple. So the idea we seemed to have of an apple with no secondary qualities is an empty one. And even Locke admitted that the idea of matter, stripped of the secondary qualities, is hard to imagine. He called it something but admitted 'I know not what'. For the idealist the indirect realist's idea of matter underlying the various sensations that we experience is a philosophical confusion.

So where are the primary qualities of objects? Berkeley argues that if an object can only be conceived with both primary and secondary qualities then our ideas of secondary qualities are inseparable from the primary. So if we accept that our perceptions of secondary qualities exist only in the mind, then our perceptions of primary qualities must be in the mind too.

> **PHILONOUS.** *Since therefore it is impossible even for the mind to disunite the ideas of extension and motion from all other sensible qualities, doth it not follow, that where the one exist there necessarily the other exist likewise?*
>
> **HYLAS.** *It should seem so.*
>
> **PHILONOUS.** *Consequently, the very same arguments which you admitted as conclusive against the Secondary Qualities are, without any farther application of force, against the Primary too. Besides, if you will trust your senses, is it not plain all sensible qualities co-exist, or to them appear as being in the same place? Do they ever represent a motion, or figure, as being divested of all other visible and tangible qualities?*
>
> *Dialogues*

Locke sometimes argues that our ideas of secondary qualities are those that are relative to the condition of the person perceiving. For example, when Locke discusses heat in the example of two hands, the fact that the water appears to be different heats suggests heat is purely a subjective reaction and nothing in the water itself. Berkeley exploits this argument for his own ends by showing that primary qualities suffer the same variability. If we are going to argue that heat and colours are not real on the grounds that they can appear different from different perspectives or to different body parts, then, by the same logic, we should argue that our perception of shape and size are merely apparent. For if an object can appear different sizes to different sized animals or from different distances, then the size cannot be real. But if the property is purely apparent, then it exists only in the mind.

A defence against Berkeley is to argue that his arguments rest on a misunderstanding of the nature of secondary qualities. Indirect realists are not saying that secondary qualities exist only in the mind, rather they are powers to cause sensations in us. Our sense data of secondary qualities may not accurately represent what is out there, but secondary qualities still exist just as much as the primary. So the temperature of the water is real – it has to do with the kinetic energy of the water molecules. But the exact way in which we sense this temperature can vary with the conditions of our sense organs.

The master argument

However, Berkeley believes he has a final knock-down argument for idealism. We have already seen that he thinks that the idea of an object which exists independently of a mind is incoherent. And to show this he asks us to try to conceive of a tree which exists outside of any mind – a tree of which no one has any awareness. In doing so, you may invoke the idea of a tree hidden deep in some uninhabited forest.

Figure 1.12
Berkeley's Master Argument
If I try to think of a tree which is independent of any mind, I must think of it, and so it is in the mind after all.

and so it ceases to exist. You come back in the room and, lo and behold, not only does it come back into existence, but the logs are gone and in their place are hot embers and ashes. Idealism seems to imply there are gaps in the fire's existence when it is not perceived. But if fires are so 'gappy' how come the fire has dwindled as if it had existed all the time? What can the idealist say to explain this? Consider also the tree which falls unobserved in the forest. If we saw it standing one day, and on the ground the next, how did it get there? How do we explain this if there has been no process, no unobserved falling-over that brought the tree to the ground? Finally consider the blind spot experiment on page 15. The idealist must claim that the circle comes in and out of existence as the book is moved. There can be no unseen circle still there when the book is in a certain position.

It seems that the world inhabited by the idealist is very different from the one we thought we lived in. Physical things have no hidden sides, no interiors and no secret aspects. They disappear and reappear without explanation, and there are no unobserved processes going on to explain the changes they undergo in the interim.

Issue 3: Regularity of the universe

A related difficulty is that idealism appears not to be able to give any explanation of why there is such regularity and predictability in our experience, nor where our ideas come from. Why, for example, do I expect to see the apple once again on reopening the drawer? Why can I be pretty sure of how this apple will taste? Indeed why do I see and hear things at all? The realist, of whatever stripe, claims to have a good explanation for why we have the sense impressions we do and why they are so regular and predictable. There exist material objects which impact upon our sense organs and cause us to see, hear or taste them. Matter retains certain properties when we are not perceiving it, so when we do come to perceive it we can expect it to produce the same sensations in us. It is because of the independent existence of matter that our experience hangs together as it does. Idealism appears to have no parallel explanation, and the whole world of ideas we inhabit appears nothing short of miraculous.

Issue 4: The trap of solipsism

We have seen that the indirect realist's commitment to the idea that I only have direct access to sense data within my mind can lead to scepticism about the existence of anything beyond the mind. Since idealism is effectively embracing this sceptical conclusion, then it too seems to fall into solipsism. The whole of my experience amounts, it would seem, to an extended dream and I cannot know about the existence of anything beyond my own experience, namely the external world and other people. The master argument itself is often held to lead directly to solipsism: if it is impossible to conceive of anything beyond my own mind, then only my mind can be known to exist.

Berkeley's defence

In response to the complaint that idealism cannot explain the regularity of our experience, Berkeley would simply question the materialist's use of matter to this end. Why, he would ask, should we suppose matter to behave in a regular way? What account does the materialist have of this? Is this not at least as miraculous as Berkeley's claim that our sensations exhibit regularity? So when it comes to explaining regularity, realism and idealism are in the same boat.

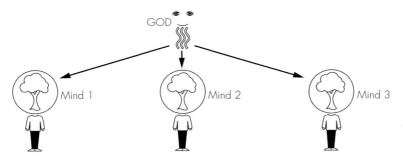

Figure 1.14 Idealism
Nothing can exist unperceived. So physical objects are just collections of 'ideas' or sense data appearing to minds. God plants these ideas in all of us and perceives the world, thereby keeping it in existence.

But what of the gappiness of objects? Berkeley's idealism as so far characterised appears to fly in the face of our common-sense understanding of the nature of physical things, and threatens to reduce idealism to absurdity. Given that Berkeley believes his position to be in accordance with common sense he could hardly be claiming that the world disappears every time I close my eyes – and indeed he does not.

He claims that objects do continue to exist when not perceived by me, because they continue to be perceived by God. God is a permanent perceiver of all that exists and, by perceiving the universe, Berkeley's God ensures that physical objects retain the kind of continuous existence that realists and common sense would claim for them. Berkeley's God also deals with the other issues we identified above: the questions of where my perceptions come from, why they are regular and whether anything exists outside of my mind. Berkeley recognises that the origin and regularity of our sense data need an explanation, but believes he has shown that they cannot come from matter – for reasons we have discussed. So could they come from within me? If so solipsism would be true. Berkeley rejects this possibility too on the grounds that I have no control over my sense experiences. So what other external source could there be for my sense experience? Well, the regularity and predictability of experience strongly

anthology
1.13

suggests the involvement of a good and extremely powerful intelligence. So he concludes that sense data are produced in me by God.

Berkeley's considered position is neatly summed up in a limerick by Ronald Knox:[29]

There was a young man who said, 'God
Must think it exceedingly odd
If he finds that this tree
Continues to be
When there is no one around in the Quad.'

to which the reply is:

Dear Sir: Your astonishment's odd;
I am always about in the quad.
And that's why the tree
Will continue to be
Since observed by, Yours faithfully, God

Criticisms of Berkeley's idealism

Issue 5: Can God be used to play the role he does?

The use of God to shore up a philosophical position is often regarded as evidence that there is something seriously wrong with it. And Berkeley is often accused of bringing God in purely so that he can escape from the difficulties that idealism leads to. Yet, arguably, there is no independent reason to suppose either that there is a God or, if there is, that he plays the role Berkeley casts him in. To use God in this way expressly to solve a problem is often regarded as intellectually dishonest since it masquerades as an explanation while in fact it explains nothing. If whenever there is something that we can't explain we turn to divine intervention then we could eliminate all mysteries. All philosophical difficulties could be explained away as miracles, a bit like 'solving' a puzzle about the world by explaining sagely that God moves in mysterious ways.

Moreover, we might complain that positing the existence of God goes against Berkeley's principle that we cannot conceive of anything beyond the mind. And worse, since God is a mind, and all that we can conceive of must come from sense perception, it would seem to be impossible to have a coherent idea of God, or any other minds.

Berkeley is aware of this difficulty and accepts that his idea of God (and other minds) is not like other ideas; not, that is, an image of some set of perceived qualities. Nonetheless he believes the inference to the existence of God is a justified inference in the same way as we are justified in believing in other minds generally.

I can be fairly certain that other people and their minds exist on the basis of their use of language. For language is a complex series of signs, and it is inconceivable that they merely appear to refer to ideas in other minds. In the same way the regularity of our sense experience is like a language indicating the presence of an intelligence orchestrating it. God, in other words, is continually speaking to us through our senses. And I can have the idea of other minds, including God's, by analogy with my own mind, which, even though I don't have a perception of it, I intuitively recognise as that which has my ideas. Moreover, given that matter is an incoherent concept, and yet that there is nothing contradictory in the notion that minds can have perceptions, it follows that a mind must be the basis of all that exists.

While the materialist thinks his use of God is dishonest, at least God is supposed to be an intelligence, and so it makes sense that he would do things in an orderly way. So he provides a good explanation, argues Berkeley, of the regularity and predictability of experience. The idea that some mindless substance called matter should behave in a regular and orderly fashion and so account for the origin and regularity of experience is, according to Berkeley, a far bigger cop-out than an appeal to God. In fact, it's worth being clear that, as far as Berkeley is concerned, God doesn't enter his theory to save it. Rather Berkeley's whole argument amounts to a demonstration of God's existence. If his arguments succeed in showing that matter cannot exist, then the only way to explain the orderly appearance of sense impressions is by positing the existence of some intelligence producing them.

Berkeley's view of space and time

Berkeley rejected the scientific orthodoxy of his day, according to which space and time are absolute; that is, they exist independently of the spatio-temporal relations between objects as if they were infinitely great containers in which objects and events take place. He argued that absolute space is an abstraction from our ideas of bodies and their relative positions, and absolute time is an abstraction from our experience of successive events, and since space and time cannot be perceived in themselves, then we cannot have a genuine idea of them.

According to Berkeley's picture, the spatial and temporal relations that obtain between objects are generated from within my sense experience and so the space and time of which I am aware is essentially private to me. Since my ideas of spatial relations are as subjective as colour, space is nothing more than the product of the spatial relations that we perceive and has no existence beyond this. Time is similarly nothing over and above the perception of the succession of ideas within each mind.

Criticism

But if space and time are private, and each of us occupies a world completely distinct from everyone else's, then it is difficult to make sense of our common-sense view that when, for example, we arrange to meet on the 18.25 from St Pancras, we succeed because we converge on the same point in an objective spatio-temporal order. So how does Berkeley account for the public time of clocks, which is so fundamental to the way we arrange our ordinary affairs?

For practical purposes Berkeley argues that there is no problem. Even if no *objective* time exists, we can still operate with a *public* time since we are able to use our perception of standard measures of time, such as the revolution of the earth or clocks. God underwrites our perception of such standards so that they are inter-subjectively regular enough to allow us to arrange to meet, catch trains and so forth. There is no need to suppose there is an objective time over and above this.

God may be able to establish an objective spatial order by perceiving all of his creation and so sustaining them and their relations in existence. It is more difficult for God to provide an objective framework of this sort for time. This is because there can be no succession of ideas in the mind of God since he is thought to be IMMUTABLE or unchanging. But if time is purely subjective and exists only in finite minds like ours, then when I am not conscious of its passage, it does not pass. Indeed, the very idea of time passing while no ideas are perceived to succeed one another is contradictory for Berkeley, so that no time can pass while I am in a dreamless sleep. This, however, seems problematic, in part because clock time appears to show that time has passed while I was unaware. Consider also watching someone else sleeping. In this situation, on Berkeley's view, there is no passage of time for them – it is as though their time has frozen while mine continues. And yet, common sense strongly suggests that time is passing while they are blissfully unaware of it. After all, if I make a loud noise and wake them up, this event seems to have taken place in time and to have caused the person to go from a state of unconsciousness to consciousness. Yet, for Berkeley there is no such thing as an unconscious state, since a mind without ideas it is conscious of is not a mind at all. At the very least, this understanding of time appears not to square with Berkeley's claim that his philosophy is in accordance with the common understanding.

Summary

In this section we have examined various considerations raised against the idea that we perceive the world directly. The facts that:
- our senses are sometimes deceptive,
- we may perceive the same thing differently from different positions or under different conditions and
- our perception of something does not occur simultaneously with what causes it

all are taken by indirect realists to show that what we are directly aware of cannot be things as they are in themselves. Rather, they have urged, perception involves a direct awareness of a mental component – the sense data or appearance – which mediates between us and reality. The world as it appears to us becomes a representation of reality which may be fairly accurate in some respects, but highly misleading in others (as if we are watching a movie of the world, rather than looking directly at the world itself). The arguments for indirect realism are, however, not universally accepted and there are some strategies that we have explored by which direct realism may be defended. Moreover, indirect realism also leads us into serious difficulties. In particular it raises sceptical concerns about our knowledge of reality because of the gap it introduces between the immediate objects of perception, which are held to be certain, and the world beyond them, the nature of which must be inferred. Berkeley's idealism is one striking attempt to cut to the heart of such concerns by questioning the indirect realists' right to maintain a belief in a world beyond experience. If we only have access to ideas in our own minds, argues Berkeley, then we have no reason to suppose there is anything beyond the mind. Indeed, the very idea of a non-mental reality is incoherent. Idealism is the view that all that exists are minds and their ideas, a position which may appear counter intuitive, but which Berkeley himself claimed was in tune with common sense. This is because he is not denying that what we think of as physical objects exist, as it is often mistakenly supposed. Rather he is saying that objects just are what is perceived, and no more. In other words, he is denying the existence of what indirect realists call 'matter': that unperceivable 'I know not what' which Locke and others claim causes our perception.

it. As with practical knowledge, knowledge by acquaintance need not involve any capacity to give a verbal report of what it entails. I may know the taste of pineapple without being able to describe it and without knowing any facts about it. Some philosophers regard knowledge by acquaintance, particularly with our own sense data, as the foundation of all empirical knowledge. The claim is that all of our knowledge is built up from our acquaintance with shapes, colours, sounds and tastes and without these elements there would be no knowledge at all. Without the input of the senses our minds would be a blank slate, or, to use the Latin term, a *tabula rasa*.

3 Factual or propositional knowledge (knowing 'that')

This is knowing *that* something is the case. So, for example, we speak of knowing *that* 2 + 2 = 4, or *that* the earth orbits the Sun, or *that* Shakespeare wrote *Hamlet*. Unlike the other two types of knowledge, when we know some fact, what we know can, in principle, be expressed in language. Thus if someone claims to know that Shakespeare wrote *Hamlet*, he or she claims that the sentence 'Shakespeare wrote *Hamlet*' is true. What is asserted by a sentence, that is to say, what it means or affirms about the world, is called a PROPOSITION and for this reason factual knowledge is often called propositional knowledge. A good way to remember the meaning of this term is to think of this kind of knowledge as *proposing* that the world is one way, rather than another. So saying that you know that Paul McCartney wrote 'Let it Be' is to *propose* a certain version of the world is true (as opposed to a version where John Lennon, or someone else, wrote the song). Hence the term *propositional* knowledge.

The other two forms of knowledge outlined above don't have to involve any propositions about the world. A bee can know how make honey without resorting to any claims about how the world is or isn't. Likewise, knowing what vanilla tastes like doesn't involve understanding any propositions. Any claim to propositional knowledge is usually preceded by the word 'that'. For example, I know *that* it is snowing in Scotland or Taz knows *that* Arsenal were unbeaten during the 2002–2003 season. The word 'that' sets up the proposition that the person claims to know.

It's interesting to note that these three different forms of knowledge are distinguished in many languages. French, for example, has *connaître* (for acquaintance) and *savoir* (for propositional knowledge) and *savoir-faire* (for practical knowledge). German has both *kennen* and *wissen*, whereas English just has *to know*.

Three kinds of knowledge

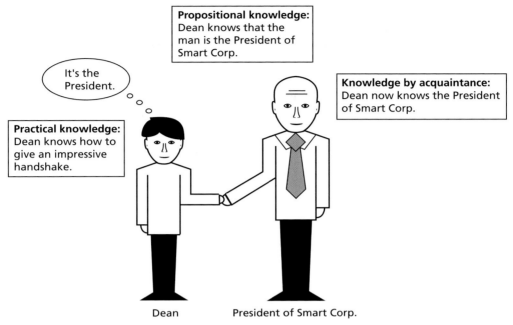

Figure 1.15 Three different kinds of knowledge. Dean is meeting the president of Smartcorp. The three forms of knowledge all come into play.

▶ ACTIVITY

Revisit the list of knowledge claims above.

1 Do all of the examples fit neatly into one of the three categories of knowledge (practical, acquaintance and factual)?
2 How do you usually come to gain each kind of knowledge?
3 Which type of knowledge do you think you have the most of?

There is no easy answer to the last question! However, there are interesting differences between the kinds of knowledge in terms of how they are acquired/transmitted. I can be taught 'know *how*' by others; for example, helping me tie my laces. Also other people can introduce me to new forms of knowledge by acquaintance; for example, by giving me liquorice for the first time – although I actually have to experience this myself to have the knowledge of the taste. I cannot learn this by reading about the taste or talking to others.

Because propositional knowledge involves language, this means it can be passed swiftly and rapidly through books, the internet, lectures, and so on. This form of knowledge seems more or less exclusive to humans and is the cause of the rapid spread and growth of technology in the last few thousand years. With a simple click of a mouse we are now able to access much of the propositional knowledge that has been gained in the current and preceding lives of billions of people. Our 'know-how' and 'know of' however, are not so easily transmitted.

This chapter is primarily concerned with factual, propositional knowledge. We will examine the conditions under which a person might legitimately claim to know a fact. Before we begin properly we need to explore some related key words.

Because factual knowledge is expressed in language it seems to involve holding *beliefs*. A swallow does not need to have any specific beliefs to fly south (know-how), or to know its chicks (by acquaintance) but propositional knowledge is different. If I have knowledge of certain facts, I *believe* certain propositions to be true; in other words, I *assent* to these propositions. Because it deals with knowing facts, and so with having beliefs, these beliefs can be either *true* or *false*. These key terms, namely 'belief', 'proposition', 'fact' and 'truth' have somewhat ambiguous meanings in ordinary English, so if we are to make headway in our analysis of knowledge it is important that we give working definitions of these terms (see **Figure 1.16**).

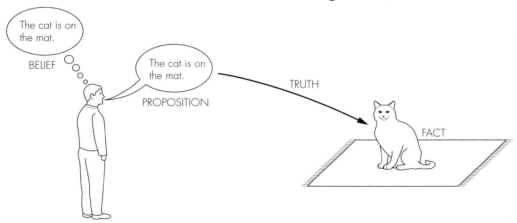

Figure 1.16 Beliefs, propositions and facts

■ A *belief* is a thought which is about the world. It is a mental representation which claims that something is the case. Beliefs can be true or false. In the figure, Sam has the belief that the cat is on the mat.

■ A *proposition* is what a statement says or asserts about the world. Like beliefs, propositions can be true or false. When Sam utters the sentence 'The cat is on the mat' he is expressing the proposition that the cat is on the mat.

■ A *fact* is something that is the case in the world. Here the fact is the cat's being on the mat. Facts can't be true or false, they just are.

■ *Truth* is a tricky concept, but one account of truth is that it involves a correspondence between a belief or a proposition and the world. If Sam's belief that the cat is on the mat corresponds with the world; that is, with the facts, then it is true. So his belief will be true if the cat is indeed on the mat.

Knowledge, certainty and ordinary language

Having given brief definitions of some key terms (*belief*, *fact*, *proposition* and *truth*), it is worth quickly reminding ourselves of what the undertaking of this chapter is. The chapter aims to explore the concept of knowledge and to see whether a definition can be reached. However, giving a definition of knowledge could involve one of at least two different things. We could be trying to give a definition of what the concept of knowledge *should* be (this would be a prescriptive account of knowledge) or we could be trying to give a definition of what the concept of knowledge *is*, in its ordinary usage (this would be a descriptive account of knowledge). We are aiming for the second kind of definition, although it is often very tempting to slip into the first kind of definition. To see how easily this slippage can occur, consider the following activity:

▶ **ACTIVITY**

I You know who will win the best actor Oscar.

2 You know what you will do tomorrow.

3 You know there is no life on the Moon.

4 You know that you are looking at a book right now.

5 You know who you have spoken to today.

6 You know where you were born.

7 You know if you currently are in pain or not.

8 You know that you are experiencing black ink-coloured lettering sensations that seem to spell out words and sentences.

9 You know that you exist.

  a) How many of these things would you agree to knowing? All of them?

  b) But how many do you *really* know?

  c) Can you think of ways in which you could be mistaken about each one?

It seems there is very little we can be certain about; after all …

  1 … the best actor or the bookies' favourite does not always win.

  2 … your plans for tomorrow could suddenly change with the weather/world events.

  3 … there may be living organisms living in lakes deep beneath the surface of the Moon.

  4 … you could be dreaming and not looking at a real book.

  5 … some of the people you think you have spoken to today might have been other people in disguise or even clones.

  6 … people (for example, your parents) could simply have lied to you about where you were born.

If such doubt is possible then can you really be said to *know* any of these things? What about numbers 7–9; is it possible to doubt these statements too? Perhaps these are harder to doubt and might be the only statements you would count as *proper* knowledge?

What these considerations are designed to show is that we intuitively link the concept of knowledge with the concept of certainty. However we also intuitively believe that we are capable of knowing a lot of things and these two INTUITIONS can be contradictory. Here are our two intuitions:

a) We can only know things if we are certain about them.

b) We know lots of things.

The more we emphasise certainty a), the less we are likely to actually know b). The more we emphasise b) it seems that knowledge is less about certainty a). This conflict relates to two different purposes we may have in seeking to define knowledge; prescriptive or descriptive. We might intuitively be inclined to say that we *should* only count things we know for certain as knowledge (prescriptive), whereas in ordinary language we *are* inclined to count lots of things as knowledge, and not require certainty (descriptive). The danger in giving into our intuition about certainty is that we will no longer be analysing/describing the concept of knowledge as it is used in ordinary language. Instead we would be trying to explore how we might want to use the concept of knowledge, or even simply exploring the concept of certainty itself. Either way, we will not be analysing the concept of knowledge as it is used in ordinary language.

For the time being we will leave the concept of certainty behind. But if knowledge does not need to involve certainty, what *does* it need to involve? Most theories suggest it must involve some form of JUSTIFICATION, and this will be one of the key concepts in this chapter.

Propositional knowledge

What, then, is factual/propositional knowledge? (From now on we will use the term propositional knowledge.) A question like this is hard to answer directly. It is difficult even to know how to begin.

A non-technical answer might be that propositional knowledge is the ideas and thoughts inside a person's head that relate to the world. However, not all ideas and thoughts inside our heads would count as knowledge. A more detailed answer is clearly needed. A promising approach, first adopted by Plato, is to ask what must be the case when someone knows something. Under what circumstances do we say that someone has knowledge? Answering this question involves looking for the conditions or criteria which would establish that someone knows a proposition. If we can list these conditions and so say exactly when someone does and does not know something, then we will have a pretty good idea of what propositional knowledge is. In order to clarify this approach it will be useful to abbreviate the expression 'someone knows a proposition' to 'S knows that p'. Here 'S' stands for the subject (the person doing the knowing – for example, Sharon), and 'p' for the proposition that she knows (for example, that Paris is the capital of France). So we need to determine what conditions must be satisfied in order for us to assert 'S knows that p' (Sharon knows that Paris is the capital of France).

▶ **ACTIVITY**

1 To get started on our search for a definition of 'knowledge', let us try to distinguish it from belief. Begin by writing a short list of things you would normally claim to *know*, and another of things you merely *believe*. These may be things that you know or believe have happened or exist. Try not to be too influenced by sceptical arguments and simply use the terms 'know' and 'believe' as they would be used in everyday life.

2 Having done this, consider what has to be the case for you to claim that you know something as opposed to simply believing it. What makes the knowledge claims different from the belief claims?

3 Now read on to see how your answer compares with Plato's.

Socrates was a famous ancient Greek philosopher. He was renowned for engaging others in dialogue and examining interesting ideas and concepts such as love, justice and knowledge. Socrates liked to challenge conventional thinking which led to some clashes with the authorities. Socrates was eventually accused of impiety (not believing in the gods) and corrupting the youth of Athens. He was tried and sentenced to death by drinking hemlock. It is likely that had he wished, he could have escaped to live in exile. However, he chose to remain in Athens, his city of birth, and willingly drank the hemlock that ended his life.

Socrates attracted many disciples, usually young men, who were interested in philosophical discussion. One of these disciples was Plato – who would have been about 29 when Socrates died. Plato was born in Athens in around BC430 into a relatively wealthy aristocratic family. After the death of Socrates, Plato travelled widely before returning to Athens as the age of 40 and founding perhaps the first proper college in western society, known as the Academy. The school went on to last for nearly a thousand years. The great philosopher Aristotle was one of its first students.

To aid the teaching in his school, Plato wrote many dialogues, all concerned with philosophy. In many of the dialogues, Socrates is the main character and he usually engages in a debate about a philosophical issue. Indeed it is primarily through the writings of Plato that we know of the life and teachings of Socrates.

Plato on true belief and knowledge

Having begun to think about the differences between knowledge and belief, we can now examine how Plato approached the problem. In his dialogue, the *Meno*, he tries to work out the difference between someone having a true belief and someone having knowledge. He begins by pointing out that true belief has much in common with knowledge. Indeed, it would seem that the two are equally valuable as guides to action. Socrates, the character expounding Plato's views, explains his reasoning to his fellow debater Meno, as follows:

> **Socrates:** *Let me explain. If someone knows the way to Larissa, or anywhere else you like, then when he goes there and takes others with him he will be a good and capable guide, you would agree?*
>
> **Meno:** *Of course.*
>
> **Socrates:** *But if a man judges correctly which is the road, though he has never been there and doesn't know it, will he not also guide others aright?*
>
> **Meno:** *Yes, he will.*
>
> **Socrates:** *And as long as he has a correct belief on the points about which the other has knowledge, he will be just as good a guide, believing the truth but not knowing it.*
>
> **Meno:** *Just as good.*
>
> **Socrates:** *Therefore true belief is as good a guide as knowledge for the purpose of acting rightly.*[1]
>
> Plato, *Meno*

Here Plato is arguing that so long as my beliefs are true then they are as useful to me and to others as if I had knowledge. So why, the question arises, should we prefer knowledge to true belief? Are they in fact the same thing and if so why is knowledge so highly prized? Socrates' answer has many facets, but we will focus on just one aspect, which contrasts the stability of knowledge with the flightiness of belief.

> **Socrates:** *True beliefs are a fine thing and do all sorts of good so long as they stay in their place; but they will not stay long. They run away from a man's mind, so they are not worth much until you tether them by working out the reason ... Once they are tied down, they become knowledge, and are stable. That is why knowledge is something more valuable than right belief. What distinguishes one from the other is the tether.*[2]
>
> Plato, *Meno*

This all sounds rather cryptic. What can he mean by beliefs failing to 'stay in their place'? What is to 'tether them by working out the reason'? Plato seems to be saying that part of the reason we value knowledge is that it is more steadfast than mere belief since it is backed up by reasons or evidence. The evidence acts as a kind of glue, which retains the belief in the mind by giving us good reason to continue believing it. By contrast, a belief for which we have no evidence – even if it happens to be true – has nothing to make it stick in the mind. If I have no good reason for believing a proposition, it will not take much for someone to dissuade me from it. But if I know it, I will not readily withdraw my assent. So Plato is suggesting that it is a kind of tethering that converts belief into knowledge. To have knowledge is to have a true belief secured by reasons. In another dialogue, the *Theaetetus*, Plato offers other considerations in support of the idea that knowledge is more than mere true belief.

Socrates: *Now, when a jury has been persuaded, fairly, of things which no one but an eyewitness could possibly know, then, in reaching a decision based on hearsay, they do so without knowledge, but get hold of true belief, given that their verdict is fair because what they have been made to believe is correct.*

Theaetetus: *Absolutely.*

Socrates: *But if true belief and knowledge were identical, my friend, then even the best juryman in the world would never form a correct belief, but fail to have knowledge; so it looks as though they are different.*[3]

Plato, Theaetetus

Plato's point here is that we can hold true beliefs that we would be reluctant to call knowledge because of the nature of the evidence supporting them. A juror can come to a correct decision on the balance of evidence presented in court. But if the evidence available to him were circumstantial and less than absolutely conclusive we would be reluctant to call this knowledge. By contrast, an eyewitness to the events in question could indeed be said to know. Consider also the example of a gambler who believes that the next number on the roulette wheel will be red. Even if he happens to be right, we would be reluctant to say that he truly knew. These examples show that the manner by which one acquires a true belief, or by which one *justifies* it, is important to its counting as a piece of knowledge. Because of basic considerations such as this, Plato is led in the *Theaetetus* to consider the view that 'true belief accompanied by a rational account is knowledge'[4] or, as we might say, knowledge is a *justified, true belief* – that is, a true belief for which the believer has adequate reasons or evidence.

So it seems we have an early candidate for a definition of factual knowledge. A person knows something if they have a BELIEF THAT is *true*, and that has a good *justification*.

Experimenting with ideas

1   Think up your own examples, like those above, to illustrate the difference between having a true belief and having knowledge.
2   The last activity (on page 55) involved writing down some things you claimed to believe and other things that you claimed to know. Go back to these statements and see if the missing ingredient in the two cases is indeed the degree of justification for the belief.

To test whether the *justified, true belief* account of knowledge seems plausible, consider the following example. Innocence and Pete the Cheat are playing cards (see **Figure 1.17**). Innocence has a strong feeling that the card on the top of the deck, about to be turned over, is the Queens of Spades. She has no particular reason for this feeling though. In the game she needs it to be a Queen and just has a strong hunch that it is the Queen of Spades. Lo and behold, the card is indeed the Queen of Spades! Innocence has a true belief; however as this was just a guess/hunch we would we say that she *knew* it? Probably not. This would seem to imply, as Plato suggested, that a true belief is not enough to grant knowledge. Now, Pete the Cheat also had a very strong belief that the card on the top of the deck was the Queen of Spades. It was his deck and some of the cards had tiny markings on the back which the casual observer would not notice. It was a marked deck! Pete could see that the card on the top of the deck had a mark on it that indicated it was the Queen of Spades. When turned over it was, indeed, the Queen of Spades! Pete had a true belief, however, in this case as his belief was justified. Would we say that Pete *knew* it? Probably yes. So, on the basis of this example, it seems that a defining knowledge as a *justified, true belief* has some merit. However as we will discover in remainder of this chapter, philosophy is rarely this straightforward!

Knowledge as justified, true belief

The definition of knowledge as justified, true belief is the traditional one. If it is correct, it means that if someone knows a proposition, then three conditions must be satisfied. The person must *believe* the proposition, it must be *true* and it must be *justified*. These conditions can be set out as follows.

S knows that p if and only if (for example, Sharon knows that Paris is the capital of France if and only if ...):

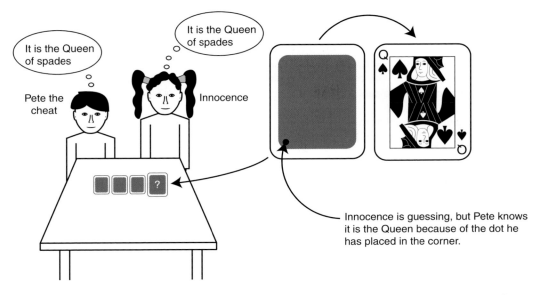

Innocence is guessing, but Pete knows it is the Queen because of the dot he has placed in the corner.

Figure 1.17 Innocence and Pete the Cheat are playing cards. Innocence has a belief that the card on the top of the deck is the Queens of Spades. Pete also has the same belief; however, his is justified as they are playing with his marked deck of cards.

1　S believes that p (the belief condition; for example ... Sharon believes Paris is the capital of France)

2　p is true (the truth condition; for example ... Paris is indeed the capital of France)

3　S has adequate or sufficient evidence for p, or is justified in believing p (the evidence condition; for example ... Sharon has read that Paris is the capital of France in a trustworthy encyclopaedia).

This means that the proposition 'S knows that p' is true if and only if S believes that p, p is true and S has adequate justification for her belief. These three conditions are said to be individually NECESSARY and jointly SUFFICIENT for saying that 'S knows that p'. So you need each one to have knowledge and if you have all three then you definitely have knowledge. This kind of definition of a concept is what philosophers call a *logical analysis* of the concept.

Experimenting with ideas

1　Read the scenarios given below. Using your common-sense intuition, decide in each case whether the person in bold knows the fact in question.

2　Then check to see whether:
　　a) the person believes the fact (the belief condition)
　　b) the fact is true (the truth condition)
　　c) the person would be justified in believing it (the evidence condition).

3　If all three conditions are met then according to the JTB (justified, true belief) definition this should be a case of knowledge. If one or more of the conditions are not met, then this is not a case of knowledge. Did using the three conditions match your own intuitions in each of the cases?

4 Consider whether justified, true belief is a good analysis of the concept of knowledge. What problems could the definition run into? How good must the justification be? (Remember: we are looking to establish the criteria for the everyday concept of knowledge, and justification need not be perfect for knowledge to be claimed in everyday parlance. So avoid ruling out examples just because absolute certainty is not established.)

a) Davina thinks that monkeys are more intelligent than humans because her mate told her so.

b) Ravi reckons the Sun will set at 19:02 on Sunday having read as much in the paper. And it does.

c) The forecast says there is a 50–50 chance of rain tomorrow. Looking at the sky, **farmer Clare** is convinced it will be dry. It stays dry the whole day.

d) Having been told by his parents and having read books and watched DVDs on the subject, young **Victor** is convinced that Santa Claus exists.

e) Hamid is convinced that Pluto is the furthest planet from the sun because Mickey Mouse told him so in a dream.

f) **Tamsin** learns from a textbook that *Hamlet* is Shakespeare's longest play (which it is).

g) Wanda watches five DVDs of Shakespeare plays and concludes by their length that *Hamlet* must be Shakespeare's longest play.

h) Colin is going out with Simone. However, at a party he drunkenly, yet inexcusably, kisses Fiona. No one sees a thing. Back at college Nigel is secretly in love with Simone. To try to get Simone and Colin to split up he makes up a rumour, telling Brian that Colin and Fiona got off at the party. Later on **Chanise** hears this rumour and believes it.

i) Samma has been dating Joel for five years now. She knows that he is faithful to her. She just knows it in her heart.

In the activity you have been testing the justified, true belief (JTB) analysis of knowledge. In other words, you have been considering whether each condition is necessary by asking whether we can do without *belief*, *truth* or *justification*. You may also have considered a slightly different question when you got to scenario h), namely whether or not together the conditions are sufficient. In other words, you may have been wondering whether someone who has all three conditions definitely has knowledge. It is important to recognise that these two questions are distinct. In the following discussion of the traditional analysis of knowledge we will treat each question separately. First, we will ask whether the three conditions are *individually necessary*. This means seeing whether we need each one by seeing if we can do without any. Second, we will examine whether they are *jointly sufficient*. This means seeing whether having all three definitely guarantees you have knowledge, and involves looking at odd cases where someone seems to have a justified, true belief, but not knowledge.

Necessary and sufficient conditions

Necessary and sufficient conditions can seem like complex ideas, but the principle behind them is fairly commonplace. If an element is necessary then without that element you could not have the thing in question. Being a man is a necessary condition of being a father. If you are not a man, then you cannot be a father. The definition of a necessary condition can be summed up as: *X is a necessary condition of Y if without X you cannot have Y.*

Having a necessary condition isn't always enough to have the thing in question though. For example, being a man is a necessary condition of being a father, but it alone is not enough. Not all men are fathers. Other conditions need to be met in order to be a father. If having certain necessary elements/conditions always guarantees having the thing in question then these elements are called sufficient. For example, being unmarried and being a man are sufficient conditions for being a bachelor. Every time you have an unmarried man, you have a bachelor. There is nothing more you need; the two elements are sufficient. (They are also necessary – you cannot be a bachelor without being a man or without being unmarried.) The definition of sufficient conditions can be summed up as: *X and Y are sufficient conditions of Z if the occurrence of X and Y guarantees the occurrence of Z.*

Experimenting with ideas

Often it can be hard to articulate all of the sufficient conditions of a concept. Think about all of the elements that, if present, would guarantee you were looking at a square. Having four sides is not enough as not all four-sided objects are squares. Having four sides of equal length is not enough either (consider a four-sided object drawn on a ball, with equal sides, but not with angles of 90 degrees).

a) Look at points 1–3 below. Which of the elements are necessary for the concept in question? In other words could you have the concept in question without the particular element?

b) Are the elements jointly sufficient for the concept? In other words, do the elements together always yield the concept?

1 Elements are – *three angles, three lines* and *red*. The concept is **triangle**.
2 Elements are – *water, drops* and *falling*. The concept is **raining**.
3 Elements are – *owning a valid ticket, the six numbers on the ticket are the same as the lottery draw, the ticket is for the right draw*. The concept is **a person having a winning ticket for the lottery jackpot**.

In example 1, having three angles and three lines are necessary conditions for a triangle, but red isn't. Three angles and three lines are not jointly sufficient though, as there are many combinations of three angles and three lines that are not triangles. The lines have to at least join together and enclose a space to be a triangle.

▓ In example 2 the three elements seem to be necessary. If there is no water there can be no rain. (Although can't it rain frogs? Or blood?) The water would need be falling (otherwise it is mist or just a cloud) and there would need to be drops rather than a big sheet of water. However, they are not jointly sufficient, as someone holding up a watering can would create water, drops and falling without it raining. So the three elements being present do not guarantee rain; other elements are needed.

▓ In the last case, the three elements would each seem to be necessary. Together they also seem to be sufficient. If all these three elements are together then surely the person has won the lottery? However, maybe you can come up with a counter example? Either an example of someone who has won the lottery jackpot without one of these elements being present or an example of all three elements being present and yet the person not having a winning ticket for the jackpot.

Returning to the concept of knowledge and the conditions of truth, justification and belief (JTB), we will now explore whether each of the elements is necessary for propositional knowledge and whether together they are jointly sufficient to guarantee knowledge.

Are the JTB conditions individually necessary?

1 The belief condition (B)

Do you need to believe something to know it? The belief condition says that a necessary condition for your knowing that p is that you *believe* that p. In other words, you must believe that the proposition is true, or hold that what it says really is the case. This is certainly plausible. After all, it appears that you cannot know something to be true if you do not even believe it. So, for example, it is incoherent to say that you know that it is raining when you do not believe that it is. Nonetheless, philosophers have disputed the belief condition by arguing that knowledge and belief are *separable* so that each can exist either with or without the other.

Some philosophers have even claimed that the two are mutually *incompatible*, or in other words that if you have one you cannot have the other. While Plato in the *Meno* adheres to the view that knowledge entails belief, in a later work, *The Republic*, he develops an incompatibilist view known as INFALLIBILISM (see page 74). There he reasons that since knowledge is infallible and belief is fallible, they must be fundamentally different ways of apprehending the world.[5] To believe is to be ambivalent about the object of one's belief. Knowledge involves no such hesitation. So to know something does not entail also believing it, but rather involves going *beyond* mere belief. There is no need to discuss Plato's argument in detail here, but one might defend such a position by pointing out that people often speak as if knowledge and belief were distinct, as when tennis players say, 'I don't believe I will win, I *know* I will'. Does this not imply that to come to know something is to cease to believe it? In fact it is doubtful that it does, for surely this is just a more emphatic way of saying, 'I don't *just* believe that I will win, I know I will'?

The view that one can have knowledge without belief has also been defended by philosophers who claim that knowledge is more about how one acts than about what beliefs one might entertain. So it is argued, for example, that knowledge is more about responding correctly to questions than it is about any state of mind. If I forget that I have learned the history of the Civil War and am quizzed on it, it might be that I am able to give correct answers but believe them to be mere guesses. Since I am guessing, I seem not to have belief, and yet my getting the answers right suggests I do have knowledge. Despite this, it would seem that some tendency to assent to a proposition is required of knowledge. Perhaps just choosing an answer, however unsure I may be, is sufficient to count as belief. So long as I am disposed to assent to a proposition then I can be said to believe it, and, in this minimal sense, belief certainly seems necessary for knowledge.

However, in cases of action and abilities, some people have knowledge without any form of assent. Consider the following example.

Clara can't drive. Her friend Jared has just got his provisional licence and is going to take them both on a trip to San José. Jared drives over to pick up Clara. He reveals that his satnav is broken and that he has never been to San José. Clara goes every Saturday with her dad to a rock climbing venue; however, Clara doesn't pay much attention to the route and she also claims not to know the way to San José. Her dad laughs and says that of course she knows it. They set off and as Jared starts driving she realises, one by one, that she recognises the roads and that she does know the route after all and directs them safely to Route 101 which leads to San José.

Before setting out Clara did not believe that she knew the way to San José. But did she know it?

She was certainly able to get them there. Is it possible that she did know the way, without believing she did? Her father certainly would claim that she knew the way having driven her there over 30 times.

Perhaps she was being modest; she did really believe, but pretended not to, much like someone might say 'I don't believe it!' when they clearly know (and believe) that they have just won the Oscar for best director. Maybe Clara did really believe she could find the way and so did know.

Also this example might be considered a case of know-how rather than propositional knowledge which we are currently examining. Swallows can know the way south, without having specific propositional beliefs, so the example is unfair as the two sorts of knowledge are very different. However, as this case involves road directions, it can fairly easily be turned into a sequence of propositional beliefs rather than just a specific ability to get from A to B.

Consider this. Clara herself may have individually believed that:

- Kings Road leads to Humboldt Road
- Humboldt Road turns into Glenpark Way
- Glenpark Way turns into San Bruno Avenue
- San Bruno Avenue leads into Bayshore Boulevard
- Bayshore Boulevard leads to Route 101
- Route 101 leads to San José.

If asked, she may have been able to give any one of these road changes; however, she may not have ever put this information together in her mind and so did not believe that she knew the way to San José, or even believe a specific fact that the shortest way from her house to San José involves six road changes. Is this possible? If so, then maybe belief is not a necessary condition for knowledge.

Belief though is certainly a necessary condition for someone to claim they have knowledge. It makes no sense to say 'I know that Paris is the capital of France, but I don't believe it.' Someone claiming knowledge of a fact will always believe the fact too. However, other people might be more inclined to attribute knowledge on behalf of a person without that person themselves claiming a belief. My history teacher may claim that I did know the facts about the Civil War, even though I felt I was guessing. Clara's dad may claim that she did know the way to San José despite her not believing it.

Despite the odd, vaguely plausible counter example, the philosophical consensus certainly claims that belief is a necessary condition of knowledge. If a person does not believe a fact, then they cannot know it.

2 The truth condition (T)

Does a fact need to be true for you to know it? The truth condition is fairly uncontroversial. It says that if you know something it must be true. To test this condition try to think of a case where you knew something that was in fact false. Is this possible? Often we *claim* to know something that turns out to be false, but this doesn't mean that we actually do know it. Thinking you know something is not the same as actually knowing it.

Consider Raquel, a cavewoman living thousands of years ago. She believes that the earth is flat. She has compelling evidence for this belief. First, it looks flat. Second, if the ground were curved then things would roll off towards the edges and eventually fall off, and so on. Does she know that it is flat? Surely not. If she knows that the earth is flat, then the earth must be flat. If it is not flat then Raquel cannot know that it is. Of course, she may well have excellent evidence and be completely convinced and we could understand why she would claim to know, but this by itself is not sufficient for knowledge.

People sometimes talk as if Raquel does have knowledge. They might say that thousands of years ago people knew that the earth was flat, and now we know that it is round. But when they use the word 'know' in this way they are probably using it as a synonym for 'were convinced'. Strictly speaking, this is not knowledge, but simply a well justified, but false belief. So it seems that the proposition 'S knows that p' entails that p is true, and it cannot be true if p is false. In other words, you cannot know something if it is false no matter how good the justification for your belief may be.

One important point to draw from this is that whether or not a person knows something cannot be established by *internal* criteria alone (meaning internal to their mind). Raquel cannot simply inspect her belief to determine whether it counts as knowledge. By examining her mind she can establish that she fulfils two of the conditions for knowledge: she has a belief for which she has good justification. She knows this because these two criteria are internal, they are directly accessible to her, since they are 'in her mind' as it were. But for it to count as knowledge it must also be true. Her belief must actually correspond with reality, and this is an *external* criterion. So a justified, false belief is not knowledge, and truth is considered to be a necessary condition of knowledge.

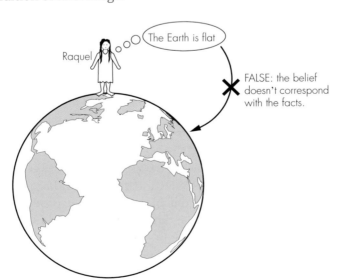

Figure 1.18 Knowledge is impossible without truth. Raquel the cavewoman believes the earth is flat, but in fact it is round. Since her belief doesn't correspond with the facts it is not true. And if it is not true it cannot count as knowledge. The truth condition is 'external' since, unlike the belief and evidence conditions, it is not 'in her mind'.

3 The evidence/justification condition (J)

As we have seen, Plato argued that we are reluctant to grant someone knowledge if they have acquired a true belief by inadequate evidence, or by sheer luck; and a third condition is needed. So if S claims to know that p then she must be able to justify it by appeal to evidence, since otherwise she is simply making an unsubstantiated assertion. A good way of illustrating this point is to consider the example of a racist juror. Suppose the juror comes to believe that a defendant is guilty purely on the basis of the colour of his skin. Let us also suppose that, as a matter of fact, the defendant is guilty. In this case, the juror has a true belief. But is it knowledge? It is generally thought that the answer here must be no since the juror has no good justification for her belief. Her belief is based on irrational prejudice, not on the evidence presented to her in court.

So an *unjustified*, true belief is not knowledge. We need the justification criteria to distinguish knowledge from lucky guesses, though quite how 'justified' a belief needs to be to count as knowledge is not clear. As we will see below, the issue of what counts as proper justification becomes quite complex. However, for the time being it may be useful to think of a belief being sufficiently justified, if the type of justification given is one that is usually good enough to attribute knowledge (although, as we will see on page 86, this is a circular definition).

Is the justification condition really necessary? Do you always need some form of justification to truly know something? In the activity on page 60 above, isn't it possible that Samma just knows in her heart that her partner is faithful? Maybe her claim to knowledge is based on the evidence of her partner's behaviour and so is justified, but could it just be based on the feeling in her heart? Many people would claim to know that God exists or to know that they will go to heaven and they may have no rational justification for this, just a very strong feeling and belief. However, most people would doubt whether this would count as knowledge at all – specifically *because* there is no rational justification. But consider this case:

John has a rare gift. If you give him any date in the future, say 15 March 2123, he is able to tell you what day of the week this will be (for example, a Monday). He is unable to say how he does this, though he is incredibly accurate: 15 March 2123 will indeed be a Monday.

Would you say that John knows this? This is a case of true belief but with no rational justification. As we discuss later, some philosophers claim a reliable process that produces the true beliefs is what counts as knowledge (see RELIABILISM, page 84). Justification, though nice, may not always be necessary.

This possible counter example aside, for the moment we will assume that knowledge does require justification. We will also assume that it requires belief and truth. Assuming all three are necessary, the next question is: are they all jointly sufficient?

Are the JTB conditions jointly sufficient?

We have seen why philosophers have felt that each condition is individually necessary; and hence that you can't do without any one if you want to have knowledge. But if the traditional account of knowledge is right, we must also show that the conditions are jointly sufficient; in other words that if you have all three then you are guaranteed to have knowledge. So is justified, true belief sufficient for knowledge? Does J + T + B = K? As you may have seen in the activity on page 59, the J + T + B definition seems to match many everyday uses of the word 'knowledge', but maybe there are examples of J + T + B that don't equate to knowledge.

Gettier-type objections to the traditional analysis

The best way of showing that the JTB conditions are *not* sufficient would be to give examples of JTBs that do not count as examples of knowledge. In 1967, one philosopher, Edmund Gettier (1927–) did just this. Gettier published a short paper entitled 'Is Justified, True Belief Knowledge?' The paper was only three sides long, but has had a large impact and led to many other philosophers writing papers, chapters and books exploring its consequences. Gettier himself never published any philosophy again.

His paper gives examples of *beliefs* which are both *true* and apparently *justified* but which we are inclined not to count as examples of *knowledge*. In other words, while accepting that the three conditions are individually necessary, he questioned whether they were jointly sufficient. The examples he and others have subsequently used have become known as Gettier counter examples.

Gettier gives two examples in his famous paper. The first involves two men, Smith and Jones, both going for a job interview. Gettier writes:

Suppose that Smith and Jones have applied for a certain job. And suppose that Smith has strong evidence for the following conjunctive proposition:

d) Jones is the man who will get the job, and Jones has ten coins in his pocket.

Smith's evidence for d) might be that the president of the company assured him that Jones would in the end be selected, and that he,

anthology
1.14

Smith, had counted the coins in Jones' pocket ten minutes ago. Proposition d) entails:

e) The man who will get the job has ten coins in his pocket.

Let us suppose that Smith sees the entailment from d) to e), and accepts e) on the grounds of d), for which he has strong evidence. In this case, Smith is clearly justified in believing that e) is true ...[6]

Gettier's language is a bit formal (he specialises in logic!) but what he is claiming is this: Smith has good evidence for believing that Jones will get the job and good evidence that Jones has ten coins in his pocket. From this he then goes on to believe the proposition 'the man who will get the job has ten coins in his pocket'. Now, as it turns out there is an unexpected change of events and Jones does not get the job. Smith does. Also, by coincidence, Smith has exactly ten coins in his pocket (he did not know this earlier). This leads to a possible counter example in the JTB account of knowledge. Did Smith know proposition e) 'the man who will get the job has ten coins in his pocket'?

   a) Smith certainly was *justified* (to some extent) for his belief (he had counted Jones' coins and been told by the president of the company that Jones would get the job).
   b) Smith's belief was *true*.
   c) Smith had a *belief* that the man who would get the job had ten coins in his pocket.

Smith had a *justified, true belief* that 'The man who will get the job has ten coins in his pocket', but would you be willing to say that Smith knew that the man who would get the job has ten coins in his pocket? If you are not willing to say that Smith knew it then it seems that having a justified, true belief is not the same thing as having knowledge. The three elements are not sufficient conditions. Either the account is the wrong approach or some extra element is missing.

   Most people would claim that Smith did not have knowledge. His belief about the coins is a true one because of luck. After all, Smith did not know how many coins he had in his own pocket. As suggested earlier we have a strong intuition that knowledge should not involve luck and so Gettier's examples convinced most philosophers that the account knowledge as a justified, true belief needed some forms of modification or patching up. The rest of this chapter consists of looking at these attempts to amend the definition.

   Before we move to look at these, it is worth exploring some more 'Gettier-style' counter examples, where a justified, true belief seems to fall short of being knowledge.

Experimenting with ideas

Consider the Gettier-style counter examples below. Then answer the following questions.

1 Do you think the person in each of the examples has knowledge?
2 Do you think the person has a justified, true belief?
3 Do you think these examples mean that having a justified, true belief is not the same thing as having knowledge?
4 Do these examples have anything in common?
5 Can you come up with your own Gettier-style counter example showing a case of a justified, true belief that we are unlikely to accept as a case of knowing?

Example 1

Imagine that one evening you watch a nature programme and you hear David Attenborough say that the killer whale is the fastest swimming sea mammal. As a consequence you acquire the belief that the killer whale is the fastest sea mammal. As a matter of fact this belief is true: killer whales are indeed the fastest of all sea mammals. Moreover it is justified since David Attenborough is a reliable source of information about wildlife. So here is a clear-cut case of a justified, true belief. However, unremarked by you, the evening in question was that of the first of April, and the nature programme was a spoof littered with amusing falsehoods about the natural world. Given this extra fact, could you still be said to know that the killer whale is the fastest sea mammal?

Example 2

Imagine you ride into town at around noon and look up at the clock tower to check the time. The clock says 12 o'clock and so you come to believe that it is 12 o'clock. In fact it is 12 o'clock. Checking a clock is an excellent justification for your belief and so we have here an example of justified, true belief. However, unbeknown to you, the clock has in fact stopped. And the fact that it was telling the correct time at precisely the moment when you chanced to look up at it is a remarkable coincidence. Can you be said to know at that moment that it is 12 o'clock?

Example 3

Jonathan comes home from work early in order to watch the world triple-jump championships. He doesn't know it but the BBC are having technical difficulties with their broadcast, so to keep the viewers happy they show a replay of the triple jump final from four years ago, and in the mayhem forget to put on the symbol that shows it to be a repeat. Jonathan switches on the TV and is excited to see Richard Long win the event with a jump of 18.27 metres. Naturally he does not realise this was a replay. As it happens, while the replay was being shown, Richard Long did actually win this year's triple jump, remarkably with a jump of 18.27 metres. Does Jonathan know that Richard Long won the triple jump?

Example 4

Today London is hosting a Boris Johnson look-alike day for charity. Thousands of Londoners are roaming the streets dressed up as the dishevelled politician – sporting appropriate wigs, and so on. Many of them are very convincing. Taz has just landed at Heathrow airport and knows nothing of the charity day. She takes a taxi to her hotel in Park Lane. While the taxi is driving into the centre of London she passes many Boris Johnson look-alikes, but does not really notice them. As she gets out of the taxi to pay she glances up and for a few seconds sees a man riding past on a pink bike looking just like Boris Johnson. It was, in fact, the real Boris Johnson. She stares in surprise for a moment. She goes into the hotel and texts her friend all about it. Does Taz know that Boris Johnson was riding a pink bike that morning?

Example 5

On the very same day Luke was travelling to his office. (Unlike Taz, he knew about the Boris look-alike charity event). Outside his office Luke saw a 'Boris' cycle past on a pink bike. He was completely convinced it was the real Boris. It wasn't; it was a very good impersonator. Luke, seeing the fake and believing it to be real then formed a belief that Boris Johnson was riding a pink bike that day, which of course he was. Does Luke know that Boris Johnson was riding a pink bike that day?

In each of the cases the people have a *true belief* that seems to be reasonably *justified* and so all three conditions of the JTB have been met, yet many would argue that they don't have *knowledge*. All of these cases involve a belief that is somehow coincidentally true. There seems to be a strong element of luck involved in each of these cases and we are not inclined to award knowledge on the basis of luck.

Although each of these examples involves luck, there are some important similarities and differences between the cases.

In example 2 you were was looking at something broken and unreliable that coincidentally was right. In example 3 Jonathan was watching the wrong event, which just luckily happened to match the real event in some ways. Another coincidence. Both these, in some way, involve a kind of false belief about what they were watching, that luckily turned out to be accurate. In these cases neither person had seen the real thing; they saw something false that was coincidentally true. These two examples match Gettier's own examples in this regard.

In examples 1 and 4 something subtly different is going on. In example 1 you heard a true fact about a mammal in a programme that contained lots of other falsehoods. However, the fact you heard was true and your belief was not coincidentally true; it's just that in the context of the April Fool's programme it was lucky that the thing you remembered was one of the few true facts.

Likewise in example 4: Taz actually saw the real Boris and formed her belief based on seeing the man himself. There is no coincidence. It is just that the context of the Boris Johnson look-alike day makes this seem a bit lucky, particularly as she was not aware of this. Contrast this with example 5. Luke saw a fake Boris believing it to be real and formed a belief that Boris Johnson was riding a pink bike that day. In this case Luke saw the wrong person and his belief was luckily true, whereas Taz saw the right person, but the context makes it seem a bit lucky. Who are you more inclined to say knew that Boris was on a pink bike – Taz, Luke or neither?

Examples 1 and 4 are examples of 'fake-barn' Gettier-style counter examples. The original fake-barn scenario is roughly this: A man, Barney, is driving, unknowingly, through a place called fake-barn county, where, by the side of the road they have built lots of fake barns consisting just of a barn front with nothing behind (like on a movie set). The driver does not pay much attention, but then looks to the side and sees a big red barn. On the basis of this he believes there is a big red barn by the road. However, it just so happens that this is the only real barn in the whole area! Did he know there was a big red barn there? He saw a real barn with his eyes, believed there was a real barn and there was a real barn. The luck involved is that it happened to be the only real barn for miles and he had no idea that the others were fakes. Like examples 1 and 4, this relies on the wider context making the belief seem luckily true. In the other cases a false belief/assumption then turns out to be coincidentally true.

Examples 4 and 5 show these two different types together. Luke's belief relies on the coincidence of the fake Boris and the real Boris both being on a pink bike. This is what we will call a STANDARD Gettier example. In contrast, Taz's belief was based on seeing and believing that it was the real Boris, which it was, so there is no error here. The only element of luck was that she did not know it was a look-alike day and so it could easily have been a fake that she saw. In other words, the context meant that there was a bit of luck involved. This is a fake-barn-style Gettier counter example.

Some people may be inclined to say that Taz *did* know that Boris was on a pink bike and that the person *did* know the fact about the killer whale. As we will see below, the fake-barn-style cases come into the discussion quite a bit and in some cases philosophers have argued that these do count as knowledge and are not counter examples at all. However, all of these examples seem to throw doubt on the idea that knowledge is simply justified, true belief. How are we to react to such problem cases?

Reactions to Gettier

Initially perhaps the most attractive response is to defend the traditional account by arguing that the reason that we are reluctant to say that these people have knowledge is simply that their beliefs are not justified in the proper way. So the idea would be that we need to define our notion of justification more strictly so as to rule out these counter examples. For example, we ought not to trust the BBC since it is always possible that the programme makers are pulling our legs or running the wrong footage. And we ought not to trust clocks since they may have stopped. However, this line of argument faces two related problems. First, it is difficult to see how one could define '*proper* justification' in such a way as to prevent Gettier-type examples arising. So, while we might be inclined to say that one is only justified in believing what the BBC say about wildlife if one has first checked the date, or cross-referenced what they say against an encyclopaedia, it would seem that further Gettier-type scenarios can always be dreamt up. One could be deceived about the date; the encyclopaedia might contain a misprint, and so on. Second even if we did succeed in defining 'proper justification' in such a strict way as to eliminate the possibility of error, this creates another problem. A method of acquiring beliefs that could avoid the risk of ever going wrong in cases like Gettier's would be terribly strict, and even infallible. As we say above on page 54, this would involve us in saying that we don't really know the things we think we know and so entails a radical redefinition of our ordinary concept of knowledge. Thus, for example, we could no longer rely on the testimony of others since it is always possible that they are mistaken or have reason to lie. We would have to say that I don't really know most of what I think I know about the natural world, since I have learned a lot of it from unreliable sources such as the BBC. And, it would seem that I can hardly ever be said to know the time since I acquire my beliefs about the time almost exclusively by checking a single watch or clock.

Although neither of these solutions seems ideal, these are the main approaches that philosophers have taken in the face of Gettier-style counter examples to the concept of knowledge. Some have tried to articulate what would count as the 'proper' justification for a knowledge claim (see below on reliabilism, 'No false lemmas', page 81) while others have claimed that only justification that somehow 'guarantees' knowledge is good enough (infallibilism).

Summary of JTB and Gettier

According to the classic definition, knowledge is justified, true belief. Gettier came along and gave examples that seemed to be JTBs, so should be classed as knowledge, but which our intuition tell us are not cases of knowledge. This of course raises big doubts about the validity of the definition. For the rest of this chapter we will explore a range of alternative theories of knowledge, most based on variation of the classic JTB definition. Although each theory is different, they all attempt to overcome the Gettier examples in a similar way. They seek to show that, according to *their* definitions, the Gettier examples would not be classed as knowledge in the first place, so the fact that our intuitions would not class them as knowledge is no longer a problem.

Infallibilism and certainty

Earlier we noted that one of the intuitions we have about belief is that it should involve a level of certainty. Here we will explore this idea further and look at different ways in which certainty has been used to shore up the concept of knowledge. There are three different theories that we look at:

1 Knowledge as the **feeling of certainty**. In this theory knowledge must be a justified, true belief of which you feel certain (K = JTB + feeling of certainty).

2 Knowledge as an **infallible** belief. In this theory knowledge must be a justified, true belief where the justification is so strong that it rules out any other possibilities and means that the belief *must* be true (K = JTB + infallibility. Although many proponents of this claim that knowledge does not involve belief so really it would be K = JT + infallibility).

3 Knowledge as a fairly certain belief, where the **relevant alternatives** are not possible. In this theory knowledge must be a justified, true belief where the justification is very, very strong and rules out most relevant alternatives (K = JTB + no relevant alternatives are possible).

Feeling of certainty

Some have suggested that the feeling of certainty should be another necessary condition for truth – in other words knowledge is a justified, true belief of which you feel certain. The problem with this is that certainty is quite a subjective feeling. Let us consider whether this is correct through an example. Imagine that you are on a famous quiz show on TV and have managed to get through to the last round where you have a chance to win a million pounds. All you have to do is answer the question correctly. However, if you get the answer wrong you risk losing nearly half a million of the winnings you have so far accumulated. So the pressure is on. The question is posed: 'Who wrote *Meditations on First Philosophy*? Is it a) Desmond Tutu, b) Descartes, c) the Dalai Lama or d) David Beckham?' In such a circumstance, even though you have studied philosophy and have excellent evidence that Descartes is the correct answer, you might experience doubts. Could the book in which you read about Descartes be a hoax? Did Beckham write philosophy between matches? Is it a trick question? Despite your doubts, you plump for the correct answer: Descartes. So, did you know this was the answer?

If feeling certainty is a necessary condition for knowledge, the answer would be that you did not. But according to the plain old JTB account of knowledge you did, since, despite your hesitancy, you had a justified, true belief. So which view is correct? It is clear that doubts can creep in even when we have good evidence for beliefs that are true. In such cases, we will not claim to have knowledge, and this is the reason that they seem not to be cases of knowledge. However, the JTB account says that someone's reluctance to claim to know doesn't necessarily show that they don't know. In the example of the quiz programme, it may simply be that you are a very sceptical and diffident person. You may be particularly afraid of making a fool of yourself on national television. You may be scared at the thought of possibly losing a fortune. But such psychological facts about you do not warrant the conclusion that you do not have knowledge.

This is perhaps clearer if we imagine another contestant in the same situation who has none of your worries. They are naturally confident and always think they are right. They have exactly the same evidence as you that Descartes wrote the *Meditations*, having read the same book on the subject. Do they have knowledge? Presumably they do. But if they do then surely you do too, since the only difference lies in the degree of conviction you have in your beliefs. So the conclusion appears to be that subjective certainty – that is, about how confident one is of the truth of one's beliefs – does not have any bearing on whether or not one knows. It cannot be a sufficient condition for knowledge; after all, many politicians are convinced their policies are the right ones, but few of us would say that they know them to be.

Furthermore, adding a subjective 'certainty' condition does not overcome any of the Gettier counter examples outlined above. In each of these cases the person could have a justified, true belief that they felt certain about – but they would still not have knowledge.

Infallibilism

Gettier-style counter examples rely on cases where the believer seems to have reasonable justification for their belief, but where there is a large element of luck involved in their belief being a true belief. And, as we saw with Plato above on page 57, we are not inclined to award 'knowledge' to anyone on the basis of luck. One way to remove this element of luck from the process is to require the justification to be so strong that the truth is guaranteed. In other words to claim that knowledge can only be allowed if the belief is infallible (meaning impossible to be wrong).

Infallibilism (sometimes called the guarantee condition) is the theory that we should only count as knowledge those things which we cannot rationally doubt. Under this theory most justified, true beliefs would not count as knowledge – only those beliefs that cannot be rationally doubted. In contrast to the theory above, infallibilism is *not* the claim that we must feel certain in our beliefs to have knowledge. It is the much stronger claim that we should only count as knowledge those things which we cannot rationally doubt.

▶ ACTIVITY

1 Which of the following beliefs cannot be rationally doubted?
2 Which of these have alternative possibilities to the belief being true?
3 Are points 1 and 2 above asking the same thing?

   a) You believe that it will rain tomorrow.
   b) You believe that $2 + 2 = 4$.
   c) You believe that one day dogs will start to speak.
   d) You believe you currently are in pain or not.
   e) You believe that you are experiencing black ink coloured lettering sensations that seem to spell out words and sentences.
   f) You believe that you are reading a book.
   g) You believe you know that you exist.
   h) You believe you ate breakfast this morning.
   i) You believe that it is possible to doubt things.
   j) You believe the Sun will rise tomorrow.

Most infallibilists would claim that only b), d), e), g) and i) would count as knowledge as these cannot be rationally doubted. Consider the example of pain. If you are in pain you cannot be wrong about this. There are no alternative possibilities where you are feeling pain, but this might somehow be an illusion. As no alternatives are possible, your belief is *infallible* and so you know that you are in pain. With most beliefs the external world needs to match up with my beliefs for them to be true; however, when I am considering my own mind there no are external facts with which my internal knowledge needs to match up. My knowledge of my pain, and my pain, are the same thing. Without a gap between the belief and an external reality, there is no space for the sceptic to exploit, and this is why such knowledge is thought to be infallible.

Descartes was assuming an infallibilist approach to knowledge in the *Meditations* when trying to find a belief that could not be doubted, where no hypothetical alternatives were possible. His plan was to doubt all of his beliefs, so that only those that cannot be rationally doubted would remain. He could then build up a system of knowledge where every belief was infallible.

> *Some years ago I was struck by how many false things I had believed, and by how doubtful was the structure of beliefs that I had based on them. I realized that if I wanted to establish anything in the sciences that was stable and likely to last, I needed – just once in my life – to demolish everything completely and start again from the foundation.*[7]
>
> Descartes, *Meditation 1*, page 1

As we saw in the Introduction, he concluded that he could *know* that he existed as this was impossible to rationally doubt (as someone must be doing the doubting!). Descartes called these infallible beliefs clear and distinct ideas and these would be the building blocks of his new system of knowledge (see the diagram on page 166). Descartes also would have counted b), d), e), g) and i) as examples of clear and distinct ideas that cannot be doubted.

Infallibilism: Knowledge and belief

Although we are using examples of beliefs here, some holders of the theory of infallibilism claim that we should distinguish belief from knowledge. They claim that knowledge is not a kind of belief; it is a separate thing. Imagine that you are in your bedroom and you hear an engine-style noise coming from outside your house. According to this version of the infallibilism you would know that you are experiencing a certain kind of revving noise at that moment. You cannot be wrong about this, even if you are dreaming or hallucinating. No alternatives are possible whereby you think you are experiencing a noise but you are not. This is infallible, so you know that you are experiencing a noise. You might *believe* that the noise is caused by a car outside, but you cannot *know* this, as there are other possible alternatives. In claiming there is a car outside you are making an inference and you may be wrong. In this way some infallibilists claim that belief and knowledge are different things.

Beliefs only occur when doubt *is* possible and knowledge occurs when it is impossible. To show this difference the philosopher Price cites the example of pain. When you are in pain, you *know* you are; you cannot be wrong. He claims that it makes no sense to say you *also* believe you are in pain, as you know you are.[8] It is just not an issue of belief. Someone else may observe you and infer that you are in pain. In this case the person would hold a *belief* about your pain. They would not know you were in pain – as there is the possibility of an alternative explanation/error (you could be faking it!). But there is no possibility of your being wrong about your pain, and so you *know* that you are in pain. Knowledge involves no other possibilities but beliefs involve other possibilities, and therefore may involve erroneous inferences.

▶ **ACTIVITY: Belief or knowledge?**

Are some infallibilists right to distinguish belief and knowledge? For each of the following decide:

1 Is this a case of knowledge?
2 Is this a case of belief?
3 Which of the cases of knowledge are also cases of belief?

   a) Shaffique knows that God exists.
   b) John knows he is in pain.
   c) Alison knows that Arsenal will win the Champions League next year.

d) Billie knows she is awake.

e) Reuben knows he ate cornflakes for breakfast.

f) Casper knows that Shakespeare wrote *Hamlet*.

g) David knows that dinosaurs once roamed the planet.

h) You know you are reading a book.

The standard theory of knowledge suggests that it is a form of justified belief. However, some infallibilists suggest that belief and knowledge are different beasts. This activity might make you lean one way or the other. Question 3 is the important one. If you feel that the cases of knowledge involve belief, then you side with the standard theory. If you feel that none of the cases of knowledge involve belief then you may agree, along with some infallibilists, that knowledge is not a form of belief, but a different type of thing. This means that you would not agree with the claim earlier (page 62) that belief is a necessary condition for knowledge.

Evaluation of infallibilism

Should we adopt infallibilism? On the positive side, infallibilism is not open to Gettier counter examples. None of the examples given would count as knowledge in the first place as all are open to some doubt/alternative explanations. By restricting knowledge to only those things that cannot be doubted then there is no room for Gettier counter examples to thrive as these all rely on beliefs that are merely plausibly justified – which might be false, but turn out to be luckily true. Another positive feature of this theory is that it accords with our intuition that knowledge involves a level of certainty – although in this case it is absolute certainty!

The main criticism of the theory (and it is a big one) is that it goes against our intuition that we can know lots of things. Infallibilism would imply that we have very little knowledge. We can know logical truths (things that are true by definition), such as a triangle has three sides. This cannot be doubted as there are no alternatives. We can also know facts about our minds, such as the sensations we experience. We may also be able to know one or two other things through careful, undoubtable reasoning, such as 'I exist'. In the *Meditations* this is about all that Descartes establishes with certainty (he establishes more if you accept his proof of God!).

Under the theory of infallibilism this would be the extent of our knowledge. We would not be able to claim to know that the Sun will set, that England once won the World Cup, that you had a cup of tea this morning, that milk is white, and so on. Now this may not be a problem. It may be that our common definition of knowledge needs such radical revision. This is certainly the approach that many philosophers, such as Descartes, have taken in the past. However, most contemporary philosophers are reluctant to pursue such a radical redefinition of our ordinary view of what counts as knowledge. To diverge too radically from common usage, they argue, involves our leaving behind the very concept we set out to analyse. Only by holding some sort of connection with ordinary usage and our ordinary intuitions can we be said to be analysing the concept of knowledge at all. We should be asking how we know what we know, and so getting clear about what our concept of knowledge actually is. We should not seriously be wondering whether we really know what we commonly suppose we do. Infallibilism seems to be prescribing what our concept of knowledge *should* be, rather than analysing/describing what it *is*.

Learn More

Relevant alternatives

Infallibilism appeals as it equates knowledge with certainty and this seems intuitive. However, because sceptical arguments introduce cunning alternative possibilities that cannot be eliminated, then it seems there are very few things we can know for certain. The theory of relevant alternatives is a softer version of infallibilism and claims that we do not have to eliminate *every* possible alternative to claim knowledge – we just have to eliminate the *relevant* ones.

Imagine you have a friend, Billie Baxter, who has been travelling around Asia for the last three months. You bump into her on the High Street this morning and catch up for ten minutes, admiring her tan, and so on, before parting ways. Do you now know that Billie Baxter has returned from her holiday? According to the theory of infallibilism you cannot know this as there are many alternative possibilities. You could be dreaming or hallucinating; you could be a brain in a vat; it could have been a robot disguised as Billie Baxter or even Billie Baxter's secret twin Amy. As you cannot eliminate these possibilities completely then you cannot claim knowledge. As we have seen, this makes the total of what we can actually know rather small. The theory of relevant alternatives claims that we do not have to be able to eliminate all alternatives to claim knowledge, just the relevant ones. Sceptical considerations such as being a brain in a vat, or a Robot Billie are just not relevant. In this case you would have knowledge. However if had you just glanced at Billie Baxter from the other side of the road, you would not have knowledge, as other alternatives – such as your seeing someone that looked like Billie Baxter – are relevant and possible.

This approach to defining knowledge by only considering the relevant ways a belief could be wrong has parallels with other everyday concepts such as *empty*. An absolute concept of empty does exist (a perfect vacuum). However, we can happily say that a cup is empty even though there is dust and air in it and tea stains. These things are just not relevant to it being 'empty'. A tissue or some lemonade in the cup would be relevant and stop us saying that it was empty.

Likewise with knowledge, we do not need absolute infallibility (emptiness); we do not need *all* alternatives to be eliminated (such as a possibility of being asleep); as long as the relevant alternatives are not possible, then you can claim knowledge. This is shown in **Figure 1.19a** where John is looking at a tree. The possibilities that he is dreaming or being deceived by a demon are not relevant so this is an example of knowledge. Whereas in **Figure 1.19b**, there are other relevant possibilities – John might be looking at a bongo antelope rather than a zebra, so John does not know there is a zebra near the bushes; he only believes this. One problem with this theory is that stating what would be a relevant/irrelevant alternative is a slippery business and seems to depend on each context. However, some would say this is not a problem, and it mirrors the vagueness with which we use the word in everyday life.

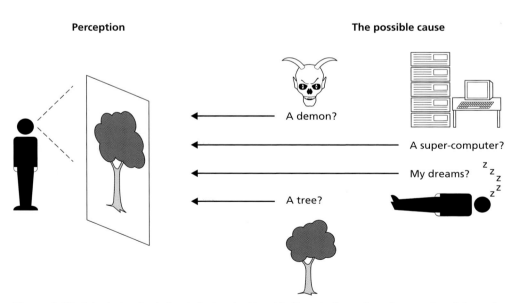

Figure 1.19a John is standing in front of a tree looking at it. Does he know there is a tree there? According to infallibilism, he does not know as there are alternative explanations that could explain his perception. Rational doubt is possible so the belief there is a tree is not infallible, and so John can only believe there is a tree there; he cannot know it. The theory of relative alternative would say that these alternative possibilities are not relevant. As there are no relevant alternatives John can know there is a tree in front of him.

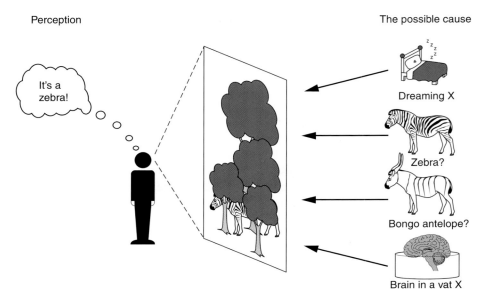

Perception   The possible cause

It's a zebra!

Dreaming X

Zebra?

Bongo antelope?

Brain in a vat X

Figure 1.19b On safari John can see a black and white shape in the far distance. Does he know there is a zebra there? Infallibilism would say no as there are other possible alternatives. The theory of relative alternatives would say that the possibilities of dreaming or a super-computer are not relevant. However, the possibility it is a bongo antelope is a relevant alternative. So John would not know there was a zebra there; he would only believe it.

How does the relevant alternative theory cope with Gettier?

Learn More

As deciding what counts as a relevant alternative can be a slippery affair, the answer to this question is also a bit slippery. With the standard Gettier examples, many would not count them as examples of knowledge if we set a strict standard for knowledge and include the possibility of lots of relevant alternatives. Smith, or even the president of the company, may be wrong about who will get the job (Gettier's example, page 67); clocks may well be broken (page 69); replays of sporting events are often played on TV (page 69). These could be classed as relevant alternatives, so in these cases the beliefs would lack the level of certainty needed to count as knowledge in the first place.

The cost of this approach is that account of knowledge becomes much stricter and does not match our everyday use. Also other Gettier examples can be generated which involve even more coincidence, and someone holding the relevant alternative theory would either have to restrict the cases of knowledge even further or simply concede that the Gettier cases are a problem.

The situation gets even worse for the relevant alternative theory when we consider the fake-barn-style cases. When Taz glances up, sees the real Boris and believes he is on a pink bike, is it a relevant alternative that, unknown to her, it might be Boris look-a-like charity day? If it is relevant, then, again, knowledge seems impossible. Every time I see an apple in shop window then it *could* be Fake Apple Day, or Make Lifelike Things Out of Wax Day. If these are considered relevant alternatives then very little indeed can count as knowledge and the relevant alternative theory starts to resemble infallibilism.

No false lemmas

Before we explore this theory it is worth noting that a LEMMA is not some kind of suicidal furry animal. *Lemma* is a term used in logic and mathematics, formally meaning a subsidiary proposition that is assumed to be true and is used to demonstrate another proposition. For our purposes, a lemma can be taken to mean a belief or assumption that is held to be true and is used to justify a piece of knowledge.

Previously we have explored how the concept of 'certainty' might, or might not, feature in the account of knowledge. Here we explore a different approach to saving the JTB account of knowledge from the problem of Gettier, which involves trying to pinpoint why it is that some seemingly 'justified' beliefs can be 'luckily' true. The suggestion is that in Gettier's own example the 'justification' for the belief should not be considered valid because it involves, or relies upon, a false belief. Specifically Smith's belief that *the man who will get the job has ten coins in his pocket* was based on the *false* belief that Jones would get the job.

Smith's reasoning might have proceeded like this:

a) I believe that Jones has ten coins in his pocket (having seen them).

b) I believe that Jones will get the job (having been told as much).

c) I believe that the person that gets the job will have ten coins in his pocket.

However, b) is a false belief/assumption. It is a *false lemma*. Gettier gives two examples in his famous paper and both involve the use of a false assumption in the believer's reasoning. This theory claims that knowledge is a justified, true belief, where the justification is not based on a false assumption. To put it more formally it claims that:

Knowledge = J + T + B + N (where N means = No false lemmas)

This theory adds an extra 'external' element to the account of the knowledge. A believer may have strong justification for a given belief but if her belief was based on a false lemma and is 'luckily' true, then even though it may feel to her like a case of knowledge, it is not one. This seems a reasonable addition to the account of knowledge. In most cases, when we justify a belief using a false lemma, the belief itself will turn out to be false, and so would not count as knowledge.

For example, imagine you were checking the football results in the back of a Sunday newspaper, but without realising it was a paper that was a year old. In doing this you have made a false assumption/lemma. As a result, most of the beliefs you form as to Saturday's football scores will simply be false in the real world. However, if one of them happens to be true by coincidence then we would not want to count this as knowledge either, as we don't want knowledge to be based on false beliefs that luckily turn out to be true.

How does the no false lemmas theory cope with Gettier?

The no false lemmas theory copes well with the standard Gettier cases. We should expect this, as it was one of the first attempted 'solutions' to the Gettier problem and the two cases presented by Gettier both rely on false lemmas to justify the belief. However, soon after this theory was put forward, other Gettier-style examples were generated which did not seem to involve the obvious use of a false lemma.

In Gettier's case the false lemma is obvious. Smith believed that Jones would get the job (he didn't). In our example of the charity day (page 70), Luke believed he had seen the real Boris and he had not.

However, in other cases it is not so clear that a false belief was involved. Consider the example of the broken clock. You see the time on a clock and believe it to be twelve o'clock and even though the clock is broken the time is coincidentally right. In this example your thought processes might go something like this:

    a) You believe it is roughly the middle of the day.
    b) You see a clock that says twelve o'clock.
    c) You believe it is now twelve o'clock.

In this case your belief that it is twelve o'clock is not based on any obvious false lemma. You had a rough belief about the right time, which was true. You saw a clock, which did indeed say twelve o'clock. No assumption was false, yet you would not have knowledge. As such, the theory of K = J + T + B + No false lemmas must, on the face of it, not work, as this looks like a case of J + T + B + N *not* equalling K.

Learn More

From no false lemmas to no-essential-false-assumptions

It may be possible, however, to resurrect a different version of this theory if we also include tacit or hidden assumptions when we consider what might count as a false lemma. Revisiting the case of the clock, if we included assumptions as well as consciously held beliefs, we could outline the reasoning process as follows:

    a) You believe it is roughly the middle of the day.
    b) You see a clock that says twelve o'clock.
    c) You (tacitly) believe that the clock is working.
    d) You believe it is twelve o'clock.

This version of the reasoning process includes the new assumption c). It is unlikely that you actually stop and think about this every time you look at a clock: in other words, it is not a consciously held belief. However, you could argue that it is an essential assumption that you make in concluding that it is twelve o'clock. As this is a false assumption, then you do not know it is twelve o'clock and this particular Gettier problem no longer exists.

As we saw above, the no false lemmas theory can cope with some of the standard Gettier examples by claiming they would not count as knowledge in the first place. And by modifying this theory to include hidden assumptions, the no-essential-false-assumptions theory can cope with an even wider range of standard Gettier cases. However, both theories run into trouble with the fake-barn-style cases.

Consider the example of the Boris look-alike day. Taz believed Boris was riding a pink bike, and the stages involved in her forming this belief were very simple:

a) Taz sees someone in London looking very like Boris Johnson riding a pink bike.

b) Taz believes Boris Johnson was riding a pink bike.

In this case there are no false lemmas and there do not seem to be any essential false assumptions either. We cannot reasonably claim that Taz is assuming that it is not Boris Johnson look-alike day, as Taz has never heard of such a day. Although it is hard to define what might reasonably count as a hidden assumption when arriving at a belief, it would be hard to come up with a definition that would include this as an assumption!

Lycan, the philosopher who devised the no-essential-false-assumptions theory, takes the unusual step of not arguing with this conclusion.[9] He agrees that fake-barn cases do not involve any essential false assumptions, but instead he claims that these are actual cases of knowledge. Taz does know that Boris is riding a pink bike. This counter example is not a counter example at all. It is simply a case of knowledge.

▶ **ACTIVITY**

Let us reconsider those fake-barn cases. Do you agree with Lycan that they count as knowledge?

1   Example 1 on page 69: you hear a true fact in an otherwise fallacious spoof documentary (you do not realise it is a spoof). Do you now know that the killer whale is the fastest sea mammal? There are no false lemmas. There are no essential false assumptions. (Well, you could claim that there is an assumption the programme is not a spoof documentary, but we will overlook this.) Do you know the whale-related fact?

2   Example 4 on page 69: does Taz *know* that Boris is on a pink bike?

3   The fake-barn case itself on page 70: does Barney know he is looking at a big red barn?

These cases all seem to involve an element of luck, although the luck is derived more from having a true belief in a rather haphazard context, rather than simply having a belief (based on a false belief) that is coincidentally true. Our intuitions seem to suggest that knowledge shouldn't involve luck, so should we rule out the case or not? Luck can of course be involved in acquiring knowledge without ruling it out. We may discover many things about the world by chance; however, this is different from holding a belief that is luckily/coincidentally true. The fake-barn cases seem to raise something of a problem with our luck intuition. Yes, there is luck involved, but there is no false belief/coincidence involved either. Perhaps it is up to you the reader to decide whether these cases count as knowledge or not . . .

Summary of false lemmas

Gettier's initial counter examples rely on someone holding a false belief, then making another belief based on this that is luckily true. The no false lemmas theory was devised to overcome these counter examples by showing that they were based on a false PREMISE, and so were not true. The no-essential-false-assumptions theory expands on this by ruling out knowledge in cases, not just involving false premises, but also false assumptions. This overcomes a wider range of possible counter examples. However, the fake-barn cases involve neither false premises nor assumptions. According to both these theories these should then count as knowledge, but our intuition about luck suggests that they do not. Lycan, in defending his theory, suggests that, yes, they do count as knowledge. The fake-barn counter examples are not counter examples at all, as they count as knowledge.

Reliabilism (R + T + B)

So far we have explored the idea that knowledge is justified, true belief. Through Gettier we have seen that there are examples of JTBs that we would not count as knowledge and have explored different ways of amending the standard account to try to overcome these counter examples. So far the approaches we have looked at have tried to shore up the idea of what counts as knowledge-worthy justification. Suggesting that adequate justification must either rule out all other possibilities and so guarantee the truth (infallibility) or that adequate justification must not be based on any false premises or assumptions. Below we will explore two very different approaches. The first approach (reliabilism) ignores the whole idea of justification and instead explores the sorts of processes that tend to lead to knowledge. The second approach explores the sorts of qualities a good 'knower' might have.

A reliable process

The theory of reliabilism, or rather of the theory *process reliabilism* that we will be exploring here, can get quite complicated. However, at its heart is a fairly simple idea. Consider these two cases:

1 You read in *Viz*/the *National Enquirer*/the *Beano* that a man in China has fifteen fingers.
2 You read in *The Guardian*/*The Times* that porcupines are mostly nocturnal.

Can you be said to know that the Chinese man has fifteen fingers? Probably not. Can you be said to know that porcupines are mostly nocturnal? Probably yes.

One key difference between the two is that the information in the second case is from a reliable newspaper. There may be other factors at play as to why we might attribute knowledge in the second case but not the first, but the reliability of the source is likely to be a key factor. The more reliable the source the more likely we are to say that the person *knows* the fact.

But what do we mean by a reliable newspaper? It could mean that it doesn't rip easily, or is always printed on time and available in the shops. In this case, however, we mean that a reliable newspaper is one that tells the truth with a high level of regularity. The more often a source or process produces the truth the more reliable it is.

Reliabilism is a theory of knowledge that claims the reliability of the process involved in generating a belief is the key factor in whether we should call it knowledge or not. Formally the theory claims that knowledge is a true belief that is produced by a reliable process (K = T + B + R).

Experimenting with ideas

1 On a scale of 1–10 rank how reliable you think each process below is for arriving at the belief (1 is not reliable and 10 is reliable).
2 Which of the cases would you class as examples of *knowing*?
3 Do your answers to question 1 correlate to your answers to question 2?
4 If you enjoyed this activity, then repeat it with the examples on page 60.

   a) Wishfully believing that it will not rain today.
   b) Adding 6 and 4 in your head to make 10.
   c) Eating hallucinogenic mushrooms and believing the Moon is alive.
   d) Reading (and believing) on www.conspiracies4ever.com that the Prime Minister is a reptile.
   e) Believing that you will have children because of the pattern of lines in your hand.
   f) Seeing your friend up close and believing he is back from his holiday.
   g) Seeing a black and white shape in a field far away and believing there is a cow.
   h) Seeing and hearing a cow up close and believing there is a cow in front of you.
   i) Multiplying 246 and 327 in your head to give 80,442.
   j) Reading (and believing) on Wikipedia that Nelson died at the Battle of Trafalgar.
   k) Remembering what you ate for breakfast on your third birthday.
   l) Remembering what you ate for breakfast this morning.
   m) Seeing the hands on an old church clock point to 12 and believing it is twelve o'clock.
   n) Guessing (correctly) that Arsenal would beat Liverpool 3–1.

What this activity may show is that there is a strong correlation between how reliable a process is for producing/arriving at the truth and whether we would attribute knowledge. A reliabilist would claim that this is precisely because knowledge is a true belief that is produced by a reliable process (K = T + B + R).

How reliable a process needs to be for knowledge to be attributed is a matter of debate; some might count tricky mental arithmetic as reliable and others not. But this elasticity precisely matches our ordinary concept of knowledge, where some are more willing to attribute knowledge than others. In general, processes such as wishfully believing, seeing when hallucinating, glimpsing from a distance, complex mental arithmetic, remembering things from a long time ago and guessing do not often regularly produce a true belief. As a result, they are not reliable and the beliefs they generate should not be classed as knowledge. On the other hand, processes such as seeing things up close, simple arithmetic and reading from a trustworthy source tend to produce true beliefs and so are reliable and should be classed as knowledge. This seems to accord with our intuitions since we would tend not to attribute knowledge in cases that involved one of these unreliable processes, but would in cases involving the reliable ones.

Reliabilism and justification

Notice that the account of reliabilism suggests that K = T + B + R, not that K = **J** + T+ B + R. The J is missing in the definition. Reliabilism is *not* saying that knowledge is a *justified*, true belief that has been formed by a reliable process, it *is* saying that knowledge is a true belief that has been formed by a reliable process. In other words, the idea of a reliable process is not in addition to the justification condition, it *replaces* the justified condition. It is more or less claiming that what we mean by a justified belief (for the purposes of knowledge) is a belief which is produced by a reliable process.

Up to this point in the chapter we have frequently mentioned the idea of a *justified*, true belief, but haven't really considered what might count as suitable justification. Defining justification can be very difficult and often ends up as a kind of circular definition. For example:

> **Question:** *How justified does a belief need to be to count as knowledge?*
> **Answer:** *It needs to have knowledge-worthy justification!*

This would count as a circular answer or definition (we gave such a definition earlier on page 66)! Circular definitions involve repeating the terms to be defined in the definition itself. Consider a different case:

> **Question:** *How big does a ball need to be to be classed as a football?*
> **Answer:** *It needs to be as big as a football!*

A reliable process

1)

The farmer sees the sheep and clicks the counter as each one enters the field. This is a reliable process as his counter works perfectly; he gets it right nearly all the time. The farmer **knows** he has nineteen sheep in the field.

2)

This farmer just looks in the field and makes an estimate. He believes there are twenty sheep. This process is not reliable. Even if it is true, he does **not know** this.

Figure 1.20 A reliable process.

Circular answers or definitions add no new information and do not really help. Process reliabilism is a way out of this circle. The theory gives an account of justification that, in turn, doesn't rely on the idea of justification.

Consider the following example:

a) An experienced vet picks up a guinea pig, examines it and concludes it is a male.

b) A ten-year-old boy notices a guinea pig twitch its ear when he calls it 'Hector', so concludes it is a male as 'Hector' is a boy's name.

In both cases they are right – the guinea pig *is* a male. However, there is a big difference in their justifications. But what do we mean by this? Rather than get into complex accounts of justification, process reliabilism keeps it fairly simple. In case a) the vet will reliably get the sex of guinea pigs right. He is trained and has the skills needed. Because of this there is a process at play that yields a high level of accuracy. This is what we mean when we say the vet's belief is justified. In case b) there is not a high level of accuracy and so the belief is not justified.

Reliable process or justification: which is best?

Some people have criticised this idea of equating the 'justification' required for knowledge with concept of a reliable process. The criticism argues that a justification is a different sort of thing from a reliable process, so they cannot be equated. One difference, they claim, is that justifications are *internal* to the believer. This means they involve conscious thoughts that the thinker is aware of, and as such, the believer can tell you why and how their beliefs are justified; for example, 'I saw it with my own eyes', 'John told me'. However, being a part of a reliable process does not necessarily involve conscious thought processes. The reliable processee (person involved in the reliable process) cannot necessarily tell you that the process is reliable, or necessarily explain the process. In this sense, reliable processes are *external* to the believer (even though they *may* involve cognitive processes). The criticism concludes that as justifications are internal and reliable processes are external, they cannot be the same thing.

Another related criticism is that 'justifications' involves *reasons* for beliefs, whereas reliable processes involve *causes* and so they cannot be the same thing. There is a whole literature on the differences between reasons and causes but this is the essential difference:

- *I turned the light on because it was dark.*
  This is a reason (which usually involves a thought).
- *I turned the light on because my eyes detected a lack of light and this triggered a sequence of neurons in my brain which eventually cause my finger to move and flick a switch.*
  This is a causal explanation (which does not involve thoughts).

Some people argue that reasons and causes can be the same thing, whereas others would say they are always different and reliabilism is mistaken in overlapping the two.

However, these criticisms of reliabilism can also be seen as a strength – depending which way your intuitions about knowledge lie. Consider this example from earlier:

John has a rare gift. If you give him any date in the future, say 15 March 2123, he is able to tell you what day of the week this will be (for example, a Monday). He is unable to say how he does this, though he is incredibly accurate.

He's right: 15 March 2123 will indeed be a Monday – but would you say that John knows this?

He certainly has a belief that is true. You would not say his belief is lucky, as he seems to have an ability to predict the day. However, he does not seem to have any sort of justification that a person who typically knows what day a future date might be would have, such as 'I have a spreadsheet that works out the days', or 'I looked it up on a calendar website' or 'My phone can tell me'. According to the JTB definition, John would not know what day of the week it would be as he lacks this sort of justification. Does this seem right though? Maybe you agree with this verdict.

Others would argue that John does know. Although John lacks an obvious justification, he does seem to have an ability to tell what the day will be. There seems to be a reliable process involved whereby John can tell the day, even though John could not describe the process. This example, depending on how you judge it, either highlights a weakness in reliabilism by showing that a reliable process is not the same thing as a justification and is not a necessary condition for knowledge. Or it highlights a strength showing how our ordinary concept of justification is not a necessary condition of knowledge and is better replaced by the idea of a belief being produced as part of a reliable process.

The idea of (non-human) animals having knowledge is another potential criticism or strength of reliabilism. According to most versions of the JTB account of knowledge, animals are unlikely to have knowledge as they could not justify their beliefs. Reliabilism, however, would disagree. Animals have evolved to have reliable processes of vision, hearing, memory, and so on that enable them to eat the right food and avoid the right dangers. Although animals may not have propositional knowledge (for example, 'I know that ...'), they certainly have *know-how* and are able to accurately interact with the world precisely because they have reliable processes. In this sense, a reliabilist would claim that animals do have knowledge.

As with the previous argument, this can either be seen as a strength or a weakness of reliabilism. If you believe that animals cannot have knowledge then it is a criticism. However, if you believe that animals can have knowledge then it seems that reliabilism can explain this better than the JTB account.

Reliabilism and Gettier

How does reliabilism fare with Gettier counter examples? It fares fairly well with the standard cases. Gettier counter examples involve cases where the believer has a justification, but somehow the belief is 'luckily' true and, in general, any belief that is true because of luck is not going to be part of a reliable process.

► **ACTIVITY**
1 Revisit the Gettier counter examples above on page 69.
2 For each case, decide if the process leading to the belief was a reliable one or not.

Example 1

Although watching a BBC nature programme is usually a reliable way of getting true beliefs, watching a spoof documentary is not a reliable way of getting true beliefs. So, according to reliabilism, this would not count as knowledge in the first place. Although the viewer may believe it is true, this is irrelevant. There was no reliable process involved as spoof TV programmes are not reliable sources of beliefs. (This highlights the difference between the internalist JTB approach where the viewer, not knowing it was a spoof, would feel justified, and the externalist reliabilist approach where this is irrelevant. It is not important if the viewer feels justified; what *is* important is if there is a reliable process [there wasn't] and it does not matter if the viewer is aware of this or not.) This case also shows that there is flexibility in how we describe a process – for example 'watching a BBC documentary' or 'watching a BBC spoof documentary' – and this is a potential weakness of the theory as it is not always agreed what process is in play in the formation of a belief.

Example 2

The case of the clock is fairly straightforward, but highlights the same issue with reliabilism. Looking at a clock is generally a fairly good way of telling the time. Looking at broken clocks is not though. Analysed this way, this would not be a case of knowledge as the process was not reliable.

Nonetheless, this process can be described/analysed in lots of different ways. Looking at old clocks is generally less reliable than new ones. Looking at clocks from a distance is less reliable than from close up. Looking at clocks without your glasses on (supposing that you wear glasses) is less reliable than with them. How a process is described can affect how reliable we think it is, and, in turn, whether it is appropriate to attribute knowledge. However, it is not clear how a process should be described and how detailed or general the description should be. Trying to articulate what might count as a reliable process both in general terms, such as 'seeing relatively near objects', and in very specific instances (sometimes called token instances), such as 'seeing an object on a foggy Tuesday with bleary eyes', has proved to be a problem with the theory of reliabilism. If we defined a process narrowly enough, for example – 'Amy looking at a peach from 10 metres away on an overcast day' – then each case becomes unique and we are unable to say whether the process, in general, is reliable. It will either be 100 per cent reliable or 0 per cent reliable as there is only one such case! If we make cases too general – for example 'watching a documentary' – and claim it as reliable, then the theory cannot cope with legitimate exceptions such as 'watching a spoof documentary'. Getting this balance right has proved a problem for the theory of reliabilism.

Example 3

Watching last year's replay (even unknowingly) is not a reliable way of getting accurate the result of this year's competition. So there is not a reliable process and this would not count as knowledge.

Reliabilism and fake-barn cases

Example 1 is actually a fake-barn case and reliabilism can deal with this fairly well, by classing the process as an example of watching a spoof documentary, which is unreliable. Example 4 and the real Boris Johnson spot is a little trickier. In this case it is not obvious that there was an unreliable process at play. Taz had a close-up perceptual experience (albeit a glance) and saw the real Boris: this caused her to believe that Boris was cycling on a pink bike that day. This is a true belief caused by the perceptual encounter with the real Boris Johnson. So reliabilism should class this as knowledge, but many people would be inclined to say that this is not a case of 'knowing', as there is an element of luck involved. The same problem occurs in the case of fake-barn county (see page 70). The driver saw the real barn among the fakes. It is not clear that there is an unreliable process at play, so again reliabilism should class this as knowledge.

How should the reliabilist respond?

There are a few different approaches. One is to simply claim that Taz does have knowledge. Yes, there is an element of luck involved in that she isn't aware of the broader context (the look-alike day), but nevertheless a reliable process was in play so this should count as knowledge. Taz has good eyesight and saw Boris reasonably close up. (This approach of accepting that there was knowledge in the fake-barn style cases was also used above as a defence for the no-essential-false-assumptions theory.) This defence is simple, but may not convince everyone as it goes against the intuitive idea that knowledge should not involve luck.

in a suitable way. This may seem very similar to reliabilism; however, the focus is on the virtues of the person (the AGENT) rather than on the process.

▶ **ACTIVITY**

1 Write down the names of five people you know. This could include celebrities.
2 Rank the five in order of their intellectual virtue.
3 Rank the five in order of who is likely to be a source of knowledge.
4 What does this activity tell you?

Formally speaking, virtue epistemology might state that knowledge is a true belief brought about by a virtuous intellectual disposition, or, in other words, a virtuous true belief. So K = V + T + B.

One problem with the shift in focus from the process to the faculties is that it makes the theory prone to standard Gettier counter examples. For example, you may be standing in the hallway and hear a meowing sound coming from the lounge. Because of this you believe a cat is in the lounge. You are right: a cat *is* in the lounge. However, it wasn't the cat that you heard meowing: someone had put on an audio track of animal noises, featuring meowing. It would be hard to claim you had knowledge in this case, although your belief was the result of your virtuous intellectual faculties working well. So the simple account of knowledge as a true belief coming about as the result of virtuous intellectual dispositions needs some refining. In this case, reliabilism would be able to say that the *process* of hearing an audio track of animal noises is not a reliable way of forming accurate beliefs about the animals in a particular room. But by focusing on just a person's faculties and intellects, virtue epistemology cannot use this defence. However, other defences are possible.

Triple A rating ('AAA')

Ernest Sosa (1940–) gives a more nuanced account of virtue epistemology.[10] He often compares cases of knowing with cases of athletes performing a particular task. His most famous example is that of an archer shooting an arrow. In accurately shooting an arrow, Sosa identifies three key elements:

1 **Accuracy** – whether it hits the target. A shot is accurate if it hits the target. Accuracy is only a measure of whether the arrow hits the target, so an accurate shot can come about through luck or even with low levels of skill, as even an unskilled archer will sometimes hit the target!

2 **Adroitness** – how skilfully it was shot. An adroit shot is a skilful one. It is important to note that not all adroit shots will hit the target; for example, a sudden gust of wind or

the target moving might make the shot miss. However, adroit (skilful) shots will hit the target more often than non-adroit ones.

3 **Aptness** – the shot hits the target *because* it was adroit. An apt shot is one that is accurate, and is accurate because it was adroit. Note that not every accurate, adroit shot is apt! It is possible to hit the target with a skilful shot, but for it not to be apt. A footballer may take a skilful free kick that a gust of wind pushes away from the target, only for the ball to hit a defender and deflect into the back of the net. *Goal!* The strike was skilful (adroit), the free kick was accurate but it was *not* apt. It did not go in the goal *because* it was skilful – luck was involved. So not every accurate, adroit performance is apt.

Sosa suggests this 'AAA' model for analysing skilful performance can also be applied to intellectual performance and knowledge. An *accurate* belief is one that is true. An *adroit* belief is one that is formed by an intellectual virtue, a reliable cognitive process such as seeing up close, simple mental arithmetic, deduction, and so on. An *apt* belief is one that is true *because* of the intellectual virtue!

Sosa suggests that knowledge, or what he calls 'animal knowledge', is the same thing as apt belief. Moving away from his terminology, Sosa's claim is that knowledge is a true belief that was

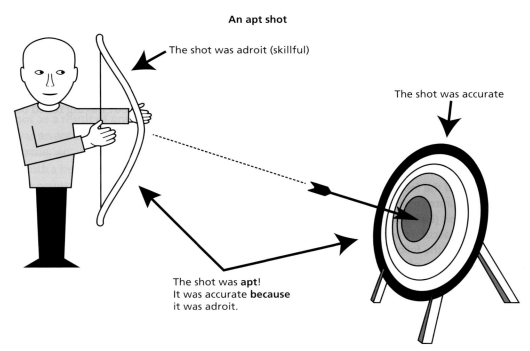

An apt shot

The shot was adroit (skillful)

The shot was accurate

The shot was **apt**!
It was accurate **because**
it was adroit.

Figure 1.21a An apt shot. This shot was apt. It was accurate and it was accurate because it was adroit (skilful).

Summary of virtue epistemology

Virtue epistemology is a new and sometimes complex area of philosophy, of which we have only explored a small part. It tries to analyse knowledge by exploring the relationship between beliefs and the intellectual virtues that bring them about. Beliefs that are true because of exercising of intellectual virtue count as knowledge. This theory can cope well with standard Gettier counter examples. However, the analysis of the fake-barn case becomes more complex and Sosa introduces the distinction between animal and reflective knowledge to account for this scenario.

Summary

In this chapter we have explored how philosophers have attempted to analyse the concept of knowledge. Focusing on propositional knowledge, we saw how the standard definition of knowledge as justified, true belief can be traced back to the writings of Plato. However, Gettier's famous paper in 1967 puts a spanner in the works. It gives two examples of justified beliefs that are true, but luckily so, and that we would not class as cases of knowledge. The standard definition needed reworking.

The rest of the chapter examined several different theories that attempted to analyse knowledge in a way that avoids the Gettier-style cases. There are a lot of other theories besides. Gettier's short paper has given birth to a mini-industry in the philosophical world, with hundreds of articles and books devoted to trying to solve the problem. At times the writing becomes very technical and detailed, with increasingly complex theories and counter examples. Gettier's name is even used as a verb sometimes! If a theory of knowledge has some counter examples that it can't explain away then it has been 'Gettiered'.

Other philosophers have stood back from all the endless debates and wondered if the whole approach might be flawed. Earlier we saw that it can be very difficult to give the necessary and sufficient conditions for a simple concept such as rain. If this is a difficult enterprise, then attempting to give some simple conditions that explain every account of knowledge might seem like a foolish enterprise. Human knowledge is a vast and complex domain covering anatomy to apple types to astrophysics. And that's just the 'A's! Maybe the use of the word 'know' is very vague, context-dependent and even subjective and there is no simple definition that will cover all cases. Perhaps the concept of knowledge is not analysable after all.

1.3 The origin of concepts and the nature of knowledge

The previous two chapters have explored different aspects of knowledge. We have examined how we account for our perception of the world and analysed the CONCEPT of knowledge itself. In this chapter we will explore the sources of knowledge.

We all claim to know various FACTS about the world – the price of tomatoes, who wrote *Hamlet*, our birth dates, that 2 + 3 = 5. But where does this knowledge ultimately come from? In other words, what are the basic sources of knowledge? Take the example of *Hamlet*. Perhaps I learned who wrote *Hamlet* from a teacher at school. But where did the teacher gain their knowledge? Perhaps they got it from a book. But this simply leads us to the further question of where the author of the book gained their knowledge. In the end it seems there has to have been an original source of this piece of knowledge. Searching for the ultimate sources of knowledge has been a central quest in philosophy.

Experimenting with ideas: Where does knowledge come from?

1 Using the word 'know' in its everyday sense, write down five things that you know.
2 For each of these things try to trace the knowledge back to its origin.
3 Have a look at the origins of knowledge you have identified. Do they have anything in common? Are there any 'ultimate' sources of knowledge?

Sources of knowledge

Traditionally philosophers have identified four ultimate sources of KNOWLEDGE: experience, REVELATION, REASON and INNATE IDEAS.

Empiricism

EMPIRICISM is the view that the ultimate source of knowledge is experience. Empiricists argue that we are born knowing nothing. Everything we know, they claim, comes to us through our five senses. All our knowledge, indeed all our thoughts, must ultimately relate to things we have seen, smelled, touched, tasted or heard. The spirit of empiricism is embodied in literature and myth in the figure of the wise traveller: someone who has set out and explored the world, has had many great and varied adventures, and finally returns with the wisdom of experience.

Gnosticism

Another view of the origins of human knowledge claims that genuine wisdom is only to be gained by means of divine revelation (page 179). This view is sometimes called gnosticism. Again, we find this idea personified in myth and literature in the figure of of colours, sounds, tastes and smells, except perhaps what it recalls of its limited experiences in the womb. It gradually learns to recognise faces, where to find milk, which foods it likes, and so on. What we as adults consider the most basic pieces of knowledge about our world, such as that objects fall downwards, or that day follows night, would at one point in our lives have been novel discoveries.

The philosophical view that all our ideas and knowledge come from the senses is known as empiricism, and so the *tabula rasa* thesis is primarily associated with empiricist philosophers. The earliest of these in the modern era is the English philosopher John Locke (1632–1704). The first book of his main work in the theory of knowledge, the *Essay Concerning Human Understanding* (1690), is devoted to refuting the view – associated with rationalist philosophers – that we are born with certain 'innate ideas': ideas that exist in the mind but which have not been derived from experience. The subsequent books try to show how the human mind is able to acquire the knowledge and ideas of which it is capable exclusively from sense experience and from the mind's ability to reflect upon itself and its own operations.

anthology
1.15

Let us then suppose the mind to have no ideas in it, to be like white paper with nothing written on it. How then does it come to be written on? From where does it get that vast store which the busy and boundless imagination of man has painted on it – all the materials of reason and knowledge? To this I answer, in one word, from experience. Our understandings derive all the materials of thinking from observations that we make of external objects that can be perceived through the senses, and of the internal operations of our minds, which we perceive by looking in at ourselves.

Locke, *An Essay Concerning Human Understanding*, II, 1, par. 2

Sense impressions and concepts

To see how this is supposed to work we need first to make clear an important distinction between sense experiences and *concepts*. At any moment, much of what we are conscious of is what we are actually sensing. So I am now aware of the tea I am drinking because I am actually seeing, tasting and smelling it. But I am also able to think about tea when I am not actually in its presence. This is an important ability since without it we would only ever be conscious of what we are sensing at the present moment. If we couldn't think about tea while we were not actually experiencing it, then we could not recognise it on the next occasion, nor could we hold any beliefs about it, such as that it is a good drink to wake up to, or that it is made by pouring boiling water onto dried leaves. So concept formation is crucial to knowing about the world. Understanding its mechanism is going to be central to any theory of knowledge.

Empiricism claims that all our concepts, like that of tea, are formed out of sense experiences. It is only because I have encountered tea that I can have the concept of tea, and so can form beliefs about it. We also have various inner impressions ranging from physical sensations of pleasure and pain to emotions such as jealousy or sadness. These are also an important source of concepts.

At first glance, this view seems inadequate to account for the complexity of the mind, since we surely possess all kinds of concepts of things we have never experienced. For example, we are able to imagine all kinds of fantasy creatures, such as unicorns and dragons, that do not exist in reality and which we have never encountered. I am able to imagine green aliens with eyes on stalks and spiky legs, which I have never actually witnessed with my senses. However, on closer inspection I have to concede that the elements out of which I have composed my imaginary alien do indeed come from my own experiences. Its colour is derived from my perception of grass and leaves; the antennae are obtained from seeing butterflies and its spiky legs are stolen from crabs. It seems that all the elements of my imaginary alien friend have, in one way or another, come from my sense experience of the world. The only novel thing is the arrangement of the elements. And this, argues the empiricist, is true of anything I can imagine or conceive. As Hume writes:

> But although our thought seems to be so free, when we look more carefully we'll find that it is really confined within very narrow limits, and that all this creative power of the mind amounts merely to the ability to combine, transpose, enlarge, or shrink the materials that the senses and experience provide us with.
>
> Hume, *Enquiry Concerning Human Understanding*, Enquiry 1, section 2

anthology 1.16

Locke and Hume both distinguish between simple and complex concepts, or what they call 'ideas'. Simple ideas consist of a single element such as the idea of red. Complex ideas involve various simple ideas merged together – for example, a gold mountain or a unicorn. All simple ideas must ultimately derive from simple impressions. For example, my idea of red must have come from my SENSE IMPRESSIONS of red.

Hume also claims that we have inward impressions (feelings) and outward impressions, such as seeing a tree. In other words, not all impressions are sense impressions; my emotions such as anger or feeling pain, for example, count as impressions too. And my idea of anger will come from my impression of anger. So not all our ideas are derived from sense experience, as some ideas, such as sadness, will be derived from our inward impressions.

One important consequence of this theory is that all of our ideas, our concepts, thoughts and imagination must have come from our impressions. This is, of course, the central claim of empiricism. But, for a moment, consider its consequence. The claim is that everything in our imagination must have come from an impression.

▶ ACTIVITY

To help you consider the theory of empiricism, try the questions below.

1 Is it possible to imagine a brand new colour you have never experienced before?
2 Do you think someone who is colour-blind from birth could ever know what red is?
3 Construct your own alien or made-up creature and then identify how your construction is derived from experience.
4 Can you think of any ideas that are not ultimately derived from experience?
5 Do your answers to these questions tend to support empiricism? Or do they raise difficulties with it?

We have seen that the traditional empiricism of Locke and Hume claims that our imaginations can rearrange the basic elements we acquire from experience but that we cannot invent these elements for ourselves. We can now flesh out the details of this picture of how our minds work. We have, on the one hand, simple impressions: that is, the information gained through experience, typically via the senses (sometimes called SENSE DATA). These are the basic elements that come into the mind, which cannot be broken down further into smaller elements. Examples of simple impressions might be the sight of red, the smell of tea or the sound of a trumpet.

Figure 1.23 Where our ideas come from. Following the arrows backwards we can see that all ideas, both complex and simple, derive from impressions.

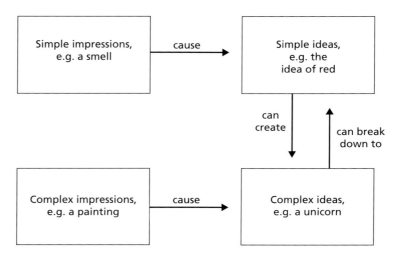

108

On the other hand, we can also think about the things we experience when we are not actually perceiving them. I can think of the colour red or a nice cup of tea even when I am not presently experiencing them: in other words, I can form concepts. To do this, according to the empiricist, the mind retains the basic sense experience as a kind of copy or image. This copy is stored in the mind so that we can think about things we are not experiencing and recognise them when we encounter them. For example, I acquire the concept of red from first observing it and my mind stores the concept as a kind of image of the original sensation. Armed with this concept, I am able to recognise some new experience as being an experience of red.

In the same way, my concept of tea is formed from the various sense experiences I have had of tea from seeing, smelling and tasting it. My concept of tea, therefore, unlike that of red, is complex, since it is formed out of the various simple elements of its smell, colour, taste, and so forth. Once I possess the tea concept, the next time I encounter some tea I can recognise it. Having the concept of tea also enables me to distinguish it from coffee, biscuits and everything else. Simple concepts, like red, can be acquired only if one has experienced the relevant impression and so for every simple concept there must correspond a simple sense experience. This means a person born blind cannot have the concept of red, or any other colour because they have not had the simple impression of red. But, as we have seen, I can concoct new, complex concepts of things I have never experienced by rearranging simple elements.

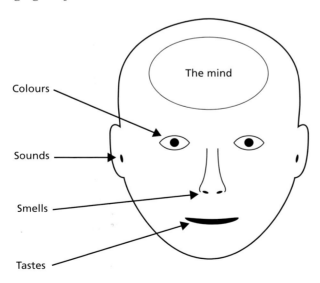

Figure 1.24 No concepts without impressions. The *tabula rasa* thesis is saying that all our ideas or concepts are derived from impressions, so that there can be nothing in the mind that does not originate with impressions.

Experimenting with ideas

To see if this theory of no concepts without impressions works, try to trace the following complex ideas back to the impressions from which they derive:

1 Sherlock Holmes
2 dragons
3 chocolate pizza
4 friendship
5 God
6 beauty
7 the number 3

Are some of the ideas harder than others? Later we will discuss some of the difficulties with the empiricist account of concept formation that this activity raises.

Hume's empiricism

So empiricism claims that all of our concepts, ideas and imaginings must ultimately be derived from our impressions. Hume believed that this picture of the mind gives us a means to clarify our thinking on a range of philosophical issues by allowing us to make our concepts more precise. The process of tracing concepts back to experience, Hume believed, could be used to reveal their true nature, often demonstrating that they are rather different from what we had supposed. Since philosophical progress can only be made once we are clear about the concepts we are using, the investigation of the origins of our concepts became in Hume's hands a starting point for his investigations into several important philosophical issues.

These investigations, however, sometimes seemed to show that a concept cannot be traced back to experience, suggesting that it cannot be a genuine concept at all. So what is it then? Hume's answer is that it is a kind of error. We may think we have a concept because we have a word, and the word seems to be the sign for a concept. But when we look closely we may discover that it is not a concept at all. Such apparent concepts are to be treated with suspicion and rejected as confusions.

This point is most obvious if we consider a made-up word like 'wagglytoth'. We have no idea of what a wagglytoth is because we cannot trace any such concept back to sensations or emotions. We have nothing to 'picture', as it were, when we use the word, and so the word is meaningless. On other occasions, however, we may use words that seem to have concepts attached to them. In such cases, Hume argues, we should ensure that there is indeed a lineage we can trace back to experience and so establish that there really is a concept there. If we fail, we must reject the concept as empty or non-existent. In this way the empiricists' idea that all knowledge comes from experience becomes a critical tool by which to reject certain sorts of concept as unthinkable, and hence reject certain areas of enquiry as unknowable. To see how this critical tool works in practice, let us consider some of the philosophical problems Hume hopes to solve with it.

What is God?

Many philosophers claim that we are born with the idea of God – it is innate. Hume disagrees and offers a different account of where the concept of God, as a supremely powerful, infinitely wise, all-loving being, comes from. Clearly we haven't encountered God, and so it cannot come directly from him. So the concept must have come from our experiences of powerful, wise and loving people that we have encountered. Having encountered such qualities in people, we then imagine their being extended without limit.

The idea of God – meaning an infinitely intelligent, wise, and good Being – comes from extending beyond all limits the qualities of goodness and wisdom that we find in our own minds.[2]

Hume, *Enquiry Concerning Human Understanding*, Enquiry 2, page 8

Thus, although God may have made man in his own image, the concept of God is made in man's own image according to Hume. This invites the conclusion, radical in Hume's day, that God doesn't exist.

Who am I?

What does the word 'I' refer to? The idea of my self, Hume claims, cannot be based on any one sensation – the smell of tea, the memory of falling off a bike, the feeling of anger – as these feelings and emotions change constantly. If you look into yourself you never find any impression of something that corresponds to your idea of your self. But if the idea has no source in sensation, then it cannot be a proper concept. Hume concludes that the idea that I have a self is a kind of illusion. The words 'I' or 'self' are really just the name for the entire series of sensations and thoughts that make up your life. There is no thing, no essential me, that we are aware of, existing independently of the sum of conscious experiences which constitute my mind.

What is morality?

Hume points out that our concepts of good and bad cannot be traced back to any particular sensations. After all, you can't see the EVIL of an action, or smell the goodness of someone's character. So where do we get such concepts from? According to Hume, they come from the 'inner' sensations that are our own emotions. We condemn and praise different actions ultimately because of the way they make us feel. This insight is the basis for Hume's moral theory, which shows how our concepts of good and bad stem from our emotions.

Thus Hume engages with many of the big debates in philosophy, using the simple principle of empiricism. How successful he is in each of these areas is debatable, but in the philosophical discussions of religion, the self and morality Hume remains a very important figure. However, it is his treatment of the concept of causation that has led to the most discussion.

Learn More

Hume on causation

We are all aware of causes and effects. A dog's tails knocks a glass, the glass falls over. The dog has caused the water to spill. The water in turn causes the ink on the essay to run, and so on. Every minute we can witness multiple examples of causation all around us, but where does the concept come from? What would an empiricist say? At first sight it seems obvious. We can see that the dog has caused the water to spill. We can see the effect of the water on the ink. We observe the one thing causing the other and, like anything else, the concept of causation derives from sensation.

However, Hume points out that things are not as simple as we might suppose. Using his example, consider observing one billiard ball approaching another, striking the second and the second moving off. Here it seems we have a clear case of observing one ball causing the other to move. So surely this must be the origin of our concept of causation? However, when we look more closely at this experience, it becomes clear that all we ever saw was one ball approach and come into contact with another; we heard a sound and saw the second move off; we never actually witnessed any sense datum corresponding to the cause. Imagine that all the time there were elaborate magnets under the table and that these moved the first ball up to the second, and then a separate magnet moved the second ball away, such that the first ball did not cause the second to move at all. Would this look any different? The answer must be no; but if there is no difference between the first and the second case, then we must conclude that indeed a cause is not something we actually experience in the sense impressions themselves, as the sense impressions are the same whether or not there was a cause.

So it seems that the concept of cause is not drawn from the senses. So where does it come from? Some would suggest that we are born with the idea. It is somehow 'in' us all along. This would be to claim that the concept is 'innate' and such an approach is usually associated with rationalism, which asserts that reason, not experience, is the ultimate source of knowledge. Obviously, as a good empiricist, this is not Hume's solution. An empiricist must either deny that we really have such a concept, or attempt to redefine it. Hume actually elects to do both. He claims that we tend to use the word 'cause' to link together experiences that frequently occur together. In other words, we notice patterns that repeat themselves and come to regard them as governed by causal laws. This is something that our minds do automatically for us. Imagine you clap your hands and a split second later you hear thunder in the distance. You would probably think nothing of it. Imagine the same thing happens again a minute later. Again, you would put it down to coincidence. But imagine the same thing happens a third, fourth, fifth and sixth time. Eventually you would begin to suppose that your clapping was causing the thunder. But this supposition cannot be based simply on the sense impressions involved for there is nothing different about the first clap than about the sixth. The only difference is in the repetition, the constant occurrence, of the two events. By the sixth clap your experience of the event feels very different; it now starts to feel like a causal event.

Thus Hume suggests that what we mean and experience as cause and effect is really just the constant conjunction of events. The feeling of one event inevitably following the other is the result of repetition, and is little more than custom or habit. Instead of claiming that the concept of causation is meaningless, Hume suggests that it refers to the feeling of anticipation that arises in our minds when we come to expect one event to follow another, because it has done in the past. In this way he is able, true to his empiricist convictions, to trace the source of our concept of cause back to experience: in this case, not an experience of something external to us, but the internal feeling of expectation we develop that one event will follow another.

Figure 1.25 If every time you clapped your hands you heard a thunder clap, it wouldn't be long before you developed the conviction that the one was the cause of the other. According to Hume, the feeling of anticipation you would have of an imminent thunder clap whenever you clapped your hands is the source of our ordinary idea of causation.

Learn More

Logical positivism

Some philosophers have taken Hume's approach further and turned it into a theory about meaning. They have argued that sentences are only meaningful if they are connected in some way to the world and our impressions. Such sentences describe the world either truly or falsely. For example, 'The teacher of the class is a tall man with a beard' is meaningful because it tries to tell us something about the world. It is irrelevant for this theory of meaning whether a sentence is actually true; false sentences are still meaningful because they still 'paint a picture' of the world that we can understand. For each meaningful sentence, because it 'paints a picture of the world', we would know how to go about checking whether it was true or not. We would know how to verify it. However, for other sentences it is hard to see how we might go about verifying whether is true or not. Consider these two:

1 'Twas brillig and slithy toves did gire and gimble in the wabe.[3]
2 Jesus is the Way, the Truth and the Light.

The first sentence is clearly nonsense. We would not know how to go about verifying its truth, so, according to logical positivism, this shows that it is meaningless. Many logical positivists would argue that the second sentence is meaningless too, as it is not very clear what would count as a verification of the claim. As you can imagine, this theory caused a lot of controversy (see page 319 for a more detailed account) but at its heart is the idea that our thoughts and concepts somehow must relate to our experience of the world.

Summary of concept empiricism

Concept empiricism is the simple idea that all ideas must derive from impressions. This simple idea, empiricists claim, has the power to explain how all of our ideas are created, including those from the imagination. Hume used this simple idea to examine some of the central questions in philosophy. In each case he took a difficult concept and looked to find out from which impressions it was derived. If he could not find such impressions then he suggests we should treat the concept with suspicion. By exploring how our concepts link to impressions (or fail to link easily) Hume was challenging traditional thinking, which often assumed that we are born with such ideas.

However, to be convincing, concept empiricism relies on the *truth* of the claim that all of our ideas can be derived from our experiences, in other words of the idea of the *tabula rasa*. And we will now turn our attention to some issues that might make us doubt the truth of this central claim.

Issues with concept empiricism

Here we will explore some criticisms of the claim that our concepts must come from our impressions. One of the chief criticisms is that some of our ideas may be innate and so not derived from experience; however, as the theory of innate ideas forms its own section in this chapter (page 124), the text below focuses on other potential issues with concept empiricism.

Criticism 1: Does the concept of 'simple ideas' make sense?

Locke and Hume give examples such as red, cold and sadness as examples of simple impressions and define them as concepts that can not be broken down or analysed into anything simpler. But how precisely are complex concepts like that of a unicorn to be analysed into these simple ones? In the case of a unicorn the initial answer must be a horn and a horse, but it appears that these can be further analysed. The concept of a horn might be composed of simpler concepts, perhaps including hard and pointy; the concept of a horse would be composed of a kind of bundle of innumerable simple concepts derived from various impressions one can have of horses, including those of neighing and snorting, galloping and trotting, of hooves, nostrils, shanks, manes, and so on. Are the parts of which the horse is composed – the hooves, the mane – simple? Or must we analyse these into elements? Perhaps a mane is a complex concept, somehow composed of a bunch of the hair concept. The trouble with this suggestion, however, is that a mane doesn't necessarily appear to the senses as a collection of hairs; not unless we examine it closely.

So how closely do we need to examine such things to determine the point where analysis stops and we have found simple impressions? And even a horse hair appears not to be a simple concept, since it is in turn analysable into the concepts of its colour, texture, length, and so on. The qualities of the hair – say, dark, coarse, thin – may be very different from those of the mane – shiny, wavy, thick. So it does not seem that we can straightforwardly move from the hair concept to the mane concept. What of neighing? Is it a simple concept? Presumably it needs to be analysed into its constituent sounds and it is certainly true that I can hear different tones in the neigh of a horse. And yet the sense impression which gives us the concept of a horse neighing seems complete in itself and if we were to break it down into moments of sound we would appear to lose the essence of the concept. What of galloping? Is this is a complex concept? What are the simple ones of which it is composed?

Such questions begin to show some of the difficulties empiricists are going to have to address when working out the details of their theory that concepts derive from impressions and which impressions are to count as simple.

▶ **ACTIVITY**

Consider the following concepts. Which do you think are simple? That is, which do you think cannot be analysed into any simpler concepts? What do your reflections suggest about the feasibility of discovering absolutely simple ideas?

1	Moon	6	Poetry
2	Triangle	7	The number two
3	Beauty	8	The taste of an apple
4	The sound of a G chord on a guitar	9	Mother
5	Fairness	10	The colour orange

On a related point, you may think that that the empiricists' claim that we cannot imagine a colour we have never seen is fairly plausible. However, this is not the same as to say that we cannot form the *concept* of this colour. To see the point, take the example of ultra-violet, a colour in a wavelength too short for the human eye to detect. Now, we are able to form the concept of such a wavelength of light even though we can't see it, suggesting that the concept here is not to be identified with a copy of any sense experience. In a similar way a blind person could form the concept of red as being that colour which occurs in a particular part of the light spectrum, without ever being able to imagine what it is like to see this colour. So, again, the concept need not be identified with a copy of any impression.

Criticism 3: Do all complex ideas/concepts relate to sense experience?

We explore this criticism of concept empiricism further when examining the possibility of innate ideas (page 124 below). However, without needing to claim innateness, there are other concepts that it is hard to see as straightforwardly deriving from sense experience. These also pose a problem for concept empiricism.

Concepts don't have to relate to experience

Difficulties arise when we consider that we seem able to have a concept of something without ever having experienced it. I can have the concept of tea even if I have not tasted it, and, similarly, I can form the concept of Spain even though I have never been there. Consider also the concept I have of an atom, something that is too small for us ever to have any sense experience of. How is this concept formed? Certainly, while such concepts might have their source in experience, the way in which they are derived from experience seems to be more complex than a simple matter of copying sense impressions, whether they be inner or outer. With the concept of Spain, it seems implausible to say that my concept is a series of images of Spain gleaned from travel brochures and trips there, and when it comes to abstract concepts the difficulties get worse. How do I acquire the concept of justice or freedom? It seems very difficult to relate such concepts merely to patterns within experience and ultimately to patterns of sense impressions. After all, neither justice nor freedom looks or smells like anything; nor can they be equated with inner emotions or feelings. In fact, they don't seem to be things that we have sense experience of at all.

Note here that it is possible that you have some sort of image in your mind when you think of justice – the scales of justice perhaps, or a wise-looking judge in a wig. Similarly, the thought of justice might produce a certain feeling within you – a warm righteous glow in the chest perhaps. But even if you do enjoy such images and feelings when contemplating the concept of justice, they cannot be identified with it, since the concept involves all kinds of connections with other concepts that cannot be explained in terms of such impressions. Indeed, it is quite likely that other people will have very different images and feelings in mind when they think of justice, and yet they still have the same *concept* as you. So it seems that what we *imagine/picture* when thinking of justice is not the same as what we *think of* and therefore that the concept is not reducible to a copy of any impression of inner or outer sense. Again this brings us up against the obscurity of the relationship between the concept and experience.

An empiricist could argue that the fact that it is very difficult to explain abstract concepts in terms of sense experience is why such terms are notoriously vague. They could claim that if we could pin them more closely to experience then we would have greater clarity, and this is what Hume argues when conducting his examinations of concepts such as *God*, *self* and *cause*. With a concept like justice there might be a complex route back to experience; one terribly hard to trace, but nonetheless somehow it would find its origins in observation of just acts, and hearing about just judgements in law courts, and the associated inner feelings produced. The empiricist might also argue that if we lived in a world without fair/just behaviour of any kind, in some kind of anarchic dystopia, we would be unable to form the concept precisely because we would have no experience of it.

Do relational concepts derive from impressions?

Further difficulties arise with relational concepts such as 'being near' or 'far', 'next to' or 'on top of'. If I form the concept of a cat from seeing a cat, then how do I form the concept of the cat being *on* the mat? I can't actually see the 'on-ness': all that appears in sensation is the cat and the mat. Obviously it is on the mat, but the recognition of this fact and the understanding of the relationship involved is not something we acquire by copying any sense impression.

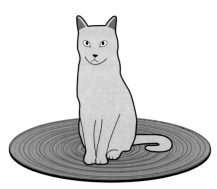

Figure 1.27 I have sense impressions of a cat and sense impressions of a mat, but what impression relates to the on-ness?

Summary of Descartes' trademark argument

Descartes attempted to show that our idea of God can only be caused by God and is innate, but there are many powerful criticisms of his approach.

However, 'God' is not the only concept/idea that philosophers have claimed is innate and below we look at other candidates.

Some instincts are innate

A baby knows how to suckle from its mother, it knows to cry when hurt. It seems that there are many things that a baby knows how to do that cannot be derived from experience. Do these count as innate ideas or as types of genuine knowledge? Hume claims that if we are to regard such things as ideas then we are using the term 'ideas' very loosely indeed, and suggests that we should leave it to refer to thoughts rather than instincts. The question of knowledge is harder to dismiss. Claiming that a baby knows how to suckle doesn't seem, at least on the face of it, to be an unreasonable use of the verb 'to know'. There are, of course, limits to how the word can be meaningfully pushed. Do birds know when to migrate? Does a heart know how to beat? Do raindrops know how to make the pavement wet? We need to have some sort of criteria for what we are to count as knowledge and what is simply an ability or function. Part of the problem might be that there are at least three distinct senses of the verb 'to know' in use in the English language: know how; know by acquaintance; and know that (see pages 49–50).

Most people, however, would classify the baby's suckling as a clear-cut example of practical knowledge – of *know-how*. This may give empiricists a way of salvaging their theory from the claims of innate knowledge. They can acknowledge that the baby knows how to suckle, but deny that this counts as knowledge of the world. It is simply an instinct to behave. There is no factual knowledge accompanying the suckling, such as that a woman has breasts or that breasts contain milk. The empiricist can still maintain that all of our knowledge of the world must be derived from experience and at the same time allow that humans are born with certain instincts to behave in certain ways.

However, this empiricist defence might not satisfy all. Some behaviourist philosophers have claimed that all forms of knowledge really amount to practical knowledge. After all, it is the ability to behave in a certain way that makes us inclined to attribute knowledge to anyone in the first place. For example, factual knowledge can be seen as the ability to answer certain questions or to do well in exams. Scientific knowledge is the ability to make accurate predictions about the world. The claim is that all knowledge is the knowledge of *how* to behave in a certain way. Now the empiricist wants to dismiss 'instincts', claiming they represent *know-how* and don't provide factual knowledge about the world. However, if all our knowledge boils down to knowing *how* to behave, then the distinction between the knowledge of the baby and the scientist is less clear. It should be noted, though, that the behaviourist's account of knowledge is not widely accepted.

Morality

Another area in which philosophers have thought we may have innate concepts is morality. It may be that we have an innate sense of what is right and wrong so that we can all recognise when something is fair or unfair, for example, without the need for it being taught. Is a moral conscience the voice of God within us? Does a child have an innate recognition of the correct way to divide a cake between four equally greedy mouths? A glance at playground disputes might make us sceptical of this view. On the other hand, do we then acquire our moral sense from socialisation, from our parents and schooling? Is it based on our inner impressions, our feelings of sympathy as Hume argued? Several moral theories claim that our moral concepts cannot be derived from our sense experience. In this regard they must be considered innate. One of the most important of these theories is intuitionism.

Moral ideas are known intuitively

Moral 'intuitionism' has had a long history, and the great debate among these moral philosophers was over where our intuitions come from. Some philosophers, such as Francis Hutcheson (1694–1746), said our moral intuitions stemmed from an internal, God-given, moral sense (analogous to our other five senses) through which we could intuit what was right and wrong. Others said our intuitions stemmed from a rational faculty in our mind that had the power to grasp moral truths (analogous to our capacity to grasp mathematical truths).

The British philosopher G.E. Moore (1873–1958) provided some powerful arguments to suggest that our moral concepts cannot be based on things that we see in the world. Morality cannot be equated with anything from our sense experience. So what do we mean by 'good'? The answer that Moore reached by the end of his seminal work *Principia Ethica* is that 'good' cannot be defined, but is known intuitively. This is why his approach is known as intuitionism. Because 'good' is indefinable, it cannot be reduced to elements that we can observe in the world, such as 'the greatest happiness', or to 'what people desire', or any other such non-moral good. In order to clarify what he means by indefinable, Moore likens the word 'good' to 'yellow'. If we try to say that 'yellow' means 'light travelling at a particular frequency' then we are simply wrong – yellow refers to what we see when we see yellow objects, not to 'light-vibrations'. So for Moore 'yellow' is clearly comprehensible to us, yet we are not able to define it in terms of anything else. The same goes for 'good': we know what it is when we see it, but we cannot define it in any other terms.

But for Moore it is important to note that moral properties are unlike natural properties such as 'being yellow', as we do not observe them through our ordinary senses. Moral judgements are evaluative rather than factual and so cannot be justified by purely empirical observation. Moral terms are *self-evident* and can only be known by what Moore calls INTUITION.

Criticism

Moore and others suggest that our moral concepts cannot be derived from our impressions and must be innate. Hume agrees that our moral ideas are not derived from sense impressions; instead he claims they are derived from our sentiments, in particular from our emotion of sympathy. It is our feelings of sympathy that give rise to our moral ideas and intuitions. For Hume, however, our emotions are still impressions – inner impressions. It may be true that our emotional responses to the world are to some degree innate, in the same way that the baby's suckling response is innate; but our responses are not the same thing as having moral ideas. We are not born with moral ideas. We are born with emotional faculties and, upon having certain sense impressions, these may generate emotions and it is from these that we later derive our moral ideas. So our moral ideas are not born in us; they develop over time as our sense impressions trigger various inner impressions.

Numbers

Plato argues that our concepts of numbers are innate on the grounds that we never have any sense experience of them. The number two is not a thing you can encounter with your five senses. We encounter couples, pairs of gloves, braces of pheasants, and so forth, in the world, but never the number two itself. It is as though what we experience is always an *example* of 'two-ness', but never the real thing. If the number is not something encountered in the physical world, Plato concludes, it must be something we encounter in some other realm, a realm of pure thought, which is independent of the senses.

The empiricist's response to this is to say that we can acquire the concepts of different numbers by abstracting from the experiences of collections of objects in the world. After several encounters with objects in threes I can work out what they have in common. The concept of three is some kind of copy of this common denominator. However, this still leaves us with the problem of how we acquire the concepts of numbers which we haven't yet encountered. I have the concept of 5381 and yet I may well never have encountered a group with this many members. Descartes makes a powerful argument against the empiricists along similar lines in his *Meditations on First Philosophy* where he points out that we can form the image of geometric shapes such as triangles and pentagons in our mind's eye, suggesting the possibility that our concept of these shapes derives from a sense experience of them copied into an image retained in the mind. But, he points out, I am equally capable of understanding the concept of a figure with a thousand sides, and yet I can form no clear image of this shape in my mind. He concludes that geometric shapes are conceived not in the imagination as kinds of copies of sensations, but rather by the intellect. Like Plato, he argues that our grasp of numbers and geometric shapes is not grounded in the senses.

Beauty, justice and universal concepts

Plato goes further, arguing that concepts like 'beauty', 'justice' and other universal concepts are not things we ever perceive in the world. We encounter beautiful things or just acts, but never *beauty* or *justice* as such. He concludes that we must acquire these concepts from somehow observing the essential nature of beauty or justice with our minds and not with our senses. Plato also points out that our ability to recognise an action as just or a person's face as beautiful appears to require that we understand what beauty and justice are. However, if the *tabula rasa* thesis is true, at birth we can have no such understanding. But this means that we would be unable to recognise a beautiful face the first time we saw one. Not yet having acquired the concept of beauty seems to imply that we could never recognise beautiful things. How then could we ever hope to learn what beauty was from experience?

Conceptual schemes

Causation

We looked earlier at the claim that there must be conceptual schemes in place prior to anything counting as an experience (page 120). Immanuel Kant claimed our knowledge of certain concepts such as causation are not directly derived from the world, but rather form part of the conceptual scheme through which we experience the world. In this way Kant might be said to claim that we have innate knowledge of, for example, causation. Other concepts that Kant claims must pre-exist experience include unity, necessity, substance, space and time.

Deep grammar

As previously mentioned, Noam Chomsky has argued that our ability to learn language is not simply derived from our experiences. Our exposure to language is not sufficient to account for how quickly we learn it. He argues that we have an innate capacity to learn language, which enables us to pick up the structure and grammar of language on the basis of rather limited evidence. He also claims that all languages share the same deep grammatical structure and uses this to support the thesis that a language-learning faculty is a universal aspect of our biological make-up. In other words, he makes use of a universality argument to support his claim (we explore this argument below page 138). Although Chomsky would not claim that we are born with specific innate ideas, he does claim that our brain/minds are hardwired with structures that we do not derive from experience. This claim that our minds have existing structures in place prior to birth is known as nativism. Like innatism, it is a challenge to the idea of the *tabula rasa*, which claims our minds are like a blank slate.

Criticism of innate ideas

Although there are many potential candidates for innate ideas, the whole concept of innatism has drawn criticism, which we explore below. Specifically included are several of the criticisms presented by John Locke alongside the defence of innate ideas provided by Leibniz and so we start with some brief contextual background on these two philosophers.

Locke and Leibniz on innate ideas

John Locke (1632–1704) was one of the first philosophers to put forward a detailed account of empiricism. The first section of his *Essay Concerning Human Understanding* (1690) is devoted to refuting the view – associated with rationalist philosophers – that we are born with certain 'innate ideas'. The rest of the *Essay* attempts to show how the human mind is able to acquire all of its knowledge and ideas exclusively from sense experience and from the mind's ability to reflect upon itself and its own operations.

At the time of writing innatism was a commonly held belief among both philosophers and the general population.

Nothing is more commonly taken for granted than that certain principles ... are accepted by all mankind. Some people have argued that because these principles are (they think) universally accepted, they must have been stamped onto the souls of men from the outset.[5]

Locke, *An Essay Concerning Human Understanding*, I, 2, par. 2

Locke's arguments against innate ideas may not convince all, but they are of historical significance. Locke was challenging the orthodox thinking of the day, which is never easy to do, and his arguments form part of a wider 'modern' movement of basing our thoughts and beliefs on evidence and reason rather than tradition and dogma. In this way Locke was championing the cause of scientific method as it attempted to free itself from religious doctrine. In his *Essays,* Locke modestly portrayed his role as an 'under-labourer' clearing the way for others, such as his good friend Isaac Newton.

> *The commonwealth of learning is not at this time without master-builders, whose mighty designs, in advancing the sciences, will leave lasting monuments to the admiration of posterity: but every one must not hope to be a Boyle or a Sydenham; and in an age that produces such masters as the great Huygenius and the incomparable Mr. Newton ... it is ambition enough to be employed as an under-labourer in clearing the ground a little, and removing some of the rubbish that lies in the way to knowledge.*
>
> **Locke, *An Essay Concerning Human Understanding,* Epistle to the Reader**

Gottfried Wilhelm von Leibniz (1646–1716), like Descartes, was another great polymath. Most of his life was spent working in the courts of various European royalty and consequently his studies in philosophy, maths and science were all conducted in his spare time. Much of his philosophy was carried out with correspondents through the exchange of letters – he wrote over 16,000 in his lifetime. He was also a great mathematician and discovered calculus at the same time as Isaac Newton.

Leibniz was also a contemporary of Locke. As a rationalist, he found some of the empiricist ideas of Locke very challenging, so he published a defence of his own philosophy entitled *New Essays on Human Understanding.* As Leibniz was responding directly to Locke, below we outline some of Locke's main criticisms of innate ideas and set out Leibniz counter criticisms of these at the same time.

Criticism 1: The theory of innate ideas is unnecessary

anthology
1.19

> *Some people regard it as settled that there are in the understanding certain innate principles ... I could show any fair-minded reader that this is wrong if I could show (as I hope to do in the present work) how men can get all the knowledge they have, and can arrive at certainty about some things, purely by using their natural faculties, without help from any innate notions or principles.*[6]
>
> **Locke, *An Essay Concerning Human Understanding,* I, 2, par. 1**

Locke claims he will be able to persuade you of the truth of empiricism, which is the theory that *all* ideas come from the senses, and so the theory of innate ideas would, by implication, be seen as false. The key issue at stake though is whether experience alone *is* enough to explain all of our knowledge and ideas, which has been discussed in detail previously.

Locke develops this line of reasoning further:

> *Everyone will agree, presumably, that it would be absurd to suppose that the ideas of colours are innate in a creature to whom God has given eyesight, which is a power to get those ideas through the eyes from external objects. It would be equally unreasonable to explain our knowledge of various truths in terms of innate 'imprinting' if it could just as easily be explained through our ordinary abilities to come to know things.[7]*

Locke, *An Essay Concerning Human Understanding*, I, 2, par. 1

Here Locke is claiming that innatism is an unnecessary theory and so it would be unreasonable to hold it. This argument implicitly relies on a principle known as 'Occam's razor' which is the idea that, wherever possible, we should always go for the simplest explanation. (The idea of the 'razor' is that we should shave off any unnecessary elements to an explanation.) Locke uses the example of our idea of colours to make the case, but suggests that it will apply to any supposedly innate idea. He argues that it *could* be the case that:

a) we are born with an innate idea of each colour.

And it certainly *is* the case that:

b) we see colours with our eyes.

The question is, why would God, or even nature, bother with a), given that b)? It is a simpler explanation to say that our idea of colour is derived from b). Claiming a) seems to add no extra explanatory value and so, according to Locke, is an 'absurd' additional claim. As outlined above, the general principal in play here is that that we should go for the simplest explanation, in other words, Occam's razor.

Criticism 2: No ideas are universally held, so none is innate

Many people in the past (and even today) have used the idea of universal consent as a justification for believing that certain ideas are innate.

> *Nothing is more commonly taken for granted than that certain principles … are accepted by all mankind. Some people have argued that because these principles are (they think) universally accepted, they must have been stamped onto the souls of men from the outset.[8]*

Locke, *An Essay Concerning Human Understanding*, I, 2, par. 2

The idea behind this argument is that all humans have different upbringings and experiences and so have different ideas. Some people like music, some do not; some are optimists, some pessimists; and each person has a unique set of tastes and preferences. Given this diversity of thought, if some ideas are held by *all* of humanity then these ideas cannot be derived from our different experiences. Instead, they must have been 'stamped on our souls from the outset'; in other words, they must be innate.

▶ **ACTIVITY**

Can you think of any ideas or beliefs that are held by everyone in the world?

Perhaps basic mathematical beliefs?

Moral beliefs?

If such universal ideas do exist, do you think they would have to exist in all minds innately or could they be drawn from experience?

One of Locke's key arguments is to attack this idea of universal consent. He wants to show that in reality, there are no universally held ideas and so there are no innate ideas. To do this he selects two commonly held candidates for innateness.

> *I shall begin with speculative principles, taking as my example those much vaunted logical principles 'Whatever is, is' [and] 'It is impossible for the same thing to be and not to be', which are the most widely thought to be innate. They are so firmly and generally believed to be accepted by everyone in the world that it may be thought strange that anyone should question this.[9]*
>
> Locke, An Essay Concerning Human Understanding, I, 2, par. 4

The two ideas Locke selects are 'Whatever is, is', which is known in the logic as the law of identity and 'It is impossible for the same thing to be and not to be', which is known as the law of non-contradiction. The particular detail of these claims is not really important. Locke wants to use what he thinks are the most likely candidates for innateness, as if he can show that *these* are not universally held, then the claim that *any* idea is universally held will be severely weakened. Locke later argues that other key candidates for innate ideas such as the idea of God, or of key moral principles, such as 'do not steal', are also not universally held.

Locke then proceeds to assert that universal consent does not exist, even for these principles:

> *Children and idiots have no thought – not an inkling – of these principles, and that fact alone is enough to destroy the universal assent that any truth that was genuinely innate would have to have.[10]*
>
> Locke, An Essay Concerning Human Understanding, I, 2, par. 5

Certainly if you asked a young child whether they believe that something can both be and not be, they are likely to stare at you in a confused manner and be lost for an answer. Similarly for knowledge of geometry or the idea of God: a child who has not been taught geometry may not be able to answer questions on it, and one who has not learned about God would have no idea of him. Because children and idiots seem to lack these ideas, Locke claims they are not universally held, and so not innate.

However, there are several potential weaknesses in Locke's argument. First, it could be the case that children and idiots do possess these innate ideas, but they are not aware that they possess them. We explore this issue in Criticism 3 below. Second, Leibniz claims that children and idiots *do* actually employ the law of identity and the principle of non-contradiction in their everyday actions, even though they would not be able to articulate these ideas in words. So, contrary to Locke, these ideas may still be held universally. Lastly, it is not clear that innate ideas need to be universally held in the first place. Certainly, not all universally held ideas are innate. Leibniz makes this point humorously by claiming that:

the practice of smoking tobacco has been adopted by nearly all nations in less than a century.[11]

Leibniz, *New Essays on Human Understanding*, Book 1, Chapter 1, page 18

Presumably even if everyone in the world smoked then it would not make smoking an innate desire! In other words, universality is not a sufficient condition for innateness.

It is not even clear that universality is a necessary condition of innate ideas either. It could be the case that God has given innate ideas to specific people only. Maybe we are born with memories and ideas from a previous life; these ideas would be innate to this life and there is no reason why they would be universally held.

To come to Locke's defence, part of his motive was to undermine the reason people gave for believing in innate ideas, and at the time of writing many thinkers *did* in fact argue for the existence of innate ideas on the grounds of universal consent (as some do today). However, undermining the idea of universal consent does not necessarily undermine the theory of innatism.

Criticism 3: Transparency of ideas

We saw earlier that Descartes claimed the idea of God must be innate within him, as only God could cause his idea of God. This may work for Descartes, but maybe not everyone has the idea of God. Even though innate ideas don't have to be universal, it does seem odd that some people are born with an innate idea and others don't seem to be. A classic defence of the innatist is to claim that we do all have the idea of God (and other innate ideas) within us, but some of us (children and 'idiots' included) may not be aware of this yet.

Locke takes issues with this defence and argues that the possibility of possessing an innate idea but not being aware of it, makes no sense.

> To imprint anything on the mind without the mind's perceiving it seems to me hardly intelligible. So if children and idiots have souls, minds, with those principles imprinted on them, they can't help perceiving them and assenting to them.[12]
>
> **Locke, An Essay Concerning Human Understanding, I, 2, par. 5**

Locke is saying that any innate ideas, if held, would be 'perceived' by the mind. In other words that our minds are transparent and we are able to perceive all of the ideas they contain. For Locke this does not mean that you are constantly aware of all your ideas at once, but that for any idea to be 'in' your mind, you must at least have thought of it, or been conscious of it at some point in the past. After all, if you have never had an idea/thought then in what sense could it be 'in' your mind?

This argument has some appeal. In what sense can I have an idea (innate or otherwise) but never be aware of it? However, maybe there are ideas/concepts/memories 'in' your mind that you have never been conscious of, or experienced at any point? Perhaps you have observed events without realising them (subconsciously), and can recall these at a later stage. Maybe you 'absorbed' a song that was playing in the background, without being consciously aware of it. That song is not immediately accessible and transparent in your mind, in that you cannot recall it, but it may be recognisable if you heard it again. So presumably it must have been 'in' you somewhere. If these examples are possible, then surely an innate idea too could be 'in' your mind, without you being aware of it yet.

Leibniz puts forward this very idea in his *New Essays*. In articulating this view – the idea of taking in information subconsciously – Leibniz was substantially ahead of his time (although he doesn't actually use the term *subconscious*). If this idea is plausible then it would seem to undermine one of Locke's key arguments, as it may be possible to have innate ideas of beauty, or of mathematics, that are only awoken by the appropriate stimulus later in life. Indeed, on the basis of good evidence Chomsky suggests that we do have an innate ability to learn language, but this only comes into play if we are exposed to other language speakers.

anthology
1.20

Criticism 4: How can we distinguish innate ideas from other ideas?

As we have seen, some innatists suggest that children do possess innate ideas, but may only become aware of these later in life. In this way an innatist might claim that having an innate idea, for a child, means having the ability to have that idea. So the ideas of geometry may not enter your mind until later in life, but the capacity to have these ideas was innately in you all along.

Locke rejects this by saying that this 'ability' approach could be true of all ideas, so how can we distinguish the innate ones from the non-innate ones? In other words he is suggesting that the capacity to see colours and taste chocolate, and so on, must also be in you from birth, which would mean that everything the mind could ever know would be 'innate' in this sense. Even innatists don't hold this. So the problem for the innatist is that if it is possible that we have innate ideas, but that they only come into our minds in later life, then how can we tell which ideas are the innate ones and which are the ones derived from experience?

Once again Leibniz takes issue with this criticism of Locke's. Leibniz suggests that we *can* distinguish innate ideas from the non-innate ones, even if they emerge later in life, because innate ideas are true in a different way – they are *necessarily* true.

Leibniz makes a distinction between what he calls 'necessary truths or truths of reason' and 'truths of fact'. Truths of fact are established by the senses. These truths lack necessity. It may rain on one day, but not the next. It is true that I am now alive, but one day I won't be. The truths are CONTINGENT on events in the world and this is why they can only be derived from the senses. On the other hand necessary truths, such as the truths of mathematics, or logical principles, such as the law of identity, are not derived from experience. These truths have a different status from other truths in that they will always be true. Two and three will always be five, not just today, but every day. The eternal nature of these truth means they cannot be established by experience, but only by reason, and so in this sense are innate.

Leibniz claims that although young children may not be able to know many of the truths of mathematics (even most adults do not!), once they do understand a truth, the mind immediately recognises that this truth has an eternal application and that such truths are different from truths of fact. In this way, contrary to Locke's claim, Leibniz claims that there is a way of distinguishing innate ideas from non-innate ideas, even though the ideas may not be made aware to the mind until later in life.

On this view, all the propositions of arithmetic and geometry should be regarded as innate, and contained within us in a potential way, so that we can find them within ourselves by attending carefully and methodically to what is already in our minds, without employing any truth learned through experience or through word of mouth. Plato showed this, in a dialogue where he had Socrates leading a child to abstruse truths just by asking questions, not telling him anything. [We explore this dialogue on page 168.] *So one could construct the sciences of arithmetic and geometry in one's study – with one's eyes closed, even – without learning any of the needed truths from sight or even from touch.*[13]

Criticism 5: Reliance on the supernatural

Many versions of innatism hold that all humans possess certain key ideas – about God, mathematics, morality, and so on – and that these ideas are universally held because they have been placed in our minds by God.

We have seen in criticism 2 above that Locke argues there are no such universal ideas. In criticism 1 he also argues that, through empiricism, all our ideas can be explained naturally. In this way there is no need to rely on any supernatural being (God) in the explanation of any of our ideas.

However, not all forms of innatism need rely on the supernatural. Chomsky has argued that our ability to rapidly acquire language is only possible through an innate possession of a 'universal grammar'. Others have argued that we are born with moral intuitions, or born to experience the world in certain ways, for example as a sequence of causes. Some argue that through evolution our brains have become 'hard wired' to respond to the world in certain ways, and, in this sense, some of our abilities and ideas are innate. This non-supernatural form of innatism is usually called *nativism*. In this way innatism does not have to involve the supernatural.

Summary of concept empiricism

So far in this section we have explored the theory of concept empiricism. This is the theory, encapsulated in the idea of the *tabula rasa*, that all of our ideas and concepts must be derived from our impressions. It is claimed, by Hume and others, that this simple theory has the power to transform and 'solve' many traditional philosophical ideas. However, the idea of concept empiricism itself has generated a whole new area of philosophy, including many criticisms. One of the key areas of contention is the possibility of innate ideas, which has a long tradition and is deeply embedded in the beliefs and ideas of many philosophers and theologians. We explored different ideas that might be claimed as innate, including

Descartes' trademark argument for the existence of God, before looking at Locke's criticisms of innatism.

Knowledge empiricism

So far we have focused on ideas and their origins; empiricists and the idea of the *tabula rasa;* and rationalists and the claim of innate ideas. Here we move away from exploring the origins of individual ideas and concepts and consider the broader domain of human knowledge and how this is constructed. Does all our knowledge come from the senses too?

▶ **ACTIVITY**

Consider the following potential knowledge claims:

1 How many of these knowledge claims are derived solely from sensory input?
2 How many rely mainly on sensory input, plus some reasoning?
3 How many do not rely on sensory input at all (other than to know the meaning of the words)?

   a) The cat has just got off the bed.
   b) Water boils at 100°C on the surface of the earth.
   c) God loves the world.
   d) London is the capital of England.
   e) Wayne Rooney once played for Everton.
   f) The switch was flicked, causing the light to come on.
   g) 2 + 3 is 5.
   h) All bachelors are unmarried.
   i) The Sun will rise tomorrow.
   j) It has been raining so the grass in my garden will be wet.
   k) It is wrong to kill the innocent.
   l) All swans are white.

This activity might show that analysing how our knowledge relates to the senses is not always a simple affair. Propositions a) and e) above seem to be straightforward; however, the other propositions seem to stray beyond the senses in different ways.

Proposition b) seems to be derived from the senses (although most people will have simply read this in a book, rather than used a thermometer, but presumably someone has used their senses at some point!). However, it is not a straightforward sensory claim. First, it is hard to sense a 'centigrade'. We can sense the effects of temperature; for example, steam rising, mercury expanding, sweating and feeling hot. How we experience centigrade itself is not that clear. Furthermore, we only ever experience individual *instances* of water boiling at 100°. We cannot observe the 'law' that it always will do this. Some may even argue that as the centigrade scale itself based on the freezing (0) and boiling (100) points of water at sea level, then this truth can be known without observation. If we define 100°C as the boiling point of water, then that water boils at 100°C is true by definition.

Proposition c) is a tricky one. Some people may claim that they can observe this at work in the world. However, most would not claim this can be derived from the senses. As we explore on page 319, logical positivism, an extreme form of empiricism, would suggest this makes sentence c) meaningless.

Proposition d) seems to be derived from the senses, although it is not easy to observe a 'capital' city directly. The idea of a 'capital' describes a relationship between a city and a country and is not something that could easily derive directly from observing anything about the city. You would have to learn this fact through language, either online, in a book or on radio or TV.

Proposition f): switches being flicked can be derived from sight or touch. However, it is much harder to say how the 'cause' was derived from sense impressions. Hume suggests that it isn't (see page 112).

Proposition g): very strict empiricists such as John Stuart Mill would claim that even mathematical truths are just generalisations from sensory experience. But most empiricists would concede that mathematical truths are derived from reason.

Proposition h): our concepts of men and marriage are derived from the senses; however, there is no need to do a survey of unmarried men to see how many are bachelors. This truth can be worked out in terms of the meanings of the words alone. This makes it an ANALYTIC truth, which can be known through reason.

Proposition i): we can't directly observe the future, so this claim uses a form of reason (induction) based on how the world has behaved in the past, which is gained via the senses.

Proposition j): I cannot directly see my garden, but did observe the rain. This seems to be an inference based on a sensory experience, which again is a kind of inductive reasoning.

Proposition k) is much trickier! We observe situations and have moral reactions to them, but we certainly don't observe moral laws directly. Some would claim that this moral rule can be derived largely through reason; others would claim it is a generalisation based on inward impressions (emotions); others would say it is known innately or through revelation; and yet others still would say it is nonsense. It is hard to say where we derive k) from without first articulating a philosophical theory.

Proposition l): again, this is a generalisation. You can observe instances but not the general claim (unless you observed all the swans in existence).

Foundationalism

It seems obvious that much of our knowledge comes from the senses. We are bombarded with images, sounds and smells every day and on top of this our minds are full of memories of previous sensory input. As the examples above show, whether all of our knowledge comes from the senses is not clear at all. Others have doubted whether many of our beliefs gained from senses should be classed as knowledge at all, as such beliefs seem to lack a level of certainty (see INFALLIBILISM on page 74).

An important distinction to note is that empiricism is a form of FOUNDATIONALISM. This means that it is a theory of knowledge which claims that all of our belief and knowledge have an underpinning 'foundation'. For empiricism, this foundation is our sense impressions.

Empiricists argue that, as sense experience accounts for our *ideas*, it is also the ultimate source of our *knowledge* of the world. One reason for thinking this is, again, the idea of the *tabula rasa*. Empiricists also stress the point that we tend to appeal to our own experience when trying to justify our claims to know things. If I want to convince you that I know there is chicken across the road, a good way to justify my belief is the fact that I can see one.

Figure 1.32
Empiricist
foundationalism

The empiricist foundationalist regards knowledge of sensations or sense impressions as the basis for all our factual knowledge about the world. Knowledge of sense impressions is immediate and incorrigible. On this basis we infer the existence of the physical world. So all our knowledge of the physical world is ultimately justified in terms of knowledge about our own sense impressions.

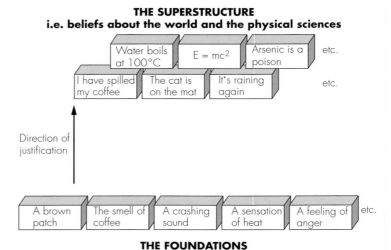

THE SUPERSTRUCTURE
i.e. beliefs about the world and the physical sciences

Water boils at 100°C $E = mc^2$ Arsenic is a poison   etc.

I have spilled my coffee   The cat is on the mat   It's raining again   etc.

Direction of justification

A brown patch   The smell of coffee   A crashing sound   A sensation of heat   A feeling of anger   etc.

THE FOUNDATIONS
Things we are immediately aware of such as colours, sounds and smells, as well as emotions and feelings; sometimes referred to as sense impressions, 'sense data' or the 'given'.

The empiricists claim that the foundations of our knowledge are our sense impressions (sometimes also called sense data). Our sense impressions are a solid foundation as they seem to be INCORRIGIBLE – meaning that they are beyond doubt. There is no new evidence that could come to light which could lead me to correct my claim to know that I am having a sensation of a certain sort – be it seeing a purple patch, experiencing a smell of lavender or suffering from a headache. I know I am having these sensations, whether or not purple things, lavender or even my own head exist. I cannot be brought to doubt that I have a headache no matter what sceptical scenarios one might raise.

It is on the basis of our sensations that we infer the existence of objects and events, mostly without being aware of doing so. I open the fridge and have a yellow and round visual experience – from this I infer that there is a grapefruit before me. I have an aural barking experience, and infer the existence of a dog outside. In these cases we move from our basic sense impressions to a belief about the world. However, in moving from one to the other there is the possibility of error: it may be a toy grapefruit in the fridge; it may be a dog impersonator outside my window. I may even be dreaming. Because there is an inference involved, there is always room for doubt. But when it comes to experiencing the sensations themselves, no inference is necessary. They are presented immediately to my mind and so knowledge of them allows no room for error. That I am experiencing a yellow, round shape cannot be doubted, regardless of what is actually causing it. This is why, according to the empiricists, our sense impressions form the foundation of our knowledge.

Scepticism of the world

One philosophical difficulty that empiricism has faced is the challenge of scepticism. While our sense impressions themselves may be impossible to doubt, this absolute certainty is hard to transfer to our beliefs about the world, since the world does not always match our sense impressions. A standard example of sense deception is that of a straight stick which appears bent when half immersed in water (see page 2). If I see a bent stick, when it is in reality straight, then sensation is misleading me about how the world is. But if sensation is misleading me, then the empiricist project to ground knowledge of the world in sensation looks flawed. Beyond our immediate experience too, our knowledge of the future or even of the past seems to leave much room for error. Maybe the future will be different from the past; maybe my memory is unreliable.

Descartes explored all these doubts in the *Mediations* (see page xiii). The challenge for empiricism is to move from the foundation of our 'certain' sense impressions to holding other beliefs about the world, without losing this certainty. Descartes' demon is the ultimate sceptical challenge. Here is a modern-day version.

Consider this science-fiction story:

It's the year 2560. Scientists know an enormous amount about the workings of the human brain to the point where they are able to keep brains alive suspended in a vat of chemicals and nutrients. One fiendishly clever (yet slightly mad) scientist is working on a pet project of his own. He has acquired a brain which he plays with in his secret laboratory. With the brain kept alive in the vat of chemicals, the scientist has carefully wired up the brain's input and output nerves to a powerful computer. The computer is able to send a complex array of electrical impulses which mimic precisely those that a normal brain-in-a-body would ordinarily receive from its environment through its senses. The computer interacts with the brain in such a way as to

our ideas and knowledge operate within our minds. In doing so he puts forward an account of empiricism, similar to that of John Locke, which argues that we should be able to trace all our ideas and concepts back to sense impressions. Hume also provides an account of how our reasoning relates to the world, which involves dividing the areas of human understanding into two distinct camps.

> *All the objects of human reason or enquiry fall naturally into two kinds, namely relations of ideas and matters of fact.*

Hume articulates these two areas of thoughts in more detail.

> *The first kind include geometry, algebra, and arithmetic, and indeed every statement that is either intuitively or demonstratively certain ... That three times five equals half of thirty expresses a relation between those numbers. Propositions of this kind can be discovered purely by thinking, with no need to attend to anything that actually exists anywhere in the universe. Matters of fact, which are the second objects of human reason, are not established in the same way; and we cannot have such strong grounds for thinking them true. The contrary of every matter of fact is still possible, because it doesn't imply a contradiction and is conceived by the mind as easily and clearly as if it conformed perfectly to reality.*[14]
>
> **Enquiry Concerning Human Understanding**, Enquiry 1, section 4, page 11

Relations of ideas and matters of fact

Hume is suggesting that all of our attempts to understand the world can be divided into two areas. 'Relations of ideas' concern logic and mathematics and, although we need sense experience to understand the concepts, Hume suggests that our reasoning in this area does not depend on how the world actually is. Two and three will always make five and we do not have to check this by observing facts in the world. The truth of such claims lies in pure reason alone. Such truths are true by definition and the opposite would be impossible. Consider the example of triangles. We do not have to observe every triangle in the world and then make the generalisation that they have three sides. Triangles have three sides by definition and we can work out their properties using reason. Because these truths are not derived from observing the world, they do not tell us anything new about the world. Such truths consist of working out what must already be the case from a given starting point (this process is known as deduction). The truths generated are certain as they are true by definition.

In contrast, 'matters of fact' can only be derived from experiencing how the world is. It may seem obvious that (most) objects fall down toward the earth or that fire burns, but this is only known through experience. Hume claims that our knowledge in this area consists of observing how the world is, and then generalising from experience. This process is known as induction. In terms of reasoning about matters of fact we can never be certain, we can only achieve degrees of probability or confidence. We may feel absolutely certain that the Sun will rise tomorrow – but maybe it won't. All of our scientific laws are just based on observations of how the world has been in the past and there is always the possibility that this will change tomorrow. We assume that the past will resemble the future, but again this is only on the basis that in the past, the future has previously resembled the past. So we are generalising from experience again.

Hume defines the difference between the 'matters of fact' and 'relations of ideas' using several different, but related, criteria. This table below summarises the differences between the two areas of understanding. (Note that some of the terms we use in the table were actually not used by Hume, but have been coined afterwards. However, Hume was referring to the same concept, albeit by another name.)

Area of thought	Relations of ideas	Matters of fact
Covers	Mathematics, geometry, logic.	Facts and generalisations about the world.
Examples	2 + 4 = 6.	Barak Obama was a US president. Water can turn into ice.
Certainty level	Absolute.	Not 100 per cent certain. Different levels of probability.
How we know	By thinking alone. (Can be known as *a priori*.)	By experience. (Can be known as *a posteriori*.)
Reliance on how the world is	None. Truth does not rely on how the world is, or even the existence of objects. (Would be true in all possible worlds = a necessary truth.)	Complete reliance on how the world is. Relies on the existence of objects and how they operate. (Would not be true in all possible worlds = a contingent truth.)
Is the opposite conceivable?	No. It is true by definition (an analytic truth).	Yes, the opposite is conceivable and possible. It is not true by definition (a synthetic truth).

Hume's division of human thought into these two areas is one of his most influential passages of philosophy. By separating out the areas of human understanding and clarifying what each is capable of, Hume sets out the limits of what each area can achieve. 'Matters of fact' (including science) cannot achieve absolute certainty and also can never *fully* explain why the world is as it is. We can explain some aspects of world in terms of other generalisations, for example explaining a light bulb shining in terms of electricity and electromagnetic radiation. But in the end, all of our explanations are based on observing how the world actually is, and generalising from it.

On the other hand, 'relations of ideas' can achieve absolute certainty – but only because they tell us nothing new about the world. This form of reasoning only concerns definitions and logical truths.

These two distinct areas of thought make up the two prongs of what has become known as Hume's fork (see **Figure 1.35** below). Hume's fork became a key discussion point in philosophy. Many previous philosophers (rationalists) had tried to use reason alone to show how the world must be. This was partly in the hope of achieving certainty and partly because they thought that reason could penetrate the ultimate truths about the world, in a way that our unreliable senses could not. According to Hume these 'rationalists' were simply wasting their time. You can only learn about the world by experience, and you cannot have certainty. On the one hand, we can study maths and logic using reason, and on the other we can observe the world and see how it is. Reason alone cannot tell us about the world. Once we have observed the world, reason may be able to help us deduce some further elements and truths, but by itself reason cannot tell us about the world.

Hume realised that his 'fork' had powerful consequences for the writings of many other philosophers and he was not frightened to spell this out.

> *When we go through libraries, convinced of these principles, what havoc must we make? If we take in our hand any volume – of divinity or school metaphysics, for instance – let us ask,* Does it contain any abstract reasoning about quantity or number? *No.* Does it contain any experiential reasoning about matters of fact and existence? *No. Then throw it in the fire, for it can contain nothing but sophistry and illusion.*[15]

Hume, *Enquiry Concerning Human Understanding*, Enquiry 1, section 12, page 86

Hume is suggesting that books that try to tell us what the world is like using reason alone should be burnt! In the twentieth century Hume's fork evolved into the theory of logical positivism – as we saw on page 113. This theory claimed that sentences are only meaningful if they are either true by definition (relations of ideas) or hypothetically verifiable (potential matters of fact). In this way, the two prongs of the fork were used to suggest that sentences involving neither are not only 'illusions', as Hume claims, but actually meaningless.

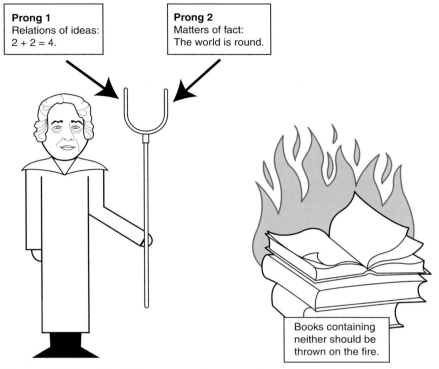

Prong 1
Relations of ideas:
2 + 2 = 4.

Prong 2
Matters of fact:
The world is round.

Books containing
neither should be
thrown on the fire.

Figure 1.35 Hume's fork. Hume suggests that our understanding is limited to these two areas – matters of fact and relations of ideas.

Hume's fork is a powerful claim and in the following text we will see if it is justified. First, we will clarify some key terms and then explore whether, as the rationalists claim, reason alone, unaided by the senses (sometimes called pure reason), can tell us anything substantial about the world.

Some key philosophical terms

We will look at four pairs of terms that will have a bearing on the debate as to whether reason can provide us with truths about the world independently of the senses:

- *A PRIORI* and *A POSTERIORI* knowledge
- analytic and synthetic truths
- necessary and contingent truths
- inductive and deductive reasoning.

A priori and *a posteriori* knowledge

The terms *a priori* and a *posteriori* refer to the way in which we acquire knowledge. Truths that can be known independently of experience, without the use of the senses, are said to be *a priori*. The term can also be applied to the truths themselves: an *a priori* truth is one which can be known *a priori*. Truths that can only be known via the senses and so are dependent on experience are

153

termed *a posteriori*. The claim of innatism and rationalism is that *a priori* knowledge of the world is possible. The strict empiricist, on the other hand, claims that all knowledge is derived from the senses and so is *a posteriori*. A good way of remembering these terms is that *a priori* knowledge can be known *prior* to any experience. So I know that if I put three apples into a basket containing two already, then I will have five apples. Because I can know this for certain prior to doing it, it means that 2 + 3 = 5 is knowable *a priori*.

Analytic and synthetic truths

You can tell that some sentences are true simply through an examination of the meanings of the terms involved. Such truths are termed ANALYTIC. An analytic truth is true by definition and so cannot be denied without contradiction. For example, it is analytically true that a square has four sides. To say that a square does not have four sides is to contradict oneself. That a bachelor is unmarried is also an analytic truth. I can tell this is true just by looking at the terms involved; I do not need to go out into the world and conduct a survey of actual bachelors. Contrasted with analytic truths are SYNTHETIC truths, which are not true simply by definition and can be denied without contradiction. For example, it is a synthetic truth that the dinosaurs died out, or that John, a 43-year-old bachelor, is miserable. Dinosaurs might have continued to dominate the earth if the asteroid that ultimately wiped them out had been on a slightly different course. John might not have been miserable if he had met the girl of his dreams. These possibilities are conceivable since there is no contradiction in them.

Analytic truths are also known by other names – *tautologies* or *logical truths* – and, as with *a priori* knowledge, they do not seem to rely on the senses to be known.

Necessary and contingent truths

There are competing definitions of NECESSARY and CONTINGENT truths, but one way of seeing the distinction is to imagine there are worlds just like this one, but each different in one or more ways. No matter how much these worlds differ, some propositions will have to be true in all of them, for example that 2 + 3 = 5 or that a bachelor is unmarried. These truths are termed necessary. Necessary truths are *necessarily* true as there is no world possible in which they are false. Some propositions, however, will only be true of some worlds: for example, that Tony Blair was the Prime Minister of the UK in 1999. It is possible to imagine a world in which another politician was the leader. Such truths are termed contingent, because they could have been otherwise.

Term	Examples	What does it apply to?	What distinction does it pick?
A priori	A bachelor is unmarried 2 + 3 = 5 An object is identical to itself	Knowledge (or truths)	Knowledge/truths that can be known independently of the senses, via reason.
A posteriori	John is a bachelor It rained yesterday	Knowledge (or truths)	Knowledge/truths that can only be known through experience / sense impressions.
Analytic truths (sometimes called tautologies or logical truths)	A bachelor is unmarried 2 + 3 = 5	Sentences (propositions) and the manner in which they might be true	Propositions that are true because of the meanings of the terms alone. Propositions whereby the opposite implies a contradiction.
Synthetic truths	John is a bachelor It rained yesterday	Sentences (propositions) and the manner in which they might be true	Propositions that are not true because of the meanings of the terms alone. Propositions whereby the opposite implies no contradiction.
Necessary truths	A bachelor is unmarried 2 + 3 = 5 An object is identical to itself Water = H_2O (this is a bit controversial)	Truths	Truths that are true in all possible worlds. Truths whereby the opposite is impossible.
Contingent truths	John is a bachelor It rained yesterday Tony Blair was the Prime Minister	Truths	Truths that are only true in this world and maybe some other possible worlds, but not in all possible worlds. Truths whereby the opposite is possible.

Types of truth and ways of knowing

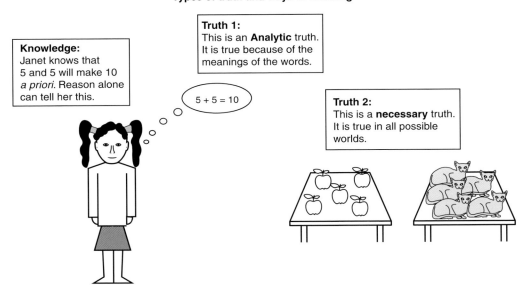

Knowledge:
Janet knows that 5 and 5 will make 10 *a priori*. Reason alone can tell her this.

5 + 5 = 10

Truth 1:
This is an **Analytic** truth. It is true because of the meanings of the words.

Truth 2:
This is a **necessary** truth. It is true in all possible worlds.

Figure 1.36a Types of truth and ways of knowing (1). Janet works out that five apples and five cats makes ten objects. **155**

Figure I.36b Types of truth and ways of knowing (2). Janet sees a boy with a balloon.

The rationalist challenge

One feature that may immediately strike you is that these terms all seem to be saying similar things. In other words doesn't all *a priori* knowledge simply consist of analytic truths, which in turn are the same as necessary truths?

There is no easy answer to this question, and philosophers have held very different positions. Hume's fork suggests that truths established as 'relations of ideas' are all analytic, necessary and knowable *a priori*. Truths established as 'matters of fact' are synthetic, contingent and only knowable *a posteriori*. The consequence of this, he claims, is that 'relations of ideas', established by reason cannot tell us anything new about the world.

However, rationalists would disagree and claim that we can have *a priori* knowledge of the world. In other words, we can have knowledge gained by reason, not via the senses, which is substantial and not just true by definition (analytic). To use the philosophical terms, they would claim that synthetic *a priori* knowledge is possible. However, empiricists may claim that the only things we can know *a priori* are analytic truths, and these tell us nothing about the world, as they would be true even if there were no world. In other words they claim that synthetic *a priori* knowledge is not possible.

To clarify these ideas, consider the 'Rationalist challenge' table below. Hume's fork claims that boxes A–F cannot be filled with any valid propositions as the columns all relate to 'matters of fact' and the truths that can be gained by the senses, and the rows all relate to 'relations of ideas' and truths that can be gained through reason.

Hume's fork suggests that the two domains are separate and, as such, reason alone cannot tell us anything new or substantial about the world (that is anything *a posteriori*/synthetic/*contingent*) but can only generate knowledge/truths that are *a priori*/analytic/necessary. The rationalist, however, would claim that some of the boxes can be filled. In this debate, box A is the key one – the possibility of synthetic *a priori* knowledge. For example, several rationalists suggest that claims such as *every event has a cause* can be put in this box. They claim this is not true by definition, but can be known through reason without checking with experience. Hume and others disagree. Descartes' *cogito* also seems to establish a truth for box A and Descartes hoped that by doubting everything and using reason alone that he could establish many more truths in this box. We will explore his attempts, and those of other rationalists, later.

Rationalist challenge

	A posteriori	Synthetic	Contingent
A priori		A Every event has a cause? I exist	B
Analytic	C		D
Necessary	E Water is H$_2$0?	F	

▶ **ACTIVITY**

1 Read through the following statements and decide whether they are:
   a) *a priori* or *a posteriori*
   b) analytic or synthetic
   c) necessary or contingent.
2 Can any of these statements be placed in the 'Rationalist challenge' table above?

   1 Everyone wants what is good.
   2 The square root of 81 is 9.
   3 All bachelors are unmarried men.
   4 Some bachelors have penthouses and throw wild parties.
   5 Mammals exist which have beaks like ducks, and which lay eggs.
   6 God exists.
   7 All things eventually decay and die.
   8 Material objects occupy space.
   9 Two parallel lines will never meet.
   10 Nothing can come from nothing.
   11 Water is H$_2$O.

You may have noticed that we already placed the final statement ('Water is H_2O') in box E of the 'Rationalist challenge' table. This is by no means without dispute. The claim that water being H_2O was discovered by experience and so is not knowable *a priori*, but only *a posteriori*. It is also claimed that water will be H_2O in every possible world. If there is a world in which there is a wet, tasteless substance that plays exactly the same role of H_2O, but is in fact a different chemical formula, then, the claim goes, this will not actually be water. It will be something like water, but not water, as water is necessarily H_2O. If this line of reasoning is accepted then it would allow lots of truths to be entered in box E of the table.

This may seem like a good result for the rationalist, though sadly they are not really interested in box E. The truths in box E can only be discovered by the senses (*a posteriori*) and, as their name suggests, the rationalists were only interested in truths that could be established by reason alone (*a priori*). Hence their interest in box A. Rationalists would be interested in filling box B, but this seems a challenge too far, as it involves working out by reason alone something that could easily have been otherwise. Although, as we will see below, Spinoza claimed that box B could also be filled in, but it could only be filled in by God! And the truths in this box are not really contingent anyway; they only appear that way to mere humans.

Induction and deduction

Another useful distinction drawn by philosophers is between two forms of reasoning: DEDUCTION and INDUCTION (see pages 206–207 for more on this)

Inductive reasoning is associated with science and empiricism and involves looking at how the world works and generalising from this. Deductive reasoning is used in mathematics and logic and is associated with rationalism. The rationalist idea is that from self-evident or innate ideas, it is possible to deduce what must also be the case about the world, without the need for observation/experience.

Rationalism
What can be known through reason alone?

 Experimenting with ideas

You are suddenly kidnapped and cryogenically frozen in a top-secret laboratory. You are awoken at some unknown point in time and space. (It is over 20,000 years later – though you don't know this.) You are in a completely dark room and feel quite weightless. A voice pierces the darkness. It asks you to work out as much as you can about the new 'world' you are in. You are asked to come up with a list of things that you know will be true in this world. If the list is broad enough and *all* items are true, then you will be freed to see this brave, new world.

Create a list of possible truths about this new world.

If you have explored some of Descartes' ideas, you may be tempted to claim that you can know that you exist. It may be tempting to assert that other intelligent beings must exist too, as you have been awoken and spoken to. However, this could just be a pre-recorded message – you may be all alone!

Rationalists would claim that this list could be populated with a range of truths. For a start, they would claim that truths of mathematics and of logic would also be true in this world. They claim these could be demonstrated *a priori* and so do not rely on your needing to experience the new world. Some would add other truths to the list, such as that every event will have a cause, that an object cannot both be and not be at the same time. Others would suggest you could claim truths about geometry, such as that the angles of a triangle will add up to 180 degrees. Possibly logical truths might be claimed, such as that all bachelors are unmarried. Maybe you could claim other truths gained from your knowledge of the earth, such as water is H_2O?

Some rationalists would claim that we can build up whole systems of substantive truths about the world that do not rely on the senses, and that could be established in such a darkened room. Before we look at their claims we will briefly consider what this possibility might mean for the idea of the *tabula rasa*.

A priori knowledge and the *tabula rasa*

Can *a priori* knowledge tell us about the world? The empiricist would say no, as this would seem to undermine the *tabula rasa* thesis, which claims that all our concepts must come from the senses. There are two different ways in which the empiricist might deny the claim to *a priori* knowledge:

1 Claiming that all knowledge is in fact *a posteriori* and that *a priori* knowledge doesn't exist
2 Claiming that *a priori* knowledge does exist but that it is all analytic (true by definition) and tells us nothing about the world.

1 There is no *a priori* knowledge at all

Strict empiricists such as John Stuart Mill (1806–1873) have claimed that we obtain *all* our knowledge, including mathematical knowledge, via experience, and that there is therefore no *a priori* knowledge at all. They claim that we observe that two apples and three apples make five apples, that two lizards and three snakes make five reptiles, and so on, and it is from such observations that we can generalise that $2 + 3 = 5$. The argument is that mathematical laws are discovered in much the same way as other laws about the world. For example, just as we see the Sun rise each morning and thus generalise that it will rise every morning, or observe that delicate objects dropped from certain heights tend to break,

159

so we observe how objects behave when grouped together and make empirical generalisations, which are the laws of addition. The difference between mathematical truths and other empirical truths is only that the evidence for them is more consistent. As we have seen, using the past as a guide to the future is called inductive reasoning. And the claim here is that maths is another form of induction: we observe how the world has worked in the past and then believe it will work that way in the future again.

However, this conclusion is not very satisfactory. It places mathematical claims on the same level as empirical generalisations and it seems clear that this is wrong. For example, on the basis of my previous experience, I might conclude that the number 3 bus will probably take 30 minutes to get me to work today, but I'm not very certain about this. I do, however, feel very certain that if I give the driver £1 and a 50-pence piece then I will have given the driver £1.50. Of this I am sure. Not every delicate object is certain to break when dropped from a height, and eventually the Sun may not rise. And even if delicate objects did always break, and the Sun did always continue to rise, it is at least *conceivable* that this might not be the case. Yet surely 2 plus 3 will always be 5, and we just can't imagine waking up one morning and finding that they were now 6. Such an idea appears to make no sense: 2 plus 3 just has to make 5. From this we can see that the truths of maths don't have the same features as truths gained by induction. The former are certain and impossible to conceive otherwise; the latter are not certain and possible to conceive otherwise. The reason for this difference, argue the rationalists (and most other empiricists such as Hume), is that the truths of maths are not empirical generalisations: they are not inductions based on the evidence of the senses but are deductions based on logical reasoning. As they are deductions, they can be demonstrated to be true, so they are certain and beyond doubt.

2 *A priori* knowledge does exist but it is all analytic and tells us nothing about the world

So most philosophers would conclude that *a priori* knowledge is at least possible. However, can this form of knowledge tell us anything substantial about the world?

As we saw above, analytic truths are true in virtue of the meaning of the terms. Because of this they can be known *a priori*. Take the example of the proposition: 'All sisters are female.' I don't need to conduct a survey of sisters to justify my belief that this is true. I would be wasting my time if I did. I can know this simply in virtue of understanding the terms involved. To take another example, contrast the proposition: 'No one can steal the Queen of England's property' with 'No one can steal his or her own property'. In the first case, to establish whether or not it is true I would have to make various enquiries into the security surrounding the Queen. So establishing its truth would involve more than just thinking about the meaning of the proposition. But in the second case, I can see that it must be true just by understanding what the terms involved mean. It is impossible to steal one's own property just because stealing *means* taking someone else's property (without permission).

Some empiricists argue that all *a priori* truths are analytic. As analytic truths tell us only about the meanings of the symbols, they tell us nothing new about the world. So box A in the 'Rationalist challenge' table (page 157) cannot be filled. An empiricist may recognise that there are truths of reason, but regard them as empty of empirical content and so useless as a basis for knowledge about the physical universe. In so doing the empiricist can retain the basic point that it is only experience that can provide interesting or new information about the world.

Reason's usefulness lies in unpicking implications and truths that are already present in the knowledge we have. So, for example, if I knew that Shakespeare wrote *Hamlet* and I later found out that *Hamlet* was a tragedy, I would be able to deduce, by reason alone, that Shakespeare wrote at least one tragedy. However, in doing so I would not be gaining any new knowledge but merely teasing out facts I knew implicitly already.

Can reason provide us with new knowledge about the world?

Is synthetic *a priori* knowledge possible? Or is *a priori* knowledge limited to analytic truths and the unpicking of the implications of truths already known, or can it tell us new facts about the world?

To answer this we will consider:

- the relationship between mathematics and the world
- whether rationalism can generate knowledge beyond the mathematical and the analytic.

Mathematics and the world

The relationship between mathematics and the world is not easy to describe and represents a significant philosophical problem in itself. Here we can only summarise some of the main positions and see the implications for the claim that we can gain significant knowledge of the world *a priori*.

Geometry

One of the easier areas to discuss is that of geometry – the study of shapes. The foundations of geometry were established by the pivotal Greek mathematician Euclid. In his book the *Elements*, Euclid sets out what is known as an axiomatic system; that is to say, a system in which all the propositions are derived from a small set of initial axioms and definitions. These initial axioms and definitions are thought to be self-evident. For example, among those in Euclid's axioms are the following:

- *All right angles equal one another.*
- *A circle is a plane figure contained by one line such that every point on it is the same distance from the centre.*[16]

From these axioms, Euclid then proceeds to prove a host of further propositions, for instance:

- *If a straight line falling on two straight lines makes the alternate angles equal to one another, then the straight lines are parallel to one another.*[17]

Through the careful use of reason, Euclid is able to establish a large and systematic body of truths all derived from his initial axioms and definitions. Euclid's system was undoubtedly the inspiration behind many of the rationalists' attempts to gain knowledge through reason. First one establishes a series of truths that cannot be doubted (axioms) and then one builds from this point to establish a complete system of truths.

Regarding geometry it would seem that the truths established through reason do indeed apply to the world. We are able to construct bridges and buildings that rely on matter and space behaving in the ways described by geometry. We can even correctly predict the angles and properties of shapes that have never before existed. Geometry seems to be telling us new facts about the nature of physical space, facts that have genuine application and are not just true by definition. So it would seem that with geometry we have an example of how we can gain substantive knowledge of the world independently of the senses.

Criticism

However, is this really the case? It can be argued that geometry is simply working out the logical implications of a given set of initial assumptions. Once these axioms have been established then the other truths can be analytically deduced. These other truths follow deductively from the axioms. They are essentially claiming conditional truths along the following lines:

Given that a straight line is the shortest distance between two points and that parallel lines never meet, triangles and squares will have certain properties x, y and z.

So perhaps geometry is not adding any new facts beyond the initial assumptions: it is simply working out their implications. And, where did we get these initial assumptions from? If they are ultimately derived from experience, then the whole system is grounded in experience after all and we are not gaining any new knowledge *a priori*.

Further, the truths established by Euclid's geometry are not even true of the world. In most instances they are simply very good approximations. It seems to be the case, following the work of Einstein and others, that the world is in fact non-Euclidean – which means that the axioms that Euclid based his theories on are not actually true. It turns out that, in real space, parallel lines do actually cross: it is just that this can't be observed on the scales that the human eye deals with. It seems that we need to carry out experiments and careful measurements in order to determine the actual properties of space, and that they cannot be worked out by reason alone.

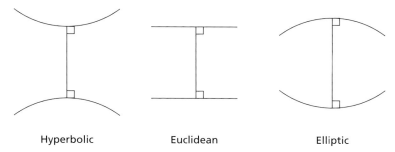

Figure 1.37 Euclidean and non-Euclidean space. In Euclidean space parallel lines never meet and stay the same distance apart. However, this is not true in other possible geometries such as hyperbolic and elliptic. Further it is also suggested that the world itself is not Euclidean, it merely appears to be on the scale relevant to the human eye.

Hyperbolic   Euclidean   Elliptic

There are many different possible geometries that would each follow from a different set of axioms and all of them are perfectly intelligible. This means that the axioms of any geometry are not true by definition (analytically true) as the opposite is conceivable. It seems we have to actually look at the world using our senses and see which of the many possible geometries actually applies to the universe we live in.

Algebra

Unlike geometry, numbers themselves don't seem to be describing anything as tangible as space. Despite this, the truths of numbers seem to apply to almost every aspect of the universe. But what do these numbers actually describe? There are a range of possible answers of which we outline only three:

1 **Platonism:** Earlier we saw Plato suggest that numbers describe ideal entities that exist independently of the human mind. As he believed they exist outside of the mind, Plato was a *realist* about numbers. According to this view, mathematicians are trying to work out the relationships between these various entities (numbers) and these seem to apply to the world we inhabit too. Despite being over 2000 years old, Platonism is still one of the main theories in the philosophy of maths. If true it would imply that reason can tell us about the world independently of the senses.

2 **Empiricism:** As described above, empiricism is the view that mathematical truths are just generalisations from experience. This is not widely held today, but if true would imply that mathematics can only be known *a posteriori*.

3 **Logicism:** Bertrand Russell and Alfred Whitehead, following the work of other philosophers, attempted to show that it is possible to derive the truths of mathematics from a set of more basic truths about logic – for example, that 'A or not A' *is necessarily true*. Their masterpiece *Principia Mathematica* famously contains a proof that 1 and 1 makes 2, which is several pages long (see **Figure 1.38**). In this view, numbers are defined by possible sets of objects: the number 2 describes the set of all possible pairs of objects.

163

So here Descartes may have found the foundations for which he was searching. From this bedrock, Descartes thought it would be possible to deduce further truths and from these build out a whole series of truths about the world – including scientific laws. The experience of the senses would also confirm the truth of the laws, but they would be known with certainty as they were deduced via reason and not induced via the senses.

Descartes' method was the first clear articulation of the great rationalist plan. His approach was to arrive at intuitions that cannot be doubted (clear and distinct ideas) and then use deduction to establish a system of truths from these. This method of intuition and deduction could be achieved by reason alone, without the need for the unreliable senses – and so the truths could be known *a priori*.

Like Empiricism, Rationalism is a foundationalist approach to knowledge (see **Figure 1.39**). As we have seen, the Empiricists thought that our sense impressions form the foundations – the bedrock of certainty – on which our knowledge is built. However, Descartes and other rationalists believed that these foundations were 'clear and distinct ideas'. These are beliefs, perhaps innate, which can be realised through reason and are so certain that they cannot be doubted. From this solid base Descartes, and others, thought much more could then be attained through the application of reason.

THE SUPERSTRUCTURE
i.e. knowledge of the world and the physical sciences

THE FOUNDATIONS: 'CLEAR AND DISTINCT' IDEAS
i.e. knowledge of my existence, of maths and geometry; truths of reason and analytic truths

Figure 1.39 Descartes' foundationalism – the intuition and deduction thesis. All knowledge is based on a foundation of beliefs which are knowable *a priori*, and which are self-justifying. The rest of our beliefs, principally those about the physical world, are to be justified in terms of these basic beliefs. So any belief which is not ultimately based on reason is not justified and so is not knowledge. The view that all genuine knowledge is grounded in reason is termed rationalism.

This plan sounded grand, but the problem for Descartes was developing further truths on top of the *cogito*. After all, he still hasn't got rid of the idea that there is an evil demon; he has simply established that he exists. From this point Descartes tries to prove that God exists using the trademark argument (see page 125). He then argues that a good God wouldn't deceive us, so we can trust our senses and our judgements as long as we proceed with suitable care and attention. However, his proof of the existence of God is not very convincing, so for many readers of the *Meditations* Descartes' elaborate system of certainty gained through intuition and deduction starts and ends with the *cogito* and a few basic ideas about mathematics.

anthology
1.22

Although Descartes may have failed in his plan to establish a body of *a priori* truths, the method he used has had a lasting legacy. Descartes wanted to start from scratch and use reason rather than dogma or religion. This was a break from the medieval way of thinking and placed epistemology at the heart of philosophy. Method became the focus, for both philosophy and science, and this emphasis on method is one defining feature of what is termed the modern era. (Descartes is one of the first philosophers of the modern era – which might seem an odd thing to say, given that he was writing nearly 300 years ago!)

Plato and the theory of forms

Although important, Descartes was not the first to think that reason could provide important truths about the world. The fascination with *a priori* truths, especially those of mathematics and geometry, and the tendency to regard them as in some way superior to *a posteriori* truths has a long philosophical history. To regard such knowledge as having a privileged status, and to hold it as a benchmark for all other knowledge claims, is one of the main features of rationalism. In this Descartes is in the good company of Plato.

Plato founded perhaps the first proper college in western society, known at the Academy. To aid the teaching in his school, Plato wrote many dialogues, all concerned with philosophy. In many of the dialogues, Socrates is the main character and he usually engages in a debate about a philosophical issue.

It can be hard to piece together the philosophy of Plato from his dialogues, as the main character, Socrates, mainly questions others rather than putting forward a specific theory. However, across several of the plays a distinct theory emerges, known as Plato's THEORY OF FORMS.

Plato was puzzled by the problem of universals: of the relationship between a concept and an individual instance of that concept. We seem to have a concept of beauty, but never witness beauty in its pure form; only imperfectly in different people and objects. Likewise a straight line. All the lines we see in the world are not perfectly straight, yet the concept of a perfectly straight line is clear in our minds. Also puzzling is that concepts, such as numbers, are eternal and unchanging, whereas everything in the world is temporary and fleeting. (The relationship between change and permanence was a key concern for many of the earliest recorded philosophers, known as the pre-Socratics. You may have reflected on this problem yourself, because as a person you change every day and yet are the same person through all this change. How is this possible?)

To account for these puzzles, Plato believed that our souls were immortal and that, in a prior existence, we apprehended these perfect concepts or forms in their pure state. We have forgotten most of these forms but they are in us innately and, Plato believed, through a process of reasoning we can achieve a perfect understanding/apprehension once again.

Although this theory has elements that may seem far-fetched, Plato's account contains some of the classic features of innatism that have been repeated through the ages.

■ Innate ideas are 'in' us, although we might not be aware of them. Exactly like a forgotten memory is 'in' us.
■ We can realise these innate ideas through reason.
■ Innate ideas provide timeless truths.

anthology 1.23

Plato shows how these innate ideas can be realised through reason in his dialogue, the *Meno*. Socrates engages a slave boy in discussion and through questions and answers draws out of him a proof about squares (which is a simplified version of Pythagoras' theorem). The suggestion is that the boy innately has the knowledge and that reason can draw it out (see **Figure 1.40**).

▶ **ACTIVITY**

1 Read excerpt 1.23 in the Anthology extracts. Plato is presenting a similar account of innate ideas to that of Leibniz (page 142). The suggestion is that the boy has this mathematical knowledge 'in' him innately – although was not aware of it. By being encouraged to reason he is able to access this innate knowledge.
2 Do you believe the ideas were in the boy all along?
3 Does this excerpt suggest that we have innate ideas/knowledge?

Figure 1.40 Socrates' experiment with the slave in Plato's *Meno*. This diagram shows that the total area of the square EFGH is twice that of the square ABCD. This can clearly be seen since each of the four triangles (1, 2, 3 and 4) which divide ABCD is equal in area and equal to each of the eight triangles (1, 2, 3, 4, 5, 6, 7 and 8) which divide EFGH, and eight is twice four.

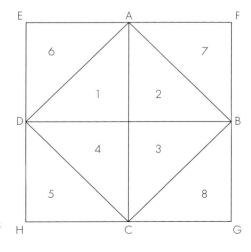

Like the boy in the dialogue, once we understand such a proof, we recognise it to be true not just of the particular square drawn, but of all squares. This suggested to Plato that such knowledge cannot derive from our experience, since our experience is only ever of particular squares. So how is such an understanding possible? Plato's answer was that our minds see the essential nature or *form* of the square and recognises truths about this, rather than about the particular example of a square I see with my eyes. Like Descartes, he thought that we have an innate faculty which recognises such truths as eternal and necessary. This furnishes us with genuine knowledge. By contrast, our understanding of empirical truths learned *a posteriori* lacks certainty. They are only ever contingently true; that is to say, they might not have been true and only happen to be true. For this reason, we can only have beliefs about them.

The precision of our mathematical thoughts contrasts with the imperfection of the world, which led Plato to suppose that mathematical and geometrical concepts do not correspond to objects in the physical world. Since he thought they must nonetheless apply to something, he posited a realm of intelligible objects which is more real than this world of imperfect, changeable objects. In this way Plato draws a distinction between a world of ideal forms – the object of knowledge – and the physical world of which only belief or opinion is possible. Such knowledge isn't restricted to maths and geometry, but also applies to other moral and aesthetic concepts, such as justice and beauty, which can also be the 'object' of knowledge, apprehended through reason.

Plato uses a variety of metaphors to describe the relation that exists between the realm of forms and the physical world. Sometimes he speaks of the form being 'present' in an object, or of the object 'sharing in' the form. Alternatively, he speaks of the object as an 'approximation', 'copy' or 'imitation' of the form.[20] The form may also be thought of as like a mould or blueprint determining what a set of objects of a certain kind have in common, while no two particulars need ever be identical. It is our recognition of the form in the particular which enables us to see that it belongs to a certain class of thing.

The problem for Plato, as it was for Descartes some two thousand years later, was trying actually to establish what these *a priori* truths are. Plato tells us that the forms exist and that we can reach them through thought alone. However, he fails to offer up a clear account of a single form for us to scrutinise. Perhaps the apprehension of a form is not the sort of thing one can discuss using language? But, until these forms are established they cannot really count as examples of *a priori* knowledge of the world.

The limits of knowledge through reason alone

So far it seems that, despite Descartes and Plato suggesting that reason alone can provide us with substantial truths about the world, nothing much has seemed to emerge. Is that because reason alone can only tell us things that are true by definition? In other words, is all *a priori* knowledge analytic? Or can reason also tell us substantial truths about the world: is synthetic *a priori* knowledge possible? Can box A in the 'Rationalist challenge' table be filled?

Few philosophers today would agree that we can acquire the precision of mathematical knowledge in the realms of aesthetics or morals. Concepts of justice and beauty are (relatively speaking) vague and may vary between individuals and cultures. But what of scientific knowledge? Descartes optimistically thought it would be possible to work out basic physical laws with mathematical certainty simply by reasoning, and without recourse to empirical observation. However, this project now seems overly ambitious. Mathematical truths alone do not seem to tell us how the world behaves. To know that if I have two marbles and then add three more marbles that I will have five marbles tells me nothing about whether or not there are marbles. The price of demanding that all our knowledge comes through reason seems to be that we end up not knowing very much.

The lack of progress that pure reason has made in telling us about the world seems to support the earlier claim that reason alone can tell us only about analytic truths and that all truths about the physical world – all empirical truths – are synthetic. As noted, analytic truths are true by definition, and the denial of an analytic truth is always an impossible contradiction. For example, a two-sided triangle is impossible. However, it is always possible that things in the world could have been different. The truths of the world are not true by virtue of the meanings of the terms themselves and their opposites do not imply a contradiction. There is no logical contradiction in supposing that there are two suns or mice that speak. Even the laws of physics could have been different. Scientists can model aspects of the universe with different laws. We can imagine all these things being different, so their denial does not imply any contradiction. This means they are not analytic truths and so cannot be established by reason alone.

I cannot work out the laws of physics, just as I cannot work out what colour my shoes are, by reason alone. Such things can be found out only by observation. This is the argument put forward by Hume. It is important because, if it is right, it shows that deductive reasoning by itself is of limited use. Experience can be the only true source of knowledge about the physical universe, and deductive reasoning can only help to work out the implications of this knowledge.

Descartes' project of establishing a body of truths, including scientific truths, through reason alone seems doomed. In Descartes' defence, he thought we could give an account of physics and the movement of objects using the concepts of geometry alone, and even went on to produce some interesting ideas in the field of optics using just this approach. It seems though, as Newton suggested, that matter also has mass, not just shape, and we have to discover the properties of mass using our senses, not pure reason. So Descartes' project did not work.

Other rationalists

Hume's claim is that the rationalist enterprise must fail. It seems to fail because reason will provide us only with analytic truths – truths by definition – whereas knowledge of the world involves knowledge of synthetic truths – truths that are not true by definition. However, Descartes was not the only rationalist of the modern era. Others followed in his footsteps and took up the challenge of establishing knowledge through reason. Two of these, Leibniz and Spinoza, avoid Hume's criticism to some extent since both of them claimed that all empirical truths about the world are not analytic truths but are necessary truths, and that these, in principle, can be established by reason alone.

Leibniz

Leibniz established a complex and contained metaphysical view of the world and it is very easy to misrepresent his views by presenting small segments of his philosophy in isolation. Leibniz believed that God existed necessarily and that by definition God is all-good, all-powerful and all-knowing. Since this NECESSARY BEING is all-good and all-powerful, it follows that the world God created would have to be the best possible world there could be. It would be nonsensical for an all-good and all-powerful God to create a less than perfect world. So the world we live in, and every event that takes place in it, takes place necessarily as part of the divine plan to maximise the good.

This may seem implausible initially. We can see perfectly well that a lot of what goes on in the world is not good. We can certainly imagine far better worlds than this one – for example, worlds without famine, or the suffering of innocent children. Leibniz defends himself against this objection by arguing that the apparent imperfections in this world appear only because we have a limited view of the whole of God's creation. Each local piece of evil is needed in order to maximise the overall perfection of the world (see page 307). So some suffering is required so that more good can be realised, just as we must sometimes endure the discomfort of taking unpleasant medicine in order to recover from an illness. If we had the mind of God and could grasp the bigger picture, we would see that these apparent imperfections are required and so could understand the reason for everything in the universe.

So, in principle at least, all empirical truths about the world could be worked out *a priori*, just by thinking about them. So, we wouldn't need to do any empirical research to know whether there will be a white Christmas this year. We could work it out, just by thinking about whether a white Christmas would be part of God's plan to produce the best possible world. Of course, in reality, humans are not up to the task of working out truths like this by reason alone. Our finite minds can't see whether snow or no snow would be best. This is why we have to do empirical research rather than reason alone.

So Leibniz would claim that box B of the 'Rationalist challenge' table could be completed, but only by God. God, knowing his will to be perfectly good, is able to work out the best possible universe by reason alone. All truths follow as a result of his goodness.

Spinoza

Benedict de Spinoza (1632–1677) was born in Amsterdam. He lived an austere life, refusing to accept his inheritance and earning his living as a humble lens-grinder. He died of consumption, probably triggered by the fine glass dust that he inhaled every day. While grinding he would contemplate philosophical ideas, often discussing his thoughts with friends and intellectuals who would frequent his workshop. Spinoza, like Descartes and Leibniz, adopted the rationalist view that the essential truths about the world should be established through reason and thus could attain the certainty of maths and geometry. His great work, *The Ethics*, starts by stating a series of definitions and axioms that he believes cannot be doubted. Inspired by the geometric method of Euclid who, using a few axioms and definitions, proves various geometrical propositions, Spinoza proceeds to try to deduce in the same manner all sorts of general or metaphysical truths.

As *The Ethics* develops, Spinoza arrives at a strange and complex metaphysical picture of the world. Spinoza was a PANTHEIST, believing that God is one and the same as the universe and, like Leibniz, he claimed that all truths are necessary, and nothing is contingent. The appearance of contingency is the result of the fact that our minds are not powerful enough to see why everything is the way it is. Forming only a small part of the universe, each human fails to see how every part of the universe (God) is connected, and it is from this that the feeling of contingency arrives, just like a tiny parasite in our bloodstream would not be aware that the blood it is in is just a small part of a wider, interconnected, living organism. So while it may seem to me that some events in the universe just happen by chance, in fact all are necessary. I have to have the cup of tea

I have just finished, as this was a necessary event. I could not have had a cup of coffee instead.

Spinoza too would claim that all truths of the world could be established by reason alone, but again, only God could do this. Spinoza claimed that this was so because all events are necessary; they only appear contingent because of our finite knowledge.

So would Spinoza claimed that box B could also be filled in by reason alone (although as all truths are necessary, not contingent, it would not really be box B in the 'Rationalist challenge' table)?

Reason and necessary truths

The rationalist views adopted by both Leibniz and Spinoza claim that the truths about the world could, in theory, be discovered by reason alone (albeit God's reason). Leibniz thought this because all contingent truths happen as a result of God's goodness and Spinoza argued that all truths are necessary and contingency is an illusion.

However, both these attempts at the rationalist enterprise are based on the supernatural (God) and this raises further difficulties. We could, though, try to imagine a modern-day version of rationalism which posits a universe that does not rely on the existence of God. We can already predict successfully the movements of the Moon and the planets by applying the relevant scientific laws to some initial starting positions. We can also predict the outcome of thousands of chemical reactions in the same way. Now, imagine this predictive power extended a million-fold, such that the behaviour of every atom could be predicted using the laws of nature and initial starting conditions.

 Experimenting with ideas

Imagine a futuristic super-computer. This perfect computer has been programmed with all the laws of the universe and the initial starting conditions at the Big Bang, down to the tiniest possible level. (For this you can assume that there is no random element in nature and that we are able to surmise initial starting conditions of particles.)

1 Would this super-computer be able to know roughly what would happen in the universe, using its reason/processing power alone?
2 Would it be able to predict how every event in the universe subsequently took place, right up to and including the event of your reading this now?
3 If possible, would this count as proof that the rationalist project, of discovering truth though reason, is possible?

Your answer to these questions may depend on whether you think humans have FREE WILL. You may also refer to Heisenberg's principle of uncertainty, which says that we cannot know both the position and the momentum of the smallest particles. These concerns aside, this thought experiment is suggesting a way that reason (albeit through a computer) could work out all truths about the universe. However, even this scenario (which contains many dubious assumptions) fails to live up to the rationalist ideal. How would the computer know the laws of nature and the initial starting conditions of the universe? These would have to be established through the senses, through observing how the universe works, and programmed into the computer. An out-and-out rationalist would have to claim that these too could be established using reason alone, by claiming that there is only one possible universe and set of natural laws that could exist. Yet this view is hard to believe – surely this is not the only possible universe. Current science suggests that universes with different laws of nature may well be possible (see page 157).

Summary of rationalism

So it seems that no matter how hard we push the case, it is simply not possible to prove substantial truths about the universe and the way it works by using reason alone. Although many philosophers have attempted to develop systems of thought based on pure reason, but beyond the world of logic, and mathematics, these systems have not produced a body of knowledge. Aside from knowing that you exist, it seems that synthetic *a priori* knowledge is not possible. Box A in the 'Rationalist challenge' table remains unfilled.

Learn More

Kant and synthetic *a priori* knowledge

Before giving up on synthetic *a priori* knowledge completely (box A), we will briefly explore the ideas of Immanuel Kant, who was the first person to define the terms 'analytic' and 'synthetic' and so use the phrase 'synthetic *a priori* knowledge'.

We saw earlier that Kant claimed we needed to apply structures/concepts to our sense data in order to have experience (page 120). For Kant this is not a conscious process, and so is to be contrasted with the sort of conceptual schemes that we develop through experience *a posteriori*. For example, after tasting some food we might subsequently classify the experience in various ways – tasty, exotic or expensive. These ways may vary from individual to individual and from culture to culture.

Kant is not talking about these types of concept. Rather, he suggests that there are fundamental categories that are applied to the raw data we receive and these combine to give us our sense experience of the world. This process is carried out automatically by the mind and, he suggests, must happen for any mind to have an experience of the world. These categories are *a priori* as they are not derived from experience. Indeed they are the precondition of any experience happening in the first place.

As outlined earlier, Kant suggests that causation is one of these categories. Hume claims that we do not seem to derive this concept from any specific sense experience and suggests that our idea of cause is brought about by a habit of the mind through experience and so is developed *a posteriori*. Kant agrees that our idea of cause is not derived from any particular impression. However, he argues that causation is one of the categories by which the raw data from the world is turned into an intelligible experience in the mind. Causation is one of the *a priori* concepts needed for any experience to occur. Because of this we cannot help but view the world as a sequence of causes and effects rather than a series of unconnected events with nothing tying them together. We experience the world as causal because the data from the world has been categorised using the concept of cause. The concept of cause is a necessary part of our conceptual scheme and without it our experience of the world would be unintelligible; it would not form part of a coherent structure.

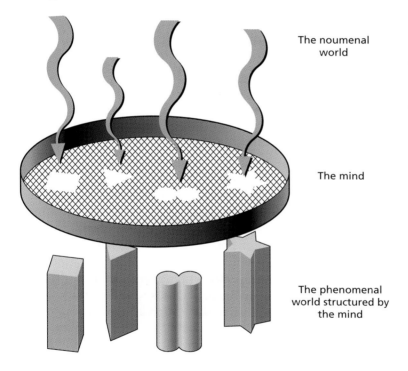

The noumenal world

The mind

The phenomenal world structured by the mind

Figure 1.41 The mind structures the experience of the world

Kant noted that the way in which we observe the world is organised by our sensory and cognitive apparatus. The way our sense organs and our brains arrange the data they receive determines how we perceive the world. Because of this we can know that what we experience will have a certain uniform structure. We can know this *a priori*.

Hume claimed that we cannot know *a priori* that every event has a cause; we only work out so-called causes by seeing events which regularly follow other events. Kant, however, claimed that we could know *a priori* that every event has a cause. This is not true by definition. It is not part of the meaning of the word 'event' that it is something which must be caused. But this, for Kant, is an example of a synthetic judgement that can be known *a priori*.

In claiming that some synthetic *a priori* knowledge was possible, Kant attempted to turn the empiricist approach on its head. Rather than ask the traditional question of how we can come to know that our understanding of the world accurately reflects reality, he claimed that reality reflects our understanding. What we can know of the world is not a simple matter of passively receiving sense impressions; the mind actively orders our experience and so gives it the particular structure it has.

According to Kant, we can know *a priori* that every event has a cause because we know that we must experience the world causally. We know that every object is a substance because we are bound to experience the world consisting of substance. As an analogy, imagine you have a black and white TV. Now you don't know for sure what picture you will see when you turn on the TV, as the schedules may change; however, you do know that whatever you see will be in black and white as this is the way that the TV has structured the experience. This you can know *a priori* (sort of).

In the same way, Kant argued it was possible to know things about the world (or the way we perceive the world) that are not true by definition (synthetic) but could be discovered by reason alone (*a priori*).

Kant's writing is impenetrably complex. His theories are hard to understand, let alone evaluate. Many of his claims are not widely supported now but his central idea that our mind in some way structures our experience is very important and echoes throughout much modern thought.

Summary

In this chapter we have explored the sources of ideas and of knowledge. Asserting the *tabula rasa* model of the mind, empiricism claims that all of our ideas and much of our knowledge comes from our impressions. In contrast, rationalism is the view that reason is the true source of knowledge. Rationalists often associate knowledge with certainty and, impressed by the certainty established in mathematics, seek to extend the reach of deductive reasoning to other areas. Rationalism often denies the idea of the *tabula rasa* and suggests that we possess innate ideas that can be drawn out through reason. Rationalists such as Plato, Descartes, Leibniz and Spinoza have tried to use reason to reach these innate ideas/intuitions and then reason outwards from these. However, it is not clear that they established the certainty they sought.

Kant started out as a rationalist, but after reading the work of Hume rejected this path and became convinced that experience must be the source of our knowledge. His famous masterpiece – the *Critique of Pure Reason* – argues, along with Hume, that pure, deductive reasoning will only establish statements that are true by definition (analytic). However, he also put forward the idea that our senses alone cannot account for all of our concepts and argued that we need concepts in order to interpret our raw sense data and so experience a world in the first place. His work made other philosophers question the simple, perhaps naïve, idea of the *tabula rasa* and since then many have suggested that our experience of the world is not a passive one where sense data simply fall into our minds. Rather, they suggest our experience is active and shaped by our language, culture and the structures of our brains/minds.

Section 2: Philosophy of Religion

2.1 The concept of God

Introduction

It is incomprehensible that God should exist and incomprehensible that God should not exist.[1]
Pascal

God said to Moses: I am what I am.
Exodus 3:13

Philosophers tend to be inquisitive meddlers, poking their noses into all aspects of human life, and trying to clarify our ideas about the world, about how we should live and what we should believe. Religion offers philosophers a rich vein of puzzling ideas that they can tap into: thinking about God ties people up in intellectual knots, and leads to strange, confusing statements – as the quotations above from Pascal and the Bible illustrate.

What particularly excites philosophers is investigating the beliefs that people have about the world, and the way we think we ought to live. Because religion deals with both these issues it is no surprise that philosophers have had much to say about religion and God over the last two thousand years. A vast body of philosophical work has built up in western philosophy around the religious traditions of Europe and the Middle East. This philosophy of religion has dealt with questions such as: 'Who is God?', 'Can his existence be proved?', 'How can God let innocent people suffer so much pain?', 'When we talk about God, what meanings do our words have?' Here we cover three of the most important groups of questions that theologians and philosophers have debated over the last two millennia:

■ **The concept of God:** In this chapter we look at what philosophers have had to say about the nature of God, and whether their description is a coherent or meaningful one.

■ **Arguments relating to the existence of God:** In Chapter 2.2 we look at three of the main attempts by philosophers to prove the existence of God, looking at how philosophical arguments are constructed and the different ways in which it is possible to prove that something exists. We then examine the problem of evil, and how religious philosophers have attempted to reconcile the pain and suffering in the world with the existence of God.

■ **Religious language:** In Chapter 2.3 we examine the meaning of religious language and the ways in which philosophers think we use, understand and make religious statements.

These topics, or clusters of questions, relating to the philosophy of religion also form a good introduction to some of the main branches of philosophy:

■ Logic and critical thinking (pages 205–290): discussions about the arguments relating to the existence of God.
■ Metaphysics (pages 178–240): discussion of the concept of God.
■ Ethics (pages 291–311): discussion of the problem of evil.
■ Philosophy of language (pages 312–350): discussion of the meaning of religious language.

Two approaches: Revealed theology and natural theology

A promising place to start an investigation into the nature of God is the sacred texts on which religions are based, such as the Torah, the Bible or the Qur'an. These books record the foundations of the religion through the REVELATIONS of certain individuals. These individuals, it is claimed, had some direct or indirect contact with God, and may be best positioned to reveal something of God's nature.

However, an alternative starting point for a philosophical investigation into the nature of God would be to look around us at the universe he is said to have created. By analysing the various features of this universe (the types of things that exist, the laws that govern it, human behaviour, and so on) we might hope to establish what God must be like.

Religious philosophers and theologians have taken both these approaches: the first is called REVEALED THEOLOGY, because it trusts sacred texts to reveal religious truths and an understanding of God; the second approach is called NATURAL THEOLOGY, because it stresses the possibility of understanding God via human reason and observation alone. There is a tension between these two methods or approaches: as potential philosophers we are naturally drawn to reason, but as potential believers we cannot put aside faith, and the goal of many religious philosophers down the ages has been to resolve the tension between these two.

▶ **ACTIVITY**

1 Write down as many words that you can think of associated with the idea of 'God'.
2 Which of these words or categories do you think come from a religious text (e.g. the Bible) and which come directly from people's experience?

Revealed theology: The God of Abraham, Isaac and Jacob

I am ... the God of Abraham, the God of Isaac and the God of Jacob.
Exodus 3:6

God of Abraham, God of Isaac, God of Jacob, not the God of the philosophers and scholars.
Pascal, unpublished note

In a note found after his death, the seventeenth-century mathematician and philosopher Blaise Pascal distinguishes between 'the God of the philosophers' and the 'God of Abraham, Isaac and Jacob' as revealed in the Bible. The implication of Pascal's words is that if we seek to know and experience God then we should turn to the Bible, and not to those religious philosophers who go far beyond the Bible in their quest to understand God. We shall see in the pages that follow how different the 'God of the philosophers' is from the 'God of Abraham'; and a question that believers might need to ask is, 'Is the God of the philosophers the God whom I actually worship?'

Natural theology: The God of the philosophers

... one God, who is the author of this whole universe ... immaterial ... incorruptible ... who is, in fact, our source, our light, our good.[2]

St Augustine

God is that, than which nothing greater can be conceived.[3]

St Anselm

By the word 'God' I mean a substance that is infinite, independent, supremely intelligent, supremely powerful, and the Creator of myself and anything else that may exist.[4]

René Descartes

> *A person without a body, present everywhere, the creator and sustainer of the universe, able to do everything, knowing all things, perfectly good … immutable, eternal, a necessary being, and worthy of worship.*[5]
>
> **Richard Swinburne**

Pascal thought that God was infinitely beyond our comprehension, and he wondered who would dare to think they could know what he was or whether he existed.[6] Despite this, philosophers down the centuries *have* dared to imagine they could tell us something specific about the nature of God, and the quotations above, which span over 1500 years of religious philosophy, are representative of the theistic philosophical tradition. What all these quotations emphasise is God's greatness and perfection. For these philosophers, God is the most perfect and greatest of beings and hence he is supremely good, knowing and powerful; he cannot change and is eternal. At the same time he is the source of all other beings: the creator of the universe.

Attributes of God

Here we examine in more detail some of the characteristics that philosophers have ascribed to God, and some of the issues that arise from claiming that God has these characteristics. These concepts have taken on technical philosophical meaning that has become part of the language of the philosophy of religion: but we should remember that these concepts have their origin both in the work of pre-Christian philosophers such as Plato and Aristotle, as well as in the Bible. Because the writings of philosophers of religion, working in a Christian tradition, can sometimes seem very far removed from the original 'revealed' texts, we have taken care to locate the origin of these concept in specific quotations from the Bible. The attributes of God that we examine here are:

- God as omnipotent
- God as omniscient
- God as supremely good
- God as either eternal or everlasting
- God as either immanent or transcendent
- God as immutable.

God as omnipotent: his infinite power

The God of Abraham was able to do anything; this is the message behind the countless examples in the Bible of what God could and did do: 'He will not grow tired or weary, and his understanding no one can fathom. He gives strength to the weary and increases the power of the weak' (Isaiah 40:28–30); 'With God all things are possible' (Matthew 19:26); 'For with God nothing is impossible' (Luke 1:37). The power of God to do anything has been termed 'omnipotence' by philosophers (from the Latin '*omni*', meaning 'all', and '*potens*', meaning 'power') and it takes a central position in God's perfection. But there has long been a question mark over the meaning of omnipotence; can God do literally anything?

There are various ways in which we can try to understand the claim that God is omnipotent. The most obvious, yet most problematic, analysis is the simple statement that:

a) *God can do anything.*

Religious philosophers such as St Thomas Aquinas grappled with the concept of omnipotence hundreds of years ago, attempting to articulate it in a coherent way. When Aquinas asks, 'Is God omnipotent?'[7] he finds an immediate difficulty as all things can be moved and acted upon, yet God is changeless ('immutable') and so there is something God can't do: namely change. There are other, related, problems with formulation a), and in *Summa Contra Gentiles 2:25* Aquinas provides a long list of things that God can't do; for example, he cannot alter what has already happened, or force us to choose something freely (see below page 200). Many theologians agree with Aquinas that God cannot change the laws of mathematics (he cannot, for example, make 2 + 3 = 6), or do what is self-contradictory, such as make something exist *and* not exist at the same time, or make something both totally black *and* totally white at the same time. These examples, and others, have led theologians to amend a) to the more qualified claim that 'If it can be done then God can do it', or more formally:

b) *God can do anything which is logically possible.*

anthology
2.25

But even this isn't quite the right formulation, as there are some things that believers agree God cannot do, even though they are logically possible. For example, Aquinas asks whether God can create anything evil, and his reply is no; God cannot sin. Now sinning isn't logically impossible, yet theologians would agree with Aquinas that God is not able to sin. Nor can God act in any other way that goes against his fundamental nature, or which contradicts the other aspects of his perfection (such as his omniscience or immutability). So, as part of an even more nuanced account of omnipotence, religious philosophers have been prepared to offer further modification to their understanding of God's omnipotence:

c) *God can do anything which it is logically possible and which doesn't limit his power.*

Theologians, then, have developed a more sophisticated understanding of omnipotence, and one that works alongside other essential perfections of God. But ATHEISTS, such as J.L. Mackie,[8] still return to the problem, eagerly pointing out the incoherence of the concept of omnipotence, and hence the incoherence of the idea of God. In the pages below (192–195), we return to some of the main problems emerging from the claim that God is omnipotent when we examine what Mackie calls the 'paradox of omnipotence'. This includes the paradox of the stone (can God create a stone so large that he cannot later move it?) and the paradox of human free will (can God create a being that he later has no control over?).

God as omniscient: his infinite knowledge

By the nature of their profession, philosophers place a high value on knowledge, and we shouldn't be surprised to find that religious philosophers consider perfect knowledge to be an aspect of God's perfection. As with omnipotence, God's omniscience (from the Latin 'omni', meaning 'all', and 'scientia', meaning 'knowing') is illustrated in the Bible by examples, rather than stated explicitly. Psalm 139:4 tells us that 'even before a word is on my tongue, O Lord, thou knowest it altogether' and Hebrews 4:13 says 'nothing in all creation is hidden from God's sight. Everything is uncovered and laid bare before the eyes of him.' However, in some parts of the Bible God's knowledge does not seem to extend so far: 'But the Lord God called to the Man [Adam] and said to him "Where are you"?' (Genesis 3:9).

Philosophers are interested in how far God's omniscience extends. Is God's knowledge only propositional, meaning it involves 'knowing that ...' something is true, such as knowing that the world will come to an end in the year 2020, or that Adam has eaten forbidden fruit? Does it involve having practical knowledge of how to do things, such as how to ride a bike or create human beings out of clay? If God is INCORPOREAL (that is, he lacks a body) or transcendent (that is, existing outside the universe), then it does not make sense to say that God knows how to engage in physical activity, although a theologian might wish to say that God knows the full set of truths about the activity.[9] Other questions we might wish to ask are 'Can God know what it is logically impossible to know, for example the area of a round square?' and 'Does God know what I'm freely about to do?' We examine the problem of free will and omniscience on pages 199–200.

A more recent philosophical problem with omniscience was identified by Norman Kretzmann (1928–1998) who argued in his paper 'Omniscience and Immutability' that there is a contradiction inherent in the claim that a perfect being can be both all-knowing and unchanging (immutable). His argument is broadly this:

anthology
2.26

1 God isn't subject to change.
2 God knows everything.
3 A being that knows everything, also knows everything in time (that is, in this, our changing world).

4 A being that knows things in time is subject to change.

5 Therefore God is subject to change – which contradicts point 1 above.

For Kretzmann this problem is highly damaging to the concept of a perfect being, and he controversially suggests that it proves there can be no such thing as a perfect being (that is, of God). Kretzmann goes on to consider some of the objections to his argument, but he focuses on those objections to statement 4, which is the claim that if God knows everything, and he knows what is going on the changing world, and he knows what is going on in our heads as we change our beliefs in this changing world, then what God knows is changing too. For example, if I know how tall a building is, and then someone adds a mast to it, then what I know has changed. If God knows everything, including what I know, then his knowledge has changed too.

In order to defend the concept of omniscience against attacks such as these, Kretzmann considers the possibility that 'omniscience' may be refined in the same way that philosophers have refined the concept of omnipotence. We saw above how it is now accepted that omnipotence does not just broadly mean 'can do anything' but that it is now better understood by theologians to mean 'can do anything which it is logically possible for God to do'. This modified explication of omnipotence rules out God having the power to do things that are logically impossible, and even rules out, perhaps, God having the power to do things which then place limits on his power (we explore this idea below in the paradox of the stone). The believer might then argue that we should try to understand omniscience within similar parameters: so, instead of stating 'God knows everything', statement 2 could be amended as follows:

2a) *God knows everything which it is logically possible for God to know and which doesn't limit his knowledge.*

If this amendment is successful, then the remaining parts of Kretzmann's argument wouldn't follow (God could still be OMNISCIENT, in the revised sense, while not knowing things that would cause him to change). However, Kretzmann does not think that these refinements help avoid the criticism that he has aimed at omniscience. The first part of 2a) states that God only knows what it is logically possible to know, but for Kretzmann that adds nothing to our understanding of omniscience: knowledge (as we saw on pages 64–65) is of things that are true, and logically impossible things are not true, so *of course* God can only know what is logically possible. What about the second part of 2a)? We saw that it appeared possible to imagine God using his power to limit his power, hence the broad acceptance that omnipotence excludes those things. But Kretzmann says that we can't think of anything that God could know that might limit his knowledge; knowledge of things isn't limiting in the way that power is. There are a number of ways in which I can use my power to limit future use of my power (for example I could lock myself up, or chop my hands off, or row to a desert island and burn my boat). But according to Kretzmann there are no ways in which my knowing something can limit my future knowledge. So Kretzmann concludes that defences of the sort proposed in 2a) do not work against his argument, and his argument against omniscience still stands.

God as benevolent: his supreme goodness

There are several ways in which philosophers have understood God's supreme goodness (also referred to as his omnibenevolence, or simply 'benevolence'). One approach emphasises the account of God's goodness that is found in the Bible, which highlights his love for his creation and in particular for human beings; a second approach interprets God's goodness as a type of perfection, influenced by the philosophy of Plato and Aristotle; the third way stresses God's goodness in a moral sense, as the source of all value. These three, and other, approaches are not incompatible, but looking at each of them in turn will help us to understand the different facets of God's supreme goodness.

'O give thanks to the Lord, for he is good, for his steadfast love endures for ever' (Psalm 106:1, and 107, 117, 118, 136, and so on). In the Bible, God's benevolence (from the Latin 'bene', meaning 'good', and 'volens', meaning 'will') is recognisable and familiar to humans. In the Old Testament it is a goodness full of passion, based on righteousness, but carrying with it the consequence of angry retribution to those who disobey him. However, in the New Testament, God's goodness becomes focused through the expression of love and mercy: 'God so loved the world that he gave his one and only Son' (John 3:16); '[God's] mercy extends to those who fear him' (Luke 1:50). It is these more personal aspects of goodness that ordinary, non-philosophical, believers may think about when discussing God's goodness. However, theologians themselves have also drawn attention to God's supreme goodness as exemplified through his love. When we come to examine the problem of evil (on page 291) we shall see that one of the reasons why the problem arises is because of the claim that God is loving (why would a loving God allow his creation to include so much pain and suffering?), but paradoxically one of the solutions to the problem of evil also depends upon seeing God as a God of Love[10] who cares deeply about his creation.

You are only one supreme good, altogether sufficient unto Yourself, needing nothing else but needed by all else in order to exist and to fare well.

St Anselm, *Prosolgion* 22

The account of God's goodness provided by religious philosophers such as St Anselm is more abstract and less personal, and influenced by the two giants of ancient Greek philosophy, Plato and Aristotle. Theologians such as Aquinas (who follow Aristotle's philosophy) view goodness as a form of perfection, meaning that there is no flaw or deficiency and that all the necessary qualities are present. On a mundane level when we say (in Aristotle's sense) that an athlete is good, we are commenting on the level of skill, speed, stamina, strength and other qualities that athletes need to have for high performance. In this sense God's goodness is not just an extra characteristic (to be added to the list, like omniscience or omnipotence), but it is the single property that includes all those other essential characteristics that make God perfect. So saying that God is supremely good is a way of capturing how complete and perfect God is, containing all the attributes (such as those described by Descartes above on page 180) necessary for perfection.

Some philosophers have emphasised the ethical aspects of God's goodness: God is the moral standard and the origin of all moral goodness. On this interpretation God's supreme goodness is seen as the source of all goodness, just as Plato's form of the good is the source for all the other forms. According to philosophers like St Augustine, God's goodness filters down through all of his creation, but all goodness has its origins in God: 'this thing is good and that good, but take away this and that, and regard good itself if you can: so you will see God … the good of all good'.[11] However, there is a problem that arises if God is seen to be the source of all moral goodness – this is known as the EUTHYPHRO DILEMMA, and we examine it on pages 195–199. In its narrower sense God's goodness could also refer to God's own moral character, and is exemplified in his love, his justice and his wisdom. Even the Bible (in the Book of Job) recognises that God's benevolence has to be reconciled in some way with the horrific pain and suffering that exists in this world and we revisit this in our examination of the problem of evil on page 291.

God as eternal or everlasting: His relation to time

You were not, therefore, yesterday, nor will You be tomorrow, but yesterday and today and tomorrow You are.[12]

St Anselm

What is God's relationship to time? The traditional view, drawn from both the philosophy of Plato and Aristotle, together with certain aspects of the Bible, is that God is eternal. In other words, God exists outside of time, he is timeless, he is ATEMPORAL. But there is an alternative, modern, understanding of God's relation with time, which is that God is not eternal (existing outside of time) but that he is everlasting (existing in time). We shall first look at the traditional view, that God is eternal.

The passage from St Anselm, above, goes on to say that God does not exist yesterday, or today or tomorrow, for these are in time and yet God is absolutely outside of time. Support for the view that God is timeless and eternal can be drawn from the opening chapters of the Bible: God in his capacity as creator of the universe (Genesis 1:1–5) must exist outside of the universe in order to create it. So as the universe consists of space and time, God must exist outside of space and time: 'The one who is high and lifted up, who inhabits eternity, whose name is Holy' (Isaiah 57:15). Support can also be found in the philosophy of Plato, who proposed the existence of a world of perfect 'forms', which existed beyond this world and which was outside of time. So the Platonic idea of perfect things being timeless already existed prior to Christian thinking and philosophers such as Augustine, Aquinas and Anselm absorbed this idea, explicitly or implicitly, into their understanding of God's perfection.

What does it mean to be eternal, or timeless? Aquinas illustrates how this might be possible by describing the perspectives of two people, one travelling along a busy road, and the other on a hill watching the travellers below. The person on the road cannot see all those people behind him, but the observer on the hill can see everyone simultaneously.[13] In a similar way, all of time is simultaneously present to a timeless God (see **Figure 2.1**). This timeless or eternal aspect of God mirrors God's position as a transcendent being, existing beyond the universe. Aquinas elsewhere offers another analogy which might also help us understand the difference between eternity and time. An hour, he writes, is part of a day and both can exist simultaneously; in the same way time is a part of eternity, except eternity both exceeds and contains time.

If neither of Aquinas' analogies helps us to imagine what 'seeing time' from the perspective of a timeless being might be like, then this is probably because we have a completely different, and limited, experience of time. The novelist Kurt Vonnegut tries to describe what it might be like to see the world from outside of time in his novel *Slaughterhouse 5*. The Tralfmadorians, a super-intelligent and advanced alien species from the planet Tralfmadore, see the past, present and future simultaneously, and they find it difficult to understand what it must be like to see time in the limited, sequential way that Billy Pilgrim experiences it (Billy is a human whom they've kidnapped for their zoo). This is how the Tralfmadorian guide tries to explain the difference to the visitors at the zoo:

> The guide invited the crowd to imagine that they [the Tralfmadorians] were looking across a desert at a mountain range on a day that was twinkling bright and clear. They could look at a peak or a bird or a cloud, at a stone right in front of them … But among them was this poor Earthling and his head was encased in a steel sphere.
>
> … There was only one eyehole through which he could look, and welded to that eyehole was six feet of pipe … He was also strapped to a flatcar on rails, and there was no way he could turn his head or touch the pipe … Whatever poor Billy saw through the pipe, he had no choice but to say to himself, 'That's life.'[14]

Figure 2.1 God is outside of time.

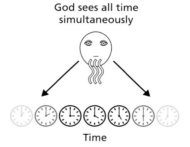

God sees all time simultaneously

Time

There is a growing modern tradition that queries the classical view that God is eternal, and looks to an alternative understanding of God's relationship with time. This new approach is perhaps more in keeping with the layperson's understanding of God and how he interacts with his creation. The contemporary philosopher Nicholas Wolterstorff (1932–) suggests that an eternal God, existing outside of time, undermines the account of God in the Bible and renders the Bible false or at best a long series of metaphors.[15] After all, if God is eternal, and exists out of time, then it does not seem possible for him to act in the world, for example through miracles, or when communicating with prophets. Most importantly, from a Christian perspective, theists do not believe that God created the world and then removed himself from it. Instead, a Christian God is understood to be a redeeming God, one who is aware of the pain and suffering in the world and one who set about giving humans the opportunity for redemption through the life, then death, then the resurrection of

Jesus. On this account, then, God, at least for a time, was very much in the world (he is 'IMMANENT' as we see below) but if that is the case then is he also 'in' time?

Throughout the Old Testament, God is described as without a beginning and without an end (Genesis 21:33, Deuteronomy 33:27, Isaiah 57:15) and, although this is consistent with God being eternal, it is also consistent with the alternative interpretation – namely that God is everlasting. 'Before the mountains were born or you brought forth the earth and the world, from everlasting to everlasting you are God' (Psalm 90:2). In this sense God has always existed, and always will, but he is not eternal (existing outside of time) but is instead everlasting, living alongside and through his creation. An everlasting God is one who, for Christians at least, is more obviously capable of a personal relationship with humans and of love for them and the world.

Criticism

There is a question, though, of whether thinking of God as everlasting (rather than eternal) limits God's knowledge and undermines his omniscience and omnipotence. Unless God existed outside of time he could not have created time (this is one of Augustine's arguments for God's timelessness[16]), in which case God cannot be omnipotent. But if God exists in time, as an everlasting God, then this suggests he does not know what is on the horizon, as it simply has not happened yet, in which case God cannot be omniscient.

God as immanent or transcendent: his relation to space

Learn More

The writers of the Bible proclaim God both as the creator of the world and as having a personal relationship with this creation: both transcendent – a term which means going beyond, or existing outside of, a limit or boundary – and immanent.

God's immanence from a Christian perspective is not the same as immanence as it may be understood in other religions, because it is specifically attached to God's being in the world and suffering through (and in) his son Jesus. The belief that God is in the world throughout his creation, held for example by the philosopher Spinoza, is often known as pantheism and this has long been held to be a heretical view within Christianity.

Criticism

To a non-believer these two attributes (transcendence and immanence) seem mutually contradictory – both cannot be ascribed to one being – and so one or the other must be given up. If theists give up the belief that God is immanent, then they become deists (holding the belief that God is an impersonal creator); if they give up their belief that God is transcendent then they will become pantheists (holding the belief that God is the world and no more).

Learn More

God as immutable: his unchanging nature

The term 'immutable' is used to refer to things that never change, and cannot change. Immutability is more difficult to understand than God's goodness, power or knowledge, because there is nothing analogous to it in our usual understanding of a person. The concept may make more sense when we consider that change only occurs in things that can be divided up into 'parts'. So, for example, people are made up of many different parts, both mentally and physically, and these parts change (for example through getting older, or through injury). But God does not have any parts either in space (God does not have a body; he is incorporeal) or in time (God does not exist over different periods of time; he is eternal). Because God is not made up of parts, and because he is perfect, he cannot change and does not need to change: he is immutable.

Figure 2.2 All God's attributes are one.

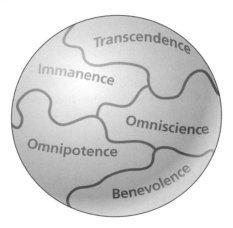

Issues with claiming that God has these attributes

Are God's attributes coherent?

We have now looked at the main characteristics of God and sketched some of the problems with these attributes. Several of the issues clustered around each attribute emerge because they don't exist in isolation, but sit alongside other aspects of God's perfection. Once the characteristics are combined with each other then further contradictions start to emerge, and the question arises as to whether the concept of God, as delineated by these eight or so characteristics, is really a coherent concept. Here we examine in more detail some of the challenges that most threaten the coherence of the concept of God. The problems that we look at are:

- Issues arising from God's omnipotence: the paradox of the stone.
- Issues arising from God's supreme goodness: the Euthyphro dilemma.

- Issues arising from God's omniscience: the compatibility of God's foreknowledge and human freedom.
- Issues arising from God's omnipotence, omniscience and supreme goodness: the problem of evil.

The idea of 'compossibility' may be helpful in this context: it is taken from the philosophy of Gottfried Wilhelm von Leibniz (1646–1716) and it captures the idea that a number of things (or people, or attributes) can exist as possibilities alongside each other, at exactly the same time, without giving rise to any contradictions.[17] The question is: are God's attributes compossible; in other words, can all these perfections co-exist in the same being at once? **Figure 2.3** below shows which attributes, when combined, lead to inconsistencies or contradictions that need to be addressed by the believer. (Obviously these inconsistencies are not a concern for atheists, and can be seen as further evidence that 'God' is not a term that refers to anything in, or out of, the universe.)

► **ACTIVITY**

In the left-hand column below are some of the properties attributed to God by believers; in the right-hand column are properties attributed to the universe by believers.

1 Try to think up as many potential problems with the concept of God as you can by combining properties from either column (e.g. 2 and D). You may find that a single property is problematic in itself or you may combine three or four properties together to create a problem.
2 How might a believer go about resolving these problems?

Properties of God	Properties of the universe
1 God is omnipotent	a) Evil exists in the world
2 God is omniscient	b) Humans have free will
3 God is omnipresent	c) There is evidence of God in the world
4 God is supremely good	d) Humans can have private thoughts
5 God is beyond understanding	e) God intervenes in the world
6 God has free will	f) The universe is governed by physical laws
7 God defines morality	g) The universe exists in space and time
8 God is outside of time	
9 God acts morally	
10 God is immaterial	

	OMNISCIENCE	OMNIPOTENCE	BENEVOLENCE	TRANSCENDENCE	IMMANENCE	ETERNAL	EVERLASTING
OMNISCIENCE	–	–	Problem of evil	Problem of free will	Inconsistent (If God has knowledge of the world he must change.)	Problem of free will	Inconsistent (If God is in time then how can he know the future?)
	OMNIPOTENCE	Problem of omnipotence	Problem of evil	Problem of divine action	Problem of creation	Problem of divine action	Problem of creation
		BENEVOLENCE	Euthyphro Dilemma	Problem of divine action	Inconsistent (If God is in the world then he is in evil.)	–	–
			TRANSCENDENCE	–	Inconsistent (God can't be both in and out of the world.)	–	Inconsistent (If God is outside the world then he is outside of time.)
				IMMANENCE	–	Inconsistent (If God is in the world then he is not eternal.)	–
					ETERNAL	–	Inconsistent (God can't be both in and out of time.)
						EVERLASTING	–

Figure 2.3 Some of the problems associated with the attributes of God.

Issues arising from God's omnipotence: the paradox of the stone

Here we examine in more detail one of the issues with the concept of omnipotence that we have already briefly discussed. The type of question a sceptic might ask about the idea of an all-powerful being is, 'Can such a being create a round square?', or 'Can they make 2 + 2 = 5?' We know that theologians are happy to concede that saying 'God is omnipotent' does not mean that 'God can do anything'; God could still be described as omnipotent, even though he is not able to perform acts that are self-contradictory or logically impossible. Both believers (such as Aquinas) and atheists (such as J.L. Mackie[18]) accept that omnipotence as a concept can be amended along the lines suggested above (page 182) to make it more coherent.

However, there is a more damaging issue that can be found in the idea of omnipotence, and this is the problem of whether an omnipotent being can use its powers to do something that will limit these powers. For example, can God create a stone so large that he cannot move it? This is known as the paradox of the stone, and an early version of this can be found in the work of the medieval Islamic philosopher known as Averroes (also known as Ibn Rushd, 1126–1198). Sceptics and atheists argue that the paradox of the stone is a strong indicator that the concept of 'omnipotence' is incoherent and therefore the whole concept of God is undermined.

George Mavrodes gives a more recent version of the paradox, together with his defence of omnipotence. His version starts with the question 'Can God create a stone too heavy for him to lift it?'[19] This question poses a dilemma for the believer, as it seems to offer two choices, both of which undermine the claim that God is omnipotent. The first choice is to say that God can create such an unliftable stone, in which case there is something God cannot do (that is, lift such a stone) and he is not omnipotent. The second choice would be to say that God cannot create such a stone, in this case there is also something God cannot do (that is create such a stone) and he is not omnipotent. So either way there is something an omnipotent being cannot do. The sceptic is likely to conclude that this is because 'omnipotence' is an incoherent concept, and if so then omnipotence isn't a possible attribute of any being, not even God.

anthology
2.27

However, Mavrodes thinks that this dilemma fails to undermine the notion of God's omnipotence (in a similar way that not being able to create a round square, and other self-contradictory tasks, also fail to undermine it). His defence explores two possibilities: the possibility that God *is not* omnipotent (which we can call assumption 1) and the possibility that he *is* (assumption 2). Let us look at assumption 1 and apply this to the paradox. If we assume that God *is not* omnipotent then the dilemma simply tells us that a being that isn't omnipotent cannot do certain things (that is, lift a certain stone, or create a certain stone). But this, Mavrodes points out, is a trivial conclusion: if someone is not omnipotent then of course their powers are limited. So the dilemma is insignificant on the basis of assumption 1. He goes on to explore assumption 2: what follows if we assume that God *is* omnipotent, and is a being with the power to do anything (including lift anything)? In which case the original question 'Can God create a stone too heavy for him to lift?' becomes 'Can a being whose power is sufficient to lift anything create a stone which cannot be lifted by him?'

For Mavrodes this clarification, based on the assumption that God is omnipotent, reveals the task to be a self-contradictory task. Now we have already seen that it is generally agreed that omnipotent beings are not limited in their power by not being able to do self-contradictory things. This takes us back to Aquinas' point that 'It is more appropriate to say that such things cannot be done,

Criticism

Another recent philosopher, C. Wade Savage, has argued that the solution proposed by Mavrodes is wrongheaded, and Savage offers a better solution to the paradox.[21] Savage suggests that Mavrodes has presented a version of the paradox (which Savage calls version A) that aims to prove that 'God is not omnipotent'. Proceeding in the way that Mavrodes does will quickly lead to the conclusion that this paradox misses its mark – because assumption 2 asks us to assume that God is omnipotent, and it obviously (and even trivially) then follows, as Mavrodes says, that the task is self-contradictory. But for Savage, version A is not really the main problem, and Mavrodes has been led astray by attacking this version. The paradox of the stone, according to Savage, is not trying to show that 'God is not omnipotent', but instead it is aiming to prove that 'the concept of an omnipotent being is logically inconsistent' and therefore that the existence of an omnipotent being is logically impossible.

Version B, as outlined by Savage, is very general and carefully avoids any reference to 'God'. It begins by offering two possibilities: the first is that a being (X) can create a stone which X cannot lift; the second is that X *cannot* create a stone which X cannot lift. In the first case, X cannot do something (lift the stone) and in the second case X cannot do something (create the stone) and therefore there is at least one thing X cannot do. But if X is omnipotent then X can do anything. Savage then concludes at the end of version B that X is not omnipotent, and that the existence of an omnipotent being is logically impossible. So it is version B that really needs to be addressed if believers wish to show that existence of God is not logically impossible.

Savage argues that the weakness in the paradox lies in the claim that 'if X cannot create a stone which X cannot lift therefore *there is a task which X cannot do (i.e. create the stone)'*. Savage does not believe that the *second* part of this claim (in *italics*) follows from the first part of this claim; and if he is correct then the rest of the paradox falls apart. His argument is a subtle one, but he asks us to imagine two beings, X and Y. X makes stones and Y lifts stones (it's a boring job, but somebody has to do it). Let us assume that Y can only lift stones that are up to 70lbs. In which case if X cannot create a stone that Y cannot lift (that is, more than 70lbs) then X really does have a limitation on his power. Let us now assume that Y is omnipotent. X can create stones that are 70lbs, 700lbs, 7000lbs, 7 billion trillion lbs, and so on, but every stone that X makes Y can actually lift. Savage argues that the fact that X cannot create a stone that Y cannot lift *does not mean that X's power is limited*.

> If X can create stones of any poundage, and Y can lift stones of any poundage, then X cannot create a stone which Y cannot lift, and yet X is not thereby limited in power.[22]

The next step that Savage takes is to say that this conclusion holds true even if X and Y are the same person. In which case the fact that X cannot create a stone that X cannot lift does not mean that X is limited in power – and omnipotence is not a logically incoherent concept. Savage concludes that the two possibilities put forward by the paradox are nothing more than the consequences of these two facets (being able to create anything, and being able to lift anything) of God's omnipotence.

anthology 2.28

than that God cannot do them.'[20] And so Mavrodes concludes that the paradox of the stone proposes a limitation (not being able to lift unliftable stones) that turns out to be no limitation at all, and the doctrine of God's omnipotence remains unaffected by this paradox.

The paradox of the stone may seem a trivial, if logically engaging, paradox, but it is essential to philosophers of religion that God's perfections are defended and clarified against such logical attacks. But the atheist may ask other, related, questions which are not trivial and do get to the heart of what it is to believe in God. The question 'Can an omnipotent God create something that later he will have no control over?' can be focused on whether God can create a being with genuine free will. This is a more serious problem for the believer since it touches on our own nature and our relationship to God. If God is truly all-powerful, then surely we would not have any power over our own actions. Everything would be under his control. On the other hand, if he were truly all-powerful he should be able to give us power over our own actions. So, once again, either way there is a limitation on his power. We explore further the idea of human free will in relation to God below on page 199.

Issues arising from God's supreme goodness: the Euthyphro dilemma

The usual format for Plato's philosophy was his dramatic dialogues in which his characters, led by Socrates, tried to define and explain a big philosophical idea: justice, love, ethics, courage, knowledge, the soul. The *Euthyphro*, which is one of Plato's earlier dialogues, is no different and it starts with two characters, Euthyphro and Socrates, engaged in conversation at an Athenian court. They quickly turn to the topic of piety, or holiness, as Euthyphro is prosecuting his father for manslaughter (his father allowed a slave to die) and he is very confident that he is doing the right thing and is acting piously. Socrates is surprised at the confidence Euthyphro shows in claiming to know what piety is; after all, piety has a close connection with the rules laid down by God (or gods), and is not easily known. Moreover, Socrates himself is at the court because he is being charged with impiety for corrupting the young people of Athens through his philosophical ideas and debates (a charge on which he would eventually be found guilty and executed). So Socrates engages Euthyphro in a philosophical discussion about what piety is, saying that it will help him in his own court defence.

As is the case in several of Plato's dialogues, Socrates' proffered ignorance of the topic under discussion is a method for revealing that the person who is so certain, and confident in their knowledge of the topic, is actually the ignorant one. And this is true here, as each definition of piety that Euthyphro offers falls apart when Socrates starts to analyse it. Euthyphro's first definition of piety is only an example, not a definition, as Socrates points out. In his second definition Euthyphro says that piety is what is pleasing to the gods, what they love; but Socrates rightly shows that the gods are divided among themselves about what pleases them, and so the same action might be considered both pious and impious according to this definition. Moving towards a third definition, Euthyphro proposes that piety means those things that *all* the gods love, and impiety is what all the gods hate. It is here that Socrates first poses the question that underpins the Euthyphro dilemma:

> *The point which I should first wish to understand is whether the pious (or holy) is beloved by the gods because it is holy, or holy because it is beloved of the gods.*
>
> Plato, *Euthyphro*, 10a

anthology 2.29

We can clarify Socrates' question here: he is asking whether God loves what is pious (good actions) because it good; or whether the action is good because it is loved by God. So is goodness separate from God (the first option) or is goodness defined by God (the second option)? Socrates points out that these cannot both be true, because if they were then we would arrive at a circular argument: 'The gods love what is good; and what is good? ... It is what the gods love.' At this point both Socrates and Euthyphro agree that the gods love what is pious (good actions) because they are pious; and in agreeing this Euthyphro is being forced to move away from the position that the gods are the most important thing when it comes to morality. We should not be surprised by this as Plato went on to propose in his later dialogues the existence of an external, objective realm, the world of 'forms', which was also the source of universal moral values.

But Socrates' question poses a dilemma that has taken on a significance beyond the one intended by Plato in his original dialogue, and this remains known as the Euthyphro dilemma. Let us now try to understand the Euthyphro dilemma in terms that give it relevance to the philosophy of religion. We have seen that Euthyphro attempts to define morality (piety) as that which is the will of the gods, or, in his phrase, that which is 'dear to God' or 'loved by the gods'. Socrates then raises the question of whether everything that the gods will, or command, must therefore be moral, or whether everything the gods command is 'moral' because they are following some external moral authority. The two choices identified by Socrates form a dilemma because they offer two equally unpalatable options to a theist:

1 Every action that God commands us to do (even cruel and despicable ones) is good.
2 Every action that God commands us to do is good because it accords with some other moral authority.

| God's commands are good simply because they come from God |  | God's commands are good because they conform to an external moral source | **Figure 2.4** The two horns of the Euthyphro dilemma. |

Let us examine the consequences of following each option, or horn, of the dilemma.

The first 'horn'

The first option assumes that God is the source and standard of all moral goodness, and that whatever he commands will automatically be good. So God could command us to do completely trivial things (such as not stepping on the cracks in the pavement) and these would be morally good. God could even command us to perform cruel, dishonest or unjust acts, which run counter to our moral intuitions. But, according to this interpretation of God's goodness, a believer would be obliged to do these things and they would be morally right because God had commanded them. It is possible to find many examples in the Old Testament of God's commands that seem to us to be morally questionable; for example, the command to Moses to commit acts of genocide while on the journey to Canaan (Deuteronomy 3:2; Numbers 31), or the command given to Abraham to sacrifice his own son Isaac:

God tested Abraham and said to him 'Abraham ... Take your son, your only son Isaac whom you love, and go to the land of Moriah and offer him there as a burnt offering.'

Genesis 22:2

Earlier on in Plato's original dialogue, Socrates asks Euthyphro why we should worship a God who could command us to do horrific acts. But this horn of the dilemma, that is, this interpretation of God's goodness, forces us into a position where any act, however terrible, is good when it is commanded by God. This is a conclusion we might wish to avoid; as Job says:

It is unthinkable that God would do wrong, that the Almighty would pervert justice.

Job 34:12

Criticism

However, Søren Kierkegaard (1813–1855) is quite prepared to accept that God may tell us to commit acts that require us to suspend our ethical beliefs, and that we would be obliged to carry out those acts. In *Fear and Trembling*, Kierkegaard defends Abraham's decision to kill his son, on the grounds that God has commanded it as proof of his faith.[23] In doing so Kierkegaard challenges the assumption that ethical values should be placed above all other values. For Kierkegaard there is a higher value, known only by God, and yet we must have faith in God's will if he commands us to perform an apparently unethical act. Such faith cannot be rationally explained, nor supported by evidence, yet faith may, in some situations, require the suspension of our ethical beliefs. It was just so with Abraham: he was, as Kierkegaard says, a 'knight of faith' and was prepared to murder his own son in the faith that he was doing it for some higher purpose or '*telos*'. Kierkegaard refers to this as the 'teleological suspension of the ethical', where the will of God comes above mere ethics.

But Kierkegaard's position is also one that many believers would be uncomfortable with. Both Aquinas and St Augustine believed that God cannot will evil because he is perfectly good, in an ethical sense. It seems tempting to reject an account of moral goodness which implies that God could tell us to do anything and it would by definition be good. In which case, what makes God's commands good?

The first horn of the dilemma throws doubt onto what we could mean by saying God is supremely good. If goodness simply means 'whatever God wills' then saying 'God is good' simply means 'God does whatever God himself wills', which seems to empty the concept of goodness of any meaning. Perhaps we should look to the second horn of the dilemma to better understand God's goodness.

The second 'horn'

We saw in **Figure 2.4** that there is a second option, which is the preferred choice of Plato, which states that goodness exists independently of God's will. In this case what makes God good, and everything he says or wills or commands good, is that these conform to some external moral authority. In this case God does not issue commands which then automatically become 'good'; instead God issues commands which are good only insofar as they comply with a moral code that lies beyond God. This approach conforms with Plato's metaphysical theory of forms in which the 'good' has an objective reality discoverable by reason. Philosophers would say that if we agree with the second option then we believe that morality has an objective status, and we would be referred to as realists or cognitivists about religious statements (see page 318 below). However, for the traditional theist this is a problematic way of accounting for the goodness of God's commands, and it raises a number of other issues:

- Objective morality does not need God. For if moral goodness lies beyond God then we can bypass God if we wish to be moral. In this case God's status as a being worthy of worship is undermined here: why should we worship a God who is bound by the same independent moral rules as ourselves?

- Objective morality limits God's power. If there is a moral law that exists independently of God then God cannot change this and determine for himself what is good and what is bad. His omnipotence is being called into question here, and God cannot command us to do what is morally wrong (for example, instruct Abraham to sacrifice Isaac) and by commanding it make it right.
- Objective morality defines God's benevolence. When we assert that God is supremely good, we are referring to an independent set of moral standards that God conforms to. So isn't it the case that it is those moral standards that are *supremely* good, and not God?

For these reasons, and others, the second horn of the dilemma seems as unacceptable as the first horn for many believers. Plato's dilemma, first proposed in a dialogue over two thousand years ago, remains very much a live issue within the philosophy of religion.

Criticism

However, both horns of the dilemma may be avoided by philosophers who do not locate goodness either in God's will or in God's commands. An alternative theological account of moral goodness can be found in Aquinas' Natural Law ethics. This moral philosophy originates in Aristotle (Aquinas made it his life's work to reconcile Aristotle's philosophy with Christian THEOLOGY) and it sees goodness as related to being good *at* something, or good *for* something. This TELEOLOGICAL account of morality looks to function and purpose in order to understand what is good. Aquinas adds to Aristotle's theory by arguing that a universe created by God, and everything in it, will have a function and purpose and it is up to us to determine what these Natural Laws are and then strive to reach our 'good'.

If Aquinas' approach works (and as always in philosophy there are many criticisms that can be made of it) then it avoids the first horn of the Euthyphro dilemma. Having created the world, in line with the Natural Law, God cannot now just arbitrarily 'decide' what is good or bad, as our nature and function (and hence what is good) have already been determined. Aquinas' theory leans towards the second horn of the dilemma by agreeing that the Natural Law is objective, but that it flows from God's omnibenevolent nature. In this way it avoids the claim that morality must exist independently of God.

Issues arising from God's omniscience and human free will

We have already looked at one of the problems that arises from claiming that God is omniscient (see above, page 183). How can we maintain that God knows things in time, when things in time change and so God's knowledge changes, while also maintaining that God is unchangeable (immutable)? Here we look more closely at another issue that emerges from God's omniscience. How can we reconcile God's omniscience with human free will? If God really knows everything, then it seems as if he must know the future, and, in particular, he must know what choices we are going to make. But if God knows what action I will perform before I decide to do it, then I cannot have chosen to do otherwise than I did. But if we cannot choose otherwise, then the actions we appear to choose are not really freely chosen at all. I may feel as though I freely choose to do some philosophy rather than watch a movie, but God knew all along that I would do some philosophy. I couldn't have done otherwise than 'choose' philosophy, and so, it seems, this choice was predetermined. It follows that the feeling of free choice is just an illusion.

Antony Kenny puts forward the problem by asking whether the following two statements are compatible:[24]

1 God knows beforehand everything that men will do.

2 Some actions of people are free.

anthology
2.30

It appears that these two statements are incompatible, and that one of them must be false. If God knows beforehand what we are going to do, then it is not in our power not to do that thing. This is because knowledge, of any kind, is of what is true, and if God knows my future actions then it must be true that I will do these future actions. There is nothing I can do to prevent it, which firmly suggests that I am not free. So, either God doesn't in fact know what we will do (we give up the first statement) or the actions of people are not free (we give up the second statement).

Now, faced with this dilemma, the believer could surrender their belief in human freedom. Perhaps we are all just robots living out our predetermined lives. But this view of humankind does not sit at all well with the notion that we are responsible for our actions, and with the associated claim, so crucial to most religious systems, that we are accountable to God for our choices. In Christian theology, for example, it is often said that at Judgement Day we will have to account for our actions before Christ, and that if we are found wanting we will be subject to eternal damnation. Now, if I have no genuine choice about the sins I have committed, then I appear to have good reason to feel aggrieved by this arrangement. If God knew I would sin, and made me so that I would sin, then what do my sins have to do with me? If I couldn't help it, why punish me? Surely on this view of human freedom God is the only person responsible for all the crimes of humanity.

Clearly then, denying humans free will has not been a popular option for believers, since it appears to put the blame for all sin onto God. But neither do believers normally wish to surrender claims to God's omniscience. So how can the problem be resolved?

Kenny highlights one of Aquinas' solutions to this problem, and that is to say that God is eternal and outside of time. This means that for God there is no future or past; or rather, future and past co-exist on a continuum laid out before his gaze. Human actions are not predetermined and we freely choose to act as we do. But, at the same time, God is able to see what actions we do happen to choose. So, just because God knows what I will do, this doesn't mean that I was somehow forced to do it. To explore this thought, consider our own knowledge of what we do. Think back to your decision to read this philosophy book rather than do something even more interesting. You now know that you chose to do some philosophy, because that is exactly what you are doing; but the fact that you *know* that you chose to read some philosophy, does not mean that you did not freely choose to read philosophy. You might have chosen to watch television instead. In the same way, the thought goes, the fact that God can know what our choices will be does not mean that they could not be otherwise. He may know that you will choose to do more philosophy next weekend. But when the choice comes, you are still freely choosing to do philosophy instead of watching television, and it is still true to say that you could, if you wanted, choose to waste away your life watching daytime TV.

According to Aquinas' solution then, God has knowledge of our actions, which to us lie in the future, but which to God are not in the future. So God does not have *fore*knowledge of our actions but he does have knowledge of them, as the point at which he knows them does not lie in the future but in an all-seeing present. However, Aquinas' solution does depend on the claim that God is eternal, and we saw above (page 187) that recently philosophers have argued that God is everlasting, and not eternal, in which case Aquinas' solution is not an option for these philosophers.

Issues arising from God's omnipotence, omniscience and supreme goodness

The final and most significant challenge to the concept of God that we examine in this book is the PROBLEM OF EVIL. This is one of the oldest and most pressing concerns faced by the believer. How is it possible that an omnipotent, omniscient and supremely good God allows such horrific pain and suffering to exist within his creation? After all, he knows about it (he is omniscient), he has the power to stop it (he is omnipotent) and he cares about stopping it (he is supremely good). It seems as if God cannot have all the perfections that we ascribe to him, otherwise he would surely do something to stop the suffering of his creatures on earth. We explore this problem in detail on pages 291–311 below.

▶ ACTIVITY

Consider the problems below. How might a philosophically minded believer respond to each of them?

1. God cannot do what it is logically impossible to do (e.g. make a stone so large that he cannot move it). Therefore God is not omnipotent.
2. God cannot create a being whom he can control yet who has genuine free will. Therefore God is not omnipotent.
3. God cannot know what a being with genuine free will is about to do. Therefore God is not omniscient.
4. God has created beings whom he knew would do evil to one another. So ultimately God is to blame for our wicked acts. Therefore God is not good.
5. God is outside of space and time. Therefore God cannot intervene in the world, and he cannot perform miracles.
6. God is present in the world, existing inside of space and time. Therefore he cannot have created space and time and cannot have created the universe.
7. God is present in the world, existing in all parts of it, including all that is evil and horrific. Therefore God is not perfectly good.
8. Ultimately, the God as described by the philosophers (omnipotent, benevolent, omniscient, etc.) cannot possess all the properties they ascribe to him. The very concept of God is an incoherent one, and belief in such a God is irrational.

Summary

One of the skills that you practise when studying philosophy is that of defining or clarifying your terms – trying to be as clear as possible what you *mean* when you are talking about an idea, a concept and in general the thing that you are discussing. This is a difficult skill to develop for a number of reasons.

1. You are normally having to define terms that other people think are significant; so in a way these are second-hand ideas that you are expected to know and think of as 'important'.
2. These terms are generated by philosophers who are often talking about ideas and concepts which you may never have come across in your life before, possibly because these concepts are obscure, or remote from ordinary experience, or possibly because the philosophers have invented these terms themselves because they are trying to describe something new.
3. Dictionaries are not much use when it comes to defining philosophical terms. This is partly because people who compile dictionaries are not philosophers (and so do not know the technical way in which philosophers use words) but partly because philosophers are describing the world in new and different ways, to help them to understand the world. Writers of dictionaries, on the other hand, are just describing how the general population happen to use a term; they are not describing anything new at all.

There are several techniques that you can use to help you to define a term, many of which have been employed since the start of western philosophy by Plato. You can think of lots of examples which illustrate a concept, and try to spot what those examples all have in common. You could look at how philosophers have used the concept in the past, and pull together a definition based on where these different accounts overlap. You could identify some very specific conditions, or criteria or features, which distinguish this concept from other ideas. As a good philosopher you should indicate where people disagree about a concept (where it is a 'contested' term), as it is rare in philosophy that there is full agreement. Many of the activities in this textbook encourage you to practise these techniques, so that eventually you will be able to define your terms with clarity and useful illustrations.

The key concept in the philosophy of religion is the concept of 'God' and this needs clarifying before you can begin to try to prove the existence of God, or ask questions about God's relationship with the world (such as why God allows such pain and suffering to exist). Being clear about what we mean by 'God' will help you to address these issues, or at least be clearer about why they are issues in the first place. We have seen that there are two approaches to investigating the nature of God. The first (called 'revealed theology') looks to the revelations of sacred texts and prophets for help in our understanding. The second (called 'natural theology') looks to human observation of the world, combined with reason and analysis, to aid our investigation of the concept of God. It is this second approach that is pursued by philosophers, although philosophers who also have faith will not want to lose sight of the first approach.

By adopting the natural theology approach, philosophers have described God in ways that help them to make sense of the world that God created, and make sense of God as a creator. Some of the key attributes of a God who created the world are that this being must have immense power (omnipotence); immense knowledge (omniscience); must be the source of values (supremely good); and must have an unusual relation with time (be eternal or everlasting). However, when philosophers have gone on to analyse these further concepts in more detail, even those thinkers who are devoutly religious, such as St Aquinas, have quickly realised that these attributes can lead to paradoxes when combined, or even incoherence if not properly defined. Three of the most important issues that arise when analysing God's attributes are as follows:

1 The paradox of the stone, which questions whether God has 'unlimited' omnipotence; for example, does God have the power to limit his own power?
2 The Euthyphro dilemma, first posed by Plato, which asks what it means to say that God is good; does it mean that

literally anything God does is good, or does it mean there is an external standard of goodness which God conforms to?

3 Is the existence of an omniscient God who knows everything (including what you are about to do) compatible with the existence of human beings who have genuine free will (which means you can change what you are about to do)?

You may have found it frustrating that these dilemmas were not easily solved, or that God was not easily defined, or that we did not dismiss some of these ideas at the very beginning because they are obviously wrong, or contradictory, or perhaps even irrelevant (if you are a devout atheist). But unfortunately that is not how philosophy, or any form of careful thinking, works. As a philosopher-in-training you need to adopt a considered approach to defining and analysing terms, to addressing problems that arise internally within these terms, to resolving as best you can criticisms made against these terms. Through this considered approach you will arrive at something you can work with: a definition and clarity to a concept that moves you forward in your thinking.

2.2 Arguments relating to the existence of God

Introduction to philosophical proofs

We have seen how philosophers have attempted to analyse *who* God is; now we turn to look at their attempts to prove *that* God is. As we are going to be looking in detail at three of the main arguments for God's existence (the ONTOLOGICAL ARGUMENT, the ARGUMENT FROM DESIGN and the COSMOLOGICAL ARGUMENT), it is worth making a few points about arguments in general.

How are arguments structured?

When we talk about arguments we are not referring to a quarrel, or some kind of personal battle of words involving a denial of everything the other person says, combined with gentle sarcasm and incisive put-downs. An argument, in the sense we are interested in, consists of one or more statements offered in support of a further concluding statement. The supporting statements, the ones that provide the justification, are referred to as the PREMISES of the argument, and the concluding statement is obviously referred to as the CONCLUSION. If a passage contains the words 'and so', 'therefore' or 'hence' then this is a good indication that a conclusion is being drawn and that an argument has been made to support the conclusion. The premises may need to be combined in order to support the conclusion, or they may support the conclusion individually. And the move made between the premise or premises and the conclusion is called an INFERENCE.

Premises

⇩ *Inference*

Conclusion

Figure 2.5 All proofs or arguments have the same basic structure.

For example:

P1: The world appears well ordered

⇩ *Inference*

C: So, someone must have designed it

P1: The world cannot have appeared out of nothing

⇩ *Inference*

C: So, someone must have created it

The goal of an argument is to convince us of the truth of the conclusion, and so to persuade us to believe it. As the conclusion rests on the supporting premises it is essential that every premise in an argument be true. This means that when constructing, or evaluating, arguments we must pay careful attention to each premise. There are various types of premise which can combine to provide grounds to support the conclusion, for example:

- general observations (for example 'politicians have always done whatever it takes to keep themselves in power')
- statements of FACT (for example 'there were only enough lifeboats on the *Titanic* to save half the passengers')
- theoretical assumptions (for example 'everything in the world has a purpose or function')
- definitions (for example 'God is a perfect being')
- HYPOTHETICAL STATEMENTS (for example 'if you eat carrots then you'll be able to see in the dark').

It is helpful to make the premises explicit when evaluating or constructing an argument, so that each one can then be weighed up and considered. As you can see from the Anthology extracts, arguments usually take the form of densely written prose, so you may have to tease out each premise, and many philosophers do this by assigning the premises numbers, and presenting them as a list. This is called presenting the argument in standard form. We have tried to do this when looking at the arguments for God's existence below. Hopefully breaking down the arguments in this way will make them easier to understand and evaluate.

As well as paying attention to the truth of each premise, we also need to consider the overall structure of the argument. You might like to think of the list of premises as a mathematical sum that 'adds up' to the conclusion. If the premises correctly add up to the conclusion – that is, if by accepting them we are forced to accept the conclusion – then the argument is termed 'valid'. However, as with any human calculation, there is always the chance that mistakes have been made. An invalid argument is one where the premises do not add up to the conclusion; in other words, the argument falls short of fully justifying the conclusion. This may be because the argument is flawed or because the argument is an inductive one (see below).

Deductive and inductive arguments

Demonstration [of God's existence] can be made in two ways: One is through the cause, and is called a priori … The other is through the effect, and is called a demonstration a posteriori.[1]

Aquinas

Valid arguments are known as DEDUCTIVE or 'deductively valid'. In a deductive argument the truth of the premises guarantees the truth of the conclusion, so long as no errors have been made. The key word here is 'guarantee'. With a deductive argument, if we accept the premises to be true then we absolutely must accept the conclusion to be true. If, as we have claimed, the goal of an argument is to persuade people to believe its conclusion, then deductive arguments must be a powerful tool; after all, if we can guarantee the truth of a conclusion, we have good reason to believe it. However, this great strength can also appear as a weakness. For deductive arguments cannot establish anything new with their conclusions: they simply reveal what is already contained in the premises. For this reason, they don't really get us beyond what is already known. Another weakness is that, while we can know that the conclusion must follow if the premises are true, we still cannot guarantee that the premises actually are true. Knowing that the conclusion has to follow from the premises is all very well, but it simply passes the buck and we still have to find a way to establish the truth of the premises. To make clearer the strengths and weakness of such arguments, take the following standard example of a deductively valid argument:

- Premise 1:   All men are mortal.
- Premise 2:   Socrates is a man.
- Conclusion: Therefore Socrates is mortal.

Here, if we accept the two premises, then the conclusion follows necessarily. The great strength of the argument is that it appears to be impossible to deny the conclusion once we've accepted that the premises are true. We might say that so long as we accept the premises to be true then we can work out the truth of this conclusion in an A PRIORI manner, in other words prior to any further experience or fact-finding, simply by teasing out what is implicit in what is already given in the premises. Everything can be done in our heads. However, this also means that we haven't really learned anything new here. The conclusion says nothing more than was already contained in the premises. Moreover, while we know that Socrates must be mortal *if* he is a man, and *if* all men are mortal, we have still to find a way of establishing that these other facts are actually true. So deductive arguments appear to leave us with further questions to address.

Notice that what makes an argument deductive is the way the premises relate to the conclusion. Deductive arguments are structured in such a way that the truth of the premises is preserved into the conclusion. But this does not mean that the premises have to be true. Take this argument for example:

- Premise 1:   All cows are green.
- Premise 2:   Socrates is a cow.
- Conclusion: Therefore Socrates is green.

This argument has the same structure as the one we considered above. And so it too must be deductively valid even though the premises are false. This is because what makes it deductive is that the premises give complete support to the conclusion irrespective of whether they are actually true. In other words if we were to accept that all cows are green and that Socrates is a cow, we would also have to accept that Socrates is green.

INDUCTIVE ARGUMENTS are often contrasted with deductive ones because they strive to reveal something new in their conclusion. This is one of the strengths of such arguments since they promise to enable us to extend our knowledge. However, because this means they have to go beyond the information contained in their premises, they lose the power to guarantee the truth of their conclusions. This means that no inductive argument can be fully valid, and at best their conclusions are only ever probably true, even if the premises are certainly true. Typically, induction occurs where an argument moves from what is known (for example, facts about the past, or particular observations) to what is unknown (for example, speculations about the future, or generalisations). Induction is frequently used in the sciences and social sciences, whenever we move from empirical data to theories about the data. A typical inductive argument might be:

1 Every raven I've ever seen has been black.
2 There are ten ravens kept at the Tower of London.
3 (Conclusion) Therefore it is likely that all ten ravens in the Tower are black.

Even if we accept the premises as definitely true, this conclusion does not necessarily follow. This is because there might be whole families of London-born white ravens, which I don't know about, or it might be that for every ten black ravens in a population two of them will be white. Just because I have only ever seen black ravens doesn't establish that they must all be black. Note that, just as with deductive arguments, we still have to accept the premises as true before the argument can be at all convincing.

Another example of an inductive argument is one where we draw a conclusion from a finite set of instances:

1 John 'Stumpy' Pepys used to play drums for rock 'n' roll legends Spinal Tap but he died in mysterious circumstances.
2 Eric 'Stumpy Joe' Childs used to play drums for Spinal Tap but he too died in mysterious circumstances.
3 Peter 'James' Bond used to play drums for Spinal Tap but he eventually died in mysterious circumstances.
4 Mick Shrimpton now plays drums for Spinal Tap.
5 (Conclusion) So it is likely that Mick Shrimpton will one day die in mysterious circumstances.

Here we have observed that these drummers are all similar to each other in one respect (they were members of Spinal Tap), and concluded that the new drummer must be similar to the others in some further respect (he will die in mysterious circumstances). Of course, the conclusion does not follow necessarily from the premises. Mick Shrimpton may be different from the others; he may evade the Grim Reaper of Rock and live to a ripe old age. So, like other inductive arguments, this one cannot establish its conclusion with absolute certainty. Here the strength of the argument will depend on how strong the similarities are between each case of drumming tragedy.

So inductive arguments vary in strength. Here is an example of a rather weak inductive argument:

My team scored while I was in the toilet. So I'd better go to the toilet again – that way we're bound to score!

The fact that my team scored on one occasion when I was out of the room, does not provide good EVIDENCE for supposing that these two things will be correlated in the future. This sort of argument just looks like superstition. But if the evidence base is stronger, we may feel more confident about the likelihood of the conclusions we draw. For example:

Every time I leave my bicycle out in the rain, the chain rusts. So if I leave it out in the rain tonight, it's likely my chain will rust.

The strength of this argument depends on how often I have observed the rain – rust correlation, but if it has happened often, then I have good reason to suppose it will happen again. We will be looking later on at the strengths and weaknesses of a particular inductive argument when we come to the design argument.

▶ ACTIVITY

Read through the following arguments, asking yourself:

1 What is the conclusion of each one?
2 Is the conclusion true?
3 Are the premises (the reasons given for the conclusion) true?
4 Which are inductive arguments, and which are deductive?
5 Which arguments do you think work, and which do not?

    a) I've split up with every person I've ever been out with, so the relationship I'm in at the moment is bound to end too.
    b) Men are incapable of driving safely, because they are prone to uncontrollable hormonal changes that can lead to road rage.
    c) If you don't believe in God you will go to hell. Stuart doesn't believe in God. So Stuart will go to hell.

d) Philosophers spend much of their time sitting around and thinking, which means their muscles weaken, and so none of them is any good at strenuous exercise such as lifting weights.

e) Paul says he had a vision of the Virgin Mary in his bedroom last night. Paul is known to be a trustworthy person and so it likely that the Virgin really did appear to him.

f) It's wrong to kill innocent people. But babies are people too, even when they're in the womb. So it's wrong to have an abortion.

g) The evil dictator denies he has any weapons of mass destruction. But we know from his denials in the past that he's a liar. So he must have them somewhere, and we should keep looking until we find them.

h) My little sister is three and she loves the adverts for toys, so your three-year-old sister should enjoy them too.

i) If God exists then he would have created a world without suffering and evil. However, examples abound of terrible suffering and evil in the world. So God cannot exist.

j) No England football team for the last 50 years has got through to the final of a major competition. So they will obviously fail in the next World Cup.

A priori and *a posteriori* knowledge

We saw that the strength of both deductive and inductive arguments will ultimately depend on the plausibility of their premises. If the premises are obviously false, then the arguments cannot be any good. So how do we establish the truth of the premises of an argument? One obvious answer is through experience. Knowledge that is acquired in this kind of a way is known as *A POSTERIORI*, meaning that it depends on, or comes after, experience. To know such things I have to have experience of them. *A posteriori* knowledge includes scientific claims, such as that magnesium burns with a bright white light or that the Earth orbits the Sun.

But philosophers have also been very interested in another way of establishing their premises that does not require reference to anyone's experiences of the world around them. Such knowledge is known as *a priori*, meaning it does not depend on experience. Examples of such knowledge come from mathematics: $2 + 3 = 5$ can be known just by working it out in your head. Its truth does not depend on doing any experiment counting real-life objects. Of course, I do need to learn the meanings of the terms involved in the expression of this sum, but that is the sole extent of the role of experience here. Alongside mathematical claims and claims that are true by definition (known as ANALYTIC; see page 154 above in the Epistemology chapter), some philosophers include truths of reason, as examples of *a priori* knowledge, such as the claim that all events have a cause, or that nothing can be created out of nothing. (For more on the distinction between *a priori* and *a posteriori* knowledge see Chapter 1.3 above, pages 153–154.)

Summary

When we come to examine the arguments for the existence of God we need to bear in mind what has just been said about arguments in general. This means thinking about the following types of questions:

- What are the premises?
- Are there any hidden premises (or assumptions)?
- Are the premises true?
- Are there any flaws in the reasoning?
- Do the premises give good support to the conclusion?
- Does the conclusion go beyond the premises?
- With inductive arguments, is the probability of the conclusion high, or are there alternative conclusions compatible with the evidence?

These questions can come in handy when you are reading the extracts in the Anthology at the back of this book – consider them to be part of the 'Argument' lens, which you use when you analyse these extracts.

2.2.1 Ontological arguments

Introduction

We can now turn to look at a specific type of proof of the existence of God known as the ONTOLOGICAL ARGUMENT. There are several different versions of this form of argument which we will examine, alongside various criticisms made of them from the time of St Anselm. We shall also look at modern perspectives on the arguments.

Ontological arguments for God's existence are supposed to be deductively valid. In other words, if we accept their premises as true, the conclusion should follow necessarily. Such arguments, if successful, would clearly represent an incredible achievement for human reason, for they promise to establish God's existence with absolute certainty! However, before we can be certain that they succeed we need to be sure that the premises used in such arguments are true. But ontological arguments also claim that their premises are unassailable since they concern only definitions and the analysis of CONCEPTS, and specifically the analysis of the concept 'God'. Because we can examine the concept of God in a purely *a priori* manner it represents a firm starting point for our argument. Thus an ontological argument should establish the existence of God with the same degree of certainty as is to be found in mathematics.

But how can an argument that proves the existence of something begin from premises that are knowable purely *a priori*? Surely, we would need to begin with some experience of the world before we could establish the existence of anything. If we want to know whether there is a black panther living on Bodmin Moor then we examine eyewitness accounts, assess the video footage, carry out autopsies on the savaged lambs and perhaps even recruit thousands of foolhardy students to trawl across the barren hills searching for panther droppings and paw prints.[1] On the basis of the empirical data (the experiences) that we have gathered we then build up a case for, or against, the existence of the beast. So here the proof of the existence of the panther begins with evidence obtained *a posteriori*. However, the ontological argument claims to be able to establish the existence of something (namely God) without needing to bother with any of this. It can be done completely independently of observation, evidence or experience. How could such a trick be possible?

Unpacking concepts

The ontological argument works by analysing the concept of God. This process of analysing a concept can be thought of metaphorically, as 'unpacking' the concept. In other words we must discover all the ideas that are essential elements of the concept. For example, **Figure 2.6** illustrates how we might 'unpack' the concept of 'triangle'. We find it contains the following ideas: it is a shape with three sides, the sides are straight lines connecting to form angles, and those internal angles add up to the sum of two right angles.

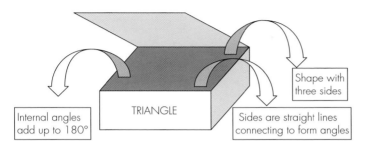

Figure 2.6 Unpacking the concept of 'triangle'.

 Experimenting with ideas

Unpack each of the following concepts into their component parts (the essential characteristics or ideas that make up each concept).

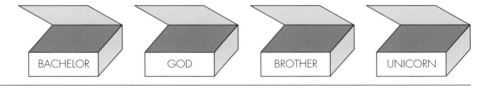

Let us now look at how we might unpack a statement about the world in order to reveal an *a priori* truth. Take the claim that Elvis' mother was female. Without knowing anything about Elvis, his mother or their stormy relationship, we can safely conclude that the claim is true. We do this through unpacking the essential elements of the key term 'Elvis' mother', as shown in **Figure 2.7**.

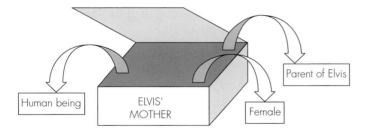

Figure 2.7 Unpacking the concept of Elvis' mother.

Our analysis, or unpacking, reveals that 'Elvis' mother' is the human, female parent of Elvis. So we can now see the obvious truth that Elvis' female parent was female.

This statement has a structure similar to the structure of many other claims; for example, that 'terrorists are a threat to national security', or that 'love of money is the root of all evil'. To assist our analysis it is useful to identify two distinct parts of such statements (or PROPOSITIONS):

1. the SUBJECT (the thing the statement is about, for example, 'love of money')
2. the PREDICATE (the properties we are claiming that the subject has, for example, 'is the root of all evil').

▶ **ACTIVITY**

For each of the following propositions, identify which part is the subject and which the predicate:

1. The Beast of Bodmin Moor is black.
2. Elvis' shoes were blue.
3. Cressida loves Prince Harry.
4. Noah counted the animals two by two.
5. The cow jumped over the Moon.
6. Humans could fly too if only they could flap their arms fast enough.
7. God exists.
8. The earth is about to enter another ice age.
9. Cain's brother was male.
10. This triangle's internal angles add up to 180 degrees.

Once we have identified the subject and the predicate we can then ask whether the claim is true. This usually means gathering empirical evidence. For example, we would need to see Elvis' shoes, or hear from someone who had, before we could determine whether they were blue. And we would need to observe Cressida's behaviour in order to work out whether she really loves the prince and isn't just in it for his mother's fabulous jewellery. However, statements 9 and 10 are special cases, as they are both true by definition or ANALYTIC. With a little analysis the predicate (for example, 'was male') can be shown to be already contained in the subject (for example, Cain's male sibling). And saying 'this triangle's internal angles add up to 180 degrees' is very uninformative to people who know what a triangle is: they know it is true by definition. This means that it is possible to know that some propositions are true *a priori* and these do not need any further empirical investigation.

So, to return to the question, one way of justifying a claim *a priori* is to show it is true by definition through analysing the concepts used in the proposition; in other words to show that the subject already contains within its meaning the property we're claiming that it possesses. With an ontological proof of God's existence a similar process takes place: by analysing, and fully understanding, what 'God' means, we shall see that the proposition 'God exists' is analytically true and hence that God must exist.

St Anselm's first ontological argument

Why then has the fool said in his heart, There is no God (Psalm 14.1), since it is so evident, to a rational mind, that thou dost exist in the highest degree of all? Why, except that he is dull and a fool?

St Anselm, *Proslogion*, Chapter 3

St Anselm (1033–1109) is widely credited with inventing ontological arguments in his book the *Proslogion* (or *Proslogium*, meaning 'The Discourse'). He writes in the preface that he was searching for a single proof of God's existence, one that would not only demonstrate that God exists, but also reveal his existence as the supreme good, depending on nothing else. In the *Proslogion* St Anselm offered at least two versions of this proof, later dubbed the ONTOLOGICAL ARGUMENT by Immanuel Kant (ONTOLOGY is the study of existence). Both proofs rely on the analysis of a particular definition of God; by fully understanding this definition we come to recognise that God must exist.

Although Anselm addresses his proof to God almost as a prayer, it may be easier for us to grasp if we present it in a standard philosophical form: with a list of numbered premises leading to a conclusion.

1 God is the greatest possible being (or as Anselm puts it 'that than which nothing greater can be conceived').[2]
2 Even a fool (someone who doesn't believe in God) can understand that God is the greatest possible being.
3 (From Psalms 14 and 53) The fool says there is no God in reality.
4 (From 2 and 3) The fool is convinced that God, the greatest possible being, exists only in his understanding (that is, in his mind) and not in reality.
5 It is greater to exist both in the understanding and in reality, than merely in the understanding.
6 (From 5) The greatest possible being, if it is genuinely the greatest, must exist both in the understanding and in reality.
7 (Conclusion from 1 and 6) Therefore God exists both in reality and in the understanding. Moreover (from 4 and 6), the fool really is a fool, as he is denying the existence of the greatest possible being, that is a being which must exist if it is genuinely the greatest!

anthology 2.31

Anselm's argument can be made clearer if we take out his passages about the fool. These passages are meant to show that the ATHEIST is guilty of an absurdity; namely, believing that something that must exist (God) doesn't exist! However, Anselm's argument works just as well if we focus only on those parts that prove God exists (and leave out the parts that reveal the fool to be a fool). There are two crucial aspects to Anselm's argument: first his definition of God as the greatest possible being; second his assumption that existing in reality is greater than existing in the understanding or mind. From these two premises it becomes clear why St Anselm believes 'So truly, therefore, thou dost exist, O Lord, my God, for thou canst not be conceived not to exist' (*Proslogion* 3). We can present the essence of Anselm's argument in standard form thus:

1 God is the greatest possible being.
2 It is greater to exist in the understanding and in reality rather than in the understanding alone.
3 Therefore the greatest possible being, God, must exist in the understanding and in reality.

 Experimenting with ideas

Who is the greatest? Have a look at the two different scenarios in **Figure 2.8**.

There are two possibilities. Either God, the greatest possible being, exists only in our minds, or he exists in our minds and in reality as well.

1 Which scenario do you think is true? (Which universe do we live in?)
2 Which scenario do you think contains the greater being?
3 Are your answers to 1 and 2 the same? If they are different how can you account for the difference?

Figure 2.8

Scenario 1: The greatest possible being only exists in people's understanding.

Scenario 2: The greatest possible being exists in people's understanding and in reality.

In scenario 1 people can imagine a powerful being, God, who has created and designed the world, who can perform miracles, who is the source of all morality, and who is omnipotent. Unfortunately, in this scenario, God exists only in people's imagination, and has not really created the world. Compare this with scenario 2 where people can also imagine such a powerful being, except in this scenario the being actually exists, and has in fact created and designed the world, performed a few miracles, and so on. The question St Anselm might ask is: which scenario has described the greater being: scenario 1 or 2? Atheists (Anselm's fools) allege we live in scenario 1, where the greatest possible being exists only in our imagination or understanding. But Anselm's point is that an imaginary greatest possible being cannot be the greatest, because it is possible to conceive of an even greater being, namely one which actually exists and so is actually able to perform miracles and create the world,[3] as in scenario 2. By comparing these two possibilities – a God who is imaginary and a God who really exists – we begin to understand that God, in order to be genuinely the greatest, must exist in reality. Another way of making the point is to consider that a God who didn't exist wouldn't be the greatest possible being, so to be genuinely the greatest he just has to exist.

The exercise above brings out some of the reasons why Anselm thinks it is greater to exist in reality than merely in the understanding. But here is another activity that might also bring out why Anselm's assumption is a plausible one.

 Experimenting with ideas

Imagine your perfect partner.

1 Write down all the amazing qualities such a person would have.
   Now suppose that there is someone, somewhere in the world, who corresponds to your fantasy.
2 Would you rather go out with the real person, or with the purely imaginary one? Why? Why not?

If, in the exercise above, you decided that you'd rather go out with someone who has all the qualities of your perfect partner and actually exists in flesh and blood as well (rather than make do with a perfect but imaginary partner) then it may seem that you are agreeing with Anselm that it is better to exist in reality rather than simply in the mind.

We seen that Anselm's ontological argument for God's existence springs from his concept of God. By analysing what 'God' means (the greatest possible being), Anselm comes to realise that he must exist, because he is the greatest, and that those who deny his existence don't really understand the kind of being he is.

Experimenting with ideas

1 The philosopher Arthur Schopenhauer (1788–1860) referred to the ontological argument as a 'sleight of hand trick' and 'a charming joke', and the argument strikes many people as suspicious in some way (see below, page 227). Have a look at each premise and each step in Anselm's argument: where, if anywhere, do you think the trickery lies in his argument? Try to formulate an objection to it.

2 What other things could you prove the existence of, using an argument like St Anselm's? Try the following format to prove the existence of whatever you like:

   1 So-and-so is the greatest possible such-and-such.
   2 It is greater to exist in reality and in the understanding.
   3 Therefore so-and-so, if it is to be genuinely the greatest such-and-such, must exist.

Issues raised by Gaunilo

anthology 2.32

Before we look at Anselm's second ontological argument, it is worth examining a criticism made by one of his contemporaries, the monk Gaunilo of Marmoutier. Gaunilo suspected that something was amiss with Anselm's argument and rejected it in his work entitled 'On Behalf of the Fool'. Gaunilo believed in God, but objected to Anselm's move from 'understanding God to be the greatest possible being' to the conclusion that 'God must exist in reality'. Gaunilo argued that we can use this method to define anything we like into existence, so long as we claim it has the property of being the 'greatest' or 'most excellent'.[4] But clearly the real existence of such things is doubtful without further evidence. And if the logic of Anselm's argument is the same as with these other examples, then it too must be unsound.

> *For example: it is said somewhere in the ocean is an island ... And they say that this island has an inestimable wealth ... it is more excellent than all other countries ... Now if someone should tell me that there is such an island, I should easily understand his words ... But suppose that he went on to say ... 'since it is more excellent not to be in the understanding alone, but to exist both in the understanding and in reality, for this reason [the island] must exist'.*
>
> **Gaunilo, 'On Behalf of the Fool', Section 6**

Gaunilo uses his counter example of the perfect island to undermine Anselm's proof, and we can summarise it as follows:

1 We can imagine an island which is the most excellent island.
2 It is greater to exist in reality than merely in the understanding.
3 Therefore the most excellent island must exist in reality.

We can see Gaunilo structures his argument in the same way as Anselm's, but it leads to a questionable conclusion: there may be no such island. For Gaunilo, using an ontological argument to prove that a perfect island exists does not actually work, as the existence of the island is always going to be in doubt until we find real evidence for it. The fact that we can imagine such an island (and, as Anselm would say, it then exists in my understanding) has no bearing on whether the island does in fact exist. Instead, according to Gaunilo, we must demonstrate as a 'real and indubitable fact' the excellence and greatness of the island. The same doubts can be raised over Anselm's argument for the existence of God. The fact that we can conceive of the greatest possible being does not imply that it actually exists, and the fool is right to say he can conceive God as not existing. Gaunilo goes on to say that the fool would be right to demand that we must prove that God is in fact (and not just by definition) the greatest possible being.

St Anselm's second ontological argument

Anselm wrote a reply to Gaunilo in which he defends his ontological argument, and draws upon his second version of it. This revolves around an extension to his definition of God, namely that he cannot be thought of as non-existent.

> *God cannot be conceived not to exist … That which can be conceived not to exist is not God.*
>
> St Anselm, *Proslogion* 3

To help us understand why Anselm makes this claim, let us once again compare two conceptions of God and ask which is the greater being: 1) a God who can be conceived of as not existing, or 2) a God who cannot be conceived of as not existing? To Anselm it is pretty clear that the second conception of God is greater: because God is the greatest possible being, it must be impossible to conceive of his non-existence. In fact the idea of a non-existent greatest possible being is a contradiction in terms, claims Anselm, and so only a fool could think that God existed only in his or her mind.

This goes some way to defeating Gaunilo's counter example. Gaunilo is right to say an island, or any other physical thing, can

3 Existence (as well as omnipotence, omniscience, benevolence, and so on) is a supreme perfection.

4 (Conclusion, from 2 and 3) Therefore God, a supremely perfect being, exists.[6]

As with Anselm's argument, Descartes' argument relies upon a particular definition of God, in this case that he is 'a supremely perfect being'. Descartes then analyses this concept of God and notes that a supremely perfect being would have to be perfect in every possible way; in other words, he would have to possess every possible perfection. So he would have to be all-powerful, all-good, all-knowing, and so on. Now, it seems clear to Descartes that existence is a perfection just as being all-powerful, all-good, and so on are. So, as Anselm argued, it is better or more perfect to exist than not to exist. And so it follows that 'existing' must be an essential property of the perfect being.

In his proof Descartes brings out what Anselm presupposes, namely that an ontological argument assumes that 'existence' is a predicate (or a property) that belongs to the concept of 'God'. By making this assumption both Descartes and Anselm are able to conclude that 'God exists' is true by definition, because the subject ('God', who contains all perfections) already contains the predicate ('exists', which is a perfection).

> *From the fact that I cannot conceive of God without existence, it follows that existence is inseparable from him, and hence that he really exists.*
>
> **Descartes, *Meditations* 5**

Descartes also agrees with Anselm on the type of existence God must have: God is a necessary being. Descartes argued that it is impossible to imagine God as not existing, just as it is impossible to imagine an uphill slope existing without a downhill slope, or imagine a triangle without its internal angles adding up to the sum of two right angles. God's existence is a part of his essence as the supremely perfect being. Because God is perfect his non-existence is impossible; in other words God necessarily exists.

Leibniz's addition to the argument

Leibniz felt that Descartes' version of the ontological argument was incomplete and that it needed an additional step to make it valid.[7] The problem he saw was that Descartes assumes that his definition of God, as a being with all perfections, is a coherent one. That is, he doesn't consider whether it is possible for all perfections to co-exist in one being. After all, we saw above when examining the concept of God that some serious questions can be raised about whether the divine attributes are compatible with each other. Just because we can use the expression 'perfect being' doesn't guarantee that we have a coherent idea corresponding to it.

So, to supplement Descartes' argument, Leibniz argues that perfections have to be considered simple and positive. That is, each cannot be defined in terms of anything else, and cannot be defined by the negation of anything else. It follows that each perfection must be self-contained and therefore that none can be shown to be incompatible with any other perfection. This means all the perfections could well be collected together in one being. And if it is possible, and existence is a perfection, then the rest of Descartes' argument goes through and God's existence is necessary.

Issues raised by Hume

Hume was an empiricist and so temperamentally opposed to the idea that we could acquire knowledge concerning what exists by the use of REASON alone. If we are to establish whether there is a beast living on Bodmin Moor then we will have to make empirical enquires; in the same way, if we are to establish that there is a God, we can only do so by reference to our experience. Arguments which try to show that God's existence can be established *a priori*, therefore, must fail. To show this, Hume has a simple argument which he regards as 'entirely decisive':

> *There is an evident absurdity in pretending to demonstrate a matter of fact, or to prove it by any arguments* a priori. *Nothing is demonstrable, unless the contrary implies a contradiction. Nothing, that is distinctly conceivable, implies a contradiction. Whatever we conceive as existent, we can also conceive as non-existent. There is no being, therefore, whose non-existence implies a contradiction. Consequently there is no being, whose existence is demonstrable.*
>
> *Dialogues*, Part 9

Learn More

In the background to this argument lies a distinction that is known as 'Hume's fork'. According to this doctrine, all claims we can make must be of two kinds: either they are 'relations of ideas', or they are 'matters of fact'. Hume's fork is discussed on pages 149–153. Relations of ideas can be recognised as true by analysis of the meanings of the terms involved and so can be known *a priori*. Importantly, this means that they would remain true (or false) no matter what happens to be the case in the actual world. The truth or falsity of all other claims, however, cannot be established by mere reflection on the meanings of the terms involved. And this means that the only way to determine whether they are true or false is by reference to experience. Thus matters of fact tell us about the way the world happens to be, but are never demonstrably true or false; while on the other hand, all relations of ideas are demonstrably true

Experimenting with ideas

To begin to see what Kant means by this, try the following exercise.

1   Imagine a piece of paper.
2   Picture it in detail in your head: what does it look like, where is it, what is it made of, how big is it? Write down a description of the paper, starting with the phrase 'The piece of paper I'm imagining is …'
3   Now add the following features to your picture-image of the paper:
    • is splattered with chip grease and batter
    • is made of eye-catching lime green paper
    • says the words 'Congratulations, you've won a trip of a lifetime' at the top
    • is scrunched up in a gutter
    • exists.
4   Which of these further features changed your image of the paper?

In the activity above your initial description of the paper contained a number of predicates, to which we invited you to add some more. These additional predicates should have enriched your original idea of the paper: in other words, they have added to the concept by giving it new properties. However, what happens when you add the last feature and imagine the scrunched-up, greasy paper existing? Does this make any real difference to your idea?

Kant thinks not. He proposes that a genuine predicate is one that really does describe the thing we're talking about and so adds a descriptive property to it and enriches our concept of it. However, 'existence' does not do this. If I think of something as existing, the idea is the same as if I think of it as not existing. The properties it has are the same in both cases. This means that existence is not a property that a thing can either have or not have.

anthology 2.34

Kant makes his point by asking us to imagine 100 Thalers (or dollars), coins used as the currency of his day; we might think of them as gold, heavy, round, musty and old. According to Kant's rule, these are all genuine predicates as they all change our concept of the '100 Thalers'. However, if we now add 'existence' to our description then nothing changes: there is no difference between our idea of '100 coins' and of '100 coins that exist'. In contrast, if we add the words 'covered in pink anti-theft paint' to the description then our concept definitely changes.

Kant concludes that 'existence' (unlike 'covered in pink anti-theft paint') is not a genuine predicate. If he is right, then ontological arguments must fail. They fail because it is essential to the ontological arguments of both Anselm and Descartes that 'existence' is a part of what we mean by 'God'. But, if 'existence' is not a predicate, then existence cannot belong to our definition of anything including 'God'.[12]

Issues raised by Schopenhauer

We mentioned before that Schopenhauer calls the ontological argument a conjuring trick and his reason for doing so is that he thinks it conceals the claim that God exists in its premises in order to then reveal it in the conclusion, much as a conjurer might reveal a rabbit that he had been hiding in his hat all along. Descartes' definition of God conceals within it from the outset the claim that he necessarily exists and the argument proceeds by revealing this presupposition through its analysis of the concept. On this way of looking at the argument it is circular and has proved nothing other than what it assumed from the outset. A circular argument like this is said to 'beg the question'.

Figure 2.11
Schopenhauer says the ontological argument is a conjuring trick which succeeds in revealing God only because he was assumed to exist all along.[13]

Issues raised by Russell

Learn More

The second criticism proposed by Kant anticipates a problem raised by philosophers of language in the first part of the twentieth century. Philosophers such as Gottlob Frege (1848–1925) and Bertrand Russell (1872–1970) thought that there was a real difference between the surface structure of language and the true logical structure that underlies it, and that we must be careful not to confuse the two. For example, on the grammatical surface a statement like 'Nothing matters' seems to have a straightforward subject–predicate structure. However, on closer inspection we find that the term 'nothing' doesn't name or refer to anything, and so is not a genuine subject. So sometimes what appears on the surface to be a subject (or a predicate), can be shown by further analysis not to be a genuine, logical subject (or predicate).

Existence quite definitely is not a predicate.[14]

Russell

The suggestion is that there is a similar deceit when it comes to the word 'exists'. 'Exists' seems to function as a normal predicate, appearing as a verb after a subject; so just as we can say that 'Bill laughs', 'Jesus saves' and 'the lion sleeps', we can also say 'God exists'. However, Frege and Russell would agree with Kant that 'exists' is not a genuine predicate, as it does not refer to any real property. Frege argued that 'exists' is really just a shorthand way of saying 'there is some object in the world that this concept refers to'; in other words to say that lions exist is to say that there are things in the world to which the concept of 'lion' corresponds. It is not to say that lions have a very special property known as existence.

Take another example. When we say 'A moon-jumping cow exists', we are not adding something new to our description of 'cow'. We are not saying 'A cow is a four-stomached ruminant which jumps over moons *and exists.*' All we are saying is that the description 'four-stomached ruminate which jumps over moons' identifies some object in the real world. **Figure 2.12** represents how Russell might analyse the claim that 'The cow that jumped over the moon actually exists.'

Figure 2.12 How Russell might illustrate the meaning of 'exists' in the statement 'A moon-jumping cow exists.'

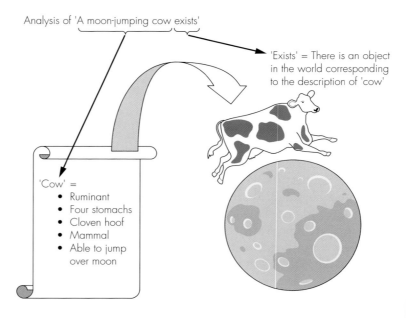

Analysis of 'A moon-jumping cow exists'

'Exists' = There is an object in the world corresponding to the description of 'cow'

'Cow' =
- Ruminant
- Four stomachs
- Cloven hoof
- Mammal
- Able to jump over moon

Another way to see the point is to contrast propositions like 'All cows eat grass' with 'All cows exist'. While the predicate 'eat grass' tells us something meaningful about the habits of cows, the apparent predicate 'exist' seems oddly tautological. For obviously all the cows that there are must exist, otherwise they wouldn't be all the cows. Similarly, while 'Some cows are mad' makes perfect sense, 'Some cows exist' is odd. By using 'exists' as a real predicate this sentence implicitly contrasts cows which happen to exist, with those that do not. But we cannot properly describe some cows as existing, as though there were others that do not, because, of course, there are not any others. There just aren't any non-existent cows. These observations suggest that to say that something exists is not to describe it or to ascribe a special kind of property to it, but rather to say simply that there is such a thing in the world.

If Russell is correct then 'existence' is not a predicate, but simply a term that informs us that there is something in the world corresponding to a particular description. When we say 'God exists' we are simply saying 'There exists a being to which the word "God" refers' (see **Figure 2.13**).

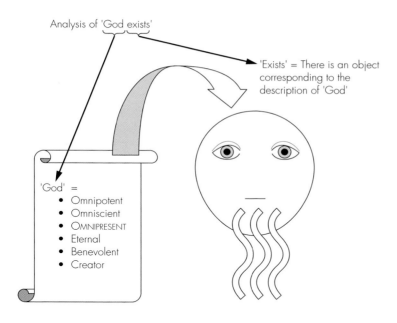

Analysis of 'God exists'

'Exists' = There is an object corresponding to the description of 'God'

'God' =
• Omnipotent
• Omniscient
• OMNIPRESENT
• Eternal
• Benevolent
• Creator

Figure 2.13 How Russell might illustrate the meaning of 'exists' in the statement 'God exists'.

Russell's analysis of existence profoundly damages the ontological arguments of Descartes and Anselm. These sought to show that 'God exists' is true by definition because existence is a property and so part of the meaning of 'God'. But if existence cannot be a property of God, in order to show that the statement 'God exists' is true, we need to find something in the world corresponding to our description of 'God', and this means producing empirical evidence for such a being.

Because of their beauty and potential power, ontological arguments have continued to intrigue and inspire philosophers of religion. In the twentieth century there have been versions or interpretations by Norman Malcolm (1911–1990), Alvin Plantinga (1932–) and Karl Barth (1886–1968) among others. Both Malcolm and Plantinga focus on claims about God's status as a necessary being; that is, one who must exist. It is difficult to do any justice to the complexities of Malcolm's and Plantinga's arguments here, but the following overviews will provide sufficient detail for our purposes.

Malcolm's ontological argument

Malcolm believes that St Anselm got things right in his second version of the ontological argument and so conceives God as a being whose existence cannot depend on anything else or which cannot be prevented from existing. In this respect God's existence is importantly different from the existence of all other things, including ourselves. Your existence depends, among other things, on the existence of your parents, and so it is conceivable, if they had not met, that you would never have been born. But in the case of God, there can be no set of circumstances which could lead to his non-existence, which is the same as to say that his existence is necessary.

anthology
2.35

We can think about Malcolm's ontological argument in the following way. Consider four possibilities concerning God's existence:

1 God's existence is necessarily false – it is logically impossible for any being that has God's properties to exist.
2 God's existence is contingently false – it is possible that a being with the properties of God could exist, but it just so happens that there isn't such a being.
3 God's existence is contingently true – it is possible that a being with the properties of God could exist, and it just so happens that there is such a being.
4 God's existence is necessarily true – it is logically necessary that any being with the properties of God exists.

Malcolm argues that possibilities 2 and 3 simply cannot apply to a being like God. This is because God is the greatest possible being, and as such he must be unlimited, independent and eternal. However, 2 and 3 suggest that his existence is contingent; that is, limited by and dependent upon other factors. For example, for Malcolm there is a crucial difference between an eternal being, and a being who just happens (contingently) to exist forever: eternity is a quality of God whereas eternal duration is not. Malcolm argues that, because God is the greatest possible being, God's existence cannot be contingent, and thus the claim that 'God exists' cannot be contingently true (or false).

This leaves either 1 or 4 as the remaining possibilities. Statements that fall under 1 are logically contradictory propositions, such as

'This square is round' or 'That bachelor is on his fifth marriage'. Malcolm argues that there is nothing logically contradictory about the claim that 'God exists'. This leaves 4 as the only remaining possibility: God's existence is necessarily true. For Malcolm this doesn't mean that 'existence' is a predicate of 'God'; instead it means that 'necessary existence' is a predicate of 'God'. Malcolm believes he has shown that because God is the greatest possible being he must be a necessary being, and therefore he must exist.

Plantinga's ontological argument

Plantinga's own ontological argument takes a slightly different approach from Malcolm's and involves reference to 'possible worlds'.[15] A possible world is the way the universe might have been. The set of all possible worlds will be all the ways the universe might have been, ranging from those that are just slightly different from this one (the actual one) – for example, the one in which you decided to skip this part of the book, the one where unicorns exist or ones in which your parents never met and you were not born – through to ones where radically different types of creature come to exist, where life never evolved, or even ones where stars and planets never formed, and so on. But not all worlds are possible. There is no possible world in which squares are round or unicorns have no horns, since these are logically impossible. By contrast a necessary truth, such as that triangles have three sides and 5 is greater than 3, is one that is true in every possible world. Similarly, what we mean when we say that 'God necessarily exists' is that God exists in every possible universe; that is, when we examine each of the universes we find that God exists in every one.

To show that God does indeed exist in every possible world, as with all ontological arguments, Plantinga begins with the definition of God as the greatest possible being or, to use his phrase, 'a being with "maximal greatness". Now, if such a being exists, then it would have to exist in every possible world, since a being that exists in all possible universes is greater than one that exists in only some worlds.

anthology
2.36

However, whether or not such a being actually exists depends upon whether it is possible; after all (as we saw in our discussion of Leibniz above) if our concept of God is incoherent, then there could not be a being corresponding to it. So is it possible? Since there appears to be no contradiction in the concept, it follows that there must be some possible world in which he exists. However, if we allow that he exists in some possible world, then, since he is a necessary being, he would have to exist in all possible worlds. And, of course, a being that exists in all possible worlds necessarily must exist in our world too.

6 The measurement of 'redshift' in the light from distant galaxies by Edwin Hubble in 1929, which supported the conclusion that the universe was expanding from an original Big Bang.

7 The evidence published by William Ryan and Walter Pitman in 1998 that there had been a 'great flood' from the Mediterranean into the Black Sea circa 5600BCE – with water pouring across the landscape at 200 times the rate of the Niagara Falls.

8 The testimony by Professor Michael Behe under oath to a court of law in the United States that certain features of the world, such as the eye, are irreducibly complex and could not be the product of evolution.

9 The lifelong charity work of Mother Teresa throughout the last century, which helped thousands of the poorest people of the world to stay alive and die in relative peace.

10 The fact that the universe exists at all.

For each observation:

a) Does it support the claim that God exists?
b) If it does, how might an atheist account for this observation?
c) Does it support the claim that God doesn't exist?
d) If it does, how might a believer account for this observation?

Can we look to the world for proof of God's existence, or will our observations point towards the opposite conclusion, that there is no God? In this chapter we look at the claim that the world provides evidence for God, in particular that the universe and everything in it seems to have been designed by a supernatural designer. This type of argument is known as the design argument. Later in the book, on pages 291–311, we examine claims that belief in God is incompatible with the horror, cruelty and suffering that are a daily occurrence among humans and every other creature in the world. This challenge to the belief in God is known as the PROBLEM OF EVIL.

Types of argument from design

Thou dost cause the grass to grow for the cattle, and plants for man to cultivate ... Thou hast made the moon to mark the seasons, the sun knows its time for setting.
Psalms 104: 14, 19

All things bright and beautiful, all creatures great and small. All things wise and wonderful, the Lord God made them all. [4]
Anglican hymn

To the writer of Psalm 104, and to millions of others throughout history who have looked up at their surroundings and wondered, the universe looks as if it has been deliberately made. From the features of earthly creatures, great and small, to the order and regularity of planetary motion, there seems to be every sign of a supernatural craftsman or artist at work – a designer, in fact, who 'made them all'. These types of arguments are known as arguments from design or TELEOLOGICAL ARGUMENTS. They are probably the most commonly cited type of argument, as anyone who has ever talked to a door-to-door evangelist will know. As Kant says:

> *This proof always deserves to be mentioned with respect. It is the oldest, the clearest, and the most accordant with the common reason of mankind.*[5]
>
> **Immanuel Kant,** *Critique of Pure Reason*

Design arguments are concerned with the specific details of the universe: why does the universe possess the particular qualities that it does and how can we best explain them?[6] These qualities include many puzzling features that scientists, philosophers and theologians have noted, including:

- the regularity and order of the world
- the way that everything in the world seems to be designed for some purpose
- the way that living things appear constructed so as to suit their environment
- the fact that life developed in the world at all
- the fact that conscious beings exist.

Before we look at the different types of arguments from design which account for these features, we should first revisit some of the technical terms that we examined above on page 210.

- Arguments from design are *A POSTERIORI*. Because teleological arguments are based on our experience of the universe they can be categorised as *a posteriori* proofs, in contrast to ontological arguments which are *A PRIORI* (see pages 212–214). The observations that form the basis of design arguments include specific observations about the way animals have been put together, the way they fit into their environments, as well as more general observations about how the earth is so suitable for life.
- Arguments from design are INDUCTIVE. Design arguments move from particular observations to a general conclusion about the whole world. Deductive arguments, like the ontological proofs of God's existence attempted by St Anselm and Descartes, are capable of providing a conclusive proof, so long as the PREMISES are true and the argument is a valid one. In contrast, an inductive argument, such as a teleological argument, cannot conclusively prove the existence of God even if it is based on true premises. At best a teleological argument can only show that God's existence is probable.
- 'Teleology' has its origins in ancient Greek thought. The word 'teleological' comes from the Greek '*telos*', which means 'end'

or 'goal', and '*logos*', which means 'an account of' or 'study of'. Hence 'teleology' literally means 'the study of final ends'. The term 'teleological' has also come to refer to the view that everything has a purpose and is aimed at some goal. So teleological arguments or arguments from design draw on evidence that the world has been designed and has a purpose in order to conclude that God exists.

Sometimes teleological arguments are referred to simply as 'arguments from design'. However, as Antony Flew and others have pointed out, the label 'argument from design' is an unhappy one.[7] The term 'from design' suggests that the conclusion (that the world has been designed) is already assumed in the premises, and hence there is hardly much argument that needs to be done. Flew proposes 'argument to design' as a better label for this cluster of arguments, and this is certainly less of a mouthful than Kant's suggestion, which was the 'PHYSICO-THEOLOGICAL' arguments (page 254 below). However, we shall stick with the usual convention and use both the common terms 'teleological' and 'argument from design'. We can identify two main types of design arguments.

Arguments from analogy

There is a tradition of teleological arguments which compare certain features of the universe with similar features of designed objects. These ANALOGICAL ARGUMENTS argue from design in that they begin by examining design in human artefacts (in this sense then they really are arguments *from* design). Similarities, or analogies, can be found between these designed objects and the world around us, and this leads to an intermediate conclusion that the world has also been designed. From here it is a short step to the final conclusion that God is the designer. Below we examine arguments from design formulated by Aquinas, Paley and Swinburne, and the issues with these arguments raised by Paley himself, David Hume and Kant.

Arguments to the best explanation

There is another type of teleological argument which seeks a different path to the conclusion that the world has been designed. Such proofs begin by noticing certain unusual properties of the universe, in particular its apparent order and purpose. They aim to show that naturalistic explanations for these properties are inadequate, and that the existence of a supernatural designer is the best explanation of these features. We can think of these as the arguments to design that Flew mentions, in that they try to demonstrate that these features are not the result of chance, but point strongly towards the existence of a designer-God.

Aquinas' argument from analogy

In his book, the *Summa Theologica*, Aquinas offers five ways in which God's existence can be demonstrated. The first three ways are all forms of COSMOLOGICAL ARGUMENT (which we examine on pages 261–290);[8] the fourth way is an argument from morality, and in his fifth Aquinas offers a version of an argument from design. It is an argument by analogy, in that it compares the natural world (the fact that it appears to have a purpose and goal) with human activity (which does have a purpose and a goal). The example Aquinas uses in his argument by analogy is that of an archer:

1 Things that lack intelligence, such as living organisms, have an end (a purpose).
2 Things that lack intelligence cannot move towards their end unless they are directed by someone with knowledge and intelligence.
3 For example, an arrow does not direct itself towards its target, but needs an archer to direct it.
4 Conclusion: Therefore (by analogy) there must be some intelligent being which directs all unintelligent natural things towards their end. This being we call God.

Criticism

The key premise in Aquinas' argument is the claim that 'things that lack intelligence cannot move towards their end unless they are directed by someone with knowledge and intelligence'. However, this is a controversial premise in so far as it very nearly assumes what the argument is setting out to prove, namely that there is an intelligent being who created the universe.

Yet we observe that most ducklings, acorns, embryos, and so on grow and develop very successfully without any interference from an intelligent being. And so the claim that some intelligent hand must directly shape the natural world simply is not supported by our observations of it.

In the five hundred years after Aquinas the success of science changed the way people saw the universe. The traditional Aristotelian view of the universe, which placed the earth at the centre surrounded by unchanging heavenly bodies, was undermined by the work of Copernicus (1473–1543) and Galileo (1564–1642). The new discoveries showed that the earth was just one planet among many revolving around the sun. Isaac Newton (1642–1727) claimed to have discovered the laws of motion that governed the movement of all objects, and the universe came to be viewed as a complex machine. Some thinkers saw these breakthroughs as a threat to Christianity – indeed the new discoveries did undermine much traditional Church teaching – but other thinkers used the new science as evidence that the universe was a glorious work of divine craftsmanship.

If the universe is machine-like then it needs a designer, just as an ordinary machine such as a watch needs a designer. This analogy between the universe and a watch was the basis for an argument from design put forward by William Paley.

Experimenting with ideas

In **Figure 2.14** there are five boxes, each containing an object. Boxes 1–4 contain a wrist watch, a pebble, a honeycomb, a coin; box 5 contains an unknown object.

1 Which of the objects in boxes 1–4 would you say have been designed?
2 What do the designed objects have in common?
3 List all the things you would be looking for in the fifth object, in order to determine whether it had been designed.

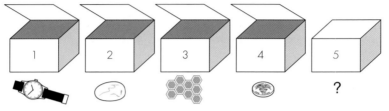

Figure 2.14 What's in the mystery box? How could we tell it had been designed?

Paley's argument from design

anthology 2.37

The Archdeacon of Carlisle, William Paley (1743–1805), put forward a very popular argument from design in his book *Natural Theology* (1802). Paley imagines himself walking across a heath and first coming across a stone, which he strikes with his foot, then finding a watch on the ground. The same question occurs to him on both occasions: 'How did that object come to be here?'. In the case of the stone, for all Paley knows it may have lain there forever. However, in the case of the watch such an answer is unsatisfactory: there is something about the presence of the watch on the heath that demands further explanation.

So what is the difference between a watch and a stone in this case? Paley undertakes two examinations of the watch, the first of which yields the most well-known version of the teleological argument. The second examination we address when we look at the criticisms that Paley anticipates of his argument (see below, page 244). What Paley actually notices at this first examination of the watch is that:

■ it has several parts
■ the parts are framed and work together for a purpose
■ the parts have been made with specific material, appropriate to their action
■ together the parts produce regulated motion
■ if the parts had been different in any way, such motion would not be produced.

In the activity above you might have found further features that indicate some sort of design in a watch, for example its aesthetic appearance, or its complexity. We might think of this list as Paley's criteria for (or indicators of) design, and if an object meets these criteria then Paley will take it as evidence that the object has been designed. For Paley the watch on the heath has all the evidence of what he terms 'contrivance'; that is, design, and where there is design or contrivance there must be a designer or 'contriver'.[9] He concludes that the watch must have had a maker.

▶ ACTIVITY

Draw a table like the one below.

1 Along the top row, write in your criteria for design, referring to either:
    a) the list you established in part 3 of the activity above, or
    b) the criteria Paley proposes.
2 For all the natural features listed, decide which criteria they meet.
3 Are there any natural features you can think of that do not meet any of the criteria?

Natural features	Criteria				
	I	2	3	4	5
A snake's eye					
A peacock's tail					
The changing of the seasons					
The 'flu virus					
The solar system					

Every indication of contrivance, every manifestation of design, which existed in the watch, exists in the works of nature.[10]

Paley

Having examined the watch and thereby established some criteria with which to determine whether something has been designed, Paley turns his attention to the natural world. He finds that all the indicators of design that we observed in the watch we can also observe in nature, except that the works of nature actually surpass any human design. This leads him to the conclusion that nature must have a designer wondrous enough to have designed such a universe.

We can summarise Paley's argument in the following way:

1 A watch has certain complex features (for example, it consists of parts, each of which has a function, and they work together for a specific purpose).

2 Anything which exhibits these features must have been designed.

3 From 1 and 2: Therefore the watch has been designed by a designer.

4 The universe is like the watch in that it possesses the same features, except on a far more wondrous scale.

5 From 4 and 2: Therefore the universe, like the watch, has been designed, except by a wondrous universe maker – God.

Like Aquinas' fifth way, Paley's teleological argument is thought of as an argument from analogy. Remember these arguments work by comparing two things, and by arguing that because they are alike in one (observed) respect they are also alike in another (unobserved) respect. Paley's analogy between the watch and the natural world works like this.

Figure 2.15 Paley's analogy between the watch and the universe.

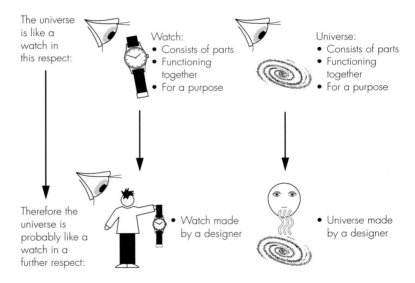

Experimenting with ideas

Read through the following arguments from analogy and answer the questions below.

a) In many ways a dog is like a cat, for example they both are warm-blooded mammals. Dogs give birth to live young, therefore cats do too.

b) A dog is like a duck-billed platypus, in that they are both warm-blooded mammals. Dogs give birth to live young, therefore duck-billed platypuses do too.

c) Just as a curry is a more stimulating dish if it contains a variety of flavours, so a nation will be more stimulating if it contains a variety of cultures.

d) Just as a window box is more interesting if it contains a variety of flowers, so a garden will be more interesting if it contains a variety of plants and trees.

e) We would not let a wild animal control its owner, because the owner knows better than the animal what is in its interests. Therefore we shouldn't let the common people control the government because the rulers know better than the people what is in their interests.

f) We would not let a child control its parents because the parents know better than the child what is in its interests. Therefore we should not let students control an A Level class, because the teacher knows better than the students what is in their interests.

g) If you suddenly found yourself being used, against your will, as a life-support device for a famous violinist and knew it would last nine months, you would not have a moral obligation to keep the violinist alive. Similarly, if you suddenly found that you were pregnant, against your will, you would not have a moral obligation to see the pregnancy through to birth.

h) If you suddenly found yourself attached to a stranger who was acting as your life-support machine for nine months, and they are the only person who can keep you alive, then you have a right to be kept alive by that stranger. Similarly a foetus, while in the womb, has a right to be kept alive until birth by its mother.

I What words or phrases indicate that an argument uses an analogy?

2 Which of the above did you think were strong analogies, and which were weak?

3 What do you think makes an analogy a strong or successful one?

Issues raised by Paley

William Paley takes great care in his *Natural Theology* (1809) to anticipate and respond to some of the criticisms that people might make of his argument from design. It is not known for certain whether Paley had read Hume's *Dialogues Concerning Natural Religion* (which was published after Hume's death in 1779), but several of the criticisms that Paley anticipates do seem to address challenges that Hume raises (and which we look at in detail on pages 247–253). We shall see that the final criticism we explore leads Paley to a second examination of the watch, and a second formulation of his argument from design.

anthology
2.38

Criticism

The first of the criticisms which Paley anticipates is that we do not generally know very much about watchmaking: we may never have seen a watchmaker at work, nor may we be able to make a watch ourselves. Does this mean that we must withhold our conclusion that a watchmaker made the watch found on the heath? Paley points out that we encounter a similar problem when we look at the products of ancient crafts and forgotten arts, and we may never know the skills that were needed to create these products, as these are lost to time. But we are still able to draw conclusions from the product itself about the artists' skills and the very fact that someone existed with the skill to create these cultural artefacts. For example, in 1902 divers recovered a piece of bronze from the bottom of the Mediterranean sea near the Greek island of Antikythera. This was no ordinary piece of bronze though, as it carried with it gears, dials, inscriptions and cogs. The so-called Antikythera mechanism puzzled scientists and historians alike, but, in the manner of Paley's abandoned watch, the assumption made of this mysterious piece of ancient craftsmanship was that it was designed for a purpose. Through a process of reverse engineering scientists have come up with several competing models accounting for the gears and cogs, the most plausible being that the mechanism was an orrery: a working model of the solar system (**Figure 2.16**) based on the highly sophisticated computational methods used in Babylonian astronomy.

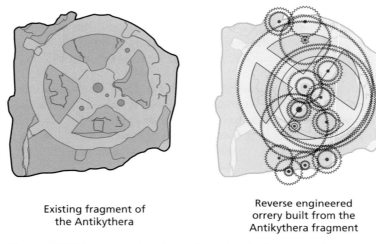

Existing fragment of the Antikythera

Reverse engineered orrery built from the Antikythera fragment

Figure 2.16 Reverse engineering to determine the function of the Antikythera mechanism.

So, even though no one had witnessed the Antikythera mechanism being constructed, the people who analysed it concluded that it had been designed and built. Paley here may be attempting to deflect Hume's criticism that we have no experience of world-making (see below, page 248) and hence cannot draw any conclusions from the basis of a world to how that world may have come about. For Paley, even though we are ignorant of the design process, it is still legitimate to infer the existence of a designer from mysterious objects that exhibit all the characteristics of design.

> *Nor would it invalidate our conclusion that the watch sometimes went wrong, or seldom went right.*[11]
> Paley

Criticism

The second criticism anticipated by Paley is that people might observe problems in the functioning of the watch; for example, an irregularity of movement, or simply a failure for it to work (after all the watch may have been lying on that particular heath for weeks before you discovered it). However, we would still be able to observe the details of the machinery, the cogs and gears, and all the qualities Paley outlined in his first examination of the watch. Paley argues that, whether or not the mechanism actually works, these qualities in themselves still lead us to the conclusion that the watch was designed. How might this apply by analogy to the universe? Many theologians and philosophers have wondered whether the universe may be considered flawed in its workings if there is an all-powerful, all-loving good God who created it. The flaw that is highlighted most frequently is the pain and suffering that are endured by creatures on this world. So is this problem of 'evil' (as it is called) one of the ways in which the world has gone wrong? For Paley, following his line of reasoning above, even if it could be shown that the existence of pain and suffering were a flaw in the workings of the universe, it would not therefore follow that God did not exist. When we come to examine the problem of evil in more detail (below, page 291) we shall look at the many defences proposed by theologians which account for why such an apparent 'flaw' exists in a universe created by an omnipotent and benevolent God.

However, the second part of Paley's quotation above '… *or seldom went right*' does seem to undermine the strength of Paley's conclusion that there is an intelligent and skilful watchmaker. We shall see below that Hume enjoys exploring fully the possible characteristics of an incompetent watchmaker, and a less-than-perfect creator of the universe (page 252).

Criticism

Paley's third issue is that some parts of the watch may have no apparent purpose. When he finds the stone on the heath he dismisses it out of hand, because it does not seem to have any purpose. So purposiveness seems to be an essential criterion for design. If parts of the watch have no purpose then does this invalidate the conclusion that it has been designed; after all, would an intelligent designer include pointless parts? Paley does not think this brings uncertainty into his argument from design, and he suggests that we can see that a part has some function (even if we do not know what it is) when that part is removed from the mechanism and the mechanism stops working.

Criticism

Paley then considers a cluster of further criticisms that question whether the features of design that we find in the watch could be explained without reference to a designer. He considers, and dismisses, the claim that the watch might arise merely out of a 'possible combination of material forms', or out of a 'principle of order', or even a 'law of metallic nature'. Paley is here rejecting the possibility that the structure of the watch may have come together out of purely random processes, a hypothesis that Hume considers as the Epicurean hypothesis (see below, page 251). He is also rejecting the claim that the watch could have come together out of purely natural processes, and the reference to a 'law of metallic nature' seems to be a dig at people who invent spurious laws of nature which have no explanatory power (or at Hume and his vegetative account of the universe, page 250). When we come to look at Darwin (see below, page 256) we shall see that, even if a law of nature cannot account for the coming together of the parts of a watch, it may be able to account for the coming together of the parts of an eye.

The possibility that the watch might not have been made by a watchmaker leads into Paley's second examination of the watch. Paley supposes that, upon this further investigation, it turns out that the watch is also some kind of watchmaking machine, capable of making other watches with all the same fine features that it has. This gives rise to the possibility that this watch-machine was itself made by a watch-machine, which in turn was made previously by watch-machine, and so on. The issue is whether this has undermined Paley's argument, by showing that the watch did not need to be designed by a watchmaker, and similarly the universe (if it arose from previous iterations of the universe) did not need to be designed by God. But for Paley this simply defers the problem, because the watch-machine which made our watch on the heath still has the same features of contrivance; that is, ordered and regulated parts, framed for a purpose. However far we go back, in terms of watch-machines, we still need to account for these features, which still indicates that there is a designer (**Figure 2.17**).

Our going back ever so far, brings us no nearer to the least degree of satisfaction on the subject. Contrivance is still unaccounted for. We still want a contriver.[12]

Paley

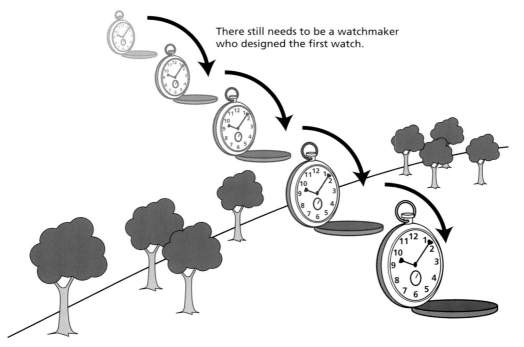

There still needs to be a watchmaker who designed the first watch.

Figure 2.17 The watch on the heath could have been made by a watch-machine. But this cannot go back forever – there still needs to be a watchmaker who designed the first watch.

Paley is here borrowing one of the features from the cosmological argument (below, page 264), namely the rejection of the possibility of an INFINITE REGRESS. We do not escape the need for a watchmaker just because we find that the watch could have been made by a watch-machine, which itself could have been made by a watch-machine. Paley is not rejecting the possibility of an infinite regress for the reasons that Aquinas' three ways or the Kalam arguments reject it (that is, because they consider it to be self-contradictory). Instead, Paley is rejecting it on practical grounds as it simply defers the question of 'Yes, but who designed *this*?' As Paley says, 'a chain, composed of an infinite number of links, can no more support itself than a chain composed of a finite number of links'.[13] Where there is contrivance there must eventually be found a contriver; where there is design there must be a designer.

Paley does consider the possibility that the question 'Who designed this?' could be done away with 'if nothing had been before us but an unorganised, unmechanised substance, without mark or indication of contrivance'. But for Paley this clearly isn't the case, as if it were then it would make no difference whether we found a stone or a watch. But it does make a difference, and the implication is that watches (and eyes and universes), unlike rocks, could not have come from unorganised, unmechanised substances. The conclusion from the first examination of the watch is that there must be a designer of this watch. But the conclusion from the second examination of the watch, raising the possibility that it was made by a watch-machine, also yields the same conclusion: that there is a skilled designer. Paley thinks that the alternative (that there is no designer) is absurd, and this is the position of the atheist.

Criticism

We can amend Paley's analogy of the watch-machine being built by a watch-machine, to introduce the idea that each generation of watch-machines is able to produce a new generation which, through mechanical processes alone, is a slight improvement on the previous generation. Or, to put it another way, each preceding generation watch-machines is slightly more primitive than the current generation. In this case we can imagine the possibility that this could go far enough backwards until there was a watch-generating mechanism that was so primitive that it perhaps could create the first proto-watch machine through a 'metallic law of nature' alone. This rather far-fetched scenario (but perhaps no more outlandish than Paley's watch-machines) is analogous to how we now think eyes, and so on, have evolved. So Paley is vulnerable here to the discoveries and theories of modern science which believe they can trace the origin of sophisticated living creatures (which Paley thinks are designed) back to 'unorganised mechanised substances'. And in this case, as Paley himself acknowledges, the question of design does not arise. For more on how evolutionary theory undermines the argument from design see the challenges raised by Darwin, below on page 256.

Learn More

Is Paley's argument an argument from analogy?

We have seen that the traditional view (held for example by philosophers such as John Hick and Brian Davies) of Paley's watchmaker argument is that it is an argument from analogy. The reasons for holding this view seem straightforward: we saw in the quotation above that Paley moves from a discussion about the watch on the heath to a discussion about the natural world. Paley believes that the indicators of design which he found in the watch are also in the works of nature, which calls to mind the very simple analogical argument given by Hume's character of Cleanthes (see below).

However, recent readings of Paley suggest that his design argument may not be an argument from analogy after all. For example, Kenneth Himma (in his 2005 article on 'The application-conditions for design inferences') suggests that Paley's argument is best read as a precursor to modern arguments to the best explanation, which have recently cited INTELLIGENT DESIGN, of the type Paley identifies, as evidence that God exists. Another contemporary religious scientist and philosopher, Del Ratzch (in his book *Nature, Design and Science*), has revived Paley's efforts to bring the supernatural (that is, God) back into our scientific understanding of design in the world. In this book, as well as his article on design arguments in the Stanford encyclopaedia of philosophy (an excellent free resource for students), Ratzch also claims that Paley's watchmaker argument is not an argument from analogy. For Ratzch, Paley's argument is to show that we all make the inference from seeing the watch to understanding that the watch has a designer, and this inference is based on particular features of design. Paley then goes on to show that we make the same inference when looking at the world, identifying those features, and realising that the world has been designed. The advantage of this reading, Ratzch points out, is that it avoids Hume's criticisms of arguments from analogy (see below, page 247).

Paley, though, does go on to refer to analogies between nature and human 'tools of art' and 'instruments' throughout the rest of *Natural Theology*, as he examines all aspects of the natural world to demonstrate God's hand in its making. For example, at the beginning of Chapter 3 (see quotation opposite).

Perhaps Paley had one eye on avoiding Hume's criticisms (of the simplistic analogy between a watch and nature), but with his other eye he saw analogies between the human and natural world everywhere he looked. One of the pleasures, and frustrations, of reading philosophy before it became 'professionalised' (that is, before academics were paid by universities to research and write philosophy) is that our neat categories of arguments ('inductive', 'deductive', 'abductive', and so on) do not quite fit over the

> *I know no better method of introducing so large a subject, than that of comparing a single thing with a single thing; an eye, for example, with a telescope ... To some it may appear a difference sufficient to destroy all similitude between the eye and the telescope, that the one is a perceiving organ, the other an unperceiving instrument. The fact is, that they are both instruments. And, as to the mechanism, at least as to mechanism being employed, and even as to the kind of it, this circumstance varies not the analogy at all.*
>
> **Paley**

poetic, lyrical, rambling, sarcastic (in Hume's case) and literary arguments written by non-professional philosophers such as Paley. For more on how to read and interpret philosophical texts see page 359 below.

Issues raised by Hume

David Hume offered some of the most memorable criticisms of the arguments from design in his *Dialogues Concerning Natural Religion* published in 1779. In this book we listen in on three fictional philosophers discussing the nature of God:

- Philo (characterised by his 'careless scepticism')
- Cleanthes (characterised by his 'accurate philosophical turn')
- Demea (characterised by his 'inflexible orthodoxy').

Near the beginning Cleanthes suggests an argument from design that takes a similar form to Paley's version. Cleanthes argues that we can see the same effects in the world as we see in all manner of machines, namely that all the parts are finely adjusted to fit each other and work towards some definite purpose. Working through the analogy, Cleanthes' conclusion is that the cause of these effects must also be similar: just as the design of a machine is caused by human intelligence, so the design of the world is caused by divine intelligence. We can see that, more clearly than Paley's version, this argument is based on an analogy (between a machine and the world), and it moves backwards from observation of the effect (the machine/the world) to a conclusion about the cause (the designer/God).

Philo responds to Cleanthes' argument with a barrage of objections, many of which are also applicable to Paley's argument written 30 years later. Hume was an empiricist, and believed that all our justifiable beliefs come from observation and experience: 'a wise man proportions his belief to the evidence' was his guiding principle.[14] Such a starting point is very close to the critical scepticism of Philo, and many commentators assume that Philo's position is also Hume's.[15]

247

We can classify the problems Philo/Hume raises with this teleological argument into three main types.

Problem 1: We have no experience of world-making

Criticism

We can only recognise that certain sorts of objects, such as machines, have an intelligent designer because we have had direct or indirect experience of such objects being designed and manufactured. So it is by observation of the way in which watches, for example, come into being in our world that we learn that they require a designer. But if we had never had any experience of manufacture, engineering or design, then we would never suppose that an object such as a watch had been designed. Hume's point is that, to know what has brought something about, we have to have experience of its being brought about. So unless we have had some experience of other universes being made we cannot reasonably claim to know whether our own universe has been made.[16]

anthology 2.39

Paley may have been thinking of Hume's attack when he responded to the first criticism above (page 241). Paley thinks that it does not matter if we have never seen a watch being made, and have no understanding of how it is manufactured. Paley asks 'Does one man in a million know how oval frames are turned?'[17] Since the answer is doubtless 'no', then how is it we nonetheless are certain that they have been designed? His answer is that there are certain intrinsic features possessed by certain objects which show that they are designed.

Criticism

Hume's point cuts deeper than this though. It is indeed possible, as Paley says, for us successfully to infer that some unfamiliar object has been designed. But this is only because we can compare it to other manufactured objects that we have previously encountered. If we had absolutely no experience, direct or indirect, of the manufacturing process, then the object would remain a mystery to us. Yet we have no experience of the process that causes universes to come into being, as the universe is unique and there is nothing we can compare it to. The only experiences we have of the universe are of its separate parts, and these parts on their own cannot tell us about the origin of the whole. As Philo says, 'from observing the growth of a hair, can we learn anything concerning the generation of a man?'.[18] For Hume, if we have no experience of this universe being designed, and if we cannot compare it to other universes that have been designed, then we have no grounds for concluding that God or anyone else has designed it.

Experimenting with ideas

The arguments in the activity above (pages 240–241) all relied on analogies. However, although two things might be similar in some respects, they might be very dissimilar in other respects.

1　Examine the table below. List the similarities and dissimilarities between each pair of things listed.

2　How might the dissimilarities you have listed damage the arguments on pages 240–241?

	Similarities	Dissimilarities
a) A dog and a cat		
b) A dog and a duck-billed platypus		
c) A curry and a nation		
d) A window-box and a garden		
e) A wild animal and the common people		
f) The child–parent relationship and the student–teacher relationship		
g) Acting as a life-support machine for a violinist and carrying an unborn child		
h) A machine and the universe		

Problem 2: Arguments from analogy are weak

An argument from analogy claims that, because X is like Y in one (observed) respect, they are therefore probably alike in some other (hidden) respect. However, arguments like this are only reliable when the two things being compared have lots of relevant similarities. A reliable example of an argument from analogy might be this: I notice that you and I behave in similar ways when we miss the nails we are hammering and hit our thumb; from this I infer that you and I have similar sensations following thumb-hammering incidents. I conclude, by analogy with my own case, that when you smash your thumb with a hammer you feel pain. This conclusion seems justified even though it is impossible for me to feel your pain. It is justified because you and I are similar in at least one important way: we both share a similar human physiology.

The question is: does a machine have enough relevant similarities with the universe to support the conclusion that they were both designed?

Criticism

In most cases complex machines are the product of many years of trial and error, with each new generation of machine an improvement on its predecessors. If the universe is to be considered analogous with the way machines have been developed then 'many worlds might have been botched and bungled' (as Philo says) before this one was created. In other words this universe may be the product of trial and error, one in a long line of 'draft' universes, and may well be superseded by a better one in the future. This line of argument is fully in keeping with the analogy and suggests that the designer of the universe would be far from the perfect being that the argument is supposed to prove.

anthology
2.40

Criticism

Hume (through the character of Philo) suggests that the universe is not even like a machine, not even a vast and complex one. Hume argues that the universe resembles something more organic than mechanical; it is far more like an animal or vegetable than 'a watch or a knitting-loom'.[19] If so, the appearance of function and purpose among the parts of the universe is due more to 'generation or vegetation than to reason or design'. And since a vegetable does not have any designer; since its organisation appears to develop by some blind natural process, we have no reason to suppose that the universe is designed. Perhaps it simply grew! Now, it may seem rather absurd to compare the universe to a giant vegetable, but this is partly Hume's point: it is only as absurd as comparing the universe to a machine. For Hume there is nothing to choose between the world–machine analogy and the world–vegetable analogy: both are equally flawed comparisons. Flawed because, as we have said, for an argument from analogy to be reliable the two things being compared need to be alike in all the relevant ways. Unfortunately in both Cleanthes' and Paley's teleological arguments the two things being compared (a man-made object and the universe) are hardly like each other at all. Therefore Cleanthes (and Paley) cannot conclude, on the basis of the analogy with a machine, that the universe has a designer.

Experimenting with ideas

Think about how you might reason backwards from the cause to the effect. Have a look at the list of effects (in the left-hand column), and the list of possible causes (in the right-hand column), and then answer questions 1–3 below.

Effect	Cause
a) A stylish and ergonomic wooden shelving unit	**A)** A five-year-old girl
b) Concentration camps	**B)** An unshaven and smelly carpenter
c) A simple metal ruler	**C)** A murderer and common thief
d) A classic racing car	**D)** An engineer working from his London garage
e) A miniature cottage made from small plastic building blocks	**E)** A power-hungry megalomaniac
f) A shoddy, badly made, wooden table	**F)** A team of world-class designers
g) One small piece of a quilt	**G)** A vegetarian who hates the sight of blood
h) A stunning sixteenth-century painting of Jesus being entombed	**H)** A 90-year-old woman
i) An efficient legal system	**I)** A smart and trendy carpenter

1 For each effect try to work out who created (or caused) it. We have connected one as an example.
2 What reasons can you give for each decision you've made?
3 What problems are there with reasoning backwards from effects to causes in this way? (Hint: G is a possible description of Adolf Hitler.)

Problem 3: It is possible that the appearance of design occurred through random processes

David Hume, again through the character of Philo, suggests an alternative to the claim that the universe, with its appearance of purpose and order, must have had a designer. Hume argues that it is at least possible that the universe is ordered and life-supporting as a result of chance and not intelligence.[20] This theory is often referred to as the Epicurean hypothesis, after the ancient Greek philosopher Epicurus (341–270BCE) who proposed that the universe exists in the way it does as a result of the random movements of a finite number of atoms. Over an infinite period of time these atoms will take every possible position, some of them ordered, some of them chaotic. It just so happens that the physical universe is currently in a state of order, and that, by chance, beings have evolved that are capable of reflecting on the universe and why it is here. Hume argues that, although this may be a remote possibility, it cannot be disregarded as a plausible explanation for the so-called design in the universe.

anthology
2.41

The Epicurean hypothesis, unsurprisingly, has not found favour with theologians, who continue to seek scientific grounds for saying that God, not chance, is the best explanation for design in the universe.

 Experimenting with ideas

A long time ago in a universe far away there lived the Yahoos, a species of self-conscious, carbon-based alien life forms. At a certain point in their intellectual evolution the Yahoos began to ponder the mysteries of the universe, where it came from and why they were here. Some of them argued that the universe was purposeful, with each part contriving to enable the evolution of the Yahoos themselves. The Yahoos believed that such a finely adjusted universe, which had resulted in the existence of Yahoos, clearly required an explanation.

1 Which explanation best accounts for the existence of the Yahoos:
   a) a teleological explanation, relying on the guiding intelligence of God; or
   b) an 'Epicurean' explanation, relying on blind chance?
2 Are there any other explanations that might account for the existence of the Yahoos?
3 Are the Yahoos justified in their belief that the universe has been perfectly adjusted so that they might come into existence? Why/Why not?

Problem 4: The argument does not demonstrate the existence of a perfect being

One of the main assumptions on which Cleanthes' teleological argument rests is that 'like effects have like causes';[21] that is, two things that are similar in their effects have similar causes. Both Cleanthes and William Paley must make this assumption if they are to conclude that the universe has a designer:

1 Machines and the universe exhibit similar features of design ('like effects').
2 Therefore they have both been designed by some intelligent being ('like causes').

Yet neither Cleanthes nor Paley examines in detail how far the likeness of causes can extend, both being happy to move quickly to the conclusion that the designer of the universe is God.

Criticism

Philo, however, takes the idea of 'like causes' and gleefully runs with it, bringing out some potential absurdities in comparing the universe with machines. He finds that by staying true to the analogy he arrives at possible causes of the universe that are nothing like a perfect, unique God. So he makes the following points:

1 Complex machines are not usually the product of a single brilliant designer. Instead teams of people are involved in their design and construction. So, by the 'like causes' principle, the universe may also have been designed and created by many gods, not by a single deity.
2 We can take the analogy to its extreme by fully 'anthropomorphising' the designers of the universe; that is, making them very similar to humans. For example, the designers and constructors of complex machines are often foolish and morally weak people. In the same way the gods who built the universe may well be foolish and morally weak. Humans involved in manufacture are both male and female, and reproduce in the usual fashion; so perhaps the deities are gendered and also engage in reproduction (like the gods of ancient Greece and Rome).
3 Where there are design faults in a machine we usually infer that the designer lacked resources or skills, or simply did not care. The universe appears to contain many design faults (particularly those that cause needless pain and suffering). For all we know this is because it was created by a God who lacked the power, skill or love to create something better (or perhaps, Philo muses, it was created by an infant or a senile God). As Philo says, the most reasonable conclusion of this argument is that the designer of the universe 'is entirely indifferent … and has no more regard to good above ill than to heat above cold or drought above moisture'.[22] This is a far cry from the all-loving God envisaged by Cleanthes and Paley and Hume makes the same point in his *Enquiry Concerning Human Understanding*. Here Hume frames his religious scepticism inside a discussion about the Greek gods (for Hume this was a safe intellectual space for an analysis of religious ideas in general, within which he could avoid scandal and prosecution). He argues, again by the 'like causes' principle, that theologians are simply not justified in concluding that God is a perfect being because of the existence of such pain and suffering in the world. Hume thinks that instead of acknowledging this, theologians busy themselves in trying to 'save the honour 'of their gods by showing why a perfect being would allow such unhappiness to exist'.

This last objection, which draws on the problem of evil (see page 298), may not be fatal for a teleological argument. Paley acknowledges the possibility of an attack from this quarter in the criticism above. But Paley argues that it is not necessary that a machine be perfect in order to be designed; all that is important is that the machine exhibits some sort of purpose. We shall see when we examine the problem of evil that the existence of God isn't necessarily incompatible with the presence of apparent design flaws (like unnecessary pain and suffering) in the universe.

It may also be possible to side-step Philo's criticisms by conceding that we can say very little about the designer of the universe purely on the basis of a teleological argument. This would take the sting out of Philo's attacks, as the conclusion of such an argument would simply be that a designer of the universe exists and would make no claims about what such a designer is like. In this case Cleanthes and Paley need only show a common thread of intent in the design of a machine and of the universe: just as the machine's design is the result of intentional action so is the universe's design. For Robert Hambourger, a modern supporter of teleological arguments, so long as we concede that the universe exhibits elements of design, even if only in parts and even if other parts are flawed, then this 'would be enough to show that something was seriously wrong with the atheist's standard picture of the universe'.[23] If we admit the possibility of design then we also admit the idea of an intentional act lying behind the design, and this would undermine the atheist's position.

Criticism

However, we have now moved a long way from the optimistic claims, made by supporters of the arguments from design, that we can see God's handiworks in nature just as we see evidence of an artisan in an artefact. Hume's Philo concludes that the very most that arguments from design are able to establish is 'that the cause or causes of the universe probably bear some remote analogy to human intelligence'.[24] Such a tentative conclusion is unlikely to persuade anyone of the existence of God, unless they already believe in him.

▶ **ACTIVITY**

Re-read Paley's teleological argument. Where do you think Hume's criticisms really hit home? For each proposed criticism decide:

a) whether it undermines a premise, and, if so, identify which premise, or

b) whether it undermines the structure of the argument, i.e. the steps it takes towards the conclusion, or

c) whether Paley (see above, pages 241–245) had already anticipated and successfully defended his argument against this criticism

d) whether Swinburne (see below, pages 250–253) successfully defeats Hume's criticisms.

Issues raised by Kant

Immanuel Kant (1724–1804), in his *Critique of Pure Reason*, examines and names of three of the most important arguments for the existence of God. The names of two of these proofs are now familiar to students of the philosophy of religion – the 'ontological' and the 'cosmological' arguments – while the name he gave to the third argument didn't really take off: the 'physico-theological' argument, or the argument from design. Kant is extremely sympathetic to arguments from design, stating that they should be treated with respect (in contrast, perhaps, to Hume's treatment of them). We owe these arguments respect, says Kant, because they are the oldest and clearest proofs, and are the ones that most strike a chord with the way we think about the world.

For Kant the physico-teleological argument works as an *a posteriori* argument, based on clear evidence of order in the world; order that could not have just come about by itself, but which must be the product of a sublime and wise cause beyond the world.

Criticism

There are several issues with this argument from design that Kant briefly considers, then passes over, possibly because he thinks that he has found a decisive flaw that renders the argument inadequate as a proof of God's existence. Kant does not think we need to criticise too strictly the analogy between the natural world and the world of human artefacts. Nor does he think that we need to question whether the argument from design actually shows that the designer of the world really does have an understanding and a will (a conclusion that its defenders wish to draw, but which Kant thinks they may not be entitled to draw). The real issue that Kant finds within the argument from design is that its conclusion is not enough to prove the existence of God in the way that its supporters want.

If we are to be careful in our use of the argument from analogy then Kant thinks we are only justified in actually specifying a cause which the argument merits. Yet the argument from design does not do this, but instead it draws a conclusion which it is not justified in making. When we look closely at the world of human artefacts (such as houses, ships and watches) then we are entitled to conclude that those artefacts have properties which indicate that they were designed by architects, shipbuilders and watchmakers. However, the architects and builders did not create these houses and ships from nothing; they used materials that already existed.

What Kant seems to be saying here is that in the first part of the argument from design ('evidence of design in the watch implies a watchmaker') we only conclude that the maker designed and put together the *form* or structure of the watch; we do not actually conclude that they also created the material (the metal, glass and leather strap) that the product was made from. When we transfer this argument, by analogy, to the universe, we are only entitled to conclude that there is a worldly architect (see over). We are not entitled to draw from the analogy the conclusion that the designer of the universe also created the materials with which they built the world. In other words the fact that there is order and harmony in the universe does not lead to the conclusion that there is a creator of the universe, but can lead only to the 'existence of a cause proportioned to' this evidence, namely to the existence of a worldly architect.[25]

William Blake, *The Ancient Days*, 1974. For Kant, the design argument can only demonstrate the existence of a designer (not a creator) of the universe.

Criticism

The 'lofty purpose', as Kant puts it, of the argument from design is to prove two things: that there is a being who created the universe and that being contains all perfections. We have just seen that Kant thinks the argument shows at most that there is an architect of the universe, not a creator. But does the argument show anything about this architect's qualities (that they are omnipotent, omniscient, wholly good, and so on)? Again, for Kant, the argument cannot stretch that far. The analogy works by our imagining the qualities needed for a human watchmaker to construct a watch, then amplifying them until they are of sufficient magnitude to account for the design of the universe. Which means that the worldly architect must have great power, great skills, great knowledge, and so on …? But, Kant says, we cannot conclude from the argument that the worldly architect has the perfect, infinite qualities normally ascribed to God: omnipotence, omniscience, supreme goodness. This is the problem, Kant thinks, with *a priori* proofs for God's existence: you cannot move from evidence in the world (for example, that the world has uncanny regularity, order, and so on) to the conclusion that God is perfect. This last step to perfection, which is the most crucial step, cannot be taken purely on the basis of observation:

To advance to absolute totality by the empirical road is utterly impossible.[26]

Kant, *The Critique of Pure Reason*, page 522

Although Kant was a devout Christian, he was also a rigorous and disciplined philosophical thinker, and he believed that God was a being who lay beyond the limits of our intellect and our experience. Kant thought it was not, then, possible to prove God's existence through *theoretical* arguments such as the ones explored here. However, Kant did think it was possible to show that there were strong *practical* reasons for believing in God, even if these reasons did not amount to a formal proof or demonstration. The practical reasons that Kant gave are that only God can give meaning to our moral actions, and we explore this 'moral' argument in another of our books.[27]

Learn More

Issues raised by Darwin

Traditional arguments from design, based on the analogy made between the natural world and human artefacts, were faced with further criticism when Charles Darwin's (1809–1882) work on natural selection was published.

Darwin had first proposed the theory of evolution by natural selection in his book *On the Origin of Species* (1859). Darwin argued that there is 'natural selection' for characteristics that enables an organism to survive. In turn this means more offspring that share these advantageous characteristics, which themselves have more offspring, and therefore the characteristic, over a number of generations, becomes more common throughout the species. Hence a species becomes more adapted to its environment (followers of Darwin are often referred to as adaptationists).

Much of the persuasive power of an argument like Paley's lay in examples of design taken from the natural world: it seemed obvious that the intricacy of a human eye and the beauty of a peacock's tail could not have come about by chance; they must have been designed. However, Darwin's research and publications provided an account of how such perfectly adapted features could and did come about, not by intelligent design, but by the struggle of every generation of species to compete, survive and reproduce.

> *The old argument from design in nature, as given by Paley ... fails now that the law of natural selection has been discovered. We can no longer argue that, for instance, the beautiful hinge of a bivalve shell must have been made by an intelligent being, like the hinge of a door by man. There seems to be no more design in the variability of organic beings ... than in the course which the wind blows.*[28]
>
> **Darwin**

Nonetheless, teleological arguments have proved to be extraordinarily robust in the face of other challenges from naturalism (theories that claim the universe can be explained in a fully naturalistic, non-supernatural, way); this is despite the success of modern physics and biology in explaining the apparent order and purpose of the universe.

Swinburne's argument from design

Richard Swinburne (1934–) has put forward an argument from design that he believes avoids the formal objections made by Hume in the *Dialogues*. At the beginning of his paper, Swinburne outlines some clear parameters within which he thinks his argument succeeds. First, he acknowledges that the argument from design cannot prove the existence of an omnipotent, omniscient and wholly good being, nor can it prove the existence of the God of Abraham, Isaac and Jacob. Swinburne thinks instead that the argument from design shows the existence of 'a very powerful, free, non-embodied rational agent' who is responsible for the order or regularity of the universe.[29] By moderating his conclusion in this way, Swinburne side-steps Kant's criticisms (above, pages 253–255).

Second, Swinburne concedes that his argument is an argument from analogy, and as such it is vulnerable to the criticism that the analogy between (order found in) human productions and (order found in) the universe may be considered by some people to be too weak to support the conclusion.

Third, Swinburne thinks we need to make a distinction between two types of regularity or order. The first type of order is 'spatial order' (or regularities of co-presence), which is the arrangement of objects in space; the parts of Paley's watch are an example of this, as are the different parts of a human eye, or the arrangement of books in a library. The second type of order is 'temporal order' (or regularities of succession), which is the pattern of the way objects behave in time; a billiard ball being moved when it is hit, or a stone falling to the ground, or a friend arriving at your house because you have asked them round. This is an important distinction for Swinburne because he thinks that most well-known arguments from design, Paley's in particular, rely on the first type of order (regularities of co-presence) to prove that God exists. This has made them vulnerable not only to Hume's criticisms, but also to Darwin's theory of evolution, which Swinburne acknowledges had a devastating effect on the traditional arguments from design. The theory of evolution explains natural 'regularities of co-presence' without any reference to God; for example, it explains how the parts of an eye evolved to work together with such efficiency and success.[30] So arguments like Paley's, which could not account for regularities of *co-presence* without reference to God, no longer succeed as evolution can now account for such regularities. Swinburne thinks that his revised argument, which is based on regularities of *succession* like Aquinas' proof (above, page 237), can avoid these criticisms.

Within these parameters Swinburne then proceeds with his argument:

1   Regularities of succession occur both as natural phenomena (as a result of natural laws) and as a result of free human action (for example, billiard balls moving and stones falling can be explained by natural laws; friends actually turning up to your house on time for once can be explained by the free action of humans).

anthology
2.43

2 Regularities of succession in the human world can be properly and fully explained by the rational choices of a free agent (for example, 'I said to my friend to turn up at seven, and she didn't want to be late, so she got her act together and rushed over on time').

3 This (point 2) is because free agents have the intelligence, power and freedom to bring about regularities of succession.

4 Regularities of succession that are the result of natural laws (for example, gravity) cannot be *explained* by reference to other natural laws.

5 However, by analogy with point 2, regularities of succession in the natural world can be fully explained by the rational choices of a free agent.

6 The universe, and its natural laws, is immense and complex.

7 Therefore (from points 5 and 3) regularities of succession in the natural world can only be fully explained by a free agent who has the immense intelligence, power and freedom needed to bring about such order in the universe.

> *An agent produces the celestial harmony like a man who sings a song.*[31]
>
> **Swinburne**

There is one final supposition we should consider, which leads Swinburne to conclude that the powerful, rational agent who shapes the universe has a different physical status from us. We humans are free rational agents who control our own bodies, and it is through our bodies that we are able to act on the universe. Swinburne argues that an agent who could directly control the whole universe cannot have a body. So we should add to point 7 that the being who shapes the universe is disembodied.

Swinburne's criticisms of Hume

Remember that Swinburne's aim in this argument is to avoid the criticisms that Hume (through the character of Philo) makes of the argument from design. Swinburne feels he has done this by building his argument on the basis of regularities of succession (not co-presence, such as the parts of an eye); and by being careful in how far his conclusion extends (he doesn't claim it proves the existence of a perfect being); and by acknowledging that it is an argument from analogy and so is vulnerable to criticisms made of analogies.

Criticism

Let us briefly go through some of Hume's criticisms, outlined above (pages 247–253) and look at Swinburne's responses.

1 **We have no experience of world-making.** Swinburne argues that Hume is wrong to criticise the argument from design on this count; after all, science does proceed by proposing and testing theories both for things they have not observed and for things which are unique. Most obviously, theoretical physicists and cosmologists propose respectable theories about the universe, which is unique. For Swinburne this suggests that Hume has an inadequate understanding of how science, and scientists, work.

2 **It is possible that the appearance of design occurred through random processes**. For Swinburne this criticism made by Hume is aimed against arguments from design that are based on 'regularities of co-presence', such as the parts of an eye. So Hume is suggesting that the current ordered state of the physical universe may be, as Epicurus suggests, the result of random processes that bring about occasional spatial order. But, for Swinburne, the Epicurean hypothesis does not apply to the more fundamental laws of physics that underpin the structure of the universe, and so this hypothesis does not apply to his version of the argument from design.

3 **The argument does not demonstrate the existence of a perfect being.** We have seen that Swinburne is prepared to concede this, and he accepts that his argument may only prove the existence of an immensely powerful, immensely intelligent, free and rational agent who is disembodied and who shapes the universe. It is unlikely that atheists will consider this to be a significant concession, as if Swinburne has successfully proved the existence of such a being then the case for ATHEISM has been severely damaged.

4 **Arguments from analogy are weak.** Finally, we know that Swinburne is prepared to concede that his argument is vulnerable to criticism from people who are not convinced by the analogy, and who are prepared to hunt out and find disanalogies.

▶ **ACTIVITY**

I Read through Swinburne's argument above, and in Anthology extract 2.43 at the end of the book.
2 Identify the points at which Swinburne is using an analogy.
3 What problems do you think there are with this analogy?
4 How might Hume, if he were writing philosophy today, respond to Swinburne?

Summary

The argument from design aims to prove the existence of God on the basis of evidence drawn from our observations of the universe. These include the observation that living beings, the components they are made up of and the environment they live in, appear to be purposeful, as well as the observation that the universe has a regularity of motion and the order of events, particularly in its physical laws. These two types of observation – of purpose and regularity in the world – are indicators for many people that the world has been designed, because these features are ones we expect to find in objects that we have designed. Thus many arguments from design proceed by what philosophers call an argument from analogy: the universe is analogous to a human artefact, and when we find that these both have general features in common (including purpose and regularity) then this suggests that they also have their origins in common, namely that they have both been designed.

Of all the proofs of God's existence, arguments from design are the most reliant on empirical observation and scientific theories. For this reason we might think that they would be the most vulnerable to scientific criticism; and yet they have consistently proved to be resilient and adaptive. Arguments from design have managed to incorporate developments like the mechanical universe of Galileo and Newton, Darwin's theory of evolution and recently the Big Bang theory. As they respond to science, so teleological arguments have shifted their focus from one special feature of the universe to another: from wondering at the place of the Earth at the centre of the universe, to puzzling over the perfect spiral of a snail's shell, to calculating the probability of carbon atoms forming. The theory of intelligent design is just such a theory, put forward by believers, which adapts in this way.

An atheist might find this unacceptable. After all, a theory that shifts and adjusts according to the prevailing intellectual wind seems to be unfalsifiable; that is to say, there would appear to be no way of demonstrating that it is false. Theories that cannot be falsified are regarded by some thinkers as meaningless, and this is an idea we will be examining more closely when we look at Flew below (page 307ff). However, the popularity of teleological arguments with ordinary believers and religious philosophers is undiminished. We are still struck by the beauty and orderliness of the universe, whether in the equations of theoretical physics, or in watching a thunderstorm above a city. To the atheist, it is a wonder that chance has led to such things and to our being here to appreciate them. But the atheist also looks at other features of the world and asks, 'How can you believe in God when this is the world we live in?' It is not the order and regularity of the natural world that strikes many atheists, but the disorder and disharmony that creates so much pain, suffering and misery. We will return to this issue when we look at the problem of evil in detail in Chapter 2.2.4 below.

2.2.3 Cosmological arguments

Introduction

> *What was it then that determined something to exist rather than nothing?* [1]
> **Hume**

COSMOLOGICAL ARGUMENTS appeal to our intuition that the existence of the universe (along with everything else) needs an explanation. In its most basic form, a cosmological argument attempts to understand and answer the question 'Why is there a universe rather than nothing at all?' Humans thirst for answers to 'why' questions, and looking up at the stars at night it is easy to move from asking 'Why are we here?' to asking 'Why is any of this here?' Many people feel that the existence of the universe demands an explanation; that there must be some reason why it is here. The cosmological arguments propose that an explanation for the existence of the universe cannot be found within the universe, but must be located in some external source or cause. This external cause, the arguments claim, must be God. Moreover, the arguments conclude that God doesn't need an explanation, and doesn't have an external cause, because God is his own cause: his existence is necessary.

So, like ontological proofs, cosmological arguments claim that God has a necessary existence (in contrast to the universe, which is dependent upon God for its existence). However, unlike ontological proofs, cosmological ones base their conclusion that God exists on our experience of the universe.[2] So the premises of cosmological arguments are knowable *A POSTERIORI*.[3] The type of reasoning generally involved in such proofs (rather than being purely deductive as in an ontological argument) is inductive reasoning. The arguments proceed from what we know of the universe through experience and draw conclusions about what lies beyond our experience, namely the existence of God. One famous exception to this is the Kalam cosmological argument. This type of argument, we shall see, is a deductive argument (although based on *a posteriori* premises).

Cosmological arguments fall roughly into two types: causal arguments and arguments from contingency. 'Contingency' in this context roughly means the dependency upon something else, but we shall examine this concept in more detail below. The cosmological arguments based on contingency are built around the claim that the universe is contingent and depends upon something outside of itself for its existence and creation (for theologians that 'something' is God). Cosmological arguments based on causation, or a causal principle, tend to move from the claim that things in the universe all have a cause to the claim that the universe itself must have a cause (and again theologians would argue this 'first' cause is God).

In this chapter we briefly sketch the origins of cosmological arguments in Plato and Aristotle before focusing on three versions of these arguments put forward by religious philosophers, and the criticisms made of these by Hume and Russell. The three formulations of the cosmological argument we look at are:

1 The Kalam argument
2 Aquinas' three ways
3 Descartes' cosmological argument.

Experimenting with ideas: Why are you doing this?

1 On the right-hand side of a piece of paper write down the following event: 'This book lands on the floor.'
2 Now just to the left of it write down another event that caused the book to land on the floor. (Perhaps you were told to drop it by a teacher, or perhaps you were bored with it.)
3 Now to the left of this event write down another event that caused the event in 2 to happen.
4 Keep going as long as you can, writing down a cause for each event.

Your sheet of paper should look something like **Figure 2.18**.

Figure 2.18 A chain of causes and effects.

You probably found that the chain of cause and effect appears to have no end and could go on for ever. But you may also have wondered how, in that case, the whole chain got started in the first place. Proponents of cosmological arguments reckon that chains like this just have to get started by something and that this something must be God.

To see how these arguments work in detail we must begin in the ancient world where they were first articulated.

The contributions of Plato and Aristotle

Shall we say then that it is the soul which controls heaven and earth.

Plato, *Laws* (Book X, 897c)

Learn More

The origins of various forms of cosmological argument lie in the works of two ancient Greek philosophers, Plato (428–348BCE) and Aristotle (390–323BCE). In the *Laws* (reproduced in Hick, ed, *The Existence of God*) Plato categorised different kinds of motion or change. His most important distinction was between things that had the power to move or change both themselves and others (which he termed 'primary movers') and things that could only move or change others once they had been moved (called 'secondary movers'). For Plato, primary movers were the ultimate source of change, as they alone possessed the power spontaneously to cause motion.

Plato argued in the *Laws* that only souls could be primary movers, and that whatever causes the whole universe to change and move must also be a soul. So Plato's contribution to cosmological arguments is the suggestion that the universe is dependent on some ultimate, intelligent primary mover.

The series must start with something, since nothing can come from nothing.

Aristotle, *Metaphysics*, Beta 4 (999b)

Aristotle also believed that all changes in the universe must come from some ultimate source. In the *Metaphysics* he put forward an argument to prove that there must be an 'unmoved mover' who is the ultimate cause of the universe. His argument asks us to consider two competing claims: that the universe has an ultimate mover, and that the universe has no ultimate mover. By showing that the second claim is not possible, he leaves us with only one option, namely that there is an ultimate mover (itself unmoved). We can represent his attack on the second claim as follows in **Figure 2.19**.

The argument we have presented here, on the basis of Aristotle's argument, is known as a *REDUCTIO AD ABSURDUM*. This means taking a point of view and reducing it to absurdity in order to show that it is false. The absurdity here is in step 3, as clearly there is a chain of movers and moved: after all the universe undoubtedly exists. But as step 3 follows on from step 2,

1. The chain of movers and moved has no beginning; there is no ultimate mover:

2. (From 1.) In which case nothing is causing the first thing to move:

3. But if nothing caused the chain there would be no chain at all (one of Aristotle's metaphysical assumptions is that 'nothing comes from nothing').

4. However, there clearly is a chain of movers and moved, as the universe around us does actually exist. So the original assumption (that there is no ultimate mover) must be false. The only other possibility is that there is an ultimate mover, one that lies behind the chain of movers and moved, and which itself is unmoved: this is the Unmoved Mover.

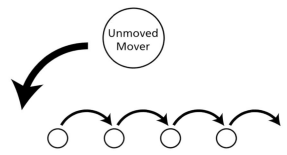

Figure 2.19 Aristotle's proof that there must be an unmoved mover.

and step 2 follows from step 1, Aristotle feels entitled to reject these claims as well. Having shown that step 1 – that the chain of movers has no beginning – is false, he has proved that there must be an ultimate mover, which itself is not moved. However, most importantly for Aristotle, the chain of movers and moved does go back in time for eternity, and the 'unmoved mover' that sustains this chain of movers and moved must be an eternal unmoved mover. This claim that the universe is eternal is challenged by the first cosmological argument that we look at, the Kalam argument.

The Kalam argument

Every being which begins has a cause for its beginning. Now the world is a being which begins. Therefore, it possesses a cause for its beginning.[4]
Al-Ghazali

Parallel to the development of philosophy in Western Europe in the Middle Ages, there was a strong philosophical tradition developing among Muslim philosophers in the Middle East who had access to the works of Plato and Aristotle. This tradition, like the Christian tradition in the West, aimed to assimilate the intellectual insights and tools of Greek philosophy within Islam, and one of the most significant Islamic philosophers was al-Ghazali (1058–1111). Al-Ghazali proposed an argument for the existence of God which has the form of a type of causal cosmological argument, and which became known as the Kalam argument. 'Kalam' means 'speech' in Arabic and it refers to the theological claims made by Islamic philosophers and the arguments put forward to support these, together with any defences or criticisms of the position. In the Christian tradition of the Middle Ages this kind of theological writing and debate was known as scholasticism, but in the Islamic world it was known as Kalam.

Al-Ghazali's argument has been recently revived by the theologian William Lane Craig (1949–, who can be seen debating this in numerous clips online), and his argument in its simplest form is presented as having the structure of a deductive argument or a syllogism. A syllogism is a particular type of deductive argument consisting of three parts: a major premise (All 'A's are 'B'); a minor premise (This is a 'B') and a conclusion (Therefore this is an 'A'). You have already met (above, page 207) an example of a syllogism which is one much repeated by philosophers (possibly because of the poignant and painful way in which Socrates did actually die):

1 All men are mortal.
2 Socrates is a man.
3 Therefore Socrates is mortal.

The foundations of cosmological arguments are based on *a posteriori* claims (Craig sometimes refers to these as 'inductive evidence'), and they differ from cosmological argument to cosmological argument. For example, they could be based on a general claim about motion or causation or contingency; but with the Kalam argument it is about *time*. This is how that structure appears in Craig's summary of the Kalam Argument[5]:

1 Everything with a beginning must have a cause.
2 The universe has a beginning.
3 Therefore the universe must have a cause.

As you can see, this presentation of Craig's argument has the straightforward form of a syllogism, but Craig does, however, move beyond this deductive argument to make a further claim:

4 Moreover, this cause of the universe must be a personal cause, as scientific explanations cannot provide causal account. This personal cause is God.

One of the assumptions underpinning the Kalam argument, and the claim being put forward in premise 2, is that the universe cannot have existed for an infinite period of time. The Islamic philosophers who had read Aristotle disputed his argument (which we looked at above) that the universe has always existed; after all, it would be hard to reconcile any of the monotheistic religions – Islam, Christianity or Judaism – with the claim that the universe had no beginning. Philosophers like al-Ghazali sought a number of different ways to show that past time could not be infinite, and hence that it must be finite and the universe must have had a beginning.

The sciences and astronomy flowered as disciplines in medieval Islam and one of the arguments put forward by al-Ghazali relied on the latest understanding of the movements of the planets in order to generate a mathematical paradox. It only takes twelve years for Jupiter to orbit the sun, while it takes Saturn thirty years to complete its orbit. If, says al-Ghazali, past time is infinite then Jupiter and Saturn must have orbited the sun the same number of times; but this is impossible as we know that Jupiter must have orbited the sun at least twice as many times. Al-Ghazali concludes from this paradox that 'infinity' is not a coherent concept, and the universe cannot have existed for an infinite past. In which case the universe must have a beginning and therefore it must have a cause, as everything with a beginning has a cause. Once step 3 of the argument has been reached, then for Craig there is a further step needed to show that the cause of the universe (the First Cause, or the unmoved mover) cannot be a naturalistic scientific cause, but instead must be a supernatural cause of immense power. For Craig, as for his predecessors, this cause is God.

Criticism

Mathematicians, at least since the time of Newton and Leibniz (who separately invented the branch of mathematics called calculus), were able to work comfortably with the idea of infinitely small numbers. However, it wasn't until the work of the mathematician George Cantor (1845–1918) that maths was able to accommodate infinite numbers, and solve some of the paradoxes described by al-Ghazali which arise from infinite numbers (see the activity below). Cantor created a new form of mathematics, known as Set Theory, which was able to accommodate both finite and infinite sets. Set Theory is now a well-established branch of maths, and because 'real' infinity is now no longer thought of as a self-contradictory idea, the paradoxes of al-Ghazali do not show that the universe must be finite.

▶ **ACTIVITY**

1 On a blank sheet of paper write out a long sequence of whole numbers starting with 1 and adding 1 each time:

    1   2   3   4   etc.

2 Underneath each number write down the list of even numbers, starting with 2.

    1   2   3   4   etc.
    2   4   6   8   etc.

3 Draw a line between the two sets of numbers:

    1   2   3   4   etc.

    2   4   6   8   etc.

4 If both sequences continue for infinity, will each list of numbers have the same number of numbers in it? Why? Why not? What puzzles do you think this raises?

Our whole universe was in a hot dense state,

Then nearly 14 billion years ago expansion started. Wait ...[6]

However, over the last 90 years another route has opened up to support premise 2 of the Kalam argument. Since Einstein first proposed his theory of general relativity and Edwin Hubble first discovered cosmological redshift, there has been an increasing scientific consensus that the universe has had a finite past. The theory of the Big Bang, as we all know it, proposes that the universe began with a burst of cosmic inflation 13.7 billion years ago (**Figure 2.20**), and, even as recently as 2014, evidence in the form of gravitational waves was found to support this theory. In this case al-Ghazali seems to be vindicated in his claim that the universe had a finite past, independently of whether his attacks on the alternative proposition (that the universe has had an infinite past) succeed.

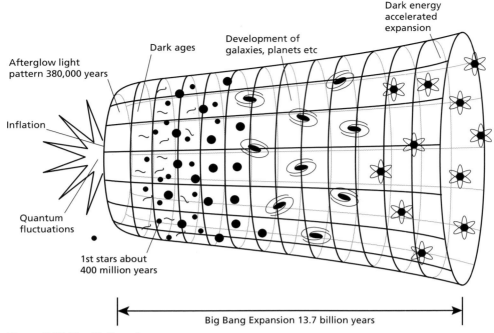

Figure 2.20 The Big Bang theory.

Criticism

Even if we concede, as most people now would, that the universe has a beginning, there are a number of other problems that face the Kalam argument. For example, do we need to concede that everything that has a beginning has a cause (premise 1 of the Kalam argument)? We shall see below (on page 288) that Russell uses another branch of modern science, quantum physics, for evidence that there are things which have a beginning but which do not have a cause. Another challenge can be made in the assumption that even if the universe has a cause (let us call it a First Cause) then this First Cause does not itself have a cause. David Hume asks why believers do not ask for an explanation for why God exists, and look for a cause of God; and if people are happy to accept that at least some things (First Causes) don't have an explanation, or a cause, then could we not be happy to accept the universe without a cause or explanation? One final argument, which we look at below, is whether the Kalam argument and other forms of the cosmological argument, really do demonstrate that the cause of the universe is God (and the kind of God that can be found in the Bible).

Aquinas' three ways

Among Christian philosophers, St Anselm put forward a very succinct cosmological argument,[7] but it was St Thomas Aquinas who explored the proofs in most detail. Aquinas made it his life's work to assimilate into Christian theology the rediscovered philosophy of Aristotle,[8] and he incorporated Aristotle's ideas in his own cosmological arguments for God's existence.

In his book the *Summa Theologica* Aquinas offers five ways in which God's existence can be demonstrated, and the first three ways are all forms of cosmological arguments:[9]

- first way – the argument from motion ⎫
- second way – the argument from causation ⎬ Cosmological arguments
- third way – the argument from contingency ⎭
- fourth way – a type of moral argument
- fifth way – a type of teleological argument (see pages 237–238 above).

The first way and the second way are both forms of causal cosmological argument, and they seek to show that certain general features of the world (causation and motion) must be dependent upon a higher source, which is uncaused or unmoved, namely God. The third way is a cosmological argument based on the contingency of the universe, and it aims to show that the universe is dependent on a necessary being: God.

Aquinas' arguments from motion and causation

Aquinas' first and second ways of proving the existence of God have a similar structure, and are 'causal' versions of cosmological argument. Both begin by noting there are features of the world that we all experience: in the first way it is the existence of motion, in the second way it is the existence of causation. One possible explanation of such features of the universe is that they have existed forever. However, Aquinas argues that this explanation must be false by showing that there cannot be an INFINITE REGRESS of movers or causers. He does so by using a type of *reductio ad absurdum* similar to the one outlined in **Figure 2.19** above. Aquinas then goes on to *show* that these features need an explanation that lies beyond the ordinary chain of motion or causation. Because an infinite regress is not possible, the only other explanation is a cause or a mover that does not fall under the ordinary rules governing causation or motion. Such a being would need no further explanation; it would be the source of all causation without itself having a cause and would be, as Aristotle said, the unmoved mover. Aquinas says that we call such a being 'God'.

We can summarise the first and second ways as follows.

First way

The first way is the argument from motion (which for Aquinas included any type of change):

1 There are some things in motion or a state of change, for example wood burning in a fire.
2 Nothing can move or change itself – in Plato's terms everything is a secondary mover.

anthology 2.44

3   Imagine everything was a secondary mover – then there would be an infinite regress of movers.

4   (*Reductio ad absurdum*) If 3 were true then there would be no prime mover and hence no subsequent movers, but this is false.

5   (Conclusion) There must be an unmoved prime mover (the source of all motion/change) whom we call God.

Second way

The second way is the argument from causation:

1   There is an order of efficient causes (every event has a cause).

2   Nothing can be the cause of itself.

3   Imagine this order of causes goes back infinitely – then there would be no first cause.

4   *Reductio ad absurdum*: If point 3 were true then there would be no subsequent causes, but this is false.

5   Conclusion: There must be a First Cause (the source of all causes) and this we call God.

► **ACTIVITY**

1   Read the Aquinas extract in Anthology extract 2.44 at the back of this book.

2   Identify in this original text where you think the premises outlined above are.

Issues raised against Aquinas' arguments from motion and causation

At the end of this chapter we shall look at some of the sustained criticisms made of the cosmological argument by David Hume and Bertrand Russell (pages 283–289), and many of these criticisms apply to Aquinas' first and second ways. But other issues have also been raised, which we shall look at here.

When we consider the chain of causation or of motion, it is easy to think of it temporally, with each event preceding and causing the next event. In this interpretation, a cause refers to the factor that brought about the effect. The chain of causation is thus one that goes backwards in time, with God, the First Cause, at the beginning starting the whole thing off, rather like a finger knocking over the first of a chain of dominos, or winding up a clockwork machine (see **Figure 2.21**).

Figure 2.21 God as the (temporal) First Cause.

Criticism

If we take the 'temporal' interpretation of causation then the cosmological argument seems to show that a First Cause, God, once existed and once created the universe. However, it is crucial to believers that God is still present to act upon the world and still cares about the world; this after all is the God of Abraham, the God described in the Bible. So the 'domino-flicking' First Cause may satisfy thinkers known as deists, but such a view is not one that a Christian philosopher such as Aquinas could subscribe to.

However, there is another interpretation of the chain of causation that lends itself better to the belief that God, as the First Cause, is acting on the world here and now. This interpretation sees 'causation' in terms of the factors that sustain an event, or keep it going once it has begun. For example, a farmer may plant a seed, and so cause the seed to grow in that patch of land, but it is the particular qualities of the seed, together with a fertile environment, that sustains its growth into a mature plant. The chain, or order, of causation can be thus seen as a hierarchical one with God as the ongoing and ultimate sustaining cause of the universe.[10]

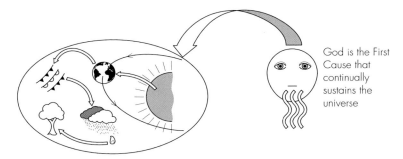

Figure 2.22 God as the (sustaining) First Cause.

God is the First Cause that continually sustains the universe

In **Figure 2.22** we can imagine tracing the cause of a tree back to its seed, then to the weather conditions that enabled the seed to grow, then to the movement of the earth round the Sun that created the weather conditions. But the cosmological argument claims to show that ultimately it is God who causes all these things.

Criticism

At first sight the first and second ways appear to rest on a contradiction. On the one hand Aquinas says that everything must have a cause (nothing can cause itself), but he then concludes that something must exist that can be the cause of itself, namely God. So the original assumption is contradicted by the conclusion.

A defender of a cosmological argument might say that this is precisely what the *reductio ad absurdum* is supposed to prove: that there has to be at least one exception to the rule 'everything must have a cause'. If there were not such an exception, then the universe would have no cause and would never come to exist. But if there is an exception, let us call it the First Cause, then it must be something without a cause, in Aristotle's terms an 'unmoved mover'. This defence has similarities to Anselm's defence against Gaunilo; namely that when we are talking about God we are dealing with a being unlike anything else, a being who has a special form of existence.

Criticism

However, a critic might come back with the response that if we are going to allow for exceptions to the rule 'everything must have a cause' then why make God the exception? Could we not just as well make the universe itself the exception? In other words we would be saying that everything that occurs within the universe must indeed have a cause, but the universe as such does not. The existence of the universe requires no further explanation: it simply is. This would rule out the need to posit God.

Alternatively, it can be asked of the cosmological argument: why must God be the ultimate cause and why is God the point at which our search for an explanation for the existence of things must end? Why, in other words, does the existence of God not require any further explanation? David Hume (1711–1776) offers a version of this criticism, which we look at below (page 284 and **Figure 2.24**).

Criticism

A further criticism arises from Aquinas' claim that an infinite regress of causes or movers is absurd. Aquinas seems to be confusing a (very long) finite chain of causes, for which there would indeed have to be a first cause to begin the chain, with an infinite chain of causes. In the first instance, it is true, if you take away the first cause, then everything else disappears. But in the second instance there is no first cause to take away; the series of causes is infinite. J.L. Mackie gives the example of a series of hooks, all hanging from each other.[11] With a finite series of hooks, each one hangs on the one above it, until we reach the last (or first) hook, which must be attached to something. Take away the wall attachment and the hooks fall – that seems to be how Aquinas is imagining the chain of causes and effects. But with an infinite series of hooks, each is attached to the one above, and so on forever: there is no first hook attached to a wall.

So philosophical critics of cosmological arguments seem prepared to admit that an infinite regress is after all possible, and that there is no need to postulate a 'First Cause'. However, by admitting this possibility such critics might be undermining a key weapon in the armoury of philosophy, what we might call the 'infinite regress FALLACY'. Philosophers often aim to show a position is flawed precisely because it results in an infinite regress. However, we've just seen that some critics of cosmological arguments are proposing an infinite regress of causes as a coherent and valid alternative to a First Cause. Such critics cannot have it both ways: either they hold onto the infinite regress fallacy, which is a useful tool against many a suspect idea, or they discard the fallacy in order to undermine such cosmological arguments. Sadowsky says that philosophers stand to lose more by jettisoning the infinite regress fallacy, than by abandoning this line of attack on cosmological arguments.[12]

Aquinas' third way: A contingency argument

Aquinas' third way is from a different tradition of cosmological arguments – ones that are based on the contingency of the universe and of everything in it. We have noted already that contingency has a close connection with the idea of dependency. So, for example, the existence of a forest is contingent upon the existence of the availability of water to the trees' roots; or the existence of our democratic system of government is dependent upon our having the freedom to vote for different parties. Contingency is also bound up with the idea of mortality or 'shelf life': contingent events occur and then stop, and contingent objects come into being then cease to be. So, once all the rivers are dammed, the forest disappears; take away our freedom to vote for different parties and our democracy will disappear. Finally contingency implies that things are not fixed: they could have been different if the past had been different. If the climate had been hotter, then the forest would never have existed; if Plato's experimental system of 'philosopher kings' had been proven to work, then there may never have been any need for democracy.

 Experimenting with ideas

What, if anything, is the existence of the following contingent upon?

1 Life on planet Earth
2 Your own existence
3 The continuing good health of your neighbour's cat
4 A successful marriage
5 Public trust in politicians
6 An acrobat balancing on top of a human pyramid
7 The whole universe

Cosmological arguments based on contingency claim that everything in the universe is contingent, and thus dependent upon something else.[13] They go on to argue that it is impossible for everything to be contingent; there must be a non-contingent being; that is, a necessary being, upon which the contingent universe is dependent. This necessary being is God. Aquinas' third way is a slightly different version of the argument from contingency. In this argument he emphasises the 'shelf-life' aspect of contingent beings; that is, the fact that they have an expiry date, they come and go, live and die, are generated and destroyed. In other words they are impermanent. Aquinas argues that if everything has an 'expiry date' then at some point everything will expire and cease to exist. Since this has not happened he concludes there must be a permanent being which has no expiry date, and which all impermanent beings depend on for their existence. Let us look at how he reaches this conclusion.

> We find in nature things that are possible to be and not to be, since they are found to be generated and then corrupted.
>
> Aquinas, *Summa Theologica* 1:2:3

Aquinas' third way can be divided into two parts as follows.[14]

Part one

1 Things in the world are contingent (they come into existence and pass out of existence).
2 Imagine everything was contingent; then there was once a time when everything had passed out of existence – that is, there was nothing.
3 *Reductio ad absurdum*: If 2 were true then there would be nothing now (as nothing can come from nothing), but this is false.
4 Conclusion of part one: Therefore not everything can be contingent – there must be at least one thing that is necessary.

Part two

5 For every thing that is necessary it either has the cause of its necessity in itself or outside of itself.
6 Imagine every necessary thing has the cause of its necessity outside of itself.
7 *Reductio ad absurdum*: If point 6 were true then (as with the causal argument outlined above) there would be no ultimate cause of necessity.
8 Conclusion of part two: There must exist a necessary being which causes and sustains all other necessary and contingent beings – this being we all call God.

In the first part of his argument Aquinas is saying that contingent and impermanent things cannot continually furnish the universe throughout its infinite existence. There must come a point in time when impermanent things all cease to exist: their expiry dates all coincide. In which case, Aquinas says, we would expect there to be nothing now. But that is plainly false: the world is still stocked full of contingent beings. Therefore there must exist a permanent (NECESSARY) being that guarantees the continuing existence of impermanent beings, even if they all expire at once. **Figure 2.23** shows how we might try to picture this: we can see there is a point at which contingent beings all expire, but a necessary being sustains the existence of the universe over this 'gap' and generates fresh contingent beings.

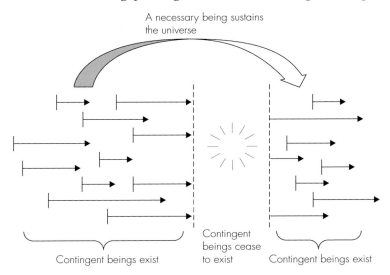

A necessary being sustains the universe

Contingent beings exist

Contingent beings cease to exist

Contingent beings exist

Figure 2.23 God as a necessary being sustaining the universe.

So Aquinas has established that there must exist a permanent, necessary being, which the universe (and the impermanent parts of the universe) depend on for their existence. In the second part of Aquinas' argument he considers whether such a necessary being is itself dependent on another necessary being, which in turn would be dependent upon another necessary being, and so on. Aquinas denies the possibility of an infinite regress of necessary beings. There must, ultimately, be a necessary being who needs no other cause, but who is the cause of itself. So Aquinas concludes that there must exist a necessary being who needs no further explanation or cause, namely God.

Aquinas' conclusion: God is a necessary being

We saw above that if something is contingent then:

- its existence is dependent on other things
- it has a 'shelf life'; it came into existence and will one day cease to exist
- it might have been different (or might never have existed) if the past had been different.

What Aquinas', and other philosophers', cosmological arguments seek to prove is the existence of a non-contingent, necessary being. In contrast to contingent beings, a necessary being:

- has an existence that is independent of everything else
- is eternal; it has always existed and will never cease to exist
- has to exist; and it is impossible that it could be different, no matter how past, present or future circumstances might vary.

It is the existence of such a necessary being, one we call God, which Aquinas believes he has proved through his third way.

Issues with Aquinas' argument from contingency

The following criticisms of Aquinas' third way should be supplemented by the criticisms offered by Hume and Russell who we examine towards the end of this chapter (pages 283–289).

Criticism

Aquinas makes a clear connection (in premise 7 above) between the argument from contingency and the argument from causation. At least one criticism applying to the second way also applies to the third way. The third way relies on a *reductio ad absurdum* in order to prove that an infinite regress of contingent (and necessary) beings is impossible. However, we saw above that Aquinas may not have got his head round exactly what an infinite regress might be, and he may have been thinking of a very long finite series. We agreed that a finite series would need to come to an end at something with a sturdy support like an unmoved mover; but an infinite series does not need such support as it never comes to an end.

Criticism

Aquinas seems to be saying that, over an infinite time period, all contingent things must come to an end, because they are impermanent, and that this would leave nothing left in existence. He concludes that there must be a necessary being that 'keeps things going' even when all contingent beings have ceased to exist. However, Mackie argues that Aquinas is committing a fallacy if he thinks that he can jump from 'every thing at some time does not exist' to 'at some time everything does not exist'.[15] Thus it might be the case that there is an infinite series of overlapping, yet contingent, things in the universe. If this were a possibility, claims Mackie, then there would be no need to hypothesise the existence of a necessary being.

Criticism

A further criticism arises from Aquinas' conclusion that God is a necessary being. Some philosophers have argued that we can talk about necessary propositions, but we cannot talk about necessary beings. The concept of 'necessity' only applies to the truth of statements, not to things that exist. In the light of this account of necessity, perhaps the real meaning of the statement 'God is a necessary being' is that 'the proposition "God exists" is necessarily true'.[16] We saw above (Chapter 2.2.1, note 9) that Hume and Kant challenged the assumption that the term 'necessary' could be applied to propositions about existence, as in the claim 'God exists'. They argued that a claim was only necessary when its denial entailed a contradiction. So, for example, we know that 'bachelors are unmarried men' is necessary because when we deny it (for example, by saying 'bachelors are married men') a contradiction results ('unmarried men are married men').[17] However, both Kant and Hume argue that existential propositions, such as 'Ghosts exist' or 'Socrates once existed', can always be denied without self-contradiction. Even Aquinas accepted that 'God exists' was not self-evident and could be meaningfully denied.[18]

Hence Kant and Hume agree that we cannot say about anything which exists that it is necessary. If this is the case (and not all philosophers agree with this analysis of necessity) then the conclusion of Aquinas' third way is seriously undermined.

Criticism

Even if we accept Aquinas' cosmological arguments as sound, we might criticise them for failing to prove the existence of a being who is worthy of worship, either the God of the philosophers or the God of the Bible. After all, it is possible to imagine a First Cause which does not have some of the essential properties of God, and which may not be personal or benevolent or omniscient.

However, when looking at the conclusions of Aquinas' arguments we should remember that he believed that there were limits to human understanding, and that his proofs had to remain within those limits. Aquinas' three ways were never intended to reveal the nature of God, only to demonstrate that there was some ultimate explanation for the existence of the universe.

▶ **ACTIVITY**

1 Have another look at the summaries of Aquinas' three ways above.
2 Now go through each criticism, identifying which part of Aquinas' arguments the criticism is aimed at: for example, identify the specific premise it undermines, or the invalidity of a particular step.

Descartes' cosmological argument

Wherein are demonstrated the Existence of God and the Distinction of Soul from Body

Descartes

The subtitle of Descartes' *Meditations* boldly asserts that inside its pages God's existence will be proved, as will the distinction between the soul and the body (the theory that became known as DUALISM). We have already seen above (page 221) that Descartes put forward an ontological argument to prove the existence of God, and this can be found in the *Fifth Meditation*. However, in the *Third Meditation* Descartes offers two further proofs of God's existence:

▪ The trademark argument
▪ The cosmological argument

The first of these proofs we have looked at in some detail in the Epistemology section of this book (pages 125–131). The central claim of the trademark argument is that Descartes has an idea of God, a perfect being, and this idea of a perfect being must have been caused by something. Descartes believed there must be 'at least as much reality in the cause as in the effect', which is known as his causal principle. Descartes' causal principle is a cousin of a family of philosophical principles, which stipulate that everything has a reason or a cause. Aristotle's claim that 'nothing can come from nothing' is a part of this family, and these principles are also referred to as the 'Principle of Sufficient Reason' which is the term coined by Gottfried Leibniz (1646–1716) and which Leibniz used to underpin his own version of the cosmological argument. Descartes uses the causal principle to show that the cause of his idea of a perfect being must itself be a perfect being. In other words, God must have planted the idea of God in Descartes' mind (imprinted on it like a trademark), and therefore God must exist. Descartes' trademark argument is an *A PRIORI* argument, reliant only on understanding God as a perfect being, and on an understanding of the causal principle (that any cause must have sufficient power to bring about the effect).

▶ ACTIVITY

Read through the following situations and decide which one of the possible causes below them – a), b) or c) – would count as having 'at least as much reality in the cause as in the effect', i.e. which cause would have sufficient power to bring about that effect:

Effect 1. A teenage girl has just won a multi-million dollar contract to advertise cosmetics for a well-known fashion brand.

a) She has been doing video blogs for a few months on her haul, the stuff she buys in shops, and now has thousands of followers.

b) Her unique look was spotted at an airport, in a fairy-tale manner, by a director of a modelling agency as she flew back to Croydon.

c) Her parents are ridiculously good-looking, rich and famous – as is she.

Effect 2. An Astrology student got the highest grade for the A Level in this subject.

a) He was naturally good at Astrology and as a result he knew in advance what the questions were going to be.

b) There was a mistake in the marking of his exam paper which had not been spotted by the exam board.

c) He had developed a systematic approach to all his subjects, working hard, redrafting each of his essays, taking mock exams and following his revision plan.

Effect 3. A window shatters in your classroom.

a) A butterfly had flapped its wings earlier in the week, causing a complex chain of meteorological events that eventually resulted in the shattering of the glass.

b) A politics student had thrown a stone from outside your class, as part of the 'People In Glass Houses Shouldn't …' campaign against government cuts, and had misjudged her own strength.

c) It was an example of SGB (Spontaneous Glass Breakage).

Effect 4. A skier on holiday says to a man at the top of a mountain 'You're my hero'.

a) He had just saved her life by pulling her from an avalanche.

b) She had just discovered that he was the author of a textbook that she found really helpful when teaching her A Level classes.

c) He had lent her some factor 50 sun-block for her nose, which he kept with him at all times (just in case).

Effect 5. You have an idea that God is defined as a perfect being.

a) This was something you read about in detail when you studied the ontological argument.
b) You understand what Power is, what Love is, what Knowledge is; you also know what 'omni' means; and you understand how to create new words using prefixes.
c) This idea must come from a perfect being in order for you to have it.

Now put Descartes' causal principle into your own words.

Descartes' version: 'The cause of something must contain at least as much reality as the effect.'

Your version:

_____

_____

Embedded in the final stage of the trademark argument in *Meditations 3*, we find a second argument, which is an *a posteriori* argument for God's existence and which you may recognise as having the form of a cosmological argument. It is prompted, as cosmological arguments are often prompted, by the search for an explanation for existence: the Kalam argument and Aquinas' arguments sought to explain why the universe existed, and what causes it to continue to exist; but Descartes has a much narrower line of enquiry, asking himself what caused him to exist and what causes him to continue existing.

This may strike us a rather self-absorbed question, and it would help to remember here the personal philosophical journey that Descartes has taken in the *Meditations* and which led him to this juncture. He began his reflections by questioning whether he knows anything for certain, and reached the troubling position where he now doubts everything that he sees and senses around him. However, he finds he cannot doubt that he is currently doubting or that he is thinking; and he arrives at the conclusion that so long as he is doubting, and thinking, then he *knows* he exists ('I think, therefore I am'). Having reached this narrow foundation of knowledge, Descartes wished to build up for himself other beliefs that he could be certain of; beliefs that were also as clear and distinct as his belief that he himself existed. When reading the *Meditations* you get a sense of the intense focus that Descartes is bringing to his task; it's almost as if we are inside his head travelling on the journey with him, which in a sense we are, as we go through the same processes he goes through in order to fully understand what he is saying. So this lonely but compelling philosophical journey inside one man's mind leads us to the point where Descartes has found another clear and distinct idea: God. But what is the cause of this idea of a perfect being? This stage of the trademark argument we examined on page 126 above, and it is just at this point that Descartes wonders:

Whether I myself, who have the idea, could exist, if no such being existed. Now from what source could I have my being?

Descartes, *Meditations*, page 127

So Descartes is now looking for the explanations that underpin *two* of the facts that he has established:

1 The fact that he has in his mind the idea of a perfect being (God)

and

2 The fact that he has a continuous existence as a conscious being.

So what power is it that both causes him to exist, and also causes him to have the idea of perfect being? We see time and again in the cosmological argument that there is a need to find an explanation, a rationale or a cause, that lies behind the very existence of the world. But Descartes (who has not at this point established any proof of an external world) is less ambitious and he simply wants to know what is the cause of his existence. What is it that sustains his continued existence from one moment to the next?

He first considers the possibility that he could be his own cause; that the power from which his own existence derives comes from within himself. Presumably then in this case all the ideas he holds (including that of a perfect being) would also have their source in himself. Descartes applies the causal principle to this; in other words the principle that the cause must be sufficiently powerful to create the effect. So in order to bring about the idea of a perfect being the cause must itself be a perfect being. As Descartes is considering the possibility here that he is the cause, then it follows that he must be a perfect being. As he clearly is not God, Descartes can reject the claim that he is his own cause.

▶ **ACTIVITY**

Write the paragraph above in the form of an argument with numbered premises, an intermediate conclusion and a conclusion (that Descartes is not the cause of his own existence).

A second possibility examined by Descartes is that he has always existed as a conscious being, in which case there is no need to look for the cause or seek any further explanation. But he rejects this idea on the grounds that we can divide our life into countless small parts, each independent of one another, and for each of these moments we can ask, 'What is causing me to exist as a conscious being?' So saying, 'I have always existed in this way' does not answer the issue at stake here, which is: 'What causes me to exist as a conscious being now and at the next moment, and the next?' For Descartes, the continuation of us, as conscious beings, from one moment to the next requires explanation: there must be something that sustains our existence. He briefly considers the possibility that he might have the power within himself necessary to bring about his continuous existence from one moment to the next. Descartes rejects this possibility on the grounds that if he had such a power then he would be aware of having it, but he is not aware of having any such power.

So Descartes cannot be the cause of his own being, nor can he avoid the issue by saying that has always been a conscious being and that there is no need to look for a cause. The cause of Descartes' idea of God, and of his existence as a conscious being, must come from something outside of himself. Could this cause be something imperfect, something like his parents for example? After all it is plausible to argue that the explanation for why we exist is that we were born to our parents. Descartes is pretty quick to reject this, as they do not sustain me as a conscious being (and did they really have the power to actually make me a conscious being?). It is at this point that we see Descartes' cosmological argument in its clearest form:

anthology
2.45

1 The existence of the idea of God in my mind needs explaining; the continuing existence of me as a conscious being also needs explaining.

2 I cannot be the cause of my idea of God (a perfect being) because I am not God (a perfect being). I cannot bring about my continuing existence as a conscious being because I do not have the power.

3 Therefore the cause of me as a conscious being, and the cause of my idea of God, must lie outside of myself.

4 Either a) this external cause is itself caused by something else, or b) it is its own cause.

5 If a) is true then either c) this other cause must be caused by a further thing, or b) it is its own cause.

6 This sequence of causes cannot run back to infinity, and eventually we will reach an ultimate cause – b).

7 The ultimate cause; that is, the thing that is its own cause, is God.

8 Therefore it is God who ultimately causes my idea of God, and it is God who ultimately sustains my existence as a conscious being.

9 Because I do have an idea of God, and because I know that I am sustained as a conscious being, therefore God must exist as the cause of both these things.

The cosmological part of Descartes' trademark argument ends here, but Descartes goes on to draw to an end his overall trademark argument with the conclusion that God, when he created Descartes, implanted the idea of God in him, in the same way that a craftsman stamps his work with a trademark (see **Figure 1.30**, on page 126, in the Epistemology section).

Issues with Descartes' cosmological argument

Several of the criticisms that apply to the trademark argument as a whole also apply to Descartes' cosmological argument. Refer to the Epistemology section (pages 125–131 above) for more details of these criticisms, and below (pages 283–289) for the criticisms offered by Hume and Russell of cosmological arguments. Descartes himself was happy to field and respond to criticisms, and these objections and replies can be found online here:

- www.earlymoderntexts.com/pdfs/descartes1642_1.pdf
- www.earlymoderntexts.com/pdfs/descartes1642_2.pdf
- www.earlymoderntexts.com/pdfs/descartes1642_3.pdf

Criticism

Is the causal principle true? Descartes' cosmological argument is prompted by his thought that something must have caused his idea of God as a perfect being. The causal principle tells us that you cannot get more out of the effect than was already in the cause; the cause must be sufficiently powerful to bring about the effect. Descartes' conclusion that a perfect being must have caused his idea of a perfect being is built on this causal principle. But as Russell and others have pointed out (see below, page 288), modern physics does appear to allow for effects which are brought about without a cause; for example 'quantum fluctuations' describes the phenomena of virtual particles appearing and disappearing temporarily in space without any cause.

Criticism

Can we infer the cause from the effect? Hume (below, page 285) gave a psychological account of causation, arguing that we develop our idea of causation by watching numerous instances of one thing happening (for example, a glass falling towards the floor) and another thing happening soon afterwards (the glass shattering). We have learned from experience to associate one kind of event with another kind of event, and we start to think of these events as joined together by something we call 'causation'. So causation, for Hume, is something that our minds add to our observations of the world, rather than something we observe in the world itself. How does this apply to Descartes' causal principle? Well, for Hume, we cannot know *a priori* what is the cause of something – we cannot work backwards from the effect to determine the cause of it – and this is particularly true if we are seeing the effects for the first time. For example, if we have never seen ice before we wouldn't be able to work out how the ice was caused: I only learn that cold weather causes water to freeze by observing water freezing in cold weather. On this account the causal principle does not even get off the ground, as we would have no idea (for those events or effects that we had not observed before, or had not observed on many different occasions) what would even count as a sufficient cause.

Criticism

Why can the sequence of causes not go back infinitely, and why are believers happy to suggest that God is the cause of his own being? We are about to look at this criticism below (page 284) when we examine Hume's critique of the cosmological arguments.

Criticism

Is Descartes' argument here a circular argument? There are specific criticisms that we can make of Descartes' argument which arise from the particular philosophical project that he is engaged with. This project is the attempt made by Descartes to establish solid foundations of knowledge, and to build his beliefs up from that point knowing he has secure foundations. One of the most damaging criticisms is known as the Cartesian Circle, and it suggests that steps which Descartes takes to establish the existence of God are not permitted at this point in his project, and that he is pulling his argument up by his own boot-straps. We looked at this criticism above (page xvii), but essentially it is this: Descartes has established that he exists as a thinking thing, and even an evil demon cannot deceive him about his own existence. From that point Descartes uses an array of 'clear and distinct' ideas (including the causal principle, the rules of logic and his idea of God as a perfect being) to prove the existence of God. Once he has proved the existence of God, Descartes argues that God, being benevolent, would not deceive him about his clear and distinct ideas. The circularity is that he relies on clear and distinct ideas to prove the existence of God, but then uses the existence of God to show that he can genuinely rely on clear and distinct ideas. If Descartes was as strict in his *Third Meditation* as he had been in his *First Meditation* then he would not have been able to use the causal principle to prove the existence of God.

Issues raised by Hume

The Scottish ENLIGHTENMENT philosopher, David Hume, in his *Dialogues Concerning Natural Religion*, presses a number of criticisms against the arguments for the existence of God, and we have already looked at those attacking the ontological argument (page 223) and the argument from design (page 247). As you would expect, Hume also raises issues, through the character of Philo, that hit home against each of the versions of the cosmological argument that we have looked at.

> *If the material world rests upon a similar ideal world, this ideal world must rest upon some other; and so on, without end. It were better, therefore, never to look beyond the present material world.*[19]
>
> Hume

The quotation from Hume above suggests that if we genuinely wish to avoid an infinite regress of causes, then we should not search for an explanation beyond the natural universe, as if we move to a supernatural cause then we may be in the same situation as the apocryphal old lady at the philosophy lecture. This story (told by Stephen Hawking, citing an incident possibly recounted by Bertrand Russell, or William James, and with a history tracing back to Hume and John Locke) is the equivalent of a philosophical urban myth. At the end of a lecture on modern cosmology the philosopher asks the audience if they have any questions, and a lady at the back of the audience puts up her hand. 'Your theory', she says, 'that the Earth and all the planets are little balls rotating around the Sun … it's completely wrong.' This particular philosopher is a patient chap, and asks her, 'What, in your view, is the right theory?' 'Well,' the lady is quick to respond, 'the Earth is a flat disc resting on the back of an elephant.' The philosopher, spotting the opportunity for the whole audience to learn about regresses, asks the lady, 'And what, exactly, is the elephant resting on?' 'A turtle,' the lady says. 'And what exactly,' the philosopher asks, 'is the turtle resting on?' 'Oh that's easy,' she says, 'it's turtles all the way down.'

Criticism

Cosmological arguments take issue with the idea of an infinite regress, or turtles all the way down. All of the cosmological arguments outlined above, both those from contingency and those of causation, try to avoid an infinite regress of explanation by giving a privileged status within the chain of causes and effects to the 'First Cause', or the thing that is supposed to be sustaining the universe. This privileged status, which the arguments hope that they have demonstrated, is caused by the First Cause itself not being subject to the same rule as the things that it has caused (the universe): unlike everything else it is uncaused, unmoved, necessary. The First Cause is its own explanation. But Hume questioned this assumption, asking why believers are happy to stop at God in their search for an explanation; instead they could continue their search and ask, 'Why God?' Alternatively, if we accept that there are some things that exist without explanation (like God) then is it possible that the universe could be one of those things, or as Hume says:

> *Why may not the material universe be the necessarily existent Being, according to this pretended explication of necessity?*[20]
>
> **Hume**

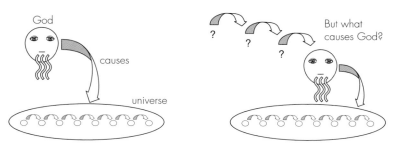

Figure 2.24 Why stop our explanations at God?

Hume suggests that seeking explanations beyond the physical universe will lead to an infinite regress of explanations. So perhaps we would do better to stop our search for explanation with the universe: either accept it has no explanation, or find an explanation for the universe that lies within the universe.

Criticism

The quotation above not only captures Hume's criticism that there is no need to look beyond the physical universe for the 'necessary being' which sustains the existence of the universe, but it also captures Hume's frustration with this 'so-called' account of necessity. For Hume, as for Bertrand Russell (see below), those cosmological arguments which talk about contingent beings (everything in the universe) and a necessary being (God) are misusing the term 'necessary'. If something is 'necessary', in the philosophical sense of that word, then it cannot be denied without contradiction. Hume points out that anything we can conceive of as existing, we can also conceive of as non-existing. So the existence of an alleged 'necessary being' can be denied without contradiction, in which case the being did not have the quality of being necessary after all. We return to Russell's version of this same criticism below (page 287) but as Hume puts it, 'The words "necessary existence" have no meaning, or, which is the same thing, none that is consistent.'[21]

In a word, then, every effect is a distinct event from its cause.[22]

Hume

Criticism

Most cosmological arguments make the assumption that there is a series of causes, such that every event has a cause. Hume put forward a view of causation that, if correct, undermines this assumption. Hume believed that we never actually experience causation; it is something our minds impose upon our perception of the world as a result of past experience. So, although we think we see one snooker ball cause another to move when it strikes it, all we in fact see is one ball move toward another until they touch, then the second ball move away (see **Figure 2.25**). We add the concept of 'cause' to this experience, once we have seen it happen frequently enough, but we can easily think of a particular event as not having this cause.[23] If Hume is right, then we have no knowledge of any 'chain of causes and effects', and this goes some way to undermining the first premise of the argument from causation. We have already seen (above, page 282) that Hume's account of causation can also be used to undermine the causal principle that Descartes uses within his cosmological argument.

However, Hume's account of causation is a controversial one that many philosophers have taken objection to. A defender of cosmological arguments such as Elizabeth Anscombe would say that Hume's concept of causation is a strange one, stemming from an unreasonably sceptical view of the world. Anscombe agrees that it may well be possible for us to imagine an event without having one cause or other.[24] For example, in **Figure 2.25** we can imagine that the first snooker ball did not cause the

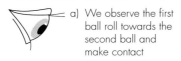
a) We observe the first
ball roll towards the
second ball and
make contact

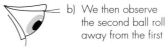
b) We then observe
the second ball roll
away from the first

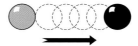

Figure 2.25 According to Hume we do not observe 'causation'.

second ball to move; perhaps it is a trick snooker table where the balls are moved by hidden magnets or wires. But even if it is possible to imagine an event without the cause we think it has, it is impossible for us to imagine an event as genuinely having no cause at all. And, so long as every event has some cause or other, then Aquinas' argument can indeed get off the ground.

But the WHOLE, you say, wants a cause.[25]

Hume

Criticism

Even if it can be shown that Hume is wrong about causation, and every event does have a cause, then theologians have to defend the cosmological argument against a further criticism made by Hume. He attacks the move that cosmological arguments make from 'every event has a cause' to 'the whole series of events has a cause'.[26] Hume argues that if we have explained the cause of each event in the series, then it is unreasonable to ask what caused the whole series. Take any series of events; let us say the separate appearance of five Inuit people in New York City.[27] Upon investigation we find that each of the Inuit is there for a different reason, and we are able fully to explain their presence in New York. According to Hume it would be unreasonable for an investigator then to say 'I agree you have explained why each Inuit is here, but I want to know why the whole group of five is here.' There is nothing more to say: an explanation of why each individual is there is enough; to demand an explanation of the whole group is unreasonable. This has become known as the FALLACY OF COMPOSITION: it is the fallacy of thinking that because there is some property common to each part of a group, this property must apply to the group as a whole. So just because a group of events all share the property of 'being caused' it would be a fallacy then to conclude from this that the group as a whole has the same property of 'being caused'. If Hume is right, then Aquinas is mistaken in thinking that there must be a First Cause that started the chain of cause and effects, and this type of cosmological argument fails.

▶ **ACTIVITY**

Which of the following claims are guilty of the fallacy of composition?

1 Every nice girl loves a sailor, therefore there is one sailor that all nice girls love.
2 Every journey has a destination, therefore there is one destination for all journeys.
3 All activities are aimed towards some goal, therefore there is one goal that all activities ultimately aim at.
4 Everyone in Tunbridge Wells voted Tory in the last election, therefore Tunbridge Wells is a Tory constituency.
5 Every proof of God's existence is flawed, therefore trying to prove God's existence is a flawed activity.

Issues raised by Russell

Bertrand Russell (1872–1970) offered a number of criticisms of the cosmological during his debate (in 1948, broadcast by the BBC) with the theologian F.C. Copleston. Towards the start of this debate Copleston puts forward a version of the cosmological argument which we have referred to as the argument from contingency, drawn from Aquinas' second way. The world, Copleston maintains, consists of beings and events which are not dependent on themselves for their own existence, but *are* dependent upon a preceding, or higher-order, being or event. If we are to explain this then we cannot go back infinitely, but must come to a being that contains within itself the reason for its own existence. In other words contingent beings are ultimately dependent on a necessary being. Russell's main criticisms of Copleston's argument are four fold:

1 Russell attacks the concept of a 'necessary being' (only propositions, he maintains, can be necessary).
2 Russell argues that causal cosmological arguments are guilty of the fallacy of composition.
3 Russell disagrees with the claim that every event is dependent on a preceding event and must have a cause (he gives as an example the discovery of certain types of sub-atomic event, drawn from quantum physics).
4 Russell rejects the idea that we need an explanation for the universe (the claim that 'God is the first cause' is for him a meaningless claim).

Let us look at each of these in turn.

Criticism

For Russell the contingency argument (both that of Aquinas and Copleston) rests on the idea of a necessary being. We saw above, on page 276, the main differences between necessity as it applies to a being, and as it applies to a statement. Well, Russell argues that there is no such thing as a 'necessary being' and there are only necessary statements, which are also analytic and which also are true by definition. A necessary proposition is one that it is self-contradictory to deny. For example: it is not possible to deny that 'all bachelors are unmarried men'; denying it would yield 'it is not true that all bachelors are unmarried men', which is equivalent (because of the meanings of the terms) to 'it is not true that all unmarried men are unmarried men', which is self-contradictory. For Russell there is no *being* for which it would be self-contradictory to deny; for any being, X, we can assert 'X does not exist' without contradiction. Russell, during the debate, does refer to the ontological argument, which is an argument that tries to prove the necessity of God's existence. But for Russell (see page 228 above) any claim about existence cannot be analytic, but must be synthetic. It is not possible to list all the attributes of a being (its essence), and then add a further characteristic – namely 'existence' – to this list because existence is not a predicate (it is not a characteristic). So if Russell is correct then the argument falls apart at its first hurdle: the search for a necessary being.

Criticism

Copleston changes his angle of attack during the debate, asking Russell if he will accept the claim 'the cause of the world exists'. Although the claim is rejected by Russell, this assertion leads to a general discussion of causation and how it can be understood and clarified. For Russell causes and causation are things we learn about from observation, which is an approach that can be traced back to Hume (see above, page 285). So Russell seems to be saying that we can ask about what causes this or that particular thing that we observe; that is, of a specific causal chains of events, but there is no need to ask of the *total chain* 'What caused all these particular things?' In order to support this position Russell gives an analogy, which is an illustration of the fallacy of composition (we encountered this above when looking at Hume's criticisms). It is true, says Russell, that every member of the human species has a mother, but it would be a fallacy then to conclude from this that our species as a whole must have a mother.[28] Similarly, every event within a series may indeed have a cause, but it is a fallacy (of composition) to conclude that the whole series must have a cause. So 'cause and effect' is taken to be a concept which applies to particular events occurring in the universe, but it is a mistake to then try to apply the concept to the universe as a whole.

Criticism

For Copleston something that is caused must either have another cause or be the cause of itself; that is, it must be a contingent being or a necessary being. So if there is an event which is caused by nothing else, nothing outside of itself, then it must be the cause of itself, which for Copleston is a necessary being: God. Russell pursues this angle of attack by questioning the idea that every particular thing in the world must have a cause (so crucial to cosmological argument).[29] Russell suggests that he is able to conceive of events that do not have a cause, and which clearly are not necessary beings. He illustrates this by drawing on the example of quantum physics, which was at the time of the Copleston debate cutting-edge theoretical science, but which is now standard technology, embedded in many of our electronic gadgets, such as flash memory in USBs and mobile phones. Since the 1920s, theoretical physics has raised the question of whether there are indeterminate events taking place at a sub-atomic, quantum level that have no cause at all (this has become known as the Copenhagen Interpretation, although there is not a complete consensus among physicists about this). Quantum fluctuations are often cited as an example of such uncaused events. Russell uses this theory to show that not all events have a cause, and that these particles that appear (for example, quantum tunnelling) are not 'necessary beings'. This invites the possibility that other events have no cause, including the appearance of the universe itself. If this is a genuine possibility then it undermines one of the key premises of causal cosmological arguments: the certainty that everything must have a cause.

Criticism

A final criticism is put very well by Bertrand Russell in the radio debate with Father Copleston. Earlier we mentioned that cosmological arguments sprung from a very real need many of us have to answer the questions 'Why are we here?' and 'Why does the universe exist?' Cosmological arguments can be seen as complex and arduous expressions of this need for an answer. To some it may seem obvious that the universe is crying out for an explanation: it must have come from somewhere, there must be a reason that it exists. However, to others it is not so obvious. The Copleston–Russell debate does eventually settle on the crucial issue of whether or not the universe is in need of an explanation. For Copleston he needs to be able to answer the question 'Why is all this here?' And his answer is God. But for Russell:

I should say the universe is just there, and that's all.[30]

Russell

In the context of the debate, Russell is arguing that it is meaningless even to ask the question 'What caused the universe?' We have already seen above Russell's reasons for saying this; namely that it is a fallacy to argue that, because the parts of the universe have a cause, therefore the whole must have a cause. But in his dismissal of Copleston's religious position, Russell is expressing something much more primitive than this: he simply does not feel a need for any ultimate answers; he does not think the universe is crying out for an explanation. For Russell the universe just is, period.

Summary

Cosmological arguments are attractive to people who feel that the universe is lacking something, and needs explaining. This feeling makes the conclusion that God is the ultimate explanation for why the universe exists more palatable. However, for people who do not see the universe in this way, a cosmological argument remains puzzling: if someone is seeking an explanation, then stopping at God seems arbitrary. Why not stop looking for explanations before you get to God? Or why not search for an explanation of why God exists? It may simply be that, as with other arguments for God's existence, they only make sense if you already have some faith. And if you do believe in God, then cosmological arguments help to reveal another facet of God: that he must be the unmoved mover, the uncaused cause and a necessary being.

You have now studied three of the most important types of arguments put forward by religious philosophers and thinkers in order to demonstrate God's existence. Of these three proofs only one type, the ontological argument, is purely an *a priori* argument, in other words it is constructed on the basis of reason alone, without reference to experience. It appears to work as an argument because it carefully analyses the concept of 'God' and in particular it highlights the special nature of God as a 'necessary' being – one whose non-existence we cannot conceive. So apparently part of the very essence of God is that he must exist.

The other two types of arguments are both built from our experience of the world. The cosmological argument draws on very general facts about the universe (for example the fact that it exists at all, or that everything must have a cause), while the argument from design uses as its starting point very specific features of the universe (for example that living things appear to be made of parts each of which has a purpose in helping that living thing to survive) and concludes from this that the universe must have been designed.

By studying these arguments for God's existence and the issues raised against them, you will have improved your critical and logical thinking skills, whether or not you agree with their conclusions. It is helpful to read an argument both in prose form (as a chunky paragraph) and in numbered form (with premises and conclusions numbered) and eventually in logical form (which uses formal symbols). By understanding how an argument is built up, what its component parts are and how it 'adds up' you will strengthen the construction of your own arguments. By finding systematic errors that can occur in our argument construction (for example the fallacy of composition or weaknesses in analogical reasoning) then you will find it easier to identify them when they occur in other proofs. By reading about counter examples or coming up with your own counter evidence, you will be better equipped to make your own arguments more robust and to find flaws in the arguments other people propose. So reading about and analysing the arguments for the existence of God has, we hope, made you a better philosopher.

2.2.4 The problem of evil

I didn't want to harm the man. I thought he was a very nice gentleman. Soft-spoken. I thought so right up to the moment I cut his throat.[1]

The multiple killer, Perry Smith

I form light and create darkness, I make peace and create evil, I the Lord, do all these things.

Isaiah 45:7

 Experimenting with ideas

1 Write down a list of ten things that have happened in the world in the last fifteen years that you regard as evil – try to be as specific as you can.
2 What do these things have in common, i.e. what makes them evil?
3 Can you categorise your examples into different types of evil?

What is meant by 'evil'?

The problem of evil remains one of the most contentious and unsettling areas in the philosophy of religion. The problem is important to believers and non-believers alike: believers because they have to reconcile their belief in a loving God with their knowledge of the terrible suffering that exists in the world; non-believers because they often claim that the existence of evil is the reason that they don't believe in the existence of God. Unlike some of the other theological issues that we have encountered (What are the attributes of God? Can his existence be proved? Is he a necessary being?) the problem of evil is encountered directly in our experience of life, and not simply through intellectual investigation. Before we outline the problem of evil in more detail we should first examine what is meant by 'evil' in the context of the philosophy of religion.

At a very general level, 'evil' is taken to refer to those unpleasant, destructive, painful and negative experiences that sentient beings have. These negative experiences can be grouped into the physical (including hunger, cold, pain) and the mental (including misery, anguish, terror), and we can summarise these two types of experience as pain and suffering.[2] Pain and suffering are commonplace in the lives of creatures on this planet, and so evil confronts us on a daily basis.

Theologians have offered other, more technical, definitions of evil. For example, St Augustine defines evil as that 'which we fear, or the act of fearing itself'.[3] The idea of fear as an evil in itself is echoed in Truman Capote's account of a horrific multiple murder (by two drifters, Perry Smith and Dick Hickock) and its aftermath in a sleepy mid-west American town in 1959. In the townspeople's panic following the murders there is a rush to buy locks and bolts to protect their homes:

> *Folks ain't particular what brand they buy; they just want them to hold. Imagination of course can open any door – turn the key and let terror walk right in.*[4]

If we apply Augustine's account of evil to the situation that these townsfolk find themselves in, then we can identify both the cold-blooded murderers and the terror they leave behind as evil. But Augustine and Aquinas are careful to argue that evil is not a 'thing' (a mysterious substance or presence, for example) but is the absence of goodness. Their account of goodness was strongly influenced by Plato and Aristotle's understanding of 'good', which contained the idea of goal or purpose. For Aristotle, 'good' refers to the complete fulfilment of a thing's natural potential. So a good can-opener is one that is excellent at opening cans; it possesses all the relevant features (the Greeks would call them 'virtues') necessary for opening cans safely and efficiently. Similarly a good oak tree is one that has all the virtues of an oak tree – it has strong roots, is disease free, efficiently photosynthesises and produces numerous acorns.

> *[Evil is] nothing but the corruption of natural measure, form or order. What is called an evil nature is a corrupt nature ... It is bad only so far as it has been corrupted.*[5]
>
> **Augustine**

For Augustine, and for Aquinas, evil is not a concrete presence or substance, it is simply the 'privation of good';[6] that is, a lack of goodness, a failure to flourish or fulfil a natural purpose. We shall see later that this account of evil is fundamental to Augustine's explanation of why it exists. Augustine sees the world, as created by God, in terms of goodness; evil is introduced only later as some disorder within the goodness of God's creation.

Two types of evil

In the activity above you might well have found that your examples of evil fell easily into two types: 'pain and suffering caused by humans' and 'pain and suffering caused by nature'. Philosophers of religion have traditionally identified two sources of evil: physical (or natural) and moral.[7] Physical or 'natural' evil refers to the pain and suffering of sentient beings that occurs independently of human actions. On the morning of All Saints' Day (1 November) 1755 the city of Lisbon in Portugal was hit by an earthquake that wrenched streets apart by 5 metre fissures and turned the city into ruins. Soon afterwards a massive tsunami swept into the remains of the city, as a result of the earthquake, and in the areas not destroyed by earth or water, a fire broke out that lasted for days. Around a third of all the inhabitants of Lisbon were burned, drowned or crushed – 90,000 people. When the French philosopher Voltaire heard the news he wrote his 'Poem on the Disaster of Lisbon' (see the extract below) that had a huge impact on European intellectuals of the day.

Mistaken philosophers who cry: 'All is well',

Approach, look upon these frightful ruins …

These scattered limbs beneath these broken marbles;

A hundred thousand wretches swallowed by the earth[.]

For Voltaire, the immense and pointless suffering of innocent people caused by the Lisbon earthquake was a troubling sign that this was not, after all, the 'best possible world'. The Boxing Day tsunami in 2004 that killed 230,000 people around the Indian Ocean is another instance of a disaster that would fall under the heading 'natural evil'. There are countless other examples of pain and suffering that could be given: the 'cloaking' device of cancerous cells that enables them to stay hidden from our immune systems and multiply their cancer unchecked; the habits of certain types of wasps to lay their eggs in caterpillars which are then eaten alive from the inside out; the mass extinction of dinosaurs 65 million years ago; the human and non-human victims of viruses, bacteria and other microscopic killers.

'Moral evil' refers to those acts of cruelty, viciousness and injustice carried out by humans upon fellow humans and other creatures, and which, for theologians, includes the concept of 'sin'. According to the American scientist and writer Jared Diamond, since the murderous genocides of Hitler and Stalin in the 1930s and 1940s, in which tens of millions of people were killed, there have been a further seventeen known genocides across the world. The soul-searching and hand-wringing after the Second World War, the creation of the United Nations, the pursuit of democracy and global capitalism have been accompanied by an increase, rather than a decrease, in the number of politicised mass murders around the world. For Jared Diamond these genocides have a close connection with tensions arising in society for geopolitical reasons: there are not enough resources to go round an increasing population and the situation is set to get worse. [8] But it was humans, not nature, who in 1994 executed around 800,000 people of Rwanda in a few weeks. As with natural evil, the suffering on this headline scale is more than matched by the daily torture and abuse of individuals around the world that goes unnoticed, unpublicised and unpunished.

What is the relationship between natural and moral evil? For some, natural evil might be seen as a consequence of human action or inaction, and hence as a subset, of moral evil. For example, crop failure, drought and starvation are often brought about by overpopulation, over-farming, the destruction of the environment, and so on. So these 'natural evils' might be read as 'moral evils', but there are other, more problematic examples for this reading. The human immunodeficiency virus (HIV), which has killed over 25 million people in the last 35 years, has been controversially seen by some as a punishment for human sinfulness. St Augustine argued that the once perfect world of the Garden of Eden has been made imperfect by the 'original sin' of Adam (pages 302–303, Free Will defence) and that the suffering caused by natural disasters and disease is God's punishment for this original moral evil.

It is also possible to regard moral evil as a form of natural evil, although this involves a philosophical view of human nature and freedom that is far removed from the teachings of western religious traditions: namely the view that humans do not hold a privileged position within the natural world. If humans are on a continuum with the rest of nature, then 'moral evil' is not distinct from the 'natural' pain and suffering caused by earthquakes, rabid dogs and malaria-carrying mosquitos. If our species is governed by the same principles as all other forms of life, then moral evil is just one specific type of the pain and suffering that all animals inevitably endure. John Stuart Mill (in *Three Essays on Religion*, 1874) argues that natural evil arises from the malfunctioning of the universe, which was originally intended for the preservation, not destruction, of life. If we assume, as Mill and Darwin did, that humans do not have a divine purpose or privileged place in the hierarchy of animals, then it is easier to see moral evil as a form of natural evil. Humans are jealous, live in close social groups, compete with one another for food, resources and mates, and have trouble controlling their violent and sometimes murderous impulses. Without any theological scaffolding, such as that of original sin, it is possible to view human actions that cause pain and suffering ('moral evil') as simply an extreme case of the 'natural' pain and suffering inflicted in the rest of the animal kingdom.

The problem of evil outlined: reconciling God and evil

Experimenting with ideas

Refer to the examples of evil you gave in the activity on page 291.

1. Which of these evils would you prevent if:
   a) you were a billionaire
   b) you were Superman
   c) you were even more powerful than Superman?
2. In the case of c) are there any evils you would allow to persist – why/why not?

The problem of evil affects all the theistic religions, which have as their object of worship a God who is the all-powerful creator of the world, and who cares deeply for his creation. We find the problem clearly stated in the works of both St Augustine and Aquinas,[9] but we can also find earlier versions dating back to the ancient Greek philosopher Epicurus (341–270BCE). This is how Epicurus frames the problem:

> *God either wishes to take away evils, and is unable; or he is able, and is unwilling; or he is neither willing nor able; or he is both willing and able. If he is willing and is unable, he is feeble, which is not in accordance with the character of God; if he is able and unwilling, he is envious, which is equally at variance with God; if he is neither willing nor able, he is both envious and feeble, and therefore not God; if he is both willing and able ... from what source then are evils? Or why does he not remove them?*[10]
>
> Epicurus

As John Hick (1922–2012) puts it: 'Can the presence of evil in the world be reconciled with the existence of a God who is unlimited both in goodness and in power?'[11] More recently, philosophers have identified at least two different formulations of the problem of evil: the logical problem and the evidential problem. The first formulation, the logical problem of evil, is an *a priori* argument put forward by atheists to show that the belief in God is false because it involves holding a set of contradictory beliefs. The second formulation, the evidential problem of evil, is an *a posteriori* argument proposed by atheists to show that the existence of evil makes it less likely that God exists.

anthology
2.46

The logical problem of evil

We can find one of the clearest statements of the logical problem of evil in J.L. Mackie's paper 'Evil and Omnipotence'.[12] Put simply, for Mackie the logical problem of evil asserts that believers are committed to holding three inconsistent beliefs:

1 God is omnipotent.
2 God is wholly good.
3 Evil exists.

There is a contradiction that needs resolving here, and Mackie argues that for any two of these propositions to be true then the third one would be false. Moreover, believing in the truth of all three propositions is an essential part of what it is to be a theist, so, as Mackie points out, the believer must hold all three to be true, and at the same time cannot hold all three to be true (because there is a contradiction).

▶ **ACTIVITY**

1 Using these three propositions do you think it is possible for an atheist to construct an argument to prove that God cannot exist?
2 Write down any additional premises that you think would be needed to make the argument watertight.
3 How might believers criticise such an argument (which premises or steps would they deny)?

Mackie states the problem more clearly by adding two further propositions that really bring out the contradiction:

4 A good being eliminates evil as far as it can.
5 There are no limits to what an omnipotent being can do.

We shall see later that Alvin Plantinga (1932–) disagrees with Mackie, but it is Plantinga who wants to make Mackie's argument as clear as possible before attacking it. He thinks that Mackie needs to add an amendment to 4, to avoid the charge that God might be all-loving and all-powerful, but might not actually know about the pain and suffering in his creation. Plantinga amends proposition 4 to:

4a Every good thing always eliminates every evil that *it knows about* and can eliminate.[13]

With these crucial additions in place Mackie believes he is able to show that all believers agree with propositions 1–5, and yet these propositions cannot be held to be true simultaneously. In which case believers must give up their belief in at least one of these statements, or they must admit that they have a 'positively irrational' and contradictory belief in God.

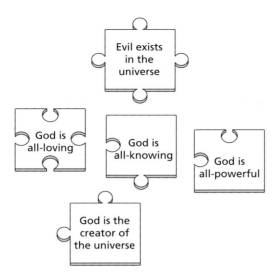

If Mackie is right, then which statement should the believer surrender? It seems undeniable that there is pain and suffering in the universe; after all, a central tenet of Christianity is that Jesus himself suffered when he was crucified, and thus believers will agree that 3 is true.[14] Proposition 5 appears to be just a simple clarification of what is meant by 'omnipotent', so believers may be happy to accept 5 as true. What about propositions 1 or 2? The contradiction would disappear if believers jettisoned some, or all, of the qualities of God, as in that case either God would not be able to do anything about evil, or he would not know that it is happening, or he would not care. But as Epicurus points out, if God does not have the will to eradicate evil (he is not all-loving) or if he does not have the power to do so (he is not omnipotent) then he would no longer be God at all. In which case the believer, in order to remain a theist, cannot give up their belief in God's power or goodness. So has the believer been revealed by Mackie to hold a set of inconsistent and contradictory beliefs?

Plantinga thinks not, and the significant disagreement with Mackie is over proposition 4. This is the crux of the argument: Mackie thinks he is able to formulate a statement that all believers will accept is true, which runs along the lines of 'good and loving creatures aim to get rid of evil'. But Plantinga argues that believers do not accept this, and that there is far more subtlety to belief in God than Mackie gives credit for. We shall see below that many proposed solutions to the problem of evil argue that evil is in some way good, or contributes to something good. In which case believers do not accept proposition 4, even in its revised versions, because they hold that getting rid of evil will in some way damage an even greater good that God intends for his creation. What these greater goods are we shall explore in detail later. But first let us turn to the other formulation, the evidential problem of evil, which accepts that 'believing in God' and 'knowing that evil exists' are not logically contradictory, but which tries to show that evil still seriously undermines the truth of theism.

The evidential problem of evil

> *God who could create the universe, is to our finite minds omnipotent and omniscient, and it revolts our understanding to suppose that his benevolence is not unbounded, for what advantage can there be in the sufferings of millions of the lower animals throughout almost endless time?*[15]
>
> **Darwin**

Darwin's experiences as a biologist brought him face to face with the daily pain and suffering of animals. For many thinkers, including Darwin, David Hume and the contemporary philosopher William Rowe, the sheer amount of evil in the world weighs against there being a God who is omnipotent and wholly good. After all, would an almighty, all-knowing, all-loving God allow such extraordinary pain and suffering to exist? Why does he not intervene to prevent earthquakes that kill tens of thousands, or viruses that kill millions? Why does he allow psychopaths and serial killers to unleash their cruelty on innocent people? Why has he permitted genocide after genocide in the last hundred years?

This is not a logical argument, as it does not aim to show that the theist holds a set of inconsistent beliefs. Instead it is posing a question: 'Given the existence of evil, which of the following is the more reasonable hypothesis?'

- ▥ H1 There is an infinitely powerful, wholly good God who created the world.

  or
- ▥ H2 There is no such God.

For Hume and Rowe, the existence of evil is clear evidence in favour of the second hypothesis. As Hume says:

> *We must forever find it impossible to reconcile any mixture of evil in the universe with infinite attributes ... But supposing the Author of nature to be finitely perfect, though far exceeding mankind, a satisfactory account may then be given of natural and moral evil.*[16]
>
> **Hume**

William Rowe cites gratuitous and pointless evil as evidence that a theistic God does not exist at all.[17] As an example of gratuitous evil, Rowe describes the suffering of a deer, trapped and horribly burned by a forest fire, which lies in agony for several days before dying. The agony endured by the deer seems to be pointless, and preventable, but Rowe accepts that such an example does not prove that God does not exist. However, he does maintain that such gratuitous evil makes it reasonable to believe in H2 and reject H1.

▶ ACTIVITY

Refer to the examples of evil you gave in the activity on page 291.

Think of as many reasons as you can why God might permit such evils to exist (write down every reason, no matter how absurd, or whether or not you believe it to be true). It may help if you consider the analogy of why loving, or generous, or thoughtful people (doctors, parents, teachers, charity workers, etc.) might sometimes allow someone to suffer, and what they hope to achieve by allowing this.

Responses to the problem of evil

Resolving the problem of evil

We have already encountered one solution to the problem of evil, which is the solution that Mackie was arguing for, namely the atheist's solution:

■ God *does not* exist, there is no such omnipotent, omniscient, benevolent being, and we should realise that humans just have to cope alone with the enormity of pain and suffering in the world.

Clearly this is not an acceptable solution to the problem of evil for people who believe in God. However, nor is it an easy or comforting solution to those people who have properly embraced a considered form of atheism.

When we speak of abandonment … we only mean to say that God does not exist, and that it is necessary to draw the consequences of his absence right to the end.[18]

Sartre

Jean-Paul Sartre (1905–1980) claimed that the realisation that there is no God, no support, no help available to us in this cruel world, gives rise to deep feelings of 'abandonment'. When we are growing up we often believe, or are told, that there is a purpose to life or some kind of meaning to existence and some reason for the suffering in the world. It is very comforting to believe that an external authority exists, someone who is there to look after to us, to support us, to give purpose to our lives and to dish out justice when we die. But for Sartre we are simply deceiving ourselves and once we realise that there is no God then the residue of our past belief (that is, our belief that there was a being who was on our side, and looking out for us) lingers and we feel abandoned, even though for Sartre there never was a God. We still deeply feel the loss of the security which we had when we believed in God. Sartre's philosophy of EXISTENTIALISM urges us to shed ourselves of our deceptions and to live more authentic lives, which means truly confronting the consequences of atheism.

For Sartre this feeling of abandonment must spur us forward philosophically: if there is no God then what else follows from this? Well, at least one of the consequences is that we must face the horror of human and animal suffering alone and without explanation, without meaning, and without any hope that people will get their just desserts in the end. Without God, Sartre claims, there is also no real possibility of any external set of moral beliefs. We are free to invent our own moral systems, or behave in whatever way we want to – an unsettling prospect for many of us. So perhaps the solution to the problem of evil arrived at by the authentic atheist – namely that God does not exist and nor does any external meaning or morality – is one of the most difficult solutions to live with in the end.

But since the problem of evil was first posed, theists have sought to resolve it without abandoning their belief in an all-powerful, all-knowing and all-loving God. There have been many theistic solutions to (or defences against) the problem of evil, but we can group the main responses into four types:

1 God *does* exist, and the enormity of pain and suffering in the world is real, but we should realise that God is *not* in fact omnipotent, omniscient and benevolent (there are several alternative Theologies to mainstream, traditional, belief in God).

2 God *does* exist, and is omnipotent, omniscient and benevolent, but we should realise that the enormity of pain and suffering in this world is *balanced by* even greater good – namely justice in the next life (we can term this the 'Afterlife defence').

3 God *does* exist, and is omnipotent, omniscient and benevolent, but we should realise that the enormity of pain and suffering is the *consequence of* an even greater good – namely humans having free will (this is known as the 'Free Will defence').

4 God *does* exist, and is omnipotent, omniscient and benevolent, but we should realise that the enormity of pain and suffering actually *leads to* an even greater good – namely humans fulfilling their potential (this has become known as the 'Soul-Making defence').

Of these, the last three preserve theism as a religious system, and solutions of this type have come to be termed THEODICIES.[19] John Hick, in his book *Evil and the God of Love*, identifies two major theodicies in western philosophy of religion: the Augustinian theodicy, which we examine below in the exploration of the Free Will defence, and the Irenaean theodicy, which we look at when we assess Hick's own Soul-Making defence. We might further categorise such solutions as either 'strong' or 'weak' theodicies. A strong theodicy provides an explanation or justification of why God permits the existence of evil within his creation. A weak theodicy (or a 'Defence') may not venture to explain why evil exists, but it does offer a defence of theism and shows that the existence of God is not incompatible with the existence of evil as the atheist claims.

Response 1: Alternative theologies

Learn More

- God *does* exist, and the enormity of pain and suffering in the world is real, but we should realise that God is *not* in fact omnipotent, omniscient and benevolent.

In the last hundred years theologians have proposed alternative interpretations of what it is to believe in God. Examples of such theologies are: theological anti-realism (see page 344), in which God is not understood as a real being existing independently of our minds; and Process Theology, where God is 'the fellow sufferer who understands', who can affect his creation through infinite persuasive powers, but cannot eradicate evil or prevent it from happening.[20] Dualist perspectives, in which God is not the only powerful deity, also offer a solution to the problem of evil, as with the Manicheans who saw a benevolent God vying with an evil deity.

Criticism
It is clear that these types of solutions lead in a direction often far away from Christian teachings, and so they are unacceptable to many believers. However, for those who have spiritual leanings, and are attempting to make sense of the universe and of evil from a position outside traditional theism, such solutions may be reasonable and plausible.

Response 2: The Afterlife defence

Learn More

- God *does* exist, and is omnipotent, omniscient and benevolent, but we should realise that the enormity of pain and suffering in this world is *balanced by* even greater good – namely justice in the next life.

The belief in life after death is one of the fundamental tenets of Christianity; it recurs throughout the New Testament, and finds support from the traditional view of God, the 'God of the philosophers' (see pages 180–181). As Hick argues, an omnipotent, personal creator would not allow his human creations to cease to exist while his aspirations and purpose for them had not been met.[21] So how does belief in life after death resolve the problem of evil? Or to put it another way: is the existence of a benevolent God compatible with a world in which there is a finite amount of suffering in this life, but an infinite amount of happiness in the next life?

> If there is any eventual resolution of the interplay between good and evil, any decisive bringing of good out of evil, it must lie beyond this world and beyond the enigma of death.[22]
>
> **John Hick**

It might be true that, from the perspective of life in this world, the cruelties and horrors seem very difficult, if not impossible, to reconcile with the existence of a loving, caring God. However, from the perspective of eternity, a limited amount of suffering in this life becomes infinitesimal compared with the potential for unlimited happiness in the next life. And belief in hell as well as heaven means that the people who inflict injustice and suffering on us in this life will be punished in the next life. The possibility of justice in the future goes part way to resolving the moral problem of evil for some people: vicious people will get their comeuppance; virtuous people will be rewarded.

Criticism

However, it seems as if the existence of hell simply defers the problem of evil to the next life, and amplifies it. If we found it difficult to reconcile the existence of a benevolent God with the existence of (limited) suffering in this life, how much more difficult are we going to find it reconciling such a God with the unlimited suffering of hell in the next life?

We will return to the idea of life after death, and examine some further philosophical problems with it, when we come to examine John Hick's parable of the Celestial City (page 325).

Response 3: The Free Will defence

■ God *does* exist, and is omnipotent, omniscient and benevolent, but we should realise that the enormity of pain and suffering is the *consequence of* an even greater good – namely humans having free will.

In many of the most influential explanations of the existence of evil, human free will is an essential element. St Augustine provides one of the earliest and best-known theodicies that takes this approach, arguing that God is good and powerful, and created a perfect world with humans to whom he gave free will. Evil was then introduced into the world because some of his creatures chose to turn away from God. Augustine places particular blame on the fall of the angel Satan from heaven and on the failure of Adam and Eve to resist temptation in the Garden of Eden. This, for Augustine, constitutes the 'original sin' of humans and resulted in Adam and Eve's subsequent expulsion from paradise by God, and the introduction of pain and suffering into their lives and the lives of all their progeny.[23] Through these sins God's creation was corrupted, and the natural goodness of the world disappeared: there was a 'privation' of the good. Augustine's theodicy thus places the blame for moral and natural evil on the freely chosen acts of God's creatures (humans and angels). So Augustine maintains that, although God created a perfect world, evil was introduced by the choices humans made, and thus it is the responsibility of humans not of God. Alvin Plantinga highlights the following line from St Augustine:

> *As a runaway horse is better than a stone which does not run away because it lacks self-movement and sense perception, so the creature is more excellent which sins by free will than that which does not sin only because it has no free will.*[24]
>
> **St Augustine, quoted in Alvin Plantinga, *God, Freedom and Evil***

So for Augustine it is clear that God has made a better world by giving some of his creatures the freedom to choose between good and evil, even if a consequence of this is that some of his creatures choose to sin and perform evil acts. A world which consisted of stones, or robots who were not able to sin because they lacked free will, is a world that is less perfect than a world which contains both free will and evil. Plantinga calls this Augustine's 'Free Will Theodicy', because it explains exactly why God permits evil.

Plantinga himself puts forward a version of what he calls the Free Will defence, which does not claim to state *precisely* what God's reason for the existence of evil might be (that would be a theodicy), but only that to show that it is *possible* that God had this as a reason. So the Free Will defence is part of Plantinga's efforts to defeat atheists like Mackie (above, pages 296–297) by demonstrating that there is no inconsistency in believing in an omnipotent, omniscient, benevolent God, and believing that God created a world with immense pain and suffering in it. Plantinga's argument is this:

1 A world with creatures who are free is more valuable than a world containing no free creatures at all.
2 God can create free creatures, but he cannot (without removing their freedom) *cause* them to do what is morally right.

anthology 2.47

3 So God created a world with free creatures capable of doing both what is morally right and what is morally evil.

4 Humans then are the source of moral evil.

Furthermore, Plantinga goes on to argue, this defence does not count against the belief that God is all-powerful and wholly good. God's goodness is what led him to create a world with creatures who had freedom (rather than creatures who were robots), and God's omnipotence gave him the power to actually create such a world. The fact that God does not prevent evil does not mean he lacks omnipotence or benevolence, as he could only prevent evil by removing our capacity for free choice, and hence removing the possibility of moral good.

As other philosophers (including both Hick and Swinburne below) point out, God does not wish to create a snug cage for his human 'pets' to live in.[25] So it is a mistake to look at the world and wonder why it is not more pleasant for humans. A much greater good than pleasure is the relationship humans can have with God, and this can only be a genuine relationship if we have free will. And, as we have seen, freely chosen evil is a terrible side effect of free will, but one that on this view is worth it.

Let us now look at some of the most important criticisms that have been made of the Free Will defence.

Criticism

The Free Will defence provides a possible reason for why pain and suffering exists in a world created by a supremely good and omnipotent God. But it only seems to account for moral evil; in other words, the pain and suffering caused by humans themselves. What of physical or natural evil? After all, humans are not responsible for the behaviour of Ichneumonidae, those wasps which, as in the *Alien* films, lay their eggs inside the body of a host so that when the larvae hatch they can eat the host from the inside out. There was horrific pain and suffering in the animal kingdom before humans evolved, and at first sight the Free Will defence does not explain why natural evils exist.

St Augustine's version of the Free Will defence, in his account of original sin, does explain why natural evil exists – it was because creatures who had been given Free Will (angels and humans) rebelled against God. First Satan, and then Adam and Eve, disobeyed God, bringing about The Fall, and Adam and Eve's expulsion from the Garden of Eden. This in turn caused God's creation to go askew, bringing pain and suffering into the world. For Augustine then, natural evil is actually just a consequence of moral evil.

Apart from the unfairness of this account (why should other animals suffer because of the decision of Eve to eat from the Tree of Knowledge?), there is also the issue that this part of the Free Will defence depends upon a literal interpretation of the first book of the Bible. For Augustine, the succumbing to temptation by Eve and then Adam in the Garden of Eden is the real origin of sin and evil. Many believers do not now read the account of what happened in the Garden of Eden as literally true, preferring to read it symbolically. Nor do many modern believers subscribe to the view that the angel Satan turned away from God, and that this too introduced evil into the world. So the Free Will defence is primarily a defence against the existence of moral evil, not natural evil.

Criticism

Antony Flew criticises the Free Will defence on the basis of the very meaning of 'free will'.[26] For Flew, freely chosen actions are ones that have their causes within the persons themselves, rather than externally. For example, when you have the chance to marry the person you love, your decision to do so will ultimately stem from the type of person you are: whether you find them funny, whether you fancy them, whether you 'click' with them, whether you trust them, and so on. As long as your choice to marry is internal to you, that is to say, powered by your own character and desires, then it is freely chosen. Flew then goes on to say that God could have created a possible world in which all humans had a nature that was good, and yet in which they were free in Flew's sense. In such a world, humans would always freely choose to do the right thing. And such a world would surely be a better one than this.

However, Flew's attack on the Free Will defence may be objected to on the following grounds. What would be the difference between Flew's 'naturally good' people, and automata or mere puppets who had been created always to act in a good way? It is important to theistic belief that God gave humans the freedom to choose to worship and love him, or the freedom to turn away from him. But, in Flew's world, God seems to have manipulated the key parts of his creation (humans) in order to bring about his desired results. Imagine a hypnotist persuading someone they were in love: what would be the worth of this love? Just as we would question the value of the feelings manipulated in someone by a hypnotist, so we might question the value of the love felt for God by the 'naturally good' humans in Flew's world. Moreover, is a God who manipulates the end results, in the way Flew describes, a God who is worthy of worship?

Criticism

J.L. Mackie offers another version of Flew's criticism, presenting it as a logical possibility, perfectly within God's omnipotent powers.[27] He argues the following:

1 It is logically possible for me to choose to do good on any one occasion.
2 It is logically possible for me to choose to do good on every occasion.
3 It is logically possible for any individual to choose to do good throughout their life.
4 God is omnipotent and can create any logically possible world.
5 Therefore God could have created a world in which we were all genuinely free, yet we all chose to do good.
6 God did not create such a world.
7 Therefore either God is not omnipotent, or he is not wholly good.

So Mackie's attack on the Free Will defence leads to a restatement of the logical problem of evil.

We have already seen that in recent years the logical problem of evil, as presented by Mackie and others, has been rigorously attacked by Plantinga, and the Free Will defence remounted. Plantinga rejects the idea that God can create an infinite number of possible worlds. For example, God cannot create a world in which humans are not created by God. And even within the possible worlds that God could create there are limitations. For example, it is possible that there is some person (Plantinga names him Curly Smith) who has a corrupt nature such that, in every possible world that God could create, he will always choose to do at least one evil action. In this case, it is not possible for God (even an infinitely powerful and loving one) to create a world in which Curly is free yet always does good actions. Plantinga would still maintain he has mounted a successful defence (what we called above a 'weak' theodicy) of evil, showing that the existence of evil is compatible with a wholly good and all-powerful God.

Response 4: The Soul-Making defence

■ God *does* exist, and is omnipotent, omniscient and benevolent, but we should realise that the enormity of pain and suffering actually *leads to* an even greater good – namely humans fulfilling their potential.

The Free Will defence aims to provide a solution to the problem of evil by showing that an omnipotent, benevolent God may not want to eliminate evil (at least moral evil) because there is a higher value at stake here, namely Free Will and the opportunity for moral goodness that stems from it. We have seen above (page 301) that John Hick referred to this approach as the 'Augustinian theodicy'. But Hick also identified an alternative tradition which gives a different account of why God allows evil to exist. In this tradition evil exists, not simply because it is caused by human free will (although for moral evil that is true), but also because a world in which there is evil enables humans to grow and develop, and provides an environment in which our souls can be forged and strengthened. This 'Soul-Making' tradition Hick traces back to another early Church father, St Irenaeus (AD130–202), and he termed this the 'Irenaean theodicy'.

The backdrop against which the Irenaean theodicy works is that this world, the world that was actually created, is a better world than the other possible worlds that God could have created. This is because this world, with all its potential for

Experimenting with ideas

You have a summer job as a shop assistant in Worlds 'R' Us – the Ultimate in Universe Shopping. One day God walks in and says he wants to buy a universe. More specifically he wants to buy the best possible universe (which he can easily do, given he is God). He browses through the billions of shelves, which contain every possible universe, and then asks you for more details of their specifications: the quantity of pain and suffering, the extent of free will, the level of DETERMINISM, the degree of order and regularity, the balance and beauty in each universe. Eventually, after examining all the billions of universes in the shop, God comes up to the counter and says 'I'll take this one'; and that is the universe we now live in.

1 What 'health warnings' or 'unique selling points' would you have told God about when selling him this universe?
2 Do you think God made a good choice? Why/Why not?
3 Was there a better universe on offer? In what way would it have been better?
4 What do you think God was looking for in a universe (what 'specifications')?

---

suffering, enables our souls to be forged, and for us to develop as human beings. It was Leibniz who put forward the idea that this was the best of all possible worlds, and we shall examine what he meant by this below, and then move on to examine an updated account of the Irenaean 'Soul-Making' theodicy in the work of John Hick.

Leibniz's theodicy

Learn More

Gottfried Leibniz (1646–1716) asks us to consider the situation of God as one of an all-powerful and good being whose task it is to select, from among all the possible universes that he could create, the one he will actually create. Now, given that God knows the whole histories of all the possible universes, and is wholly good, then the one he selected to create must be the very best one possible. Therefore the pain and suffering of this world are just some of the many essential ingredients which go into the construction of the best possible world. This means that all the evil which exists in this universe must, in some way, contribute to making it a better place than every other possible universe.

Criticism

Leibniz's position has had many critics, and the French philosopher and writer Voltaire (1694–1778) was one of the first to attack Leibniz's theodicy. In Voltaire's novel *Candide*, the character Dr Pangloss regularly announces that this is the best of all possible worlds. As the eponymous hero is tortured by religious fanatics, and as he watches his mentor Dr Pangloss hanged, Candide wonders to himself: 'if this is the best of all possible worlds, what can the others be like?'[28] What Voltaire does is to confront the cool intellectual approach that Leibniz takes to the problem of evil with the pain and suffering of the world. In so doing, Voltaire does not really refute Leibniz's theodicy; but it is certainly not easy to support Leibniz's position when faced with the concrete reality of pain and suffering.

in this life is) so that we do not know what our purpose is and must exercise our genuine free will in order to approach the good (a state of holiness).[30]

Criticism

The claim that evil exists as a means to some other good (such as spiritual maturity or noble virtues) has been bitterly contested. Hick himself acknowledges that the distribution of misery in the world seems to be random and meaningless, so that it may be heaped upon those who seem least deserving.[31]

In such cases it is hard to see what good can come of such evil. Dostoyevsky put forward a series of particularly painful examples of evil in his novel *The Brothers Karamazov*. The character Ivan Karamazov cites three cases of appalling and pointless cruelty to Russian children (to which could be added the holocaust in Belarus in 1942,[32] or the Beslan school massacre of 2004), which in his view clearly give reason to reject God and the world he has created. Ivan does not deny the existence of God, but instead, disgusted at the universe God has created, he rejects God as a being who is worthy of worship.[33]

Experimenting with ideas

Read through the following two examples given by Ivan Karamazov and answer the questions below.

1   A young girl, abused by her parents, wets her bed and is forced by her mother to eat her own excrement, before she is made to sleep in a freezing cold shed.
2   A boy throws a stone and injures a general's dog. The boy is stripped and sent out as quarry for a hunt. He is eventually caught and torn to pieces by dogs in front of his mother.
    a) How might these examples of evil be explained within Hick's Soul-Making theodicy and Plantinga's Free Will defence?
    b) Do you think these explanations are satisfactory?

Criticism

The problem Dostoyevsky poses is a question about whether the outcome justifies the method. For any theodicy that views the existence of evil as a means to an end we can ask, 'Is the end worth it?' In other words, is God justified in creating a world that contains so much pointless and gratuitous evil in order to attain certain goals? For Ivan Karamazov the answer is no – there can be no goal so worth having that young children are allowed to be tortured in order that this goal might one day be reached.

Summary

Once we have got over the use of the term 'evil' (which conjures up badly made, or even terrifying, Hollywood films full of swirling smoke, dark cellars and scuttling hands) the problem of evil becomes a compelling and genuine issue for all of us, atheists and believers alike. The enormity of the pain and suffering of humans and animals is too much for most of us to bear thinking about, so we don't. But the problem of evil, even though it stems from an issue in the philosophy of religion, forces us all to turn our attention to suffering and ask ourselves 'Why?' Perhaps for atheists there is no answer to this question: there is no reason why creatures suffer; it is pointless, senseless even, but that is life. Believers fare no better in their search for a solution because the problem of evil, clearly framed, genuinely calls into question whether a God who is powerful and loving would allow such suffering to go on, and whether such a God really does exist. Perhaps human freedom partly explains evil, at least the parts that we are responsible for (but what about the rest?). Or perhaps suffering really is good in the long term, as Irenaeus and Hick argue; or at least it is better than the alternative in which there is no suffering at all. Though neither solution rings fully true to neutral ears.

Philosophers love a knotty problem, and the problem of evil certainly is that. The ability to clearly explain, explore and resolve problems is another philosophical skill that you will need to develop. The problem of evil cannot be easily avoided, as you have seen. Once you have defined your terms (What do we mean by 'evil'?; What are the different types of evil?; What do different examples of evil have in common?) you can go on to formulate the issue and explain exactly why it is a problem. Most importantly it is a problem for believers because of their particular definition of another concept, namely 'God'. The clash between these two concepts demands a solution, and you have explored a variety of different solutions and a variety of criticisms laid against these solutions. But the problem of evil does not disappear once you close this book and you will have to weigh up which of these solutions (or others you may have thought of yourself, or read elsewhere) is the most compelling.

Ultimately our position on the problem of evil may come down to our prior beliefs about the universe. If we are committed atheists, then we may use the existence of evil to justify our atheism. However, it does not seem as if evil proves the non-existence of God. The most evil does is to show that belief in the non-existence of God is rational. From the believer's point of view the existence of evil is a lived and agonising problem. The Book of Job in the Bible underpins this, as God proves to the devil that Job will love him whatever his circumstances. The devil destroys Job's life, family, livestock, leaving him with nothing. Job's friends argue that he must have done something wrong. But throughout his trials, Job maintains his faith in God's righteousness, despite being in ignorance about why he is suffering so much. This story of faith in God, in the face of pain and suffering, is an inspiration to many believers. But the story of Job does not solve the problem of evil, it merely tells us how it is possible to live with evil and yet still believe in God. The story reassures believers, but frustrates atheists who will continue to ask how such a juggling act is possible.

2.3 Religious language

The challenges of religious language

The French monk and writer François Rabelais once described how two fictional scholars conducted a philosophical ARGUMENT using only grotesque signs and obscene gestures to convey their meaning. As one of the scholars explained: 'these matters are so difficult that human words would not be adequate to expound them to my satisfaction'.[1]

But, for most of us, words and language are indispensable to communicating complex ideas; indeed, it would be very hard to imagine how the ideas discussed in this book could be effectively communicated by any other means, such as through images, dance or mime. Language is essential for, and some would say identical with, complex thinking, and as philosophers tend to indulge in complex thought they naturally use language to do so. However, over the last hundred years or so philosophers have become ever more interested in the nature of language so that now the philosophy of language has become one of the most important areas of philosophical inquiry. The philosophy of language addresses such questions as:

■ What do words or CONCEPTS mean?
■ How do PROPOSITIONS refer to the world?
■ What is the relationship between language and thought?

Some philosophers have argued that such questions are the most important of all on the grounds that we need first to have answers to these before we can pursue any further philosophical questions. Until we understand how the medium through which we engage in philosophy works, how can we hope to do philosophy properly? Some philosophers of language also claim that many, if not all, philosophical problems arise simply because of the way in which we misuse, and so become confused by, language. According to this view, philosophical problems aren't genuine problems about the world at all; they are simply problems in the way we express ourselves. We have already seen how this approach to philosophy can work. For example, Bertrand Russell argued that a proper examination of the meanings of the words involved can reveal what is wrong with the ontological argument: this trick of proving God exists is foiled once we see how the proof misuses the term 'existence' by treating it as a predicate (see above, pages 227–230).

In this chapter we are going to look at the nature of religious language. The questions we need to deal with are:

■ What makes religious language different, and what special features does it have?

- Are religious STATEMENTS meaningful because they make true (or false) claims about the world? (Cognitivism.)
- Are religious statements meaningful irrespective of whether they are making (true or false) claims about the world? (Non-cognitivism.)

To begin addressing these questions we should first look at examples of religious language and assess the different theories of meaning that philosophers have put forward.

The nature of religious language

The philosophy of religious language looks at the meaning of both religious concepts (such as *God, omnipotence, evil*) and at religious propositions. A proposition is an assertion or statement about the world, what in an English lesson might be called an 'indicative' sentence. We all express our BELIEFS in the form of propositions; here are some examples:

- The world is round.
- I am a student.
- The grass is always greener on the other side.
- We should treat others as we would like to be treated.

Now, on the surface, religious propositions appear very much like other kinds of proposition. They appear to be giving us information about the world, telling us what the world is like or what is true of it. In other words, they appear to be FACTUALLY SIGNIFICANT. However, compare the following religious propositions with some ordinary propositions:

- God is the Father, the Son and the Holy Ghost.
- God is transcendent.
- The Lord spake unto Moses about the liberation of the Israelites.
- Our Father, who art in Heaven, hallowed be thy name.

- Jeremy Jones is a father, a son and a teacher.
- Jeremy Jones is trendy.
- Jeremy Jones spoke to Mischa about the incident in the library.
- Jeremy Jones, who lives in Hendon, has an unusual middle name.

On the face of it, both sets of propositions are very similar. However, on closer inspection, it becomes evident that propositions like those on the left – religious propositions – reveal themselves to have features that make them rather different from those of ordinary language. For example:

- Religious propositions are often contradictory or paradoxical. To say that 'God is the Father and the Son and the Holy Ghost' is to say that he is at once one and three: a claim that is rather puzzling. We can understand how Jeremy Jones might be a father and a son, because there exist separate persons, Jeremy's son and Jeremy's father, who explain these relations. It is hard to understand how God could be a father and son to himself. The claim that 'God is omnipotent' appears to be contradictory, as we saw above (page 193), because an omnipotent being both can and cannot give itself a task which it could not perform. Does this mean that such claims are incoherent or meaningless?

■ The word that is most central to religious language, 'God', refers to a being that lies beyond human experience. Many theologians have held that 'God' is a concept beyond our understanding, and that our language is woefully inadequate when it comes to talking of God. For example, the early Christian mystic Pseudo-Dionysius said this of our attempts to talk about God: 'the inscrutable One is out of reach of every rational process. Nor can any words come up to the inexpressible Good ... Mind beyond mind, word beyond speech, it is gathered up by no discourse, by no intuition, by no name.'[2] Do all our attempts to talk meaningfully about God fail, because of his TRANSCENDENT nature?

■ Religious language is also peculiar in that it often describes God in human terms. In Genesis, for example, we are told that God walked in the Garden of Eden. Does this mean that God has legs? God also spoke to Moses on Mount Sinai. Does this mean he has a tongue and lips? How are we to make sense of such talk if God is a being who is outside of space and time?

■ Finally, there are peculiarities in the uses made of religious language, for example during religious ceremony or prayer. Are we supposed to interpret prayer as a literal request for help, like dialling 999 for the fire brigade? Or are we supposed to find in it another layer of meaning, perhaps a form of worship, an expression of faith or an act of devotion?

Our task, then, is to determine whether and how religious language can be meaningful. To do this we will examine various theories of meaning and what they say about the nature of religious language.

Learn More

The idea of 'meaning'

Before turning to the theories of meaning themselves, it may be instructive to think a little about what meaning is or what we mean by 'meaning'.

Experimenting with ideas

How many different meanings does 'mean' have? What do the following examples of 'mean' mean?

1   I mean to send you a get well card.
2   Dark clouds mean rain.
3   He had a mean look on his face.
4   When your boy/girlfriend says 'I think we need a break' what they really mean is 'I've fallen in love with someone else.'
5   I mean the world to Julia.
6   Do you know what I mean?
7   The mean rainfall in Morecombe is 10 centimetres.
8   I'll report you to the police next time you slash my tyres – I mean it!

In each of these propositions the word 'mean' is used in a different way, and there are other ways too. Ogden and Richards in *The Meaning of Meaning*[3] identified sixteen different meanings of the word 'meaning', which shows how ambiguous the meaning of the word can be. But superficial ambiguity is not the only problem with 'meaning'. It seems that, although we may be able to use words happily enough, and can even explain what most words mean, it is much harder to say what it is for a word to have a meaning in the first place.

A useful starting point in giving a theory of meaning is to try to establish which sentences are meaningful and which are not. If we can establish whatever it is that all meaningful sentences have in common and meaningless sentences lack, then we should have a good idea of what makes them meaningful and so we will be well on the road to building a theory of meaning. Now obviously sentences with made-up or crazy words will not be meaningful. For example:

'Twas brillig, and the slithy toves did gyre and gimble in the wabe.[4]

clearly makes no sense. For even though some of the words are English, and even though it seems to make sense (some slithy animals are doing something like gyring in some place called a wabe), and these carefully chosen 'words' allow us to recognise the grammatical structure of the sentence, we do not really know what toves are or what it is to gimble, and so cannot make proper sense of what is being said. This suggests that the constituent parts of any sentence must be recognisable words for the sentence to be meaningful.

However, any old collection of English words is not necessarily going to make a meaningful sentence. Consider the following, for example:

With happily six the and swim.

This is clearly not meaningful because the words used are not put together in a meaningful way. This suggests that meaningfulness requires at least two conditions: that the words used are themselves meaningful, and also that they are combined in ways that follow certain rules. But what rules are these? The example we have just looked at suggests one answer: the words must be combined in ways that follow the rules of grammar. For one obvious thing that is wrong with the sentence above is that it is not grammatical.

However, to be meaningful a sentence needs more than to be composed of proper words arranged grammatically. To see this, consider the following (originally composed by Noam Chomsky):

Colourless green ideas sleep furiously.[5]

Can ideas sleep? Can something be colourless and green? Probably not. So, although this sentence is grammatical, and uses real English words that you would find in any dictionary, it is still empty of significance, because nothing clear is being communicated in this sentence.

So it seems we have identified three features that meaningful sentences possess: they use real words, they are arranged grammatically and they are trying to communicate something. So we have here the beginnings of a theory of meaning, that is to say, we have begun to consider what the criteria are by which we can determine whether a sentence or use of language is meaningful or not. However, our theory remains rather vague at this stage. In particular our third condition would need to be unpacked and examined in a good deal more detail before it became at all interesting. What exactly does it mean to 'try to communicate something'? How can we decide whether or not a sentence does this effectively?

Experimenting with ideas

Each of the following sentences uses proper words and is grammatically correct. However, it may still be that not all of them are meaningful. Read through each sentence in turn and for each decide whether it is:

a) meaningful

b) apparently meaningful (but actually meaningless) or

c) obviously meaningless.

1 It is morally wrong to believe in something without sufficient evidence.
2 It is possible to doubt everything; it is even possible to doubt whether you are doubting.
3 There is life after death.
4 Birth is one of the miracles of nature.
5 I love you.
6 One, two, three, jump!
7 What came before time?
8 God loves the world like a father loves his children.
9 Respect!
10 The universe and everything in it doubled in size last night while we were asleep.

11 There are invisible pixies that live in my fridge who disappear without trace as soon as I open the door.
12 Jesus is the Way, the Truth and the Light.
13 It is possible for an infinitely powerful being to create a stone so large that they cannot move it.
14 The universe is expanding.
15 Bondi Beach contains more than one billion particles of sand.
16 The history of all hitherto existing societies is the history of class struggle.
17 There are two mistakes in the the sentence written here.
18 It is possible to know the unknowable.
19 The sunset over Victoria Falls is the most beautiful sight on earth.
20 I am who I am.

Now make a note of all the sentences that you thought were meaningful. You may find it helpful to draw up a table as follows and list some of the features that meaningful and meaningless sentences appear to have.

A sentence is meaningful if:	A sentence is meaningless if:

What do the meaningful sentences have in common? What is it about them that makes them meaningful? Write down some criteria for what makes a sentence meaningful.

In completing this exercise it is hoped you will have come up with your own criteria for a meaningful sentence. You may have decided that all the sentences were meaningful, in which case you probably reckon that a) being grammatical and b) using genuine words are sufficient conditions for meaningfulness. Perhaps you added additional criteria to these, such as c) not being paradoxical or contradictory. Alternatively you may have thought that only the sentences that you could do something with, that you could see a practical use for in your daily life, were meaningful.

Cognitivist and non-cognitivist accounts of religious language

There are many different theories explaining what makes a sentence meaningful, and they broadly fall into two types: COGNITIVIST and NON-COGNITIVIST theories.

Often when we express our beliefs (for example, about chairs, books or electrons) we are making claims about the world. These claims take the form of propositions or statements – we write them down or say them out loud. Now these propositions are capable of being either true or false, depending on whether they describe the world truly or falsely (in technical terms, genuine propositions have a 'truth value'). For example, if you sincerely state that:

The philosophy teacher is a brilliant woman with glasses

then this statement tells us that what you believe is that the philosophy teacher is a brilliant woman with glasses. Now this statement may well be false (the teacher might be a brilliant woman with 20/20 vision), but false sentences still make claims about the world (except they are false claims).

Some philosophers (most notably the logical positivists and A.J. Ayer) have argued that sentences are only *meaningful* if they are connected in this way to the world; that is, they describe the world either truly or falsely. So the example above is meaningful because it tries to tell us something about the world, namely what your philosophy teacher is like. It is irrelevant for this theory of meaning whether a sentence is actually true; false sentences are still meaningful because they 'paint a picture' of the world. A theory that says that sentences are meaningful because they refer to the world (either truly or falsely) is known as a cognitivist theory of meaning. **Figure 2.28** illustrates the way this might happen.

Figure 2.28 Within cognitivism a judgement expresses our beliefs about the world (truly or falsely).

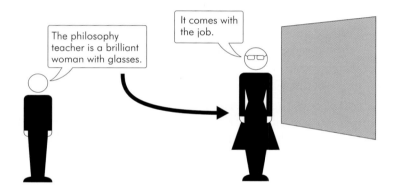

However, other philosophers have argued that there are many kinds of statements (for example, about souls, redness, beauty) which do not refer to the world at all. These types of claims are not capable of being true or false (they do not have any truth-value and are not genuine propositions). The name given to this position is 'non-cognitivism'. There are many different types of non-cognitivist theories but what they share is a rejection of the view that certain beliefs (about souls, redness or beauty) are propositional. Taking the example above ('The philosophy teacher is a brilliant woman with glasses'), a non-cognitivist might say that the term 'brilliant' doesn't refer to any property in the lecturer, but may simply be an expression of approval – that this teacher is hitting all the right spots in you as a learner.

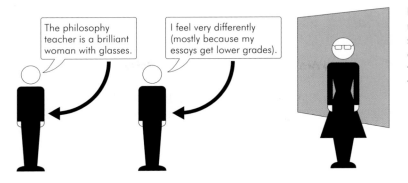

Figure 2.29 Within non-cognitivism a statement does not express a belief about the world and is neither true nor false.

So in contrast to the cognitivists, the non-cognitivists believe that statements can be meaningful even though they do not refer to the world, and even though they cannot be shown to be true or false. The many different theories which take this approach can be thought of as 'non-cognitive', and they tend to emphasise the complexity of language, and the context within which language use takes place.

Experimenting with ideas

Read through the following judgements and answer the questions below:

1 That new ring tone on your mobile is bad.
2 The morning BBC newsreader looks very fit.
3 Lying to the police is never wrong.
4 Atoms are made up of protons, neutrons and electrons.
5 The chair is bright red.
6 Your philosophy lecturer is tall.
7 It's good to fulfil your potential.
8 Everyone has a soul.
9 It was sad that her mum and dad split up.
10 The creator of the universe is all-loving.

For each judgement:

a) do you think it is objective or subjective?
b) do you think it is true/false (you are taking a cognitivist position on this statement)?
c) do you think it is neither true nor false but still expresses something (you are taking a non-cognitivist position on this statement)?

In the rest of this chapter we look in some detail at examples of cognitivist and non-cognitivist accounts of meaning, how they apply to religious language and the issues arising from these accounts. First we examine some cognitive theories of meaning, including VERIFICATIONISM in A.J. Ayer and John Hick and the debate around FALSIFICATIONISM in Antony Flew, R.M. Hare and Basil Mitchell; we then go on to look at some non-cognitive theories of religious language, including those of Ludwig Wittgenstein and his followers.

Logical positivism and the verification principle

A.J. Ayer (1910–1989) was a British philosopher who was very much under the influence of a group of Austrian philosophers known as the Vienna Circle. These philosophers (whom Ayer referred to as the logical positivists) were angered by what they took to be the gibberish that many philosophers, particularly in the nineteenth century, had a tendency to spout. They argued that language was only meaningful if it confined itself to discussing what fell within human experience. Once our language steps beyond the realms of what we can experience then it easily ventures into nonsense. These philosophers (such as Moritz Schlick and Rudolf Carnap) became known as the logical empiricists or logical positivists, which highlighted their association with the scientific movement of the nineteenth century called 'positivism'. This positivist movement argued that knowledge should be based on verifiable facts rather than on METAPHYSICS or theology, and so positivism looked to the empirical research methods of science for the foundations of authentic knowledge. The logical positivists extended this idea beyond science, applying it to the way we use language, and arguing that we must take a rigorous, logical approach to the meaning of statements.

As well as being a logical positivist, Ayer also saw himself as an heir to the Scottish Enlightenment philosopher David Hume, whose sceptical, empirical and common-sense approach to philosophy we encountered when looking at the arguments for the existence of God.

Like Hume, I divide all genuine propositions into two classes: those which, in his terminology, concern relations of ideas, and those which concern matters of fact.[6]

Ayer

The division between these two types of statements became known as Hume's fork (see above, page 152), and was a springboard for Ayer's philosophy of language. When he was in his mid-twenties Ayer wrote a book called *Language, Truth and Logic* that popularised the ideas of the logical positivists in Britain and America. In this book he used the ideas of the Vienna Circle, along with Hume's fork, and rigorously applied them to all aspects of philosophy. He defended what is known as the VERIFICATION PRINCIPLE, which is a kind of test that a sentence must pass if it is to count as genuinely meaningful. Ayer's verification principle proposes that:

anthology
2.49

- A sentence is meaningful if and only if:
  - either a) it is a tautology; that is, true by definition;
  - or b) it can – in principle – be proved to be true or false; that is, it is verifiable.
- If it isn't a) or b) then it isn't meaningful.

Ayer's verification principle claims that in order to say something that is meaningful we must know what would make our statement true or false. One way in which we can know a statement to be true is if it is true by definition, because of the meanings of the word it contains (prong 1 of the fork in **Figure 1.35**, page 153). The other way in which we can know a statement to be true is if we can check it by looking at the world and seeing if the claims it makes about the world can be proved to be true or false (prong 2). Ayer refers to these second types of meaningful statements as 'factually significant'. We saw above (page 210), when looking at arguments for the existence of God, that the first type of knowledge is referred to as *a priori*, and statements of the first type are termed *analytic*; in contrast the second type of knowledge is referred to as *a posteriori* and statements of the second type are termed *synthetic*. Let us apply the verification principle to the following statement:

Today it rained in London

and ask whether this statement is meaningful and why. We have seen that for Ayer there are two possible answers to this question:

1 It is true by definition. It does not fall into this category (although some joker may claim that part of what 'London' means is 'the city in which it always rains'; in which case the claim becomes 'today it rained in the city in which it always rains', and this is a tautology).

2 It can be shown to be true or false as a matter of fact. It does fall into this category, as it can be verified or falsified by images of wet pavements, grumpy commuters holding wet, battered umbrellas, and piles of today's free newspapers piled up and sodden outside Tube stations.

But what are we to make of other sorts of statements, like 'Today it rained in my heart'? With regards to these, Ayer, like the other logical positivists, is fairly ruthless in his application of the verification principle: it is meaningless. We should not be surprised by this as the whole purpose of the principle is to sift what is meaningful from what is not. If a proposition is not a tautology, and there is no empirical way of discovering its truth, then it is meaningless; it is a 'pseudo-proposition'. Ayer accepts that such statements may have emotional or literary significance, they may strike a chord in us or sound beautifully poetic, but they are not *factually* significant. Ayer's point is that meaningful propositions must make claims about the world; they must say that the world is this way or that way. So, if upon reading a proposition we are unsure what the world would be like if the statement were true as opposed to false (that is, if we did not know what would count as verifying it) then the proposition is not making a claim about the world after all. It is factually insignificant and meaningless.

▶ ACTIVITY

Refer to the list of propositions in the previous activity on page 316.

1 Re-categorise each proposition according to Ayer's verification principle.
2 Are there any propositions that Ayer would say were meaningless, but which to you are obviously meaningful?
3 What implications does this have for Ayer's theory?

The verification principle can be used to identify statements that look as if they are meaningful but are in fact word games, grammatical errors or simply incoherent. John Hick gives two useful examples of sentences that appear at first sight to be meaningful and about the world but which cannot be verified, and so must be nonsense according to the verificationist.[7]

The universe doubled in size last night.

There is an invisible, intangible, odourless, tasteless and silent rabbit in this room.

According to Ayer's verification principle both these sentences would be meaningless because neither of them can be verified or falsified. They appear to be making claims about the world, but when you look at them closely you see that whether they are true or false (that is, whether the world is the way they say it is) makes no difference to our experience. There is no possible experiment we could perform which could establish their truth or falsehood and so they are not factually significant.

Criticism

What of generalisations such as 'At sea level water boils at 100 degrees centigrade'? The problem with the truth of general claims like this is that they can never be conclusively proved, not even in principle, since we cannot boil all the water in the universe to confirm that it always boils at 100 degrees. This category of propositions looks as though it could represent a serious difficulty for the verification principle, as most scientific claims are of this general sort, and yet Ayer regarded science as the paradigm case of a body of meaningful claims. Note also that much of science deals with entities which are not directly observable; for example, sub-atomic particles such as protons and quarks. So how can we verify their existence, and the truth of propositions which refer to them?

Note, however, that there are claims which are meaningful according to the verification principle, even though we cannot verify them in practice. For example, it is meaningful to say that there is life on the planet Neptune, even though at present we have no means of verifying this claim. Ayer gets round this problem by differentiating between a strong and a weak version of verification, with scientific theories fulfilling the weaker conditions:

- The strong version states that a statement is meaningful if we can verify it by observation – and therefore establish its truth/falsity for certain.
- The weak version states that a statement is meaningful if there are some observations that can establish the probable truth of the statement.

So Ayer's weaker version of the verification principle is saying that a proposition counts as meaningful just if we know what observations would count towards or against the likelihood of its being true or false. For Ayer, such claims are meaningful because we could in principle verify them. Going back to the claim that there is life on Neptune, we know the kinds of things we would need to do – send a sophisticated space probe to Neptune, for example – to determine whether they are true. So the verification principle is not saying that we can as a matter of fact verify all meaningful propositions; just that we could do so in principle.

So how does Ayer's verification principle apply to philosophy, and in particular religious philosophy? Well, one implication of this for philosophers is that large swathes of what they have written and talked about over the last two thousand years will be ruled out by the verification principle. One branch of philosophy which is rendered meaningless by the principle is metaphysics: the account of ultimate reality and of what substances and beings might lie beyond our ordinary perception. A discussion of metaphysics includes discussions of supernatural beings (which cannot be observed) and God. In which case one of the most significant consequences of Ayer's theory is that it appears to make all claims about religion and about God meaningless.[8] This is because many religious claims are about something transcendent; that is to say, about objects which lie beyond human experience – for example God, heaven or life after death. But all talk about what lies outside experience is, according to the verification principle, meaningless. Statements such as 'God loves the world' or 'God is the Father, the Son and the Holy Ghost' appear to be telling us something about someone. But when we look at such statements from the point of view of verificationism it becomes clear that there are no possible ways of checking whether they are true or false. There are no experiments we could carry out or observations we could make to prove them, and so such statements are not factually significant. Importantly, then, Ayer does not regard the claim that 'God exists' as false, but rather as meaningless. Equally the claims of the atheist that 'God does not exist' are also meaningless, as they too fail the verification principle's test. For Ayer we simply cannot meaningfully talk about God.

anthology 2.50

Another area of philosophy that falls foul of the verification principle is ethics. Ethical statements which make judgements of what is right/wrong are not true by definition nor, says Ayer, can they be verified as matters of fact. In which case much of what is written in moral philosophy is meaningless, and for Ayer we should start to realise that moral judgements are simply expressions of what we feel (this theory became known as EMOTIVISM).

Criticism

There are, however, some serious difficulties facing Ayer's verification principle. The first criticism is that the principle seems far too strong since it not only outlaws religious language from the realm of the meaningful, but it also makes much of what humans speak and write about meaningless as well, including art, beauty and our inner feelings and sensations. After all, how can we prove that the *Mona Lisa* is beautiful? The verification principle makes poetic and metaphorical language meaningless: for example, I cannot verify that my love is a rose.

Moreover, it makes all ethical judgements simply a matter of personal feeling and it makes most philosophical speculation nonsense. This need not be a problem, but it certainly suggests that Ayer's notion of meaning is very different from the one we operate with in everyday life.

But perhaps Ayer's prescriptive account of meaning in general should trouble us. The philosopher Stewart Sutherland described Ayer's theory as 'conceptually restrictive and intellectually imperialistic in its character'.[9] Sutherland goes on to compare the prescriptions of Ayer (on what we can and cannot talk about) with George Orwell's invented language 'Newspeak' described in his novel *1984*. Newspeak is an artificial language that is developed by a totalitarian government with the specific intention of limiting what can be said by people. The ultimate goal of Newspeak is to enable people to speak about practical matters, and things that are permitted by the government, but to prevent people from talking about, or even thinking about, anything that might encourage heretical behaviour. This is a terrifying thought, as all human creativity, philosophy, religion, literature, theorising would be impossible within Newspeak. Rather like, Sutherland says, the effects of Ayer's verification principle, which would also rule out as 'non-sense' these areas of human activity, and eventually diminish human thought.

Criticism

A second criticism is that the principle of verification is itself meaningless according to its own criterion. The principle claims that 'for any proposition to be meaningful it must either be verifiable or true by definition'. So if this claim is itself meaningful it must either be true by definition or verifiable. However, it is clearly not true by definition. We cannot recognise its truth simply by examining the meanings of the terms it uses. But neither does it appear to be verifiable, as it is hard to see in what way the world (if the principle were true) would differ from the world if it were false. So if the verification principle is neither verifiable nor true, then by definition it must itself be meaningless!

Religious statements as verifiable eschatologically

A further significant criticism of Ayer comes from the Christian philosopher John Hick, who argued that religious statements can in fact be verified and therefore that they are factually significant and so meaningful, even according to the verification principle. There are three main aspects to Hick's approach: first, his definition of 'verification', which is different from Ayer's; second, his parable of the Celestial City, showing that verification of religious statements is possible and reasonably straightforward; third, his account of personal identity after death, showing that resurrection is possible. Let us deal with each aspect in turn.

Hick agrees with Ayer that only statements that are factually significant are meaningful, and that FACTUAL SIGNIFICANCE is judged by whether the truth or falsity of an assertion makes a difference to our experience of the world. For example, whether the statement 'There is an invisible, odourless, intangible rabbit in this room' is true or false makes no difference to our experience. Hence it is not factually significant; it tells us nothing about the world and is not meaningful. Like Ayer, Hick proposes that the factual significance of an assertion is best assessed by whether it can be verified. Hick goes on to say that verifiability should be judged by whether it is possible to remove the grounds for rational doubt about the truth of the claim in question. For example, claiming that there is a family of foxes living at the bottom of the garden can be verified if you keep finding mutilated bin bags on the path, if you have seen a red furry tail sticking out from a hole under the shed and if your night-vision goggles reveal frolicking fox cubs. Such evidence would effectively remove any serious doubts about the matter.

Now, Hick accepts that religious propositions cannot be falsified. They cannot be falsified because, if there is no God and the atheists are right, then after they die they will just be dead and they will not be able to say 'Ah-ha – there is no God, those theists got it wrong!' But Hick's argument is that although religious statements may never be falsified they can be verified, in the sense that rational doubt can be removed about their truth. For Hick it is the potential verifiability of religious statements that makes them meaningful. To illustrate how such verification is possible he offers his celebrated parable of the Celestial City:

> Two men are travelling together along a road. One of them believes that it leads to the Celestial City, the other that it leads nowhere; but since this is the only road there is, both must travel it … During the journey they meet with moments of refreshment and delight, and with moments of hardship and danger. All the time one of them thinks of his journey as a pilgrimage to the Celestial City. He interprets the pleasant parts of the journey as encouragements and the obstacles as trials of his purpose … The other, however, believes none of this … Since he has no choice in the matter he enjoys the good and endures the bad … When they do turn the last corner it will be apparent that one of them has been right all the time and the other wrong.[10]

John Hick, 'Theology and Verification'

Remember that Hick believes that the journey of our lives through this world, and its hardships and pains, are part of the process of soul-making (see above, page 309). You may also recall that, as part of Hick's theodicy, the rewards of life after death are sufficient to compensate for the suffering people experience in their lives on earth. But here it is the destination (heaven), not the journey (life), that Hick is exploring in this passage.

This parable points to the possibility of what Hick calls 'eschatological verification', that is to say, verification after our death in the next life. (ESCHATOLOGY concerns what happens at the end of things, for instance at the Last Judgement.) Hick is arguing that many religious statements, particularly in Christianity, rest on the claim that there is an afterlife, and they are meaningful because they can be verified in the afterlife. I can verify whether there is a heaven or not if, after I die, I find myself in heaven. For Hick such experience would remove grounds for rational doubt about the existence of heaven.

Hick recognises that the possibility of eschatological verification relies on the possibility of my retaining my personal identity through the processes of death, but there are certain difficulties with this idea. One important difficulty is that we all know that when people die their bodies quickly decompose. How, if the body of which you are made has dissipated, can you possibly be thought to have survived? If someone subsequently appears in heaven, in what sense can it be said to be the same person? If I am resurrected how can this new body be thought of as still me?

To answer such questions, Hick presents three separate 'thought experiments' which try to show that a person appearing in an afterlife can meaningfully be considered as the same person as someone who had lived and died in this life.

1   First Hick asks us to imagine a person, X, disappearing in America, while at the very same moment someone else, who is the exact double of X (same physical features, the same memory, and so on), appears in Australia. If this happened would you consider the person appearing in Australia to be the same as X? Hick thinks that we would.

2   Now imagine that person X, instead of disappearing, dies in America, and at the very same moment their double appears in Australia. Would we not still say they were the same person? Hick thinks that if we accept that it is the same person in the first scenario, we would have to accept that it is the same in this scenario.

3   Finally, imagine that person X dies in America, and their double now appears, not in Australia, but in heaven. Again Hick thinks that if we accept that it is the same person in scenarios 1 and 2, then we must accept it is the same in this scenario too. And if we accept that it is the same person, then we are accepting that it makes sense to talk about surviving one's death and preserving one's personal identity.

What these thought experiments are supposed to show is that resurrection is at least logically possible. And if we are resurrected in heaven, we (or at least some of us) will be in no doubt that it is heaven that we are in. For Hick there are two factors that will remove all rational doubt that we are in heaven: first, our final understanding of the purpose and destiny given to us by God; and, second, our encountering our saviour Jesus Christ. Note that Hick says that only some of us may be able to verify this, namely those who already believe in God. But, nonetheless, if it is logically possible that at least someone will be able to verify (remove rational doubt from) the claim that 'God exists', then this claim is meaningful.

 Experimenting with ideas

Scenario 1: You are a guest on the Starship Enterprise and Captain Kirk invites you to take a trip to a local planet in their matter transporter. The machine will decompose your body into its constituent atoms, channel them along a laser beam across space and recompose you on the planet's surface.

1   If you stepped into the matter transporter do you think you would arrive safely on the planet's surface as the same person?

Scenario 2: Suppose that the matter transporter does not operate over great distances, but that luckily the ingenious technicians on the Enterprise have invented a tele-transporter. The tele-transporter works by first decomposing your body and recording the precise pattern of the constituent atoms. It then transmits the pattern to the distant planet where another machine recomposes you out of local materials. Keen to cross the galaxy you agree to step into the machine. The person appearing on the other planet believes they are you.

2   Do you think you would arrive safely on the planet's surface as the same person?
3   Is your answer the same for the matter transporter? What differences are there between the two cases?

Scenario 3: Consider a tele-transporter, which does not destroy your original body, but simply creates a copy out of local materials on the planet so that now there are two of 'you'. Which one would be the real you and why?

4   Do your answers to the three scenarios in this activity cast doubt on, or confirm, Hick's claim that it is possible for you to survive your death? Why?

Criticism
One line of criticism against Hick is to question the conclusions he draws from his thought experiments. Each scenario, it may be urged, really produces a duplicate person in a new location, and so is not really the self-same person who disappeared or died. To see this, consider altering the scenarios slightly, such that in each case the original person remains alongside the double appearing in Australia or heaven. In such cases we would be inclined to think the double a different person from the original. However, this alteration to the scenario has not changed the status of the double itself, and so the double cannot be the same as the original. God could certainly create a duplicate of me in heaven on my death, but a duplicate of me is not me. Our intuitions appear to suggest that, for my personal identity to survive the process of death, there would have to be some form of bodily continuity. Simply rebuilding a perfect copy is not resurrecting the self-same person.

Criticism

A second difficulty concerns whether we truly can verify through our post-mortem experience the various religious claims in question. Consider the most obvious claims that God and heaven exist. In order to verify that we are now in heaven, or are now experiencing God, we need first to recognise that this vision in front of us is heaven (or God). But it may not be possible to recognise something we have never seen before and that lies beyond our understanding. So if, as some philosophers say, God is beyond our comprehension, then perhaps it will not be possible to recognise, and hence verify, that this is God or heaven we see before us.

The *University* debate: Flew, Hare and Mitchell

Antony Flew and falsificationism

In the mid-1950s, as part of a symposium in the journal *University*, three philosophers debated whether or not religious statements could be falsified, and whether this helped throw light onto the meaningfulness (or meaninglessness) of religious propositions. Two of the philosophers, Richard Hare (1919–2002) and Basil Mitchell (1917–2011), were believers and the third, Antony Flew (1923–2010), was an atheist, but all three used memorable parables to make their points. It was Flew who opened the symposium with an attack on the meaning of religious propositions. Like Ayer and Hick, Flew believed that propositions are only meaningful if they are factually significant, in other words if they make a genuine assertion about the world. However, unlike Ayer or Hick, he argues that it is not the possibility of verification, but more particularly the possibility of falsification, that shows whether a statement is meaningful.

Flew borrows a parable from John Wisdom's article 'Gods', written in 1944, and amends it to make his case. In the original parable Wisdom asks us to imagine two people arriving at a run-down garden. One person notices the flowers and the organisation of the plants and takes this as evidence that someone has been caring for the garden. The other person notices the weeds and the disorder and concludes that no one has been tending the garden. Wisdom's point is that although two people can be presented with exactly the same empirical evidence – it is the same garden that both are experiencing – their responses need not be the same.

This shows that empirical observation or evidence does not, by itself, determine the very different conclusions that people draw about the world. How we interpret the evidence presented to us is, at least in part, influenced by our attitudes towards it. The atheist may focus on the disorder of the universe and interpret this as evidence of the absence of any divine plan. Meanwhile, the theist attends to the order and beauty of things and sees this as evidence of the work of a divine intelligence.

Figure 2.30 Is there a gardener or not?

 Experimenting with ideas

Why do you think some people see the world as a divine creation and others as a meaningless lump of rock?

1   Read through Paley's design argument (pages 238–240) above. Think about the way that William Paley sees the world as he walks across the hills with a friend looking at the landscape, the sun setting, the birds of prey hunting. Describe how each of the following affects what he sees:
   a) His existing set of beliefs (what do you think he believes?).
   b) His expectations as to what he might observe.
   c) The suggestions that might have been made to him.
   d) His emotional states.
   e) The culture he has grown up in.
2   Read through the points Charles Darwin raised against the argument from design (see above, page 256). Think about a modern scientist walking through the same hills, observing the same features as Paley had done a hundred years before. Describe how a)–e) (above) affect what the scientist sees.

In Flew's reworking of Wisdom's gardener parable, the two people find a clearing in the jungle, containing many flowers, but also many weeds. Since they do not observe any gardener visiting to tend the plants, the sceptic reckons there must be no gardener. However, her companion, rather than give up the belief that there is a gardener, concludes that the gardener must come at night. So the two of them stay up all night keeping vigil, hoping to spot the mysterious gardener, but none appears. Again the sceptic takes this as evidence that there is no gardener, but the believer stubbornly responds that the gardener must be invisible. So they put up an electric fence around the garden and guard it with sniffer-dogs, but still they find no evidence of a gardener sneaking in to tend the land. Despite this the believer continues to maintain that there is a gardener, but now claims he is not only invisible, but also odourless and intangible, which accounts for why they have so far been unable to find direct evidence of his activity. So the believer continues to assert that there is a gardener, despite the complete lack of evidence, and each time their effort to find the gardener fails the believer simply modifies their assertion. Eventually the sceptic despairs and asks the believer, 'How does your claim that there is an invisible, odourless, intangible gardener differ from the claim that there's no gardener at all?'[11]

▶ ACTIVITY

In Flew's and Wisdom's parables what do the following represent:

a) The garden?
b) The flowers?
c) The weeds?
d) The differences in belief between the two people in the garden?

Flew is using the parable to show how a statement can start out as an assertion about the world. 'There is a gardener', but then is modified bit by bit so that it ends up not being an assertion at all. And for Flew this has significant implications for religious assertions and whether or not they are meaningful.

Flew does not use the following example, but this is a well-documented case of a religious assertion that has been modified over time, namely the assertion found in the Bible (Genesis 1.20ff) that God created humans and animals, fully formed, and that they flourished in a fully formed world that he had also recently created. According to the Christian tradition God created the universe and everything in it in six days, he rested on the seventh, and he also created the first human out of earth, and that this event happened in around 5500BC (counting generations backwards to Adam). Modern cosmology and evolutionary theory have cast serious doubts on such an assertion: in Victorian times the discovery and analysis of fossils, the work of Darwin on evolution, the work of geologists on the age of the earth; all undermined the assertions that were made in Genesis. These discoveries could have been accepted by believers as showing that the assertions made in Genesis are false. But modern theists have instead modified and qualified their claims that God created humans and animals in order to accommodate these scientific advances: God, it is now urged, created humans and animals through a process of evolution over hundreds of millions of years, and the text of Genesis is to be understood metaphorically. Another example, which theologians have themselves grappled with, is the claim that God is omnipotent, which can be modified in the light of counter examples (see above, page 182).

But such manoeuvrings worry Flew. If one repeatedly qualifies our original assertion in the light of the new evidence to avoid having to give it up, then our assertion suffers what Flew calls 'death by a thousand qualifications'. In other words the assertion has been watered down and qualified so much that the assertion no longer says anything at all.

Let us look at our own example of how an assertion can be continuously qualified. Imagine you have a friend who is convinced that Scarlett Johansson has romantic feelings for him. More than this, he claims that Scarlett Johansson *loves* him. So his claim appears to be straightforward, namely that:

Scarlett Johansson loves me.

In querying this statement you remind him that he used to love Jennifer Lopez with equal fervour. He replies that the whole J-Lo thing was just a crush, and he's moved on with his life even if she hasn't. You then explain patiently that Ms Johansson doesn't even know him; that she has never even seen him; and that it is all over the social media that she is in love with a good-looking, rich and famous person. You also explain that times have moved on, and that it's far easier to prosecute possible stalkers like him these days. However, your friend insists that Scarlett has to keep her love for him a deep secret in order to avoid a scandal in the tabloid newspapers. His original claim is now qualified as follows:

Scarlett Johansson loves me (but it is a deeply secret love).

After a while your friend admits to you that Ms Johansson's agent has recently called him, and told him to stop sending flowers, love poems and personal effects. The agent made it very clear that Ms Johansson was not interested. But your friend explains to you that the agent was merely protecting his client from the damaging effects of her passion. Eventually Ms Johansson herself contacts him online to tell your friend that if his pestering doesn't stop she will call her lawyers. Your friend tells you that he knows she is just playing hard-to-get; it's all part of the dating game. You realise that he's made a further adjustment to his claim:

Scarlett Johansson loves me (but it is a deeply secret love and she is playing hard-to-get).

Even when the court order arrives forcing your friend to keep at least two miles away from Ms Johansson, your friend explains to you that her entourage and entire legal team don't want her to become romantically involved with someone so young and so poor. He is now claiming that:

Scarlett Johansson loves me (but it is a deeply secret love, she is playing hard-to-get and her entourage and legal team are conspiring to prevent us from getting together).

Eventually you ask him if there is anything that anyone could say or do, anything that could happen, that would demonstrate to him that Scarlett Johansson doesn't love him. He confesses that nothing could come between him and Scarlett, that he knows her love for him is forever, and even if she doesn't yet realise it, deep down she will always be in love with him.

Ian McEwan's novel *Enduring Love* ends on a similar, and sinister, one-sided declaration of love. A stalker, who has finally been imprisoned, continues to write passionate letters to his victim, finding in his prison cell all sorts of signs that his victim returns this love. His thousandth letter ends as follows: 'Thank you for loving me, thank you for accepting me, thank you for recognising what I am doing for our love. Send me a new message soon.' The 'message' that the deluded man is referring to is simply the sun rising over the prison.[12]

anthology
2.52

Let us now return to Flew's argument. Flew is particularly interested in how believers surrender or adapt their assertions in the face of evidence that goes against these assertions. He uses the example of the assertion that God loves us like a father loves his children. If we point out to the theist that no father would let his children suffer what humans suffer, they typically respond by qualifying their statement and saying that God's love is a mysterious love. We saw above when examining the problem of evil how believers such as Hick and Plantinga have argued that God's love is compatible with the existence of horrific pain and suffering. So, Flew asks, how much suffering and evil must there be before the theist will admit that God does not love us, or even that he does not exist? Flew's answer to this question is that *nothing* will count against the believer's assertion that God loves us; in other words, that no amount of evidence that God does not in fact love us will ever lead believers to give up the assertion that God does love us. After all, in one of the most important books of the Old Testament, Job, who has lost everything (his family, livelihood, friends, health) and who is sitting on a dungheap wondering what on earth he has done to deserve this (nothing, actually), still asserts that 'I know my redeemer liveth.'[13]

It looks as if, according to Flew, religious assertions are not really assertions at all. Flew, like Ayer, thinks that an assertion is a genuine, meaningful assertion when it is factually significant; that is when it is making a claim about the world, saying that 'such-and-such is the case'. If you assert that your philosophy teacher wears glasses, then you are saying that 'my philosophy teacher wears glasses' is true, but you are also saying 'my philosophy teacher never wears glasses' is false. In other words your assertion is a genuine assertion because you know what the world needs to look like in order to make your assertion true *and* you know what the world needs to look like in order to make your assertion false. For Flew, then, to know the meaning of an assertion you also need to know the meaning of its opposite. But if there is no 'opposite'; that is, if you cannot imagine any circumstances in which your statement could be false, then it is not an assertion at all. And if it is not an assertion (that is, it has no factual significance) then it is not meaningful.

For Flew there are very strong indicators, based on how religious people actually respond to facts which seem to falsify their claims, that religious assertions are not falsifiable. Flew argued that religious people, rather than accept that their assertions may be false, change and qualify their assertions and keep doing this rather than give them up. We saw this in the case of the believer in the Invisible Gardener, who refused to give up their assertion that a gardener looked after the clearing in the jungle (summarised in the table below).

The believer's assertion that 'there is a gardener' cannot be falsified, but is instead modified and qualified.

Believer	Sceptic
	2 There is no gardener.
I There is a gardener.	
	Look, there are many weeds among the flowers.
I.I There is a gardener (… but he has let weeds grow).	
	We've sat here and watched and watched but we've never seen a gardener.
I.I.I There is a gardener (…but he's let weeds grow and he is invisible).	
	We've got guard dogs, but the dogs never bark.
I.I.I.I There is a gardener (… but he's let weeds grow and he's invisible and he is odourless).	
	We've set up an electric, barbed wire fence, but the fence never moves and we've never heard any shrieks.
I.I.I.I.I There is a gardener (…but he's let weeds grow, and he's invisible, and he's odourless, and he is intangible).	
	Really – how does I.I.I.I.I differ from 2?

Flew concludes that if believers cannot articulate what will make their assertion that 'God loves the world' or 'God exists' false, or if believers continue to qualify these assertions despite being given falsifying evidence, then they are not making any assertions at all. For Flew there are already strong indicators (for example, explanations of why a loving God allows so much horrific suffering) that religious statements cannot be falsified, and therefore are not meaningful. The challenge then, laid down by Flew to his fellow debaters, is this:

What would have to occur or to have occurred to constitute for you a disproof of the love of, or the existence of, God?

 Experimenting with ideas

Imagine the following people are having a conversation (similar to the one in the table above), and construct a dialogue that might take place between them:

Person A has an unshakeable belief that they will never give up no matter what the evidence	Person B wishes to provide evidence that shows person A they are wrong
I The Prime Minister believes that a certain country in the Middle East has weapons of mass destruction.	I The United Nations chief weapons inspector is carrying out thorough inspections and finds nothing.
2 Someone from the Flat-Earth Society sincerely believes that the Earth is flat and there is a conspiracy to 'prove' it is round.	2 A specialist in astronomy and geography is out to disband the Flat-Earth Society.
3 A child believes that there are monsters under their bed.	3 A mother is trying to reassure her child to help him get to sleep.
4 A fanatical England football supporter believes that the England team play the best football in the world.	4 A football historian wants to show this fan that all the evidence of past tournaments shows the England team are simply average.
5 A student is convinced that all her lecturers are out to ruin her life, no matter how helpful they might appear.	5 A counselling tutor is trying to help this student, so that she might rejoin her classes.
6 A believer is convinced that God loves the world.	6 An atheist is convinced that a loving God does not exist, because of the amount of suffering in the world.

Hare's criticisms of Flew

Following directly on from Flew's contribution to the 'Theology and Falsification' debate, two other philosophers, Basil Mitchell and Richard Hare, responded to Flew's challenge as to whether religious statements were assertions that could be falsified.

Flew's frustration with believers seemed to be related to how they accommodate and deal with evidence that apparently falsifies their assertions. We have seen that Flew concluded that this was because believers were not making any assertions at all; he based this conclusion on the fact that believers and atheists see the world very differently, and that believers have a blind spot when it comes to accepting evidence against their claims. His examples, and the parable of the Invisible Gardener, may have been selected to make the atheists' perspective appear fair and reasonable, while the believers' perspective appears to be unreasonable and defensive.

Both Mitchell and Hare try to show that the believer's and the atheist's position are more nuanced than this, and they both argue against Flew: it is not the case (as Flew suggests) that the believer is simply being stubborn in the face of some pretty obvious facts. Mitchell and Hare reject Flew's position, and both offer their own parables which also hinge on the world being seen from two different perspectives, just as Hick did through his parable of the Celestial City and Flew did in his Invisible Gardener parable. Emerging from these parables is a new understanding of how religious statements can be meaningful even though they are not straightforwardly falsifiable. Let us look at Hare's response to Flew first.

Hare gives his own parable to help us to understand the strange nature of religious statements, which we can call the parable of the Paranoid Student:

A certain lunatic is convinced that all dons want to murder him. His friends introduce him to all the mildest and most respectable dons that they can find, and after each of them has retired, they say, 'You see, he doesn't really want to murder you; he spoke to you in a most cordial manner; surely you are convinced now?' But the lunatic replies 'Yes, but that was only his diabolical cunning; he's really plotting against me the whole time, like the rest of them; I know it I tell you.' However many kindly dons are produced, the reaction is still the same.[14]

R.M. Hare

Like the person who believes in the Invisible Gardener, the paranoid student cannot imagine being wrong; his claim that 'my professors are out to murder me' is unfalsifiable. Hare concedes to Flew that the student's claim fails the test of falsifiability, and therefore it cannot count as a genuine assertion. Instead Hare proposes that we view the student's claim as something more like an expression of the student's conviction or interpretation or scaffolding that underpins his other beliefs.

Hare invented the word 'blik' to refer to such foundational interpretations and attitudes and he argued that we all have bliks. The paranoid student has a deluded, and wrong, blik; the professors (who can see that he is deluded as they all know they do not want to murder him) all have a correct blik. But the professors still have a blik, and when they say, 'The other professors really don't want to kill the student' they are expressing their own bliks. The differences between what Hare has to say about the paranoid student, and what Flew would have to say about the paranoid student are something like this:

- **Flew:** When the paranoid student says, 'the professors are trying to kill me' he appears to be making an assertion, but we know this claim cannot be falsified, therefore it is not an assertion at all. The people who tell the student, 'the professors aren't trying to kill you' are making an assertion and it is a true one.
- **Hare:** When the paranoid student says, 'the professors are trying to kill me' he is not making an assertion. He is expressing a fundamental interpretation and attitude that underpin his beliefs. The people who tell the student, 'the professors aren't trying to kill you' are not making assertions either; they are also expressing their own fundamental interpretations and attitudes that underpin their beliefs.

Hare's point is that we are all in some ways like the student in his parable; we all have bliks. We all have, and express, fundamental interpretations and foundational beliefs, that we would not let go of easily and which are, to all intents and purposes, unfalsifiable. These thoughts and principles often form the very basis for our other beliefs about the world, just as the student's paranoid blik does. In support of his concept of 'blik', Hare refers to the work of David Hume, who led the way in investigating the assumptions that we all make about the world. In particular Hume argued that we believe that all events have a cause, and we base our lives on this assumption without questioning whether it is true. Moreover, this assumption that 'every event has a cause' cannot actually be falsified, and so in Hare's terminology it is a blik.

Imagine that someone tried to falsify this belief. They might point to events for which no cause could be observed, such as the unexpected disappearance of your cat, or the sudden appearance of a puncture in your bicycle tyre. We can suppose that you spent months trying to find out how or why your cat disappeared, or hours looking for the offending object that had pierced your tyre's inner tube, but had found nothing. Would you accept such failure as evidence that these events just happened without any reason or cause? Probably not. For what you would try to do instead is hold on to your belief that 'everything has a cause', and explain away your failure to find any cause in these cases by thinking that you had not searched long or hard enough. You would probably think to yourself that given enough time and the right resources you would have found the cause. And no matter how many events the sceptic might describe that appear to lack a cause, you may well respond in the same way: refusing to give up your belief that all events have causes despite the mounting number of events cited where no cause is forthcoming. 'Cause-and-effect' is how we interpret our experience, and we rely on it when moving through the world, when conducting experiments, when planning for the future – we cannot get rid of it: in Hare's terms, it is a bilk.

For Hare many religious statements fall into the category of 'blik'. Religious statements do not just state facts about the world, but they go beyond that to express our attitude to those facts, and the value we put in those facts. So, for Hare, when believers say that 'God exists', they are expressing a blik: it is a belief that informs their perspective on the world, and in terms of which they interpret their whole lives. They may never be prepared to give it up, but the fundamental nature of the belief ensures that it remains important to them, and distinctly meaningful.

The mistake of the position which Flew selects for attack is to regard this kind of talk as some sort of explanation, as scientists are accustomed to use the word.[15]

R.M. Hare

So if bliks have meaning then it is a mistake to presume, as Flew does, that all the statements we make are assertions or propositions that can be falsified. Hare's argument represents a significant move away from a cognitivist approach and towards a non-cognitivist approach to religious language (see above, page 318). If Hare is correct then many religious statements are actually expressions of bliks, and are not assertions, yet they are still meaningful. This new approach to religious statements may

---

▶ **ACTIVITY**

Read through the following statements and answer the questions below:

1 Every event that you have experienced, or will experience in your lifetime, has a cause.
2 God loves the world that he created.
3 As you walk or run down any street (avoiding potholes, men-at-work, wobbly paving stones, sudden crevasses, etc.) the ground in front of you is basically going to be solid.
4 Someone, somewhere, loves you.
5 The cars that you sit in when you drive are not going to suddenly fall apart as you turn a corner.
6 There is life after death.
7 It always rains in London.
8 The sun will rise tomorrow (even if we may not see it because of the cloud cover).
9 Your teachers are not out to murder you.

10 The world outside this room continues to exist when the door is shut.

    a) Which of the statements above do you hold to be true? (We will call these your convictions.)

    b) How might someone get you to change your mind about these convictions (and would they be able to shake up your convictions without giving ridiculous or unlikely scenarios?)

    c) So, which of your convictions would Hare say are your 'bliks'?

---

help to prise 'meaningfulness' away from the logical positivists, and away from those who argue that a statement has to be factually significant in order to be meaningful.

Criticism

Flew gives short shrift to Hare's efforts to analyse religious statements as bliks, claiming that such an analysis is fundamentally misguided. Flew argues that religious people, when they make statements about God, about God's love and God's creation really are trying to refer to the world, to make assertions. As Flew says:

> If Hare's religion really is a blik, involving no cosmological assertions about the nature and activities of a supposed personal creator, then surely he is not a Christian at all?[16]

Flew isn't quite on the mark here, as there is a recent (controversial) movement, led by Don Cuppit (1934–) which takes an anti-realist approach to Christianity and which does not see religious statements as assertions about the world, but as expressions of value. Hare's concept of bliks would fit quite comfortably into this tradition (see also our discussion of alternative theologies on page 301 above, and Braithwaite's theory on page 344 below). However, Flew is right to think that this is not an orthodox interpretation of religious statements, and that in general when believers do make statements involving religious terms or ideas (such as 'God loves his creation') then they really are trying to make assertions about the world.

Mitchell's criticisms of Flew

Let us now turn to the third and final philosopher who took part in the symposium for the journal *University*. Basil Mitchell also offers a critical response to Flew, but from a different angle from that of Hare. He disagrees with the view that religious beliefs are unfalsifiable and he tells another parable to make his point, this time about a Stranger who may, or may not, be on the side of the Partisans.[17]

Imagine your country has been invaded and you become a Partisan; a member of the resistance movement hoping to overthrow the occupiers. One night you meet a man claiming to be a resistance leader, and he convinces you to put your trust in him and the movement. Over the months you sometimes see the man act for the resistance, but sometimes you also see him act against the movement. This troubles you: you worry that he might be a traitor, but your trust in him eventually overcomes your concerns and you continue to believe in him. Your belief that 'the stranger is on your side' is one that you do not give up, even though you see many things that suggest you are wrong.[18]

Mitchell argues that the belief of the Partisan in the resistance leader is meaningful, even though you refuse to give it up. Unlike Hare, Mitchell does not think that it is a blik because there are many occasions in which you do doubt your own belief. This doubt shows that your belief is falsifiable; that is, that you can quickly imagine circumstances under which you would give up your belief.

Mitchell's parable reflects the doubts that religious believers sometimes have when they encounter great suffering in their lives (see the problem of evil earlier, pages 291–311). These 'trials of faith' show that Flew is wrong to think that believers simply shrug off evidence that goes against their beliefs. Some believers, after all, do lose their faith in the face of painful and apparently senseless episodes in their lives.

We could take Mitchell's parable further, and develop it along the lines of John Hick's eschatological verification (see above, page 326), suggesting that one day the truth will be revealed and verified – in the parable this happens when the war is over; in real life this would happen after we die. So, by extending Mitchell's parable, we may show that a belief that 'God exists' is both falsifiable (there are trials of faith) and verifiable (after we die), and therefore religious statements are meaningful assertions about the world.

In summary then, Mitchell, although a Christian like Hare, does not take Hare's non-cognitivist approach to religious statements. Mitchell thinks that statements like 'God loves the world' are genuine statements, and factually significant. So, like Flew, Mitchell adopts a cognitivist approach, however, unlike Flew, Mitchell thinks that the statements are capable of being falsified (see the table at the end of this chapter on page 348).

Non-cognitivism: Wittgenstein, Braithwaite and Crombie

We noted above (page 318) that, while there is only one way to hold a cognitivist position, there are many ways to reject cognitivism, and so there are many different varieties or flavours of non-cognitivism. We have already encountered one non-cognitivist position: Hare's notion of 'bliks', which captures the idea that we do state convictions about the world which we are not really prepared to surrender (they are not easily falsified) but that these statements are meaningful. Here we look at three further non-cognitivist positions: the first is that of Wittgenstein, who was interested in meaning in general (not just with regards to religious statements); the second and third are R.B. Braithwaite and I.M. Crombie, both of whom were influenced by Wittgenstein.

Wittgenstein's rejection of cognitivism

Ludwig Wittgenstein (1889–1951) was one of the most significant philosophers of the last century. He was primarily a philosopher

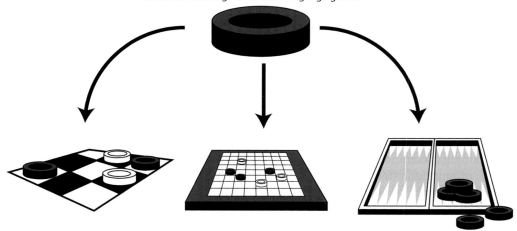

Just as a counter can have a different use in many different games, so a word can be used with a different meaning in different language games.

Figure 2.31 Just as a counter can have a different use in many different games, so a word can be used with a different meaning in different language games.

context. For example, the rules governing the use of the word 'experience' in science are very different from those governing this word in a religious context. But Wittgenstein argued that it was a mistake to think that one use of a word was better or more fundamental than another.

▶ **ACTIVITY**

1 How many different types of language games can you think of?
2 Can you describe how some of the rules of these language games differ?

Remember what Ayer and Flew claimed: that for a statement to be meaningful it must refer to the world. But Wittgenstein is now suggesting that statements are meaningful so long as they are understood by other language users in a specific context. He therefore thinks (unlike Ayer) that morality, art, poetry, and so on, are all meaningful; they are all language games. Now, when it comes to religious statements and concepts, according to Wittgenstein's approach, they are meaningful because they form part of a religious language game. Believers are users of this language; they are immersed in the practice of following its rules and, if we consider meaning to be equated with use, then such a language is meaningful to whoever is able to use the language appropriately, that is to say, to 'players' of the game.

So to understand religious statements we need to be a part of the religious language game; as Wittgenstein said, we need to be immersed in the religious 'Form of Life'. If we are not immersed in that particularly way of living, if we don't share those beliefs, or use those concepts in a familiar and regular way, then we cannot properly understand religious statements. This is the problem with cognitivist philosophers like Ayer and Flew. They think that there is only one way language can be meaningful, namely if it is factually significant; so when religious language fails to be factually significant they accuse it of being meaningless. But the error is to think that meaning lies in factual significance; that is, in statements that describe the world. The fundamental mistake made by Ayer and Flew is to treat statements from one language game (expressions of religious faith) as if they came from another (descriptions of the world): in other words to treat religious talk as if it were scientific talk and as if it were a hypothesis.

> Suppose someone were a believer and said: 'I believe in a Last Judgement', and I said: 'Well, I'm not so sure. Possibly.' You would say that there is an enormous gulf between us. If he said 'There is a German aeroplane overhead', and I said 'Possibly, I'm not so sure' you'd say we were fairly near.[22]
>
> **Wittgenstein**

For Wittgenstein, science and religion are two different language games; they are not in competition with one another, and neither can help solve the problems of the other. According to Wittgenstein, it might be appropriate for us to take a hard-nosed approach to the meaning of scientific statements, in the way Ayer and Flew suggest: scientific claims are hypotheses that need to be verified or falsified. However, religious claims about God and the Creation or Last Judgement are not hypotheses and are not subject to the same rules as scientific claims.

When a believer says 'The Creator exists' they are not using 'exists' in the same way as when a scientist says 'Duck-billed platypuses exist'. For when a believer is talking about the Creator they are also being reverential; they are expressing their faith and their understanding of the purpose of life. Although 'the Creator exists' looks very similar to a statement like 'the chairs exist', it is a much richer and resonant phrase, and is an expression of faith, of belief in the grace of God and of salvation. Atheists just do not get it, and they cannot get it unless they become involved in a religious way of life.

long as it leads to the place where they want it to go. As soon as it does not go there, rational argument is thrown out of the window and it is all 'mystery and faith'.

Finally from the point of view of the ordinary believer, the approaches of both types of philosopher (atheist and believer) are simply wrong-headed. Philosophy has little bearing on the thoughts, actions and lives of most believers around the world. When ordinary believers do come across philosophical questions ('Can God make a stone so large that he cannot move it?', 'What caused God?', 'What does "God" mean?') they may well shake their heads, and wonder in bewilderment why anyone would want to waste their time thinking about such ridiculous and obscure questions. For the ordinary believer, God is someone who is woven into every part of their lives, like breathing or thinking or feeling, and there is no more to it than that.

Perhaps we must finish with two more sobering remarks, one from a believer (Blaise Pascal) and one from an atheist (Steven Pinker), about our capacity to discover and understand metaphysical and religious truths.

Reason's last step is the recognition that there are an infinite number of things which are beyond it. It is merely feeble if it does not go as far as to realize that. If natural things are beyond it, what are we to say about supernatural things?[28]

Pascal

Maybe philosophical problems are hard not because they are divine or irreducible or meaningless ... but because the mind of Homo Sapiens lacks the cognitive equipment to solve them. We are organisms, not angels, and our minds are organs, not pipelines to the truth.[29]

Pinker

Section 3: Preparing for the exam

3.1 How to approach the exam

You will all write an essay on 'self-indulgence'. There will be a prize of half a crown for the longest essay, irrespective of any possible merit.[1]

The task set by the harassed teacher in Waugh's novel is designed to shut his students up. But many students do approach the exam thinking, 'I am going to write as much as possible'. This is not a very philosophical approach; nor is it the best approach. In this section we look at how you can do yourself justice in the final examination.

The Assessment Objectives

The AQA Philosophy specification has two Assessment Objectives. These tell the examiners what they should look for in your answers when awarding marks. So if you are to succeed in the exam it is important that you are clear both about what the different skills are that they will assess, and also which questions will assess which skills.

- **Assessment Objective 1** (AO1) concerns how well you are able to show your *understanding* of the topic, ideas, methods and arguments and your ability to explain them by identifying the key ideas and how they fit together.
- **Assessment Objective 2** (AO2) builds on your understanding and tests your capacity to *analyse* philosophical positions, theories and arguments in order that you may *evaluate* how strong they are by exploring the quality of the reasoning, considering their implications and exploring objections and counter arguments.

Across the whole of the AS examination 80 per cent of the marks are for AO1 – Understanding – and just 20 per cent is awarded for Analysis and Evaluation. This reflects the importance of being able to show good knowledge of the subject content as a grounding. So to succeed in the exam you will need to know the material covered in this book in reasonable detail and you will also be expected to understand and evaluate the main arguments developed in the set Anthology texts (see the specification for the list). Success will depend primarily on being able to explain these with precision and in good detail.

But philosophy is not ultimately about giving accounts of arguments and theories from the history of philosophy. Rather philosophy is about engaging meaningfully with the arguments for yourself and so trying to support a point of view. This, however, is not an easy skill. After all, by the time you take the exam you will have only been studying philosophy for nine months, and many of the theories and positions you will be expected to evaluate were developed over many years in complex tomes by some of the greatest thinkers in the western tradition. But while you should show proper respect for the great philosophers' arguments, you must not suppose that you should not question their conclusions. Be prepared to think for yourself about how plausible you find their arguments. And when you come to the exam, make sure that you are aware of some of the main difficulties that they face; you will need to explore these to access the AO2 marks.

However, exams are not really the time for *new* or *experimental* thinking. You need to do this during the year as you learn the material and reflect on the arguments in class and in your own writing. Rather exams are about drawing selectively on what you have learned and framing it in a way that communicates effectively in response to the precise question. So read a question carefully and make sure you are clear about its focus – that is, what precisely it is asking – before you begin to write. Make efforts to organise your material clearly and coherently so that examiners can definitely see what you are saying. In the longer questions, this means briefly planning the order you will present the ideas in and having a conclusion and an introduction (see below). In the shorter answer questions this means answering the questions concisely but precisely.

The questions

The exam is divided into two sections corresponding to the two units you have studied: Section A – Epistemology and Section B – Philosophy of Religion.

There is a total of 80 marks available; 40 marks on each section. So it is important that you divide your time evenly between both sections; that is, one and a half hours for each.

You should practise answering questions under timed conditions as only then will you get a feel for the amount you can write in the time, and so of how much depth and detail can reasonably be expected of you. Notice that the exam will be written in an answer booklet which leaves a certain amount of space for each question. This provides another indication of the approximate upper limit of the amount you are expected to write. But do not feel that you ought to fill up the space allocated for each question. It is not the quantity of writing that will determine your grade and there is a danger, when the adrenalin is pumping, that you might write far more than you should and to lose focus and ramble. You need to stay in control of your material; keep a clear eye on the question and avoid including material which does not advance your answer.

And so it is important that you take the time to think carefully through what you want to say before you begin to write.

Questions 1–4 from Section A and 6–9 from Section B are marked only on AO1. For all these questions, therefore, you should select the relevant information and explain it with clarity and precision. Stay focused on the question so as to avoid redundancy – you will lose marks if you go off topic. The amount of detail you need to put in will depend on the time available, but the better the relevant detail, the more marks you will collect.

Importantly in these answers, because marks are awarded for AO1 only, you will not be credited for evaluating the arguments and positions you discuss. So you should avoid suggesting problems, exploring counter arguments or explaining why you disagree.

Here are the approximate timings for each question. Notice that these suggested timings do not correspond precisely to the division of marks. The reason for this is that the 15-mark questions are more demanding and the marks harder to access. So if you are able to do the shorter answer questions quickly and leave yourself more time for the last question, this will help you to access the highest marks. However, you may find that you need more time to answer the shorter questions properly, in which case it may be best for you to work more slowly through them. Remember, precision is the key to gaining marks, so care needs to be taken over framing your response and this will take time. Whatever pace you work at, be sure to leave yourself at least 30 minutes for the last question.

- 2-mark questions: 1–2 minutes
- 5-mark question: 5–10 minutes
- 9-mark questions: 2 × 15–20 minutes
- 15-mark questions: 35–50 minutes

Two-mark questions

These questions will test your grasp of essential concepts that you have covered on the course and your ability to encapsulate them with precision. They may ask you briefly to outline a definition, theory or philosophical idea.

Practice questions

Write answers to the following 2-mark questions. Give yourself two minutes for each – if you know the material, it should not take long to give a short definition.

You should try to answer in just one or two sentences. Think carefully about the wording so that you are as economical and precise as possible. Illustrations or examples are not needed, and if used should be kept brief.

---

1 What is idealism?
2 What is *a priori* knowledge?
3 What is a false lemma?
4 How does Descartes define God?
5 What is natural evil?
6 What is the verification principle?

Then compare your answers with those below. Answers such as the following should attract full marks:

1 'Idealism is the view that all that exists are minds and their ideas. Objects are no more than collections of sensations immediately appearing within minds.'
2 '*A priori* knowledge is knowledge which is justified independently of experience.'
3 'A lemma is a premise taken for granted in an argument. A false lemma is one that is not true.'
4 'Descartes defines God as a supremely perfect being, or a being with all perfections.'
5 'Moral evil is the evil which is caused by human agency.'
6 'The verification principle is the claim that a proposition is meaningful if and only if it is true by definition or can be verified empirically.'

You may want to come up with your own versions of such questions and many will have answers in the glossary at the back of this book. Answers need to be accurate and to the point but do not need to be developed.

Five-mark questions

The 2-mark questions risk giving the impression that you can explain a difficult idea or argument in a sentence. Philosophical ideas are rarely so simple and the 5-mark questions require you to go further than just giving a pat definition. Rather you need to give a full explanation of a philosophical issue, and this means you must try to show that you have a detailed understanding of the complexity involved. This means doing more than simply describing. A description may fail to show an understanding of *why* someone would believe the theory or position. So what you must try to do is to make sense of it in order to show how it hangs together and what considerations support it.

You need also to demonstrate that you understand and can use accurately the technical vocabulary you have learnt. This means you cannot merely gesture at an idea with a few words, but will need to take it apart and show how it fits together. As with the 2-mark questions, you will be awarded marks here for the precision with which you can explain the ideas.

It is likely that such questions will ask you to explain the reasoning of a philosopher. Your answer will not gain full marks if it does not show awareness of the way the elements of a theory or argument are structured.

So you should be clear about the distinction between the premises and conclusion of an argument or the logical interrelations between the elements of a theory.

You may include illustrative examples to support your account, which are likely be drawn from the texts but only if these help to illuminate the ideas. Quotation, however, is not necessary.

Practice questions

Write answers to the following questions, giving yourself ten minutes for each. Be sure to reflect carefully on the wording so that your response is as clear and precise as possible.

You should try to explain the different elements of the idea and how they are connected. Examples may help to illustrate the points.

1 Outline what is meant by an innate idea.
2 Explain the time lag argument.
3 Explain what is meant by sense data.
4 Outline the idea of the *tabula rasa*.
5 Outline and explain Hume's fork.
6 Outline the theory of infallibilism.
7 Outline Gaunilo's objection to the ontological argument.
8 Explain Paley's version of the argument from design for the existence of God.
9 Outline how a religious claim might be verified eschatologically (Hick).
10 Outline the verificationist account of meaning.

Nine-mark questions (AO1)

These questions should be approached in a very similar way to the 5-markers and are likely to use similar language ('outline', 'explain'), but the difference will be in the level of detail and in the number of points you can develop to support your explanation. Questions are likely to refer to more than one position so that you need to compare or contrast them. Or, the arguments will have several steps so that you need to unpack them in depth. For this reason you will need to pay attention to the way you organise the material so that it is not just accurate, but that it is structured into a coherent whole.

So begin by identifying the key elements of the theory or argument and then, when giving your account of it, make sure you avoid merely describing, but show how it fits together into a logical structure which makes sense. It may be helpful to illustrate your answers with examples either drawn from the texts or some of your own. Examples can help to show examiners that you understand an idea because you can apply it, but take care to ensure your illustrations support your answer, as, once again, if you include superfluous material you will lose marks.

Practice questions

Have a go at writing answers to these 9-mark questions. Each response should take you around 20 minutes.

In that time you will need to go into a reasonable level of detail, so if after five minutes you find you are running out of things to say, then it is likely that you need to know the topic in more depth and so will need to revise further.

Make sure you avoid merely describing, but that you explain. And be sure to pay attention to how you organise your material so that it reads as a coherent whole.

1 Outline the argument from perceptual variation.
2 Explain the difference between inductive and deductive arguments.
3 Explain how we can acquire *a priori* knowledge.
4 Explain why Locke opposes innate ideas.
5 Outline and explain Descartes' trademark argument for the existence of God.
6 Outline a problem with the view that God is all powerful.
7 Explain why Kant objects to the design argument.
8 Explain one of Hume's objections to the cosmological argument.
9 Outline Hick's response to the problem of evil (soul-making).
10 Explain why, according to logical positivism, religious claims are meaningless.

Fifteen-mark questions (7 AO1 + 8 AO2)

These are the only questions that test your capacity to develop an argument in defence of your own judgement. So to answer them you will need to consider arguments for and against a position and then reach a conclusion which follows from what you have argued. These, therefore, are the most philosophically demanding of the questions and the AO2 marks will be the hardest to pick up. So it is a good idea to try to devote more time to this question than the marking allocation would suggest. This means that if you can leave yourself 45 or 50 minutes, this is likely to be time well spent, although not if this is at the expense of precision and clarity in your other responses.

1 Unpack the issues raised in the question …

Make sure you introduce your answer by briefly outlining what the question is asking. A helpful way to approach this can be to define the key terms, to identify and briefly explain the position identified in the question and/or outline the main alternative views relevant to the issue. It can also be helpful briefly to state what you intend to conclude. This helps make it clear to the examiner where you are trying to get to, but more importantly, it makes it clear to you, and this will help you to maintain focus and avoid tangential material.

2 Analyse some points …

Then work through a series of arguments. When selecting points for discussion, make sure they are directly relevant to the question and also explain why they are relevant. When exploring the arguments, try to avoid merely juxtaposing different philosophers' views on the topic. Rather you should examine the cogency of each view by looking at the reasons that support it and making a judgement about how strong the support is. Before moving on, say something about whether you are rejecting a position. If you are able to make each point follow from the previous point, you will help to give the essay a sense of overall development, which is something examiners will be looking for when awarding AO2 marks.

3 Develop a coherent overall argument in support of a judgement …

Having explored arguments for and against a view, avoid a conclusion which simply summarises what you have said (for example, 'I have looked at Descartes' arguments and then at Kant's objections', and so on). A conclusion is not a summary, but must be a *judgement* which responds to the question. So you will need to say that the arguments you have examined show, for example, that the ontological argument fails, or that direct realism is untenable in the face of the criticisms you have looked at. And make sure your conclusion does follow from your reasoning. If you look at arguments for and against, do not just plump for a conclusion without briefly explaining why, on balance, you find one side of the case more persuasive.

In the activity below there are some practice 15-mark questions. Notice that these use terms such as 'assess', 'critically discuss' and 'evaluate', which indicate that the examiners are awarding AO2 marks for evaluation and supporting a reasoned judgement. They may also simply present a question with no command words. But however the question is asked, the basic task, as outlined above, will be the same.

Practice questions

- Practice will be essential as preparation for answering the most demanding questions on the paper.
- For these questions give yourself 40 minutes.
- Plan the response so that it has a clear development.
- Have a clear introduction which explains the question and what your judgement will be.

- In the main body explore in detail the arguments for and against and make your own position clear.
- Give a clear conclusion which responds to the question. Make sure your judgement is supported by the arguments you have considered.

1 Can direct realism survive the objections made against it?
2 Assess whether we can know that the external world exists.
3 Is knowledge justified true belief?
4 Assess whether all our knowledge comes from experience.
5 Can reason alone provide substantive (synthetic) knowledge?
6 Is the concept of God coherent?
7 'Analysis of the concept of God reveals he must exist.' Evaluate this claim.
8 Assess whether the Free Will defence succeeds in overcoming the problem of evil.
9 'Talk of God is meaningless.' Critically discuss this claim.

Again, you may find it helpful to look at the specification and to make up your own questions. You should also make sure you are familiar with all the terminology used in the specification as questions are likely to be framed using this language. For other examples of the sorts of questions you might expect, look at the legacy specification past papers, specifically the (b) questions for Unit 1 Reason and Experience and The Idea of God, and Unit 2 Knowledge of the External World and God and the World. These are available on the AQA website, as are specimen papers for this AS Level.

3.2 How to read philosophy

Introductory textbooks like this try to summarise and clarify some incredibly complex and significant ideas. We cannot capture the depth and richness of the original ideas, so the Anthology extracts below (pages 363–393), and the original (well, translated) texts that are available online, give you a chance to get your intellectual teeth into the ideas of western philosophers in their own words.

We have included in the Anthology extracts a paragraph from each of the recommended texts in the AQA specification so that you have a quick reference, from our summary of the ideas, to the original texts themselves. When you see the Anthology extracts icon (right) in the margin of the book then you should refer to the relevant numbered extract below.

As if you needed to be told, philosophy is hard. We would argue it is the hardest 'essay-based' subject you could do at A Level because you are being asked to read, analyse and understand exactly the same material that a third-year undergraduate, or even a PhD student, might have to grapple with. It is hard because philosophical ideas and arguments are themselves so complex, so subtle and nuanced, and they rely on a web of understanding that reaches back two thousand years, past Hume and past Descartes, past Aquinas and Anselm all the way to Plato, Aristotle and Socrates. It is also hard because philosophers are not the clearest of writers:

> Lord Macaulay once recorded in his diary a memorable attempt – his first and apparently his last – to read Kant's Critique: 'I received today a translation of Kant … I tried to read it, just as if it had been written in Sanskrit'.[1]

We can excuse the fact that many of the philosophers were writing before the twentieth century, when the fashion was for longer sentences, which could be hard to follow. Even if we set aside their long-winded style, philosophers are not always clear in their explanations, they often do not refer to their source material and they introduce technical jargon to try to express their new ideas.

AQA have recommended the Early Modern Texts website www.earlymoderntexts.com as a free online source for some of the texts in the Anthology extracts. Academics on this website have 'translated' older philosophy texts into modern language so that they are more easily understood. Some of the extracts below are taken from Early Modern Texts, and so will differ from the original texts of the philosophers, and we have marked these extracts: EMT.

But there are things you can do to help overcome some of the difficulties of reading philosophy. First, do not try to work it

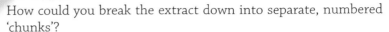

Structure

How could you break the extract down into separate, numbered 'chunks'?

- Try numbering in the margins the main points that are being made.
- Use the signposts that you have identified to break down the extract into chunks.
- Try drawing the ideas on a page, possibly as a 'mind-map'.
- Write these chunks in your own words.
- Now try rewriting the paragraph as if you were a philosopher (which you are!) by writing down the chunks, in your own words, which flow in order: 1, 2, 3, etc.

Section 4: Anthology extracts

Taken from the AQA online Anthology

Section 1: Epistemology

Russell on perceptual variation

anthology
1.1

It is evident from what we have found, that there is no colour which pre-eminently appears to be *the* colour of the table, or even of any one particular part of the table – it appears to be of different colours from different points of view, and there is no reason for regarding some of these as more really its colour than others. And we know that even from a given point of view the colour will seem different by artificial light, or to a colour-blind man, or to a man wearing blue spectacles, while in the dark there will be no colour at all, though to touch and hearing the table will be unchanged. This colour is not something which is inherent in the table, but something depending upon the table and the spectator and the way the light falls on the table. When, in ordinary life, we speak of *the* colour of the table, we only mean the sort of colour which it will seem to have to a normal spectator from an ordinary point of view under usual conditions of light. But the other colours which appear under other conditions have just as good a right to be considered real; and therefore, to avoid favouritism, we are compelled to deny that, in itself, the table has any one particular colour.

Bertrand Russell, *The Problems of Philosophy*

Locke on primary and secondary qualities

anthology
1.2

The idea of heat or light, which we receive by our eyes, or touch, from the sun, are commonly thought real qualities existing in the sun, and something more than mere powers in it. But when we consider the sun in reference to wax, which it melts or blanches, we look on the whiteness and softness produced in the wax, not as qualities in the sun, but effects produced by powers in it. Whereas, if rightly considered, these qualities of light and warmth, which are perceptions in me when I am warmed or enlightened by the

(Continued)

sun, are no otherwise in the sun, than the changes made in the wax, when it is blanched or melted, are in the sun. They are all of them equally powers in the sun, depending on its primary qualities; whereby it is able, in the one case, so to alter the bulk, figure, texture, or motion of some of the insensible parts of my eyes or hands, as thereby to produce in me the idea of light or heat; and in the other, it is able so to alter the bulk, figure, texture, or motion of the insensible parts of the wax, as to make them fit to produce in me the distinct ideas of white and fluid.

John Locke, *Essay Concerning Human Understanding*, II, Chapter viii

anthology 1.3

Leibniz on primary and secondary qualities

Philalethes: But if the relation between the object and the sensation were a natural one how could it happen, as we see it does, that the same water can appear cold to one hand and warm to the other? That phenomenon shows that the warmth is no more in the water than pain is in the pin.

Theophilus: The most that it shows is that warmth isn't a sensible quality (i.e. a power of being sensorily detected) of an entirely absolute kind, but rather depends on the associated organs; for a movement in the hand itself can combine with that of warmth, altering its appearance. Again, light doesn't appear to malformed eyes, and when eyes are full of bright light they can't see a dimmer light. Even the 'primary qualities' (as you call them), such as unity and number, can fail to appear as they should; for, as Descartes noted, a globe appears double when it is touched with the fingers in a certain way, and an object is multiplied when seen in a mirror or through a glass into which facets have been cut. So, from the fact that something doesn't always appear the same, it doesn't follow that it isn't a quality of the object, or that its image doesn't resemble it. As for warmth: when our hand is very warm, the lesser warmth of the water doesn't make itself felt, and serves rather to moderate the warmth of the hand, so that the water appears to us to be cold; just as salt water from the Baltic, when mixed with water from the Sea of Portugal, lessens its degree of salinity even though it is itself saline. So there's a sense in which the warmth can be said to be in the water in a bath, even if the water appears cold to someone; just as we

(Continued)

describe honey in absolute terms as sweet, and silver as white, even though to certain invalids one appears sour and the other yellow; for things are named according to what is most usual. None of this alters the fact that when the organ and the intervening medium are properly constituted, the motions inside our body and the ideas that represent them to our soul resemble the motions in the object that cause the colour, the warmth, the pain etc. In this context, resembling the object is expressing it through some rather precise relationship; though we don't get a clear view of this relation because we can't disentangle this multitude of minute impressions – in our soul, in our body, and in what lies outside us.

Gottfried Leibniz, *New Essays On Human Understanding*, II **EMT**

Descartes considers that he may be dreaming

anthology
1.4

At the same time I must remember that I am a man, and that consequently I am in the habit of sleeping, and in my dreams representing to myself the same things or sometimes even less probable things, than do those who are insane in their waking moments. How often has it happened to me that in the night I dreamt that I found myself in this particular place, that I was dressed and seated near the fire, whilst in reality I was lying undressed in bed! At this moment it does indeed seem to me that it is with eyes awake that I am looking at this paper; that this head which I move is not asleep, that it is deliberately and of set purpose that I extend my hand and perceive it; what happens in sleep does not appear so clear nor so distinct as does all this. But in thinking over this I remind myself that on many occasions I have in sleep been deceived by similar illusions, and in dwelling carefully on this reflection I see so manifestly that there are no certain indications by which we may clearly distinguish wakefulness from sleep that I am lost in astonishment. And my astonishment is such that it is almost capable of persuading me that I now dream.

René Descartes, *Meditation 1*

Russell on the time lag argument

The sense datum which we call hearing the thunder does not take place until the disturbance of the air has travelled as far as to where we are. Similarly, it takes about eight minutes for the sun's light to reach us; thus, when we see the sun we are seeing the sun eight minutes ago. So far as our sense-data affords evidence as to the physical sun they afford evidence to the physical sun of eight minutes ago; if the physical sun had ceased to exist within the last eight minutes, that would make no difference to the sense data which we call 'seeing the sun'.

Bertrand Russell, *The Problems of Philosophy*, Chapter 3

Descartes on primary and secondary qualities

And although in approaching fire I feel heat, and in approaching it a little too near I even feel pain, there is at the same time no reason in this which could persuade me that there is in the fire something resembling this heat any more than there is in it something resembling the pain; all that I have any reason to believe from this is, that there is something in it, whatever it may be, which excites in me these sensations of heat or of pain.

René Descartes, *Meditation 6*

Locke: The relation between our sensations and the objective property is arbitrary

How secondary qualities produce their ideas. After the same manner, that the ideas of these original qualities are produced in us, we may conceive that the ideas of secondary qualities are also produced, viz. by the operation of insensible particles on our senses. For, it being manifest that there are bodies and good store of bodies, each whereof are so small, that we cannot by any of our senses discover either their bulk, figure, or motion,– as is evident in the particles of the air and water, and others extremely smaller than those; perhaps as much smaller than the particles of air and water, as the particles of air and water are smaller than peas or hail-stones;– let us suppose at

(Continued)

present that the different motions and figures, bulk and number, of such particles, affecting the several organs of our senses, produce in us those different sensations which we have from the colours and smells of bodies; that a violet, by the impulse of such insensible particles of matter, of peculiar figures and bulks, and in different degrees and modifications of their motions, causes the ideas of the blue colour, and sweet scent of that flower to be produced in our minds. It being no more impossible to conceive that God should annex such ideas to such motions, with which they have no similitude, than that he should annex the idea of pain to the motion of a piece of steel dividing our flesh, with which that idea hath no resemblance.

John Locke, *Essay Concerning Human Understanding*, II, Chapter viii

Leibniz: The relation between our sensations and the objective property is not arbitrary

anthology
1.8

Philalethes: Now, when certain particles strike our organs in various ways, they cause in us certain sensations of colours or of tastes, or of other secondary qualities that have the power to produce those sensations. Is it conceivable that God should link the idea of heat (for instance) to motions that don't in any way resemble the idea? Yes, just as it is conceivable that he should link the idea of pain to the motion of a piece of steel dividing our flesh – a motion that in no way resembles the idea!

Theophilus: It mustn't be thought that ideas such as those of colour and pain are arbitrary, with no relation or natural connection between them and their causes; it isn't God's way to act in such an disorderly and unreasoned fashion. I hold that there is a resemblance between those ideas and the motions that cause them – a resemblance of a kind – not a perfect one that holds all the way through, but a resemblance in which one thing expresses another through some orderly relationship between them. Thus an ellipse … has some resemblance to the circle of which it is a projection on a plane, since there is a certain precise and natural relationship between what is projected and the projection that is made from it, with each point on the one corresponding through a certain relation with a point on the other. This is something that the Cartesians missed; and on this occasion you have deferred to them more than you usually do and more than you had grounds for doing.

Gottfried Leibniz, *New Essays on Human Understanding*, II **EMT**

Taken from the AQA online Anthology

367

Descartes on primary qualities

There is certainly further in me a certain passive faculty of perception, that is, of receiving and recognising the ideas of sensible things, but this would be useless to me [and I could in no way avail myself of it], if there were not either in me or in some other thing another active faculty capable of forming and producing these ideas. But this active faculty cannot exist in me [inasmuch as I am a thing that thinks] seeing that it does not presuppose thought, and also that those ideas are often produced in me without my contributing in any way to the same, and often even against my will; it is thus necessarily the case that the faculty resides in some substance different from me [...] Hence we must allow that corporeal things exist. However, they are perhaps not exactly what we perceive by the senses, since this comprehension by the senses is in many instances very obscure and confused; but we must at least admit that all things which I conceive in them clearly and distinctly, that is to say, all things which, speaking generally, are comprehended in the object of pure mathematics, are truly to be recognised as external objects.

René Descartes, *Meditation 6*

Russell: Physical objects must continue to exist when unperceived by me

If the cat appears at one moment in one part of the room, and at another in another part, it is natural to suppose that it has moved from the one to the other, passing over a series of intermediate positions. But if it is merely a set of sense-data, it cannot have ever been in any place where I did not see it; thus we shall have to suppose that it did not exist at all while I was not looking, but suddenly sprang into being in a new place. If the cat exists whether I see it or not, we can understand from our own experience how it gets hungry between one meal and the next; but if it does not exist when I am not seeing it, it seems odd that appetite should grow during non-existence as fast as during existence. And if the cat consists only of sense-data, it cannot be hungry, since no hunger but my own can be a sense-datum to me. Thus the behaviour of the sense-data which represent the cat to me, though it seems quite natural when regarded as an expression of hunger, becomes utterly inexplicable when regarded as mere movements and changes of patches of colour, which are as incapable of hunger as a triangle is of playing football.

Bertrand Russell, *The Problems of Philosophy*, Chapter 2

Berkeley: Extension is an idea in the mind

anthology
1.11

Philonous. But, as we approach to or recede from an object, the visible extension varies, being at one distance ten or a hundred times greater than another. Doth it not therefore follow from hence likewise that it is not really inherent in the object?

Hylas. I own I am at a loss what to think.

PHIL. Your judgment will soon be determined, if you will venture to think as freely concerning this quality as you have done concerning the rest. Was it not admitted as a good argument, that neither heat nor cold was in the water, because it seemed warm to one hand and cold to the other?

HYL. It was.

PHIL. Is it not the very same reasoning to conclude, there is no extension or figure in an object, because to one eye it shall seem little, smooth, and round, when at the same time it appears to the other, great, uneven, and regular?

Bishop Berkeley, *Dialogues* 3

Berkeley's 'master argument'

anthology
1.12

Hylas. If it comes to that the point will soon be decided. What more easy than to conceive a tree or house existing by itself, independent of, and unperceived by, any mind whatsoever? I do at this present time conceive them existing after that manner.

Philonous. How say you, Hylas, can you see a thing which is at the same time unseen?

HYL. No, that were a contradiction.

PHIL. Is it not as great a contradiction to talk of CONCEIVING a thing which is UNCONCEIVED?

HYL. It is.

PHIL. The tree or house therefore which you think of is conceived by you?

HYL. How should it be otherwise?

PHIL. And what is conceived is surely in the mind?

HYL. Without question, that which is conceived is in the mind.

PHIL. How then came you to say, you conceived a house or tree existing independent and out of all minds whatsoever?

HYL. That was I own an oversight; but stay, let me consider what led me into it. – It is a pleasant mistake enough. As I was thinking of a tree in a solitary place, where no one was present to see it, methought that was to conceive a tree as existing unperceived or unthought of; not considering

(Continued)

that I myself conceived it all the while. But now I plainly see that all I can do is to frame ideas in my own mind. I may indeed conceive in my own thoughts the idea of a tree, or a house, or a mountain, but that is all. And this is far from proving that I can conceive them existing out of the minds of all spirits.

Bishop Berkeley, *Dialogues I*

Berkeley's proof of God's existence

Philonous. When I say that sensible things can't exist out of the mind, I don't mean my mind in particular, but all minds. Now, they clearly have an existence exterior to my mind, since I find by experience that they are independent of it. There is therefore some other mind in which they exist during the intervals between the times when I perceive them; as likewise they did before my birth, and would do after my supposed annihilation. And as the same is true with regard to all other finite created minds, it necessarily follows that there is an omnipresent, eternal Mind which knows and comprehends all things, and lets us experience them in a certain manner according to rules that he himself has ordained and that we call the 'laws of nature'.

Bishop Berkeley, *Dialogues 3*

Gettier's counter examples: knowledge is not true, justified belief

Various attempts have been made in recent years to state necessary and sufficient conditions for someone's knowing a given proposition. The attempts have often been such that they can be stated in a form similar to the following:
(a) S knows that P IFF [IFF means 'if and only if']:
P is true
S believes that P, and
S is justified in believing that P.
… I shall argue that (a) is false in that the conditions stated therein do not constitute a sufficient condition for the truth of the proposition that S knows that P.
… **Case I**
Suppose that Smith and Jones have applied for a certain job. And suppose that Smith has strong evidence for the following conjunctive proposition:

(Continued)

(d) Jones is the man who will get the job, and Jones has ten coins in his pocket.

Smith's evidence for (d) might be that the president of the company assured him that Jones would in the end be selected, and that he, Smith, had counted the coins in Jones' pocket ten minutes ago. Proposition (d) entails:

(e) The man who will get the job has ten coins in his pocket.

Let us suppose that Smith sees the entailment from (d) to (e), and accepts (e) on the grounds of (d), for which he has strong evidence. In this case, Smith is clearly justified in believing that (e) is true.

But imagine, further, that unknown to Smith, he himself, not Jones, will get the job. And, also, unknown to Smith, he himself has ten coins in his pocket. Proposition (e) is then true, though proposition (d), from which Smith inferred (e), is false. In our example, then, all of the following are true: (i) (e) is true, (ii) Smith believes that (e) is true, and (iii) Smith is justified in believing that (e) is true. But it is equally clear that Smith does not know that (e) is true; for (e) is true in virtue of the number of coins in Smith's pocket, while Smith does not know how many coins are in Smith's pocket, and bases his belief in (e) on a count of the coins in Jones' pocket, whom he falsely believes to be the man who will get the job.

… [This shows] that definition (a) does not state a sufficient condition for someone's knowing a given proposition.

Edmund Gettier, *Is Justified True Belief Knowledge?*

Locke: our mind is like a *tabula rasa*

anthology
1.15

1. Everyone is conscious to himself that he thinks; and when thinking is going on, the mind is engaged with ideas that it contains. So it's past doubt that men have in their minds various ideas, such as are those expressed by the words 'whiteness', 'hardness', 'sweetness', 'thinking', 'motion', 'man', 'elephant', 'army', 'drunkenness', and others. The first question, then, is How does he acquire these ideas? It is widely believed that men have ideas stamped upon their minds in their very first being. My opposition to this in Book I will probably be received more favourably when I have shown where the understanding can get all its ideas from – an account that I contend will be supported by everyone's own observation and experience.

2. Let us then suppose the mind to have no ideas in it, to be like white paper with nothing written on it. How then

(Continued)

does it come to be written on? From where does it get that vast store which the busy and boundless imagination of man has painted on it – all the materials of reason and knowledge? To this I answer, in one word, from experience. Our understandings derive all the materials of thinking from observations that we make of external objects that can be perceived through the senses, and of the internal operations of our minds, which we perceive by looking in at ourselves. These two are the fountains of knowledge, from which arise all the ideas we have or can naturally have.

John Locke, *An Essay Concerning Human Understanding*, Book 2, Chapter 1 **EMT**

anthology
1.16

Hume on concept empiricism

It may seem at first sight that human thought is utterly unbounded: it not only escapes all human power and authority as when a poor man thinks of becoming wealthy overnight, or when an ordinary citizen thinks of being a king, but isn't even confined within the limits of nature and reality. It is as easy for the imagination to form monsters and to join incongruous shapes and appearances as it is to conceive the most natural and familiar objects. And while the body must creep laboriously over the surface of one planet, thought can instantly transport us to the most distant regions of the universe – and even further. What never was seen or heard of may still be conceived; nothing is beyond the power of thought except what implies an absolute contradiction.

But although our thought seems to be so free, when we look more carefully we'll find that it is really confined within very narrow limits, and that all this creative power of the mind amounts merely to the ability to combine, transpose, enlarge, or shrink the materials that the senses and experience provide us with. When we think of a golden mountain, we only join two consistent ideas – *gold* and *mountain* – with which we were already familiar. We can conceive a virtuous horse because our own feelings enable us to conceive virtue, and we can join this with the shape of a horse, which is an animal we know. In short, all the materials of thinking are derived either from our outward senses or from our inward feelings: all that the mind and will do is to mix and combine these materials. Put in philosophical terminology: *all our ideas or more feeble perceptions are copies of our impressions or more lively ones.*

David Hume, *Enquiry Concerning Human Understanding*, Section 2 **EMT**

Descartes on the impossibility of doubt

I will suppose, then, that everything I see is fictitious. I will believe that my memory tells me nothing but lies. I have no senses. Body, shape, extension, movement and place are illusions. So what remains true? Perhaps just the one fact that nothing is certain!

Still, how do I know that there isn't something – not on that list – about which there is no room for even the slightest doubt? Isn't there a God (call him what you will) who gives me the thoughts I am now having? But why do I think this, since I might myself be the author of these thoughts? But then doesn't it follow that I am, at least, something? This is very confusing, because I have just said that I have no senses and no body, and I am so bound up with a body and with senses that one would think that I can't exist without them. Now that I have convinced myself that there is nothing in the world – no sky, no earth, no minds, no bodies – does it follow that I don't exist either? No it does not follow; for if I convinced myself of something then I certainly existed. But there is a supremely powerful and cunning deceiver who deliberately deceives me all the time! Even then, if he is deceiving me I undoubtedly exist: let him deceive me all he can, he will never bring it about that I am nothing while I think I am something. So after thoroughly thinking the matter through I conclude that this proposition, I am, I exist, must be true whenever I assert it or think it.

René Descartes, *Meditation 2* **EMT**

Descartes' trademark argument

Considered simply as mental events, my ideas seem to be all on a par: they all appear to come from inside me in the same way. But considered as images representing things other than themselves, it is clear that they differ widely. Undoubtedly, the ideas that represent substances amount to something more – they contain within themselves more representative reality – than do the ideas that merely represent modes. Again, the idea that gives me my understanding of a supreme God – eternal, infinite, unchangeable, omniscient, omnipotent and the creator of everything that exists except for himself – certainly has in it more representative reality than the ideas that represent merely finite substances.

Now it is obvious by the natural light that the total cause of something must contain at least as much reality as does the effect. For where could the effect get its reality from if not from the cause? And how could the cause give reality to the effect unless it first had that reality itself?

René Descartes, *Meditation 3* **EMT**

anthology
1.19

Locke on innate ideas

Some people regard it as settled that there are in the understanding certain innate principles. These are conceived as primary notions – letters printed on the mind of man, so to speak – which the soul receives when it first comes into existence, and that it brings into the world with it. I could show any fair-minded reader that this is wrong if I could show (as I hope to do in the present work) how men can get all the knowledge they have, and can arrive at certainty about some things, purely by using their natural faculties, without help from any innate notions or principles. Everyone will agree, presumably, that it would be absurd to suppose that the ideas of colours are innate in a creature to whom God has given eyesight, which is a power to get those ideas through the eyes from external objects. It would be equally unreasonable to explain our knowledge of various truths in terms of innate 'imprinting' if it could just as easily be explained through our ordinary abilities to come to know things.

John Locke, *An Essay Concerning Human Understanding*,
Book 1, Chapter 2

anthology
1.20

Leibniz on how ideas can be in the mind and not perceived

Attending to something involves memory. Many of our own present perceptions slip by unconsidered and even unnoticed, but if someone alerts us to them right after they have occurred, e.g. making us take note of some noise that we've just heard, then we remember it and are aware of having had some sense of it. Thus, we weren't aware of these perceptions when they occurred, and we became aware of them only because we were alerted to them a little – perhaps a very little – later. To give a clearer idea of these tiny perceptions that we can't pick out from the crowd, I like the example of the roaring noise of the sea that acts on us when we are standing on the shore. To hear this noise as we do, we have to hear its parts, that is the noise of each wave, although each of these little noises makes itself known only when combined confusedly with all the others, and wouldn't be noticed if the wavelet that made it happened all by itself. We must be affected slightly by the motion of this one wavelet, and have some perception of each of these noises, however faint they may be. If each of them had no effect on us, the surf as a whole – a hundred thousand wavelets – would have no effect either, because a hundred thousand nothings can't make something!

Gottfried Leibniz, *New Essays on Human Understanding*, Preface

Hume's fork

anthology
1.21

All the objects of human reason or enquiry fall naturally into two kinds, namely *relations of ideas* and *matters of fact*. The first kind include geometry, algebra, and arithmetic, and indeed every statement that is either intuitively or demonstratively certain. *That the square of the hypotenuse is equal to the squares of the other two sides* expresses a relation between those figures. *That three times five equals half of thirty* expresses a relation between those numbers. Propositions of this kind can be discovered purely by thinking, with no need to attend to anything that actually exists anywhere in the universe. The truths that Euclid demonstrated would still be certain and self-evident even if there never were a circle or triangle in nature.

David Hume, *Enquiry Concerning Human Understanding*,
Section 4 **EMT**

Descartes' optimism on the possibility of building up knowledge of the external world

anthology
1.22

Thus I see plainly that the certainty and truth of all knowledge depends strictly on my awareness of the true God. So much so that until I became aware of him I couldn't perfectly know anything. Now I can achieve full and certain knowledge of countless matters, both concerning God himself and other things whose nature is intellectual, and also concerning the whole of the corporeal nature that is the subject-matter of pure mathematics.

René Descartes, *Meditation 5*

Plato on innate ideas

anthology
1.23

Meno. Yes, Socrates; but what do you mean by saying that we do not learn, and that what we call learning is only a process of recollection? Can you teach me how this is?
Socrates. I told you, Meno, just now that you were a rogue, and now you ask whether I can teach you, when I am saying that there is no teaching, but only recollection; and thus you imagine that you will involve me in a contradiction.
Men. Indeed, Socrates, I protest that I had no such intention. I only asked the question from habit; but if you can prove to me that what you say is true, I wish that you would.

(*Continued*)

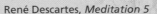

Soc. It will be no easy matter, but I will try to please you to the utmost of my power. Suppose that you call one of your numerous attendants, that I may demonstrate on him.

Men. Certainly. Come hither, boy.

Soc. He is Greek, and speaks Greek, does he not?

Men. Yes, indeed; he was born in the house.

Soc. Attend now to the questions which I ask him, and observe whether he learns of me or only remembers.

Men. I will.

Soc. Tell me, boy, do you know that a figure like this is a square?

Boy. I do.

Soc. And you know that a square figure has these four lines equal?

Boy. Certainly.

Soc. And these lines which I have drawn through the middle of the square are also equal?

Boy. Yes.

Soc. A square may be of any size?

Boy. Certainly.

Soc. And if one side of the figure be of two feet, and the other side be of two feet, how much will the whole be? Let me explain: if in one direction the space was of two feet, and in other direction of one foot, the whole would be of two feet taken once?

Boy. Yes.

Soc. But since this side is also of two feet, there are twice two feet?

Boy. There are.

Soc. Then the square is of twice two feet?

Boy. Yes.

Soc. And how many are twice two feet? count and tell me.

Boy. Four, Socrates.

Soc. And might there not be another square twice as large as this, and having like this the lines equal?

Boy. Yes.

Soc. And of how many feet will that be?

Boy. Of eight feet. ....

Soc. And now try and tell me the length of the line which forms the side of that double square: this is two feet-what will that be?

Boy. Clearly, Socrates, it will be double.

Soc. Do you observe, Meno, that I am not teaching the boy anything, but only asking him questions; and now he fancies that he knows how long a line is necessary in order to produce a figure of eight square feet; does he not?

Men. Yes.

Plato, *Meno*

Spinoza: An example of Euclid's axiomatic method applied to philosophy

anthology
1.24

Definitions

D1: In calling something 'cause of itself' I mean that its essence involves existence, i.e. that its nature can't be conceived except as existing.

...

D3: By 'substance' I understand: what is in itself and is conceived through itself, i.e. that whose concept doesn't have to be formed out of the concept of something else.

D4: By 'attribute' I understand: what the intellect perceives of a substance as constituting its essence.

D5: By 'mode' I understand: a state of a substance, i.e. something that exists in and is conceived through something else ...

Axioms

A1: Whatever exists is either in itself or in something else. As we have already seen, a substance is in itself, a mode is in something else.

A2: What can't be conceived through something else must be conceived through itself.

A3: From a given determinate cause the effect follows necessarily; and, conversely, if there is no determinate cause no effect can follow.

A4: Knowledge of an effect depends on, and involves, knowledge of its cause.

A5: If two things have nothing in common, they can't be understood through one another – that is, the concept of one doesn't involve the concept of the other.

A6: A true idea must agree with its object.

Propositions

1: A substance is prior in nature to its states. This is evident from D3 and D5.

2: Two substances having different attributes have nothing in common with one another. This is also evident from D3. For each ·substance· must be in itself and be conceived through itself, which is to say that the concept of the one doesn't involve the concept of the other.

3: If things have nothing in common with one another, one of them can't be the cause of the other. If they have nothing in common with one another, then (by A5) they can't be understood through one another, and so (by A4) one can't be the cause of the other

Spinoza, *Ethics* Part 1

Section 2: Philosophy of religion

anthology
2.25

Limits on God's omnipotence

Objection 2: Further, sin is an act of some kind. But God cannot sin, nor 'deny Himself' as it is said in 2 Tim. 2:13. Therefore He is not omnipotent …

Reply to Objection 2: To sin is to fall short of a perfect action; hence to be able to sin is to be able to fall short in action, which is repugnant to omnipotence. Therefore it is that God cannot sin, because of His omnipotence. Nevertheless, the Philosopher [Aristotle] says (Topic. iv, 3) that God can deliberately do what is evil. But this must be understood either on a condition, the antecedent of which is impossible – as, for instance, if we were to say that God can do evil things if He will. For there is no reason why a conditional proposition should not be true, though both the antecedent and consequent are impossible: as if one were to say: 'If man is a donkey, he has four feet.' Or he may be understood to mean that God can do some things which now seem to be evil: which, however, if He did them, would then be good. Or he is, perhaps, speaking after the common manner of the heathen, who thought that men became gods, like Jupiter or Mercury.

St Thomas Aquinas, *Summa Theologica*

anthology
2.26

Limits on God's omniscience

(1) A perfect being is not subject to change.
(2) A perfect being knows everything.
(3) A being that knows everything always knows what time it is.
(4) A being that always knows what time it is is subject to change.
Therefore,
(5) A perfect being is subject to change.
Therefore,
(6) A perfect being is not a perfect being.
Finally, therefore,
(7) There is no perfect being.

Norman Kretzmann, *Omniscience and Immutability*

The paradox of the stone: Proposed

A more involved problem, however, is posed by this type of question: can God create a stone too heavy for Him to lift? This appears to be stronger than the first problem, for it poses a dilemma. If we say that God can create such a stone, then it seems that there might be such a stone. And if there might be a stone too heavy for Him to lift, then He is evidently not omnipotent. But if we deny that God can create such a stone, we seem to have given up His omnipotence already. Both answers lead us to the same conclusion.

George Mavrodes, *Some Puzzles Concerning Omnipotence*

The paradox of the stone: Clarified

Stated in its clearest form, the paradoxical argument of the stone is as follows. Where x is any being:

…

(1) Either x can create a stone which x cannot lift, or x cannot create a stone which x cannot lift.
(2) If x can create a stone which x cannot lift, then, necessarily, there is at least one task which x cannot perform (namely, lift the stone in question).
(3) If x cannot create a stone which x cannot lift, then, necessarily, there is at least one task which x cannot perform (namely, create the stone in question).
(4) Hence, there is at least one task which x cannot perform.
(5) If x is an omnipotent being, then x can perform any task.
(6) Therefore, x is not omnipotent.

Since x is any being, this argument proves that the existence of an omnipotent being, God, or any other, is logically impossible.

C. Wade Savage, *The Paradox of the Stone*

The Euthyphro dilemma

Socrates: And what do you say of piety, Euthyphro: is not piety, according to your definition, loved by all the gods?
Euthyphro: Yes.
Socrates: Because it is pious or holy, or for some other reason?
Euthyphro: No, that is the reason.
Socrates: It is loved because it is holy, not holy because it is loved?

(Continued)

Euthyphro: Yes.

Socrates: And that which is dear to the gods is loved by them, and is in a state to be loved of them because it is loved of them?

Euthyphro: Certainly.

Socrates: Then that which is dear to the gods, Euthyphro, is not holy, nor is that which is holy loved of God, as you affirm; but they are two different things.

Euthyphro: How do you mean, Socrates?

Socrates: I mean to say that the holy has been acknowledged by us to be loved of God because it is holy, not to be holy because it is loved.

Euthyphro: Yes.

Socrates: But that which is dear to the gods is dear to them because it is loved by them, not loved by them because it is dear to them.

Plato, *Euthyphro* 10B

anthology
2.30

The compatibility of human free will and God's omniscience

The problem may be stated as follows. God's foreknowledge appears to be incompatible with human freedom. It does not seem to be possible both that God should know what I shall do in the future, and that I shall do freely whatever it is that I shall do. For in order for me to be able to do an action freely, it is necessary that it should be within my power not to do that action. But if God knows what my action is going to be before I do it, then it does not seem to be within my power not to do it. For it cannot be the case both that God knows that I shall do such and such an action, and that I shall not in fact do it. For what God knows must be true: and indeed what anybody knows must be true, since it is impossible to know what is false. But if what God knows is true, and God knows that I will do such and such an action, then it must be true that I will do it. And if it is true that I will do it, then it seems that nothing I can do can prevent it coming true … And if I cannot prevent myself doing a certain action, then that action cannot be free. Therefore, either God cannot know what I shall do tomorrow, or else whatever I shall do tomorrow will not be done freely.

Antony Kenny, *Divine Foreknowledge and Human Freedom*

St Anselm's ontological argument

anthology
2.31

God cannot be conceived not to exist. – God is that, than which nothing greater can be conceived. – That which can be conceived not to exist is not God.

AND it assuredly exists so truly, that it cannot be conceived not to exist. For, it is possible to conceive of a being which cannot be conceived not to exist; and this is greater than one which can be conceived not to exist. Hence, if that, than which nothing greater can be conceived, can be conceived not to exist, it is not that, than which nothing greater can be conceived. But this is an irreconcilable contradiction. There is, then, so truly a being than which nothing greater can be conceived to exist, that it cannot even be conceived not to exist;. and this being you are, O Lord, our God.

St Anselm, *Proslogion*

Gaunilo's reply to Anselm

anthology
2.32

For example: it is said that somewhere in the ocean is an island, which, because of the difficulty, or rather the impossibility, of discovering what does not exist, is called the lost island. And they say that this island has an inestimable wealth of all manner of riches and delicacies in greater abundance than is told of the Islands of the Blest; and that having no owner or inhabitant, it is more excellent than all other countries, which are inhabited by mankind, in the abundance with which it is stored.

Now if someone should tell me that there is such an island, I should easily understand his words, in which there is no difficulty. But suppose that he went on to say, as if by a logical inference: 'You can no longer doubt that this island which is more excellent than all lands exists somewhere, since you have no doubt that it is in your understanding. And since it is more excellent not to be in the understanding alone, but to exist both in the understanding and in reality, for this reason it must exist. For if it does not exist, any land which really exists will be more excellent than it; and so the island already understood by you to be more excellent will not be more excellent.'

Gaunilo, Appendix to *St Anselm's Proslogion*

anthology
2.33

Descartes' ontological argument

I can easily believe that in the case of God, also, existence can be separated from essence, letting us answer the essence question about God while leaving the existence question open, so that God can be thought of as not existing. But on more careful reflection it becomes quite evident that, just as having-internal-angles-equal-to-180° can't be separated from the idea or essence of a triangle, and as the idea of highlands can't be separated from the idea of lowlands, so existence can't be separated from the essence of God. Just as it is self-contradictory to think of highlands in a world where there are no lowlands, so it is self-contradictory to think of God as not existing – that is, to think of a supremely perfect being as lacking a perfection, namely the perfection of existence.

René Descartes, *Meditation 5* **EMT**

anthology
2.34

Kant's criticism of the ontological argument – existence is not a predicate

Being is evidently not a real predicate, that is, a conception of something which is added to the conception of some other thing. It is merely the positing of a thing, or of certain determinations in it. Logically, it is merely the copula of a judgement. The proposition, God is omnipotent, contains two conceptions, which have a certain object or content; the word 'is', is no additional predicate – it merely indicates the relation of the predicate to the subject. Now, if I take the subject (God) with all its predicates (omnipotence being one), and say: God is, or, There is a God, I add no new predicate to the conception of God, I merely posit or affirm the existence of the subject with all its predicates – I posit the object in relation to my conception. The content of both is the same; and there is no addition made to the conception, which expresses merely the possibility of the object, by my cogitating the object – in the expression, it is – as absolutely given or existing. Thus the real contains no more than the possible. A hundred real dollars contain no more than a hundred possible dollars. For, as the latter indicate the conception, and the former the object, on the supposition that the content of the former was greater than that of the latter, my conception would not be an expression of the whole object, and would consequently be an inadequate conception of it. But in reckoning my wealth there may be said to be more in a hundred real

(Continued)

dollars than in a hundred possible dollars – that is, in the mere conception of them. For the real object – the dollars – is not analytically contained in my conception, but forms a synthetical addition to my conception (which is merely a determination of my mental state), although this objective reality – this existence – apart from my conceptions, does not in the least degree increase the aforesaid hundred dollars.

Immanuel Kant, *Critique of Pure Reason*

Malcolm's ontological argument

anthology
2.35

Let me summarize the proof. If God, a being a greater than which cannot be conceived, does not exist then He cannot come into existence. For if He did He would either have been caused to come into existence or have happened to come into existence, and in either case He would be a limited being, which by our conception of Him He is not. Since He cannot come into existence, if He does not exist His existence is impossible. If He does exist He cannot have come into existence (for the reasons given), nor can He cease to exist, for nothing could cause Him to cease to exist nor could it just happen that he ceased to exist. So if God exists His existence is necessary. Thus God's existence is either impossible or necessary. It can be the former only if the concept of such a being is self-contradictory or in some way logically absurd. Assuming that this is not so, it follows that He necessarily exists.

Norman Malcolm, 'Anselm's Ontological Arguments'

Plantinga's ontological argument

anthology
2.36

Using this idea we can restate this last version of the ontological argument in such a way that it no longer matters whether there are any merely possible beings that do not exist. Instead of speaking of the possible being that has, in some world or other, a maximal degree of greatness, we may speak of *the property of being maximally great* or *maximal greatness*. The premise corresponding to (25) then says simply that maximal greatness is possibly instantiated, i.e., that
(29) There is a possible world in which maximal greatness is instantiated.
And the analogues of (27) and (28) spell out what is involved in maximal greatness:

(Continued)

(30) Necessarily, a being is maximally great only if it has maximal excellence in every world

and

(31) Necessarily, a being has maximal excellence in every world only if it has omniscience, omnipotence, and moral perfection in every world.

Notice that (30) and (31) do not imply that there are possible but non-existent beings – any more than does, for example,

(32) Necessarily, a thing is a unicorn only if it has one horn.

But if (29) is true, then there is a possible world W such that if it had been actual, then there would have existed a being that was omnipotent, omniscient, and morally perfect; this being, furthermore, would have had these qualities in every possible world. So it follows that if W had been actual, it would have been impossible that there be no such being.

Alvin Plantinga, *God, Freedom and Evil*

anthology
2.37

Paley's argument from design

In crossing a heath, suppose I pitched my foot against a stone, and were asked how the stone came to be there; I might possibly answer, that, for any thing I knew to the contrary, it had lain there for ever: nor would it perhaps be very easy to show the absurdity of this answer. But suppose I had found a watch upon the ground, and it should be inquired how the watch happened to be in that place; I should hardly think of the answer which I had before given, that, for any thing I knew, the watch might have always been there. Yet why should not this answer serve for the watch as well as for the stone? Why is it not as admissible in the second case, as in the first? For this reason, and for no other, viz. that, when we come to inspect the watch, we perceive (what we could not discover in the stone) that its several parts are framed and put together for a purpose, e.g. that they are so formed and adjusted as to produce motion, and that motion so regulated as to point out the hour of the day; that, if the different parts had been differently shaped from what they are, of a different size from what they are, or placed after any other manner, or in any other order, than that in which they are placed, either no motion at all would have been carried on in the machine, or none which would have answered the use that is now served by it. … This mechanism being observed (it requires indeed an examination of the instrument, and perhaps some previous knowledge of the subject, to perceive and understand it; but being once, as we have said, observed and understood), the inference, we think, is inevitable,

(Continued)

that the watch must have had a maker: that there must have existed, at some time, and at some place or other, an artificer or artificers who formed it for the purpose which we find it actually to answer; who comprehended its construction, and designed its use.

William Paley, *Natural Theology*

Paley anticipates two criticisms of the argument from design

anthology
2.38

Nor would it, I apprehend, weaken the conclusion, that we had never seen a watch made; that we had never known an artist capable of making one; that we were altogether incapable of executing such a piece of workmanship ourselves, or of understanding in what manner it was performed; all this being no more than what is true of some exquisite remains of ancient art, of some lost arts, and, to the generality of mankind, of the more curious productions of modern manufacture. Does one man in a million know how oval frames are turned? Ignorance of this kind exalts our opinion of the unseen and unknown artist's skill, if he be unseen and unknown, but raises no doubt in our minds of the existence and agency of such an artist, at some former time, and in some place or other. Nor can I perceive that it varies at all the inference, whether the question arise concerning a human agent, or concerning an agent of a different species, or an agent possessing, in some respects, a different nature.

Neither, secondly, would it invalidate our conclusion, that the watch sometimes went wrong, or that it seldom went exactly right. The purpose of the machinery, the design, and the designer, might be evident, and in the case supposed would be evident, in whatever way we accounted for the irregularity of the movement, or whether we could account for it or not. It is not necessary that a machine be perfect, in order to show with what design it was made: still less necessary, where the only question is, whether it were made with any design at all.

William Paley, *Natural Theology*

anthology
2.39

Hume's criticism of the argument from design: We have no experience of world-making

When two sorts of objects have always been observed to be conjoined together, custom leads me to infer the existence of an object of one sort wherever I see the existence of an object of the other sort; and I call this an argument from experience. But it is hard to see how this pattern of argument can be appropriate in our present case, where the objects we are considering don't fall into sorts, but are single, individual, without parallel or specific resemblance … To make this reasoning secure, we would need to have had experience of the origins of worlds; it isn't sufficient, surely, to have seen ships and cities arise from human artifice and contrivance … Have you ever seen nature in a situation that resembles the first arrangement of the elements at the beginning of the universe? Have worlds ever been formed under your eye; and have you had leisure to observe the whole progress of world-making, from the first appearance of order to its final consummation?

David Hume, *Dialogues Concerning Natural Religion*, Part 2 EMT

anthology
2.40

Hume's criticism of the argument from design: Arguments from analogy are weak

Even if this world were a perfect product, we still couldn't be sure whether all the excellences of the work could justly be ascribed to the workman. When we survey a ship, we may get an exalted idea of the ingenuity of the carpenter who built such a complicated, useful, and beautiful machine. But then we shall be surprised to find that the carpenter is a stupid tradesman who imitated others, and followed a trade which has gradually improved down the centuries, after multiplied trials, mistakes, corrections, deliberations, and controversies. Perhaps our world is like that ship. It may be that many worlds were botched and bungled, throughout an eternity, before our present system was built; much labour lost, many useless trials made, and a slow but continued improvement carried on during infinite ages in the world-making trade. In such subjects as this, who can determine what is true – who indeed can even guess what is probable – when so many hypotheses can be put forward, and even more can be imagined?

David Hume, *Dialogues Concerning Natural Religion*, Part 5 EMT

Hume's criticism of the argument from design: The Epicurean hypothesis

anthology
2.41

For instance, what if I should revive the old Epicurean hypothesis? This is commonly and I think rightly regarded as the most absurd system ever yet proposed; but I suspect that with a few alterations it might be given a faint appearance of probability. Instead of supposing matter to be infinite, as Epicurus did, let us suppose it to be finite and also suppose space to be finite, while still supposing time to be infinite. A finite number of particles in a finite space· can have only a finite number of transpositions; and in an infinitely long period of time every possible order or position of particles must occur an infinite number of times. So this world, with all its events right down to the tiniest details, has already been produced and destroyed and will again be produced and destroyed an unlimited number of times. No-one who properly grasps the difference between infinite and finite will have any trouble with this conclusion.

David Hume, *Dialogues Concerning Natural Religion*, Part 8 **EMT**

Hume's criticism: The argument from design doesn't prove the existence of a perfect being

anthology
2.42

That is how there comes to be so much fruitless labour to account for things that appear bad in nature, to save the honour of the gods; while we have to admit the reality of the evil and disorder of which the world contains so much. What controlled the power and benevolence of Jupiter and obliged him to make mankind and every sentient creature so imperfect and so unhappy – we are told – is the obstinate and intractable nature of matter, or the observance of general laws, or some such reason. His power and benevolence seem to be taken for granted, in their most extreme form. And on that supposition, I admit, such conjectures may be accepted as plausible explanations of the bad phenomena. But still I ask: why take these attributes for granted, why ascribe to the cause any qualities that don't actually appear in the effect? Why torture your brain to justify the course of nature on suppositions which, for all you know to the contrary, may be entirely imaginary – suppositions for which no traces are to be found in the course of nature?

David Hume, *Enquiry Concerning Human Understanding*, Section 11 **EMT**

Richard Swinburne's argument from design

Among examples of regularities of succession produced by men are the notes of a song sung by a singer or the movements of a dancer's body when he performs a dance in time with the accompanying instrument. Hence, knowing that some regularities of succession have such a cause, we postulate that they all have. An agent produces the celestial harmony like a man who sings a song. But at this point an obviously difficulty arises. The regularities of succession, such as songs which are produced by men, are produced by agents of comparatively small power, whose bodies we can locate. If an agent is responsible for the operation of the laws of nature, he must directly on the whole universe, as we act directly on our bodies. Also he must be of immense power and intelligence compared with men. Hence he can only be somewhat similar to men, having, like them, intelligence and freedom of choice, yet unlike them in the degree of these and in not possessing a body.

Richard Swinburne, *The Argument from Design*

Aquinas' cosmological argument

The first and more manifest way is the argument from motion. It is certain, and evident to our senses, that in the world some things are in motion. Now whatever is in motion is put in motion by another, for nothing can be in motion except it is in potentiality to that towards which it is in motion; whereas a thing moves inasmuch as it is in act. For motion is nothing else than the reduction of something from potentiality to actuality. But nothing can be reduced from potentiality to actuality, except by something in a state of actuality. Thus that which is actually hot, as fire, makes wood, which is potentially hot, to be actually hot, and thereby moves and changes it. Now it is not possible that the same thing should be at once in actuality and potentiality in the same respect, but only in different respects. For what is actually hot cannot simultaneously be potentially hot; but it is simultaneously potentially cold. It is therefore impossible that in the same respect and in the same way a thing should be both mover and moved, i.e. that it should move itself. Therefore, whatever is in motion must be put in motion by another. If that by which it is put in motion be itself put in motion, then this also must needs be put in motion by another, and that by another again. But this cannot go on to infinity, because then there would be no first mover, and, consequently,

(*Continued*)

no other mover; seeing that subsequent movers move only inasmuch as they are put in motion by the first mover; as the staff moves only because it is put in motion by the hand. Therefore it is necessary to arrive at a first mover, put in motion by no other; and this everyone understands to be God.

St Thomas Aquinas, *Summa Theologica*

Descartes' cosmological argument

anthology 2.45

[T]his shows me quite clearly that I depend for my continued existence on some being other than myself. Perhaps this being is not God, though. Perhaps I was produced by causes less perfect than God, such as my parents. No; for as I have said before, it is quite clear that there must be at least as much reality or perfection in the cause as in the effect. And therefore, given that I am a thinking thing and have within me some idea of God, the cause of me – whatever it is – must itself be a thinking thing and must have the idea of all the perfections that I attribute to God. What is the cause of this cause of me? If it is the cause of its own existence, then it is God; for if it has the power of existing through its own strength, then undoubtedly it also has the power of actually possessing all the perfections of which it has an idea – that is, all the perfections that I conceive to be in God. If on the other hand it gets its existence from another cause, then the question arises all over again regarding this further cause: Does it get its existence from itself or from another cause? Eventually we must reach the ultimate cause, and this will be God.

It is clear enough that this sequence of causes of causes can't run back to infinity, especially since I am dealing with the cause that not only produced me in the past but also preserves me at the present moment.

René Descartes, *Meditation 3* **EMT**

anthology
2.46

The logical problem of evil

In its simplest form the problem is this: God is omnipotent; God is wholly good; and yet evil exists. There seems to be some contradiction between these three propositions, so that if any two of them were true the third would be false. But at the same time all three are essential parts of most theological positions: the theologian, it seems, at once *must* adhere and *cannot consistently* adhere to all three.

However, the contradiction does not arise immediately; to show it we need some additional premises, or perhaps quasi-logical rules connecting the terms 'good', 'evil' and 'omnipotent'. These additional principles are that good is opposed to evil, in such a way that a good thing always eliminates evil as far as it can, and that there are no limits to what an omnipotent thing can do. From these it follows that a good omnipotent thing eliminates evil completely, and then the proposition that a good omnipotent thing exists, and that evil exists, are incompatible.

J.L. Mackie, 'Evil and Omnipotence', *Mind*, 64

anthology
2.47

The Free Will defence

A world containing creatures who are significantly *free* (and *freely perform more* good than evil actions) is more valuable, all else being equal, than a world containing no free creatures at all. Now God can create free creatures, but He can't *cause* or *determine* them to do only what is right. For if He does so, then they aren't significantly free after all; they do not do what is right *freely*. To create creatures capable of *moral good*, therefore, He must create creatures capable of moral evil; and He can't give these creatures the freedom to perform evil and at the same time prevent them from doing so. As it turned out, sadly enough, some of the free creatures God created went wrong in the exercise of their freedom; this is the source of moral evil. The fact that free creatures sometimes go wrong, however, counts neither against God's omnipotence nor against His goodness; for He could have forestalled the occurrence of moral evil only by removing the possibility of moral good.

Alvin Plantinga, *God, Freedom and Evil: Essays in Philosophy*

Soul-Making

I suggest, then, that it is an ethically reasonable judgement, even though in the nature of the case not one that is capable of demonstrative proof, that human goodness slowly built up through personal histories of moral effort has a value in the eyes of the Creator which justifies even the long travail of the soul-making process.

… For if our general conception of God's purpose is correct the world is not intended to be a paradise, but rather the scene of a history in which human personality may be formed towards the pattern of Christ. Men are not to be thought of on the analogy of animal pets, whose life is to be as agreeable as possible, but rather on the analogy of human children, who are to grow to adulthood in an environment whose primary and overriding purpose is not immediate pleasure but the realizing of the most valuable potentialities of human personality.

John Hick, *Evil and the God of Love*

Factual significance

My own version of [the verifiability principle] … was that 'a sentence is factually significant to any given person, if, and only if, he knows how to verify the proposition which it purports to express – that is, if he knows what observations would lead him, under certain conditions, to accept the proposition as being true, or reject it as being false'. Meaning was also accorded to sentences expressing propositions like those of logic or pure mathematics, which were true or false only in virtue of their form, but with this exception, everything of a would-be indicative character which failed to satisfy the verification principle was dismissed as literally nonsensical.

A.J. Ayer, *The Central Questions of Philosophy*

Taken from the AQA online Anthology

Verification principle

To test whether a sentence expresses a genuine empirical hypothesis, I adopt what may be called a modified verification principle. For I require of an empirical hypothesis, not indeed that it should be conclusively verifiable, but that some possible sense-experience should be relevant to the determination of its truth or falsehood. If a putative proposition fails to satisfy this principle, and is not a tautology, then I hold that it is metaphysical, and that, being metaphysical, it is neither true nor false but literally senseless. It will be found that much of what ordinarily passes for philosophy is metaphysical according to this criterion, and, in particular, that it can not be significantly asserted that there is a non-empirical world of values, or that men have immortal souls, or that there is a transcendent God.

A.J. Ayer, *Language, Truth and Logic*

Eschatological verification

The strength of the notion of eschatological verification is that it is not an ad hoc invention but is based upon an actually operative religious concept of God. In the language of the Christian faith, the word 'God' stands at the centre of a system of terms, such as Spirit, grace, Logos, incarnation, Kingdom of God, and many more; and the distinctly Christian conception of God can only be fully grasped in its connection with these related terms. It belongs to a complex of notions which together constitute a picture of the universe in which we live, of man's place therein, of a comprehensive divine purpose interacting with human purposes, and of the general nature of the eventual fulfilment of that divine purpose. This Christian picture of the universe, entailing as it does certain distinctive expectations concerning the future, is a very different picture from any that can be accepted by one who does not believe that the God of the New Testament exists. Further, these differences of experiential confirmation is thus built into the Christian concept of God; and the notion of eschatological verification seeks to relate this fact to the logical problem of meaning.

John Hick, *Theology and Verification*

Religious statements are unfalsifiable

anthology 2.52

Now it often seems to people who are not religious as if there was no conceivable event or series of events the occurrence of which would be admitted by sophisticated religious people to be sufficient reason for conceding 'There wasn't a God after all' or 'God does not really love us then.' Someone tells us that God loves us as a father loves his children. We are reassured. But then we see a child dying of inoperable cancer of the throat. His earthly father is driven frantic in his efforts to help, but his Heavenly Father reveals no obvious sign of concern. Some qualification is made – God's love is 'not merely human love' or it is 'an inscrutable love', perhaps – and we realise that such sufferings are quite compatible with the truth of the assertion that 'God loves us as a father (but, of course …).' We are reassured again. But then perhaps we ask: what is this assurance of God's (appropriately qualified) love worth, what is this apparent guarantee really a guarantee against? Just what would have to happen … to entitle us to say 'God does not love us' or even 'God does not exist'?

Antony Flew, *Theology and Falsification*

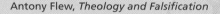

Glossary

Key terms or concepts that appear in CAPITAL LETTERS in the book are explained in the Glossary. Those words in the glossary that are in **bold** refer to terms that you can find explained elsewhere in the glossary.

Agent   A being who is capable of action. Agency and action are typically restricted to persons, because they have the capacity to reason, make a choice between two courses of action, then do what they have chosen.

Analytic   A term that describes the manner in which a proposition is true. An analytic truth is a proposition that is true in virtue of the meanings of the words alone. In other words an analytic truth is one that is true by definition, for example 'A bachelor is an unmarried man.' Analytic truths are contrasted with synthetic truths – truths that cannot be determined simply by analysing the meanings of the terms used. For example, 'All bachelors have the use of at least one kidney' is a synthetic truth.

Anti-realism   If you are a realist about something, then you believe it exists independently of our minds. If you are an anti-realist about something you think it is mind-dependent. This is closely connected to non-cognitivism. For example, in epistemology, anti-realists about perception think that material objects exist only for minds and that a mind-independent world is non-existent. (Berkeley summed up this idealist position by saying that to be is to be perceived.) An example of anti-realism in religious language is Wittgenstein's theory that religious terms need to be understood within a religious language game.

A posteriori   A Latin term that describes a belief that can only be known via experience of the world: for example, that 'snow is white' or that 'the Atlantic is smaller than the Pacific'. *A posteriori* beliefs are contrasted with ***a priori*** beliefs.

A priori   A Latin term that describes knowledge that is known prior to or independently from experience. For example, that '1,000,000 + 1 = 1,000,001' can be known independently of counting a million apples, adding another one, and then recounting them. *A priori* beliefs are contrasted with ***a posteriori*** beliefs, which are ones derived from experience.

Argument   An argument is a series of propositions intended to support a conclusion. The propositions offered in support of the conclusion are termed **premises**.

Argument from analogy   Arguments which compare two things, and draw a conclusion about one of them on the basis of their similarities are called arguments from analogy, or analogical arguments. Several well-known versions of the argument from design are analogical arguments, and these are **inductive arguments**.

Argument from design   Also known as teleological arguments, these propose that God exists on the basis of certain features of the universe: for example, observations concerning its ordered nature, or concerning the apparent design and purpose of the parts of living organisms.

Atemporal   Outside of time. It is generally agreed that God is eternal, but some theologians maintain that this means that God exists outside of time: he has no past, present or future.

Atheism/Atheist   In the tradition of western philosophy, atheism generally refers to the belief that there is no God in a Christian (or Jewish, or Islamic) sense. In contrast to **theism**.

Belief   A belief is a state of mind or thought which is about the world. It is a mental representation which claims that something is the case, or that a proposition is true. For example, you may have the belief that Westminster is in London or that cod liver oil is good for your health. A belief will have some degree of evidence in support of it but is normally regarded as weaker than knowledge, either because knowledge cannot turn out to be false, or because it requires stronger evidence.

Belief in … Belief that …   Ordinarily when we talk about beliefs we are talking about beliefs that certain things are true (for example, you might believe that Media Studies AS Level is easier than Philosophy AS Level). Sometimes we talk about beliefs in certain things (for example, belief in God, or in the new England football coach). To believe in something means not only believing that it exists but also having a certain confidence in that person or process – we adopt a positive attitude towards that person or process and are committed to it.

Benevolence   The desire and disposition to do good for others. Christian philosophers maintain that God has the property of being supremely or wholly good, which they refer to as benevolence, or sometimes as omnibenevolence.

Camera obscura   Latin for 'dark room' and referring to a room with one small aperture covered by a lens which allows the scene outside to be projected inside onto a screen by the same mechanism as a modern camera. Locke uses the device as an analogy for how the mind works. Sensations are representations of things in the physical world, which are projected into the mind as they are into a camera. All our concepts and beliefs are formed out of the sensations in our minds. We have direct access only to sensations and we make judgements about the nature of the physical world on the basis of them. So our beliefs about the world are justified in terms of beliefs about our sense experiences. The *camera obscura* analogy expresses Locke's empiricist conviction that all our concepts derive from sensation, that all knowledge is justified in terms of experience and his indirect realism about perception.

Clear and distinct ideas   The basic or self-justifying beliefs that Descartes hopes to use as foundations for his system of knowledge. Clear and distinct ideas, we are told, are those which can be 'intuited' by the mind by what he calls the 'light of reason'. In other words, they are truths of reason, truths that can be known with the mind alone. Descartes' examples of clear and distinct ideas are the basic claims of logic, geometry and mathematics. Knowledge of truths of reason, it is claimed, resists any sceptical attack, since we recognise its truth immediately. Our faculty of 'intuition' permits us to recognise the truth without allowing any room for doubt or error. For example, it is in vain to ask how I know that triangles have three sides. Such knowledge is given in the very act of understanding the terms involved. There is no further evidence I need appeal to in order to justify such knowledge.

Cogito   Latin for 'I think', and shorthand for Descartes' famous argument to prove his own existence. Descartes attempted to doubt he existed but realised that in order to doubt that this, he must exist. So his own existence was **indubitable**.

Cognitivism/Non-cognitivism   Closely related to **realism/anti-realism**. Cognitivism is a position in the philosophy of language which holds that judgements or statements must be true or false if they are to mean anything. Cognitivist perspectives on religious language include **verificationism** and **falsificationism**. Non-cognitivism is the position that statements can be meaningful, even if they do not refer to the world and the concepts of 'truth' and 'falsity' do not apply to them. An example of a cognitivist perspective in religious language comes from A.J. Ayer and the logical positivists.

Coherentism   A view about the structure of justification which claims that no beliefs are foundational and therefore that all beliefs need justification in terms of further beliefs. On this account beliefs are more or less well justified to the extent that they fit in or cohere with other beliefs in the system.

Concept   Having a concept of something is what enables one to recognise it, distinguish it from other things and think about it. So, if I have the concept of a hedgehog, I can think about hedgehogs, and recognise them when I encounter them, and tell the difference between them and hogs or hedges. Similarly, to have a concept of red is to be able to think about it, recognise it and to distinguish it from other colours. According to traditional empiricism, all our concepts are formed as kinds of 'copy' of the original sensations.

Conclusion   A statement that comes at the end of an **argument** and that is supported by the reasons given in the argument. If an argument is sound or valid and all of the premises are true, then the conclusion will also be true.

Contingent   A contingent truth is one which happens to be true, but which may not have been. In other words, it is a truth for which it is logically possible that it be false. The opposite of a contingent truth is a **necessary** one, i.e. one which has to be true and could not be otherwise, or for which it is logically impossible that it be false. For example, it is a contingent truth that daffodils are yellow, since it is conceivable that they might have been blue.

Corporeal   Made of matter. In contrast to **incorporeal**.

Cosmological arguments   Cosmology is the study of the universe as whole. Cosmological arguments for the existence of God operate by claiming that there must be some ultimate cause or reason for the existence of the universe. This explanation cannot be found within the universe and so must be found in some supernatural being, namely God.

Deductive argument   An argument where the truth of the conclusion is guaranteed by the truth of the premises. In other words it is an argument in which the premises entail the conclusion. So if one accepts the truth of the premises one must, as a matter of logical necessity, accept the conclusion. For example: either you will become a fireman or a doctor. But you can only become a doctor with a medical degree which you will never get. So you will become a fireman. A deductive argument is in contrast to an **inductive argument**. **Ontological arguments** are deductive proofs of God's existence.

Determinism   See **free will**.

Direct realism   Another term for **naïve realism**.

Dualism   Dualism about mind and body is the claim that humans are made of two distinct kinds of stuff: a material body and a spiritual mind.

Emotivism   An anti-realist position in moral philosophy, made popular by A.J. Ayer, which claims that moral judgements do not refer to anything in the world, but are expressions of our feelings of approval and disapproval.

Empiricism   An epistemological position which holds that our beliefs, and knowledge, must be based on experience. David Hume was one philosopher who rigorously applied his empiricist approach to questions in the philosophy of religion.

Enlightenment   Also known as the Age of Reason. The period of European history in the eighteenth century in which thinkers and writers were optimistic about the progress that humans could make in different fields. It was characterised by critical and analytic thinking, and meant a break with the past, including a break with Christian thinking. Some of this optimism arose from the scientific discoveries of Sir Isaac Newton, which led to the belief that similar theories and laws could be developed in other areas of human thought. Famous enlightenment philosophers include Voltaire and Hume.

Epistemology   One of the three main areas of philosophical study and analysis (see also **ethics** and **metaphysics**). Epistemology, or the theory of knowledge, looks at questions of what it is possible to know, what grounds our claims to knowledge are based on, what is true, what is the distinction between knowledge and belief. (The term is derived from the ancient Greek words *episteme* meaning 'knowledge' and *logos* meaning 'account', or 'rationale'.)

Eschatological   Eschatology is the study of the 'end of things' or the 'last things' as described from a religious perspective: this includes death, what happens after we die, the end of time, the Last Judgement, and so on. Eschatological verification is a term used by John Hick to describe the process by which religious statements can (in theory) be shown to be meaningful: if they are true then they can be shown to be true (verified) after we die.

Ethics   One of the three main areas of philosophical study and analysis (see also **epistemology** and **metaphysics**). Ethics, or moral philosophy, is concerned with questions of how we should live, what rules we should follow, how should we act, what sort of person we should try to be. Practical, or applied, ethics looks at particular issues and dilemmas that face us in the real world. Normative ethics examines the rules and principles that have been proposed to govern and judge our actions. Meta-ethics assesses the status of these rules, and at the meaning of moral claims and judgements.

Euthyphro dilemma   In the philosophy of religion this dilemma raises the question 'In what way are God's commands good?' and offers two problematic options. The first option is that whatever God commands is good, in which case his commands to commit genocide (Deuteronomy 3:2) or infanticide (Genesis 22:2), for example, are good. The second option is that God's commands are good because they conform to some external moral law, in which case we should pay attention to this moral law, rather than God.

Evidence   The reasons for holding a belief.

Evil   Philosophers usually distinguish between moral evil, which is the suffering caused by humans, and natural evil, which is the suffering brought about by natural events such as earthquakes. The existence of evil in the universe presents a challenge to believers known as the **problem of evil**.

Evil demon   A device used by Descartes to generate a sceptical argument about the possibility of knowledge of the external world and of basic propositions of arithmetic and geometry. It is conceivable that there exists an extremely powerful spirit or demon bent on deceiving me. If this were the case then all my perceptions of the world around me could be an illusion produced in my mind by the demon. Even my own body could be a part of the illusion. Moreover, the demon could cause me to make mistakes even about the most simple judgements of maths and geometry so that I go wrong when adding 2 to 3 or counting the sides of a square.

Evolution   Evolution is the process, described as natural selection by Charles Darwin, by which organisms gradually change over time according to changes in their environment and genetic mutations. Some mutations lead to traits or characteristics which make an organism better suited to an environment and more successful in having offspring that also survive and reproduce; some environmental changes mean that an organism is less suited to its environment and its offspring are less successful in surviving and reproducing. Over long periods of time, and in environmentally stable conditions, the characteristics of an organism become highly adapted to its environment and have all the appearance of being designed for that environment.

Existentialism   The name for a group of related philosophies which focus on describing and explaining what it feels like to exist as a human. Some of the key concerns revolve around the individual, the range of human experience and the significance of choice or free will.

External world   All that exists outside of or independently of the mind; the physical world.

Fact   Something which is the case. For example, it is a fact that the Earth revolves around the Sun.

Factual significance   A statement has factual significance if it tells us something about the real world. Some theories of meaning (such as **verificationism**) maintain that a sentence is only meaningful if it is factually significant.

Fallacy   An argument which is flawed either because a mistake has been made, rendering the argument invalid; or because the argument has a form, or structure, which is always invalid.

False   A term used of beliefs and propositions. A false belief is one which is not true. One account of what makes a belief or proposition false is that it fails to correspond with the facts. So, for example, the belief that humans are descended from apes will be false if in fact they are descended from dolphins.

Falsificationism   A philosophical theory about the nature of meaning. Closely related to **verificationism**, falsificationism claims that for a proposition to be meaningful we must be able to understand what would count as proving the proposition false (i.e. what would falsify it).

Forms (theory of)   Plato's theory of forms is a theory about types or classes of thing. The word 'form' is used to translate Plato's use of the Greek word 'idea' with which he refers to the type or class to which a thing belongs. Plato argues that over and above the realm of physical objects there is a realm of 'forms' to which individual physical things belong. So in the physical realm there are many tables, but there is also the single form of the table, the ideal or blueprint of the table, which we recognise not with our senses, but with the mind.

Foundationalism   A view about the structure of justification which claims that there are two sorts of belief: those which are basic or foundational and which require no justification (or which are self-justifying), and those which are built on top of the foundations and justified in terms of them.

Free will   Also known as metaphysical freedom. The idea of free will is that the self controls aspects of its own life, such as bodily movements like picking up a pencil. Many religious philosophers believe that God granted humans free will. Free will can be contrasted with determinism, which is the belief that all events in the universe are the necessary consequence of physical laws, and these laws apply to human actions as well. A determinist might claim that humans are like complex pieces of biological machinery with no real freedom of will. Some philosophers believe that these two positions (free will versus determinism) are compatible with each other, and claim that humans can have free will but are also subject to deterministic laws; such a view is known as compatibilism.

Given   The given is the raw and immediate element of experience prior to any judgement. What is given to us immediately are often termed sense data and such experience is thought to be known for certain and incorrigibly.

Good   Actions are good according to whether they bring about certain positive outcomes – these may be pleasure or happiness, or something more intangible. But 'good' also has a functional meaning, in the sense that 'good' means 'fulfilling your function well'. Aristotle believed that we have a function and hence can be good in both senses: by being good (fulfilling our function) we can reach the good (eudaimonia).

Holy   The concept of 'Holy' is used to encapsulate everything that is special and sacred about God. It can also be used to describe religious objects which share in this sacredness. Rudolf Otto described the overpowering experience of God's holiness as numinous.

Hypothetical statements   'If … then' statements which make claims about states of affairs which are not actual, but which would be if certain conditions were satisfied. Hypothetical statements are used to translate physical object language into phenomenal language in linguistic phenomenalism.

399

Language game   The phrase used by Wittgenstein to convey the idea that language has meaning within a particular social context, and that these contexts are governed by rules (in the same way that different games are governed by different rules). The way in which a sentence is meaningful therefore varies according to the context in which it occurs.

Lemma   A subsidiary belief or proposition used to justify or prove another belief/proposition.

Logical positivism   See **verificationism**.

Material   Made of physical matter. According to Descartes this involved occupying physical space. In contrast, God is thought of by Christian philosophers as immaterial.

Materialism   The view that everything in the world is made of matter and that ultimately all mental or apparently spiritual entities can be given a purely material explanation.

Metaphysics   One of the three main areas of philosophical study and analysis (see also **epistemology** and **ethics**). Metaphysics is concerned with determining what sorts of things really exist, what is the ultimate nature of reality, where the world comes from, what is the relationship of our mind to the world. (It is said that the term 'metaphysics' came about because in ancient catalogues of Aristotle's work his books on the nature of reality came after (in Greek '*meta*') his books on physics – hence metaphysics.)

Method of doubt   Descartes' sceptical method used to find certainty. Descartes found that many of his beliefs had turned out to be false, and to remedy this situation he elected to cast doubt upon all his beliefs. If any beliefs showed themselves to be indubitable, and could survive the most radical scepticism, then they would have established themselves as absolutely certain. Once he had discovered such beliefs, Descartes hoped to rebuild a body of knowledge based on them which would be free from error.

Naïve direct realism   The common-sense view of how perception works. Physical objects have an independent existence in space, they follow the laws of physics and possess certain properties, ranging from size and shape through to colour, smell and texture. When humans are in the presence of such objects under appropriate conditions they are able to perceive them along with all these properties.

Natural selection   See **evolution**.

Natural theology   Gaining an understanding of God through the use of our reason. This may be through an examination of the world around us (which leads, for example, to the teleological argument), or through an analysis of concepts (which leads, for example, to the ontological argument). This is in contrast to **revealed theology**.

Necessary   A necessary truth is one which has to be true and could not be otherwise. It is one that is true in all possible worlds.

Necessary/contingent   'Necessary' and 'contingent' are opposing terms. It is generally agreed that there can be necessary and contingent truths; but some philosophers have also used the terms to apply to beings in the world.

Necessary/contingent being   A contingent being is one whose existence depends on something else (for example, humans are contingent because their existence depends on the existence of parents, oxygen, food, and so on) A necessary being is one that does not depend upon anything else for its existence. There are both cosmological and ontological arguments that hold God to be a necessary being.

Necessary/contingent truths   In the most restricted sense, a necessary truth is one where the opposite is logically impossible; for example, that a triangle has three sides (a two-sided triangle is logically impossible and cannot be imagined). A contingent truth is one where the opposite is logically possible, for example it is true that David Cameron was once the prime minister of the United Kingdom (but it is entirely possible that this may never have happened). It is supposed by some philosophers that the proposition 'God exists' is a necessary truth, because the concept of 'God' already contains the idea of 'a being who must exist'. This claim lies at the heart of some ontological arguments.

Necessary/sufficient conditions   A is a necessary condition for B when you have to have A in order to have B. In other words, if you do not have A you cannot have B. By contrast A is a sufficient condition for B when if you have A you must have B too. In other words, having A is enough or sufficient to guarantee that you have B.

Non-cognitivism   See **cognitivism**.

Omnipotent   All-powerful. Along with **benevolence** this is one of the main attributes of God.

Omnipresent   Everywhere at once. Like **benevolence** and **omnipotence** this is one of the attributes of God.

Omniscient   All-knowing. As with **benevolence**, **omnipotence** and

omnipresence, this is one of the attributes of God. However, it is important to remember that these attributes cannot be separated from one another in God, because God is simple and **immutable**.

Ontological arguments   Ontology is the study of existence. If you were to write down everything you thought existed (cats, dogs, electrons, aliens, and so on), then this list would form your own personal ontology. If aliens were present on the list then you could be said to be making an ontological commitment to the existence of aliens (in other words you claim they exist). All believers (except anti-realists) include God in their ontology. The ontological argument is a particular proof of God's existence, and tries to show that the very meaning of the concept 'God' implies that he must exist.

Ontology   The study of being in general or of what there is.

Pantheism   The view that God is the same thing as the universe itself.

Paradox   An apparently contradictory statement or one which goes against common-sense opinion.

Perception   The process by which we become aware of physical objects including our own body.

Phenomenalism   An anti-realist theory of perception distinguished from idealism in that it claims that physical objects are collections not just of actual sense data but also of potential sense data. Physical objects continue to exist unperceived since they retain the potential to be perceived.

Physico-theological   A term used by the philosopher Immanuel Kant to describe an argument for God's existence based on particular features of the world (for

Sense data   What one is directly aware of in perception. The subjective elements which constitute experience. For example, when perceiving a banana, what I actually sense is a collection of sense data, the way the banana seems to me, including a distinctive smell, a crescent-shaped yellow expanse, a certain texture and taste. According to sense data theorists, we make judgements about the nature of the physical world on the basis of immediate awareness of these sense data. So, on the basis of my awareness of the sense datum of a yellow expanse, plus that of a banana smell, and so on, I judge that I am in the presence of a banana. In this way, we build up a picture of the physical world and so all empirical knowledge can rest on the foundation of sense data.

Sense impressions   The colours, noises, tastes, sounds and smells that one is aware of when perceiving the world. Also known as **sense data**.

Solipsism   The view that all that can be known to exist is my own mind. This is not normally a position defended by philosophers, but rather a sceptical trap into which certain ways of thinking appear to lead. For example, if it is urged that all that can be truly known is what one is directly aware of oneself, then it follows that one cannot know anything of which one is not directly aware. This might include the minds of other people (which one can only learn about via their behaviour), or, more radically, the very existence of the physical world, including one's own body (which one can only learn about via one's sense experience of them).

Soul   There are many different philosophical accounts of the soul. In some accounts it is what gives life to the human being. In others it is the immaterial part of us: that which constitutes the essence of the individual person. It is also seen as that which can survive the death of the body and so guarantee the continued existence of the person after physical death.

Statement   Indicative sentence.

Subject   In grammar, the part of a **proposition** that picks out the main object which is being described or discussed: for example, in 'the red balloon popped' the subject is 'the balloon'. In the sentence 'God is the greatest conceivable being', 'God' is the subject.

Sufficient condition   See **necessary condition**.

Synthetic   See **analytic**.

Teleological   Deriving from the Greek word *telos* meaning purpose, goal or end. A teleological explanation is a way of accounting for events by reference to their purpose or ultimate goal. For example, you notice a green shoot emerging from an acorn. A teleological explanation will refer to the purpose of this event, or to a future state that needs to be attained: 'because it is trying to grow into a tree', or 'it is searching for soil and water'. Such a teleological approach may be contrasted with efficient or mechanical explanations, which explain events only by making reference to physical factors leading up to the event. So the green shoot emerges because of certain changes in temperature and the production of enzymes, which lead to the growth of certain cells, which eventually shatters the acorn shell, and so on.

Teleological arguments   See **argument from design**.

Theism/theist Belief in one God, who is a person, who is generally held to be perfect, who is the creator of the universe, and who has a relationship with that universe. This is in contrast to atheism (the belief that there is no such God) and agnosticism (refusing to commit to either atheism or theism).

Theodicy (From the Greek *theos* – 'god' and *dike* – 'justice') The attempt to justify God's actions, and to show why, for example, a perfect God has created an imperfect world. The most common forms of theodicy are responses to the problem of evil that explain why God allows pain and suffering to exist.

Theology The study of God from a religious perspective. This is in contrast to the philosophy of religion, which starts from a philosophical perspective.

Theory of forms See **forms** and **world of forms**.

Transcendent To be outside, beyond, or removed from something. So to say that God is transcendent is to say that he exists outside of his creation, outside of space and time.

True A term used of **beliefs** and **propositions**. There are different theories of what makes a belief or proposition true. For the sake of simplicity, in this book we have been operating with the so-called correspondence theory of truth which says that beliefs and propositions are true when they correspond with the facts, that is, when what they say about the world is the case.

Verificationism A philosophical belief about the nature of meaning. Logical positivism claims that for a proposition to be meaningful it must be (hypothetically) verifiable or true by definition. Other than truths by definition most propositions make a specific claim about the universe – that it is this way or that – for example, that 'there is a cat on my mat' or that the 'leaves on my tree are green'. In such cases it is easy for us to imagine how such claims could be verified or not. However, take the claim that 'God loves the world'. How could we verify this claim? What could we look for in the world to see whether that claim is true or not? If it is not clear how the universe would look if the claim were true or not, then it is not clear what it is asserting and thus logical positivists might claim that the proposition is not meaningful.

Verification principle The rule put forward by verificationists that a statement is only meaningful if it can be shown to be true (verified): either empirically (for example, by observation) or because it is true by definition.

World of forms Plato's theory that universal concepts such as beauty and justice exist independently of human minds, in another realm. Plato called such concepts '**forms**'.

Notes

Introduction

1 Steve Pyke, Philosophers, Corneshouse, 1993, p.22.

Introduction to Descartes' *Meditations*

1 Descartes, *Meditations on First Philosophy, Meditation 1*, p.1 (online version www.earlymoderntexts.com).

2 Ibid, p.3.

3 Ibid., *Meditation 2*, p.4.

1.1

1 Hume, *Enquiry Concerning Human Understanding*, I, xii, 1, par. 117.

2 Ibid. par. 118.

3 Russell, *The Problems of Philosophy*, Chapter 1.

4 'The table, which we see, seems to diminish, as we remove farther from it: but the real table, which exists independent of us, suffers no alteration: it was, therefore, nothing but its image, which was present to the mind.' Ibid.

5 This example comes from Descartes' *Meditation 6*.

6 Thomas Reid (1710–1796) 'Men sometimes lead us into mistakes, when we perfectly understand their language, by speaking lies. But Nature never misleads us in this way: her language is always true; and it is only by misinterpreting it that we fall into error.' (Reid, *Inquiry into the Human Mind*, 1764, sec. xxiv).

7 Locke, *An Essay Concerning Human Understanding*, II, viii, par. 12.

8 Ibid.

9 Ibid., par. 13.

10 Ibid., par. 7.

11 Russell makes the same point in *The Problems of Philosophy*, Chapter 2, when he argues that 'we cannot hope to be acquainted directly with the quality in the physical object which makes it look blue or red. Science tells us that this quality is a certain sort of wave-motion'.

12 Leibniz, *New Essays*, II, viii, 13.

13 Locke, *Essay*, II, viii, par. 9.

14 This is unlike Descartes, who believed in a *plenum*; that is, the idea that matter is infinitely divisible, so no atoms, and that all of space is occupied with matter, so no void or vaccum.

15 Locke, *Essay*, II, viii, par. 9.

16 Russell, *The Problems of Philosophy*, Chapter 3.

17 Descartes thinks that because we can describe primary qualities mathematically and therefore that we can understand them 'clearly and distinctly' and argues that God wouldn't deceive us about their reality. This argument, however, ultimately relies on the existence of a benevolent, non-deceiving God, and so may not convince.

18 Locke makes an exception of our knowledge of the existence of God.

19 Locke, *Essay*, IV, xi.

20 Ibid., par. 5.

21 Ibid., par. 14.

22 Ibid., par. 7.

23 Ibid., par. 14.

24 Leibniz gives an alternative way of showing that life is not an extended dream when responding to Locke in the *New Essays*: 'a dream could be as coherent and prolonged as a man's life – that isn't metaphysically impossible. But it would be as contrary to reason as the fiction of a book resulting by chance from jumbling the printer's type together. Anyway, so long as the phenomena are linked together it doesn't matter whether we call them 'dreams' or not, because experience shows that we don't go wrong in the practical steps we take on the basis of phenomena.' (IV, iii, 14.)

25 Hume's *Enquiry*, I, xii, 1, par. 118; Russell's *Problems*, Chapter 2, p.11.

26 The meaning of the term 'idea' as used by the empiricists of the eighteenth century is notoriously difficult to pin down. Berkeley's use follows Locke's, for whom the term means 'whatever one is conscious of'. So, while including what we are here calling sense data, it would also include beliefs and concepts. Note also that Berkeley's arguments discussed above in chapter 1.1 concerning the distinction between primary and secondary qualities are in fact strategic ones, and his considered position actually denies that there is any such distinction.

27 This argument has much in common with those of Hume, who uses the empiricist claim that all genuine ideas must derive from experience to argue that we don't really have an idea of self, for example.

28 Berkeley, *Treatise Concerning the Principles of Human Knowledge* [1710]. Arc Manor, 2008: Rockville M.D. Part 1, section 10.

29 Ronald Knox, in *The Complete Limerick Book*, Langford Reed, 1924.

1.2

1 Plato, *Meno*, Penguin, 1956, 97a–b, translation modified.

2 Ibid., 97e–98e.

3 Plato, *Theaetetus*, Penguin, 1987, 201c–d.

4 Ibid., 201d.

5 Plato, *The Republic*, Penguin, 1955, pp.476–479.

6 Gettier, E., 'Is Justified, True Belief Knowledge?', in Philips Griffiths, A. (ed.) *Knowledge and Belief*, Oxford University Press, 1967.

7 Descartes, *Meditations on First Philosophy*, *Meditation 1*, p.1 (online version www.earlymoderntexts.com).

8 Price, H.H., 'Some considerations about belief' in Philips Griffiths, A. (ed.) *Knowledge and Belief*, Oxford University Press, 1967.

9 Lycan, W., 'On the Gettier Problem Problem', in *Epistemology Futures*, Hetherington, S. (ed.), Oxford University Press, 2006.

10 Sosa, E., *A Virtue Epistemology: Apt Belief and Reflective Knowledge, Volume I*, Oxford University Press, 2009.

1.3

1 Aristotle, *On the Soul*, 3.4.430a.

2 Hume, *Enquiry Concerning Human Understanding,* Enquiry 2, p.8 (online version www.earlymoderntexts.com).

3 From Lewis Carroll's poem 'The Jabbewocky' in *Though the Looking Glass and What Alice Found There*, Wordsworth, 1993, p.20.

4 Immanuel Kant, *Critique of Pure Reason*, B.75, N. Kemp Smith (tr.), Macmillan Education, 1989 [1929], p.93.

5 Ibid., par. 2 (online version www.earlymoderntexts.com).

6 Locke, *An Essay Concerning Human Understanding*, I, 2, par. 1 (online version www.earlymoderntexts.com).

7 Ibid.

8 Ibid., par. 2 (online version www.earlymoderntexts.com).

9 Ibid., par. 4 (online version www.earlymoderntexts.com).

10 Ibid, par. 5 (online version www.earlymoderntexts.com).

11 Leibniz, New Essays on Human Understanding, Book 1, Chapter 1, p.18 (online version www.earlymoderntexts.com).

12 Locke, An Essay Concerning Human Understanding, I, 2, par. 5 (online version www.earlymoderntexts.com).

13 Leibniz, New Essays on Human Understanding, Book 1; Chapter 1, p.19 (online version www.earlymoderntexts.com).

14 Hume, *Enquiry Concerning Human Understanding*, Enquiry 1, section 4, p.11 (online version www.earlymoderntexts.com).

15 Hume, *Enquiry Concerning Human Understanding*, Enquiry 1, section 12, p.86 (online version www.earlymoderntexts.com).

16 Adapted From Casey, J., First Six Books of the Elements of Euclid, Longman, 1885, available at www.gutenberg.org, p.6.

17 Ibid., p.29.

18 Russell and Whitehead, *Principia Mathematica*, Volume 1, 2nd edition, Cambridge University Press, p.362, available at https://archive.org.

19 Descartes, *Discourse on Method*: Discourse 2, in *Philosophical Writings* (tr. and ed.) Elizabeth Anscombe and Peter Thomas Geach, Nelson's University Paperbacks, 1977.

20 For example, Plato, *The Republic*, 475–476d.

2.1

1   Blaise Pascal, *Pensées* #230, Penguin, 1985, p.245.

2   St Augustine, *City of God*, Book 8, Chapter 2, Henry Bettenson (tr.), Penguin, 1984, pp.312–313.

3   St Anselm, *Proslogion*, Chapter 2 in Alvin Plantinga (ed.) *The Ontological Argument*, Macmillan, 1968, p.4.

4   Descartes, Meditation 3 in *Descartes – Selected Philosophical Writings*, Cambridge University Press, 1993, p.93.

5   Swinburne, *The Coherence of Theism*, Clarendon Press, 1977, p.2.

6   Pascal, *Pensées*, Penguin, 1985, p.150.

7   Aquinas, *Summa Theologica*, 1.25.3.

8   Mackie, 'Evil and Omnipotence' in Basil Mitchell (ed.) *The Philosophy of Religion*, Oxford University Press, 1971, pp.101–104.

9   See George Mavrodes' article 'Omniscience' in C. Taliaferro and P.J. Griffiths (eds) *Philosophy of Religion*, Blackwell, 2003, pp.236–237.

10 Hick, *Evil and the God of Love*, Fontana, 1968.

11 St Augustine, *De Trinitate* 8.3.

12 St Anselm, *Proslogion* 19.

13 St Thomas Aquinas, *Summa Theologica* 1:14:13 (reply to objection 3). Aquinas borrows this analogy from Boethius: Book 5 in his *Consolations of Philosophy*.

14 Kurt Vonnegut, *Slaughterhouse 5*, Vintage, 2000, p.83.

15 Nicholas Wolterstorff, 'God is everlasting, not eternal' in Brian Davies (ed.) *Philosophy of Religion: A Guide and Companion*, Oxford University Press, 2000

16 Augustine, *Confessions*, XI, vii.

17 See, for example, David Blumenfeld's article 'On the Compossibility of Divine Attributes', in the journal *Philosophical Studies* 34, 1978, pp.91–103.

18 Mackie, 'Evil and Omnipotence' in Mitchell (ed.) *The Philosophy of Religion*, Oxford University Press, 1971, pp.102–104.

19 George Mavrodes, 'Some puzzles concerning omnipotence', *The Philosophical Review*, 72.

20 Aquinas, *Summa Theologica* 1.25.3.

21 C. Wade Savage, 'The Paradox of the Stone', *The Philosophical Review* 76, pp.74–79.

22 Ibid., p.78.

23 Søren Kierkegaard, *Fear and Trembling*, in Alastair Hannay (tr.), Penguin, 1985, pp.83–95.

24 Antony Kenny, 'Divine foreknowledge and human freedom' in *Aquinas: A Collection of Critical Essays*, pp.256–257.

2.2

1   St Thomas Aquinas, *Summa Theologica* 1:2:2.

2.2.1

1   In eighteenth-century France, scientists and naturalists attempted to discover whether the Beast of Gevaudan (a creature that had apparently killed 140 people) really existed. For a stylish fictionalised version of their attempts see the film *Brotherhood of the Wolf*, directed by Christopher Gans (2001).

2   The philosopher J.N. Findlay argues that this definition is correct as it arises out of a genuinely religious attitude. To a believer the object of worship 'should have an unsurpassable supremacy along all avenues [and] tower infinitely above all other objects' (J.N. Findlay, 'Can God's existence be disproved?', in A. Flew and A. MacIntyre (eds), *New Essays on Philosophical Theology*, Macmillan, 1955, p.51). However, Findlay then goes on to disprove God's existence in order to show the absurdity of the ontological argument!

3   Alvin Plantinga would add to these attributes 'worthy of worship'. An imaginary God is not worthy of worship, but the supreme being must be at the very least worthy of worship, and so must exist (Alvin Plantinga (ed.), *The Ontological Argument: From St Anselm to Contemporary Philosophers*, Macmillan, 1968, p.x).

4   Gaunilo's 'On Behalf of the Fool' is reprinted in Plantinga, *The Ontological Argument*, pp.6–13. Some philosophers have had a lot of fun with the ontological argument. For example, D. and M. Haight used it to prove the existence of the greatest conceivable evil being ('An ontological argument for the devil', *The Monist*, no. 54, 1970).

5   F.C. Copleston sees Aquinas' rejection of the ontological argument as evidence of his 'empiricism' (F.C. Copleston, *Aquinas*, Penguin, 1965, p.113). Aquinas does offer five alternative proofs of God's existence, all of them based on our experience of the effects of God's existence – namely the world we see around us.

6   Descartes, *Selected Philosophical Writings*, Meditation 5, p.107. For a more detailed expansion and analysis of Descartes' ontological argument, read Clement Dore, 'Ontological arguments', in P.L. Quinn and C. Taliaferro (eds), *A Companion to Philosophy of Religion*, Blackwell, 1999, pp.323–329.

7   Leibniz, *That a Most Perfect Being Exists*, 1676.

8   Kant, *Critique of Pure Reason*, Macmillan, 1980, pp.500ff.

9   This is also the position taken by David Hume in his *Dialogues Concerning Natural Religion* (Oxford University Press, 1998, p.91), as we have seen. For both Hume and Kant a proposition is a necessary truth if, when we reject the predicate, a contradiction results. So 'Bachelors are unmarried men' is necessarily true because when we reject the predicate, and suggest that 'Bachelors are married men', then we have a contradiction. However, Kant, following Hume, argues that no statement about existence can be necessary, as it is always possible to deny something exists, without that statement being contradictory. So to say 'God does not exist' is not a contradiction, which means 'God exists' is not a necessary truth.

10   The Dutch theologian Johan de Kater (Caterus) made a similar criticism of Descartes' argument, and this was included in the first published edition of the *Meditations* as 'The First Set of Objections'. See Descartes, *Selected Philosophical Writings*, Cambridge University Press, 1988, p.136.

11   Kant, *Critique of Pure Reason*, p.504.

12   In making this point Kant relies on a principle already articulated by Aristotle: namely that being does not belong to the essence of things since existence is not an attribute or characteristic; in other words that questions of existence and questions of the nature of things are distinct. (Posterior Analytics Book 2 Internet Archive http://classics.mit.edu/Aristotle/posterior.2.ii.html.)

13   Schopenhauer, *On the Fourfold Root of the Principle of Sufficient Reason*, E.F.J. Payne (tr.), Open Court Classics: La Salle, Illinois, 1974, p.15.

14   Bertrand Russell, *Why I am Not a Christian*, Routledge, 1996, p.137.

15   Alvin Plantinga, *God, Freedom and Evil: Essays in Philosophy*, Harper and Row, 1974, pp.98–112.

2.2.2

1   The character Lucilius in Cicero's *On the Nature of the Gods*, Book II, 3–5, Penguin Classics, 1972, p.124.

2   Charles Darwin, *The Autobiography of Charles Darwin*, Barnes & Noble, 2005, p.261.

3   The film *Alien*, directed by Ridley Scott, uses a creature with similarly parasitic tendencies whose offspring are planted as eggs inside the human 'hosts', before exploding from the stomachs of their hosts once they've hatched.

4   Written by Cecil Alexander in 1848.

5   Immanuel Kant, *Critique of Pure Reason*, Norman Kemp Smith (tr.), Macmillan, 1980, p.520.

6   Terence Penelhum thinks of cosmological arguments as 'Existential' arguments, and teleological arguments as 'Qualitative' arguments. See 'Divine Necessity' in Basil Mitchell (ed.), *The Philosophy of Religion*, Oxford University Press, 1971, pp.180–181.

7   Antony Flew, *An Introduction to Western Philosophy*, Thames & Hudson, 1978, p.206.

8   Aquinas, *Summa Theologica* 1:2:3.

9   Paley, *Natural Theology*, extract reprinted in Davies (ed.), *Philosophy of Religion: A Guide and Anthology*, Oxford University Press 2000, p.257.

10   Ibid., p.259.

11   Ibid., p.254.

12   Ibid., p.257.

13   Ibid., p.257.

14   Hume, *Enquiry Concerning Human Understanding*, Section X, par. 1, Oxford University Press, 1982, p.110.

17 William Rowe, 'The problem of evil and some varieties of atheism', in C. Taliaferro and P.J. Griffiths (eds), *Philosophy of Religion*, Blackwell, 2003, pp.306–373.

18 Jean-Paul Sartre, *Existentialism and Humanism*, Methuen, 1973, pp.32–33.

19 The term 'theodicy' was first used by Gottfried Leibniz in his *Essays of Theodicy*, 1710.

20 For a succinct account of a new process theodicy as proposed by David Griffin see John Hick, *Philosophy of Religion*, Prentice Hall, 1990, pp.48–55.

21 Hick, *Evil and the God of Love*, p.374.

22 Ibid., p.375.

23 Genesis 3:14–20.

24 Quoted in Plantinga, A., *God, Freedom and Evil*, Harper & Row, 1975, p.27.

25 John Hick, *Evil and the God of Love*, Fontana, 1968, p.293.

26 Antony Flew, 'Divine Omnipotence and Human Freedom', in Flew and MacIntyre (ed.), *New Essays in Philosophical Theology*, SCM, 1955.

27 Mackie, 'Evil and Omnipotence', in Mitchell (ed.) op. cit., pp.100–101.

28 Voltaire, *Candide*, Wordsworth Classics, 1996, p.12.

29 John Hick, *Evil and the God of Love*, Fontana, 1968, p.292.

30 Ibid., pp.322–323.

31 Ibid., p.369.

32 Elim Klimov's film *Come and See* (1985) offers a compelling and graphic account of these atrocities from a child's perspective.

33 Fyodor Dostoyevsky, *The Brothers Karamazov*, Bantam, 1970, pp.295–296.

2.3

1 Francois Rabelais, *The Histories of Gargantua and Pantagruel*, Penguin, 1955, p.231.

2 Pseudo-Dionysius, 'The Divine Names' in *The Complete Works*, by Colm Lubheid (tr.), SPCK, 1987, pp.49–50.

3 C.K. Ogden and I.A. Richards, *The Meaning of Meaning*, Harcourt, 1989.

4 From Lewis Carroll's poem 'The Jabberwocky' in *Through the Looking Glass and What Alice Found There*, Wordsworth, 1993, p.20.

5 Noam Chomsky, *Syntactic Structures*, Mouton, 1957, p.15.

6 A.J. Ayer, *Language, Truth and Logic*, Penguin, 1980, p.41.

7 Hick, *Philosophy of Religion*, Prentice Hall, 1963, p.95.

8 A.J. Ayer, *Language, Truth and Logic*, Penguin, 1980, pp.151ff.

9 S.R. Sutherland, 'Language, Newspeak and Logic' in A. Phillips Griffiths ed., *A. J. Ayer, Memorial Essays*, Cambridge, 1992, p.78.

10 John Hick, 'Theology and Verification' in Basil Mitchell (ed.), *The Philosophy of Religion*, Oxford University Press, 1971, pp.59–60.

11 Antony Flew, *Theology and Falsification* in Mitchell (ed.), *The Philosophy of Religion*, Oxford University Press, 1971, p.13ff.

12 Ian McEwan, *Enduring Love*, Vintage, 1998, Appendix 2.

13 Job 19:25. For an updating of the story of Job see the Coen brothers' film *A Serious Man* (2009).

14 A. Flew, R.M. Hare and B. Mitchell, *Theology and Falsification* in Mitchell (ed.), *The Philosophy of Religion*, Oxford University Press, 1971, p.16.

15 Ibid., p.17.

16 Flew, ibid., p.22.

17 Ibid., pp.18–19.

18 It is unlikely, but possible, that the film director Paul Verhoeven had read Mitchell's parable when writing the script for his gripping film about the Dutch resistance movement *Black Book* (2006).

19 Ludwig Wittgenstein, *Philosophical Investigations* #43, Blackwell, 1981, p.20.

20 Ibid., #23, pp.11–12.

21 Ibid., #23, p.11.

22 Ludwig Wittgenstein, *Lectures and Conversations on Aesthetics, Psychology and Religious Belief*, Blackwell, 1970, p.53.

23 R.B. Braithwaite, 'An Empiricist's view of the nature of religious language' in Mitchell (ed.), *The Philosophy of Religion,* pp.72–91.

24 I.M. Crombie, 'The Possibility of Theological Statements' in Basil Mitchell (ed.), *The Philosophy of Religion*, Oxford University Press, 1971, pp.23–52.

25 Moses Maimonides, *The Guide of the Perplexed*, Hackett, 1995, p.82.

26 I.M. Crombie, 'The Possibility of Thelogical Statements' in Basil Mitchell (ed.), *The Philosophy of Religion*, Oxford University Press, 1971, pp.48–51.

27 This well-known Socratic principle is articulated in several dialogues by Plato, although never in this precise form. For example, see *The Republic* 394d (Penguin, 2003), *Euthyphro* 14a (in *Last Days of Socrates*, Penguin, 2003) and *Sophist* 224e (Dover, 2003).

28 Blaise Pascal, *Pensées*, Penguin, 1985, p.85.

29 Steven Pinker, *How The Mind Works*, Penguin, 1998, p.561.

3.1

1 Evelyn Waugh, *Decline and Fall*, Penguin, 2003, p.38.

3.2

1 Brand Blanshard, *On Philosophical Style*, Manchester University Press, 1954, p.1.

Selected bibliography

AQA have provided a list of texts that you will be expected to understand and be able to evaluate. This list can be found in the AQA specification, and the texts themselves can be accessed via the AQA online Anthology.

Below are some further books that will help in your understanding of the issues within Epistemology and the Philosophy of Religion.

Epistemology

Audi, Robert, *Epistemology: A Contemporary Introduction to the Theory of Knowledge*, Routledge, 1998

Cole, Peter, *Theory of Knowledge*, Hodder & Stoughton, 2002

Descartes, *Meditations on First Philosophy*, in Sutcliffe, F.E. (tr.), *Discourse on Method and the Meditations*, Penguin, 1968

Everitt, Nicholas and Fisher, Alec, *Modern Epistemology: A New Introduction*, McGraw-Hill Inc., 1995

Hospers, John, *An Introduction to Philosophical Analysis* (second edition), Routledge and Kegan Paul, 1967

Morton, Adam, *A Guide through the Theory of Knowledge* (second edition), Blackwell, 1977

Russell, B., *The Problems of Philosophy*, Oxford University Press, 1912

Trusted, Jennifer, *An Introduction to the Philosophy of Knowledge* (second edition), Palgrave, 1997

Philosophy of Religion

Copleston, F.C., *Aquinas*, Penguin 1965

Davies, Brian, *Introduction to the Philosophy of Religion*, Oxford University Press, 1993

Davies, Brian (ed.), *Philosophy of Religion: A Guide and Anthology*, Oxford University Press, 2000

Hick, John, *Philosophy of Religion*, Prentice Hall, 1990

Hick, John (ed.), *The Existence of God*, Macmillan, 1964

Hitchens, Christopher, *The Portable Atheist*, Da Capo Press, 2007

Hume, David, *Dialogues Concerning Natural Religion*, Oxford University Press, 1998

Mackie, J.L., *The Miracle of Theism*, Oxford University Press, 1982

Mitchell, Basil (ed.), *The Philosophy of Religion*, Oxford University Press, 1971

Plantinga, Alvin, ed., *The Ontological Argument: From St Anselm to Contemporary Philosophers*, Macmillan, 1968

Quinn, P.L. and Taliaferro, C. (eds), *A Companion to Philosophy of Religion*, Blackwell, 1999

Swinburne, Richard, *The Existence of God*, Clarendon Press, 1979

Taliaferro, C. and Griffiths, P.J. (eds), *Philosophy of Religion*, Blackwell, 2003

General philosophy

Blackburn, Simon, *Think*, Oxford University Press, 2001

Honderich, Ted (ed.), *The Oxford Companion to Philosophy*, Oxford University Press, 1995

Martin, Robert, *There are Two Errors in The Title of this Book*, Broadview, 1998

Morton, Adam, *Philosophy in Practice*, Blackwell, 1998

Rosenberg, Jay, *The Practice of Philosophy*, Prentice Hall, 1976

Warburton, Nigel, *Philosophy: The Essential Study Guide*, Routledge, 2004

Index